FOR MORE THAN BREAD

Clarence E. Pickett

Clarence E. Pickett FOR
MORE THAN
BREAD

An autobiographical account of twenty-two years' work with the American Friends Service Committee

Little, Brown and Company · *Boston*

FIRST EDITION

*Published simultaneously
in Canada by McClelland and Stewart Limited*

PRINTED IN THE UNITED STATES OF AMERICA

Preface

THE American Friends Service Committee is a co-operative enterprise of literally hundreds of people. The publishers of this volume suggested that I should write the history of the work of this Committee from 1929 to 1952 from an autobiographical point of view. "This," I said, "is no one-man show. It has not been my achievement." But I could not in good conscience argue against the logic of the publishers that a book written from a personal point of view might well be more interesting than simply a straight history of events. So I agreed to undertake the combination of autobiography and history, and the account which follows is the result.

"But who is the author of this volume?" I can hear someone ask.

I was born in a little Quaker colony eighty miles south of Chicago on a bright October Sunday morning in 1884. But I have no memory of childhood life in Illinois. The depression of '87 almost broke my father's slender fortunes as a farmer, and he traveled westward to Kansas to explore the possibility of resettlement. That same year our home was re-established in the central part of Kansas, in another Quaker colony.

On a corner of the land which my father purchased and on which he was able to make a small down payment was a little Quaker academy named for Stephen Grellet, a French Quaker. This academy and the Quaker Meeting and community were, I am sure, the great attractions of the locality for my father.

From his exploratory visit, he had been much depressed by the low grade of work horses he found in the Kansas community, and he felt a kind of missionary call to improve the breed. Therefore, when we moved he brought from Illinois two mares and one stallion of Percheron stock. To this day, the horses around Glen Elder, Kansas, still reflect the improved breed which my father introduced.

It was in this simple rural environment where neighbors worked together, exchanging labor, helping each other in sickness, and maintaining a high level of community responsibility, that I grew up. In the periphery of the Quaker community were many kinds of settlers, some of whom indulged in practices which my parents thought threatened the moral tone of the area. There were drinking and dancing and card-playing, all of which were completely excluded by our family and neighbors. I still remember the sense of bewilderment that came to me as a growing boy when, one Fourth of July evening, my father took me to see the fireworks in town, and allowed me to stand by a platform that was erected in the town square, to watch the social dancing. I have a notion that he may have enjoyed it quite as much as I. But of course we did not participate.

The religious life of our community was deep and genuine. The ministry in the Quaker Meeting was contributed by neighbors who themselves were farmers. We had no official clergy. Later, an evangelist who brought into the fold some of our non-Quaker neighbors was invited to remain as a pastor, and we became a part of what is known in Quakerdom as the pastoral system.

The Friends Academy building burned down shortly before I was old enough to enter. But I had had the privilege of attending a little district school also located on the corner of our farm, and later I went to a newly established high school in Glen Elder. It was here that my contact with the wider world was begun. The principal, who incidentally was the sole teacher, had been imported from New England. He was a Quaker minister named Elam Henderson — a man of quiet, gentle spirit, who seemed to me to have remarkable knowledge and culture.

We lived three and a half miles from town. The first two years

I drove a horse and a little basket cart back and forth. The next year I graduated to a bicycle, which was the pride and joy of my life. Summers were spent working on the farm, where we had a long, hard struggle with a debt of $2500. With low prices for our products and frequent crop failures, it was often not an easy undertaking to pay the interest on that debt. I do not remember a time, however, when we didn't have enough food to eat, and I was never conscious that we were poor. By today's standards, living was very primitive.

We had a good-sized house and the traveling Quaker ministers who came to visit our little country Meeting usually stayed in our home. Glimpses of other horizons came to me when Henry Stanley Newman, a British Quaker who edited the paper called *The Friend* and also operated an orphanage, was our guest for several days. On Monday morning he helped me turn the washing machine that did the family laundry, and while we spelled each other at this monotonous job he pictured to me the beauties of the countryside in England. There is no doubt in my mind that here was the beginning of some of my yearning to see and know a wider world, and my belief in the importance of a broader experience.

When I was eight, my older sister Minnie was sent to Japan by Friends of Philadelphia to teach in the Friends Girls' School which had been established in Tokyo. Deep down in my inner heart there were forming resolves to follow in some fashion the kind of life that she was leading.

Meanwhile, I was learning to handle horses, milk cows, feed hogs, to cultivate crops, to endure heat and keep up courage when the hot wind destroyed the corn crop and consequently our hope of emerging from debt. I was the youngest of eight children, and as my brothers and sisters established homes of their own I was left to care for the farm, with considerable responsibility for my father and mother.

No member of our family had enjoyed the privilege of college training. But the contacts with visiting ministers who stayed in our home, the experience of my sister and that of one of the boys in our community who had gone to college, all had conspired to develop in me a hunger to know something of what is called higher education. Also, my mother vouchsafed to me one day that she hoped I would be a missionary. This was her conception of the life which called for the fullest dedication to religious service. I am sure that this comment from my mother, made one morning when the two of us were working in the garden, had as deep an influence on me as any other one thing that ever happened. I never became a missionary in the formal sense, but I saw that I had an inward response to the real concern she was expressing. She wanted me to work with human beings and for their betterment.

For two years after I finished high school I remained on the farm and during the winter taught the local elementary school. By the end of that time the debt on the farm had been paid off. We had been able to get a local neighbor to rent some of our land, and this opened the way for me to fulfill my cherished ambition. It was decided that I should go to Penn College, located at Oskaloosa, Iowa.

Life at Penn College then was very simple; but to me it offered a rich treasure of wider association, with teachers well trained and deeply dedicated. Here I was introduced to fields of knowledge which I had only vaguely known existed. Most of my fellow students planned to be schoolteachers, farmers, or ministers. There was a sprinkling of those who planned to be foreign missionaries.

I discovered in college that I had some gift in public speaking. I was interested in people. I had met a few ministers whom I greatly admired. Especially did this apply to Ellison R. Purdy, who was minister at the Meeting which I attended regularly while I was in college. I think it was his influence, coupled with the fact that I was able to secure scholarship assistance, which led me to go to theological seminary with the plan of becoming a minister.

Again, at Hartford Theological Seminary I experienced a delightful sense of an expanding world. I came into contact with people from many regions, and with fields of scholarship new to me. In retrospect I find that I have by no means accepted the patterns of theological thought which were laid before me as the product of able, staunch theologians, nor have I fully accepted the interpretations of the Scriptures that were given. Both fields of instruction had the effect of inspiring me to do my own thinking, and this exploration has been more valuable than if I had too readily accepted what was taught.

Soon after I had entered Penn College, I had watched Lilly Peckham walk down the street, and was greatly impressed by her. She was unknown to me, and she was further along in college than I. It took me a long time to get up courage to have a talk with her. . . . After college she went to the West Coast to teach school, while I finished college and then entered Hartford Seminary for three years' study. Patiently and impatiently we waited to be married until I had completed my graduate work. I believe that today's more common practice of marriage during student days may be much more sensible, but it was almost unheard of then.

We began our life together in Toronto, Canada, where I was minister of the Friends Meeting. Then in 1917 I was asked to return to the Meeting alongside Penn College. Part of the attraction to go back to this community was the fact that now the United States was in the World War, and I had developed a strong sense of responsibility for the difficult decision that many young men were having to make regarding their response to the military draft. From 1917 to 1919 we had a warm fellowship with men in college and in the Meeting who were making these deep emotional and spiritual decisions. I never took the position of urging men to claim conscientious objection to war, but rather discussed with them the issues involved in making a decision.

In the summer of 1912 I had visited England with my intimate friend Alexander C. Purdy, a college and seminary classmate. I have always been grateful that I was able to see England before the devastation of the First and Second World Wars. The beauty of the countryside charmed me; the quality of social thinking intrigued me. The sense of public responsibility was much further developed with them than with us. Although at that time there was a great deal of the external appearance of class consciousness, one could see and feel the effects of social revolution that was well under way. The social application of religious faith was beginning to be the focus of much of my attention.

In 1919 I was asked to become secretary of the Young Friends Movement, which involved the younger generation of Quakers throughout the United States. I had taken a live interest in this organization from its inception. The coming of the war had made us all realize the importance of rethinking our position as members of a religious body which by tradition and official pronouncement refused to participate in war, but sought with diligence for a way of life which did away with the occasion for war. The work of this younger generation seemed to me to correspond to the stage of development I had reached. So I worked with this group until 1922, when I became professor of Biblical literature at Earlham College, in Richmond, Indiana. Here I carried on the same quest for a way to apply the teachings of our religious faith and our Christian heritage to the social problems of our times.

In 1929 I was astonished to receive an invitation to become executive secretary of the American Friends Service Committee, whose headquarters were in Philadelphia. This quite overwhelmed me. I had been acquainted with the Committee's work, and thought of it as the great growing edge where the conscience of American Quakers was applied to the social order in which we lived. I knew that the undertaking was beyond me, yet it offered opportunities for growth, which I hoped I might live up to.

By now, two daughters, Rachel and Carolyn, had come into our home. We had lived a relatively simple and uncomplicated life. Lilly Pickett and I knew that for me to become secretary of the American Friends Service Committee meant living in a great metropolitan area, it would involve a great deal of travel in this country and abroad, and it would mean more separation than we liked. I realized that it took more courage for the family to face these changes than for me. But it seemed to us to be the right step to take, so from 1929 to the present this has been the scene of our labor.

The field of my religious training presupposed a clear definite sense of call to a particular kind of service. I must confess that this has never happened to me. The daily shaping of events has made virtually inevitable most of the decisions that have been taken. I have never aspired to a particular job or asked for one; nor have I been "stricken on the road to Damascus" as was Paul and had my way clearly dictated to me from the heavens. The entire course has been a maturing of family and personal decisions. In perspective I should say in all humility that my life has been characterized by an inadequate, persistent effort to try to find a workable harmony between religious profession and daily practice.

The pages that follow are a record of my twenty-two years with the American Friends Service Committee. They are by no means a complete history of the Committee's work during this period. I could not hope to be that exhaustive. I have touched on the program at points where I have been best acquainted with it, but literally hundreds of persons have carried out important pieces of work which are not so much as referred to. I should think that probably the most useful thing I have done at AFSC is to help open the way for a good many people to work at home and abroad, at hard jobs, sometimes for little or no pay, and often to be able to look back on such service as the richest experience of their lives.

The names of a few of those with whom I have worked are mentioned. But only a very few. Others whose names aren't there are just as precious in this fellowship of service. But I must here say that a great deal of what has happened could never have come about without the devoted and intelligent help of Blanche Cloeren Tache, who has been my secretary throughout this entire work with the American Friends Service Committee.

I hope that the way events are set forth in these chapters fully acknowledges that whatever has been accomplished is the result of wide participation. Above all, I hope that the book maintains a devout sense of reverence and gratitude to the Divine Spirit into whose channels of mercy and developing purposes for humankind we have consistently tried to find our way.

Contents

To Lilly P. Pickett, whose understanding and devotion made possible my share in the twenty-two years of work recorded here.

I
Economics and the Spirit

Were all superfluities and the desire of outward great-
ness laid aside, and the right use of things univer-
sally attended to, such a number of people might be
employed in things useful as that moderate labor with
the blessing of Heaven would answer all good purposes, and a sufficient number would have time to
attend to the proper affairs of civil society.

While our spirits are lively, we go cheerfully
through business; either too much or too little action
is tiresome, but a right portion is healthful to the body
and agreeable to an honest mind.

— JOHN WOOLMAN
A Word of Remembrance
and Caution to the Rich

1. Marion, North Carolina

Iᴛ is Norman Thomas calling from New York," said my secretary. It was the fall of 1929. I was still new to the business of being executive secretary of the American Friends Service Committee, and was just getting acquainted with its operations. Long-distance calls to our office were not very frequent in those days. In fact, I am not sure but there was a certain sense of flattery in being called up by someone as far away as New York. Here is what Norman had to say.

There was a bitter strike in a textile mill in Marion, North Carolina. Six strikers had been killed; others were injured. A feeble union had exhausted its relief funds. More than nine hundred persons had nothing to eat, and little to wear. Many of them were ill. Could the Service Committee* undertake to relieve their distress?

Norman Thomas himself was already working on the problem as chairman of the Emergency Committee for Strikers' Relief. Identified as he was with the striking workers and the cause of unionization, which did not then have the wide public support which it has today, he yet felt a crying need in that bitter industrial situation for some nonpartisan work of relief and healing of the spirit. This was the basis of his appeal to us, and it was not easy to argue against his premise of our interest in reconciliation.

It was the beginning of winter; nine hundred people eat food pretty fast. Where were the funds to come from? Who could ad-

---

* Ours is not the only "Service Committee" in the United States, but in this volume the term means AFSC unless otherwise designated.

minister such an enterprise? I had not been on the job long, but I knew that on our Board were some persons who tended to be a little suspicious of trade unions. Nevertheless, here was a real situation involving men, women, and little children who were hungry. And clearly there was need for human understanding in a bitter conflict. Of course there was precedent in the Service Committee's history for such domestic action. Back in 1922 in West Virginia, and again in 1928 in Pennsylvania, the Committee had, for brief periods, fed and clothed children of striking and otherwise unemployed coal miners. "I'll see what can be done," was the only answer I could give Norman Thomas.

James Myers, Industrial Secretary of the Social Service Commission of the Federal Council of Churches, had already gone to North Carolina to appraise the Marion situation. He found conditions appalling. In the ensuing days, telegrams from him and from Norman Thomas impressed upon us the urgency of the need as well as our Committee's special qualifications for serving in such a situation.

On October 18, by previous arrangement, James Myers attended a meeting of our Board of Directors and presented an official request for AFSC co-operation from the Federal Council of Churches, and a carefully prepared memorandum:

> I interviewed employers, workers, labor leaders, ministers, county and state officials, including the Governor and state and federal conciliators, spoke at the funeral of the strikers killed in front of the gates of the Marion Manufacturing Company on October 2nd, and visited in the homes of the strikers and others in the mill villages. I am convinced that a situation exists at Marion which is characterized by hate, fear, suspicion, unredressed wrongs, and the immediate need of relief in the form of warm clothing, proper food, medical and nursing care, milk for little children, money to pay for moving. . . . I am convinced that large numbers of Christian people everywhere will be quick to respond to this human need and unwilling that an economic conflict shall be settled by the pressure of hunger and privation. . . .

Personal interviews convinced me that many were working

12 hours a day and some over 12 hours. The manufacturers, when questioned on the matter of hours before the first strike, replied, "No one was working over 12 hours a day to the Company's knowledge." The state law prohibits any employee working over eleven hours a day. Wages according to the president of the Marion Manufacturing Company averaged $14 a week. Workers interviewed reported weekly earnings ranging from $5, $7, $9, $11, $12; and $16 and $18 a week for weavers....

A number of workers met out in the woods secretly and decided to send one of their number "to find a labor union organizer to come and help them form a union." This was done and a local of the United Textile Workers (AFL) was formed and charter obtained before "outside" leaders arrived to help conduct the first strike which was occasioned by discharge of a number of employees who joined the Union and were found out.

This report then described violent actions on the part of both strikers and officers of the law, the settlement of the first strike, persistent discrimination against union members, a second walkout on October 2, scuffling, and the shooting by the armed deputies. Now the mills were getting back into operation with nonunion labor. "We have a total of eight or nine hundred people without support because they were laid off by the mills," the report stated, and went on to cite sample cases:

Interview, Oct. 13th, with Mrs. R. (splendid type of woman). Her oldest son, 18 years old, one of the strikers killed by the Sheriff's forces. Husband died last year. Has five children still living. Boy 16. Girls of 14, 9, 7, 3. Mrs. R. herself has worked in the East Marion mill for two years in the spool room, averaging about $7 a week. Hours 6 A.M. to 6 P.M. "No time to go off at noon when plenty of yarn." Works on piece work. Says she wants to get work somewhere else as she keeps thinking of her boy and can't stand the thought of working in this mill any more. Very sweet small children with her.

J.L.W. Weaver. Worked for Marion Manufacturing Company 13 years. Discharged before first strike because belonged to the Union and informed that was the only reason. His daughter (15 years old) also discharged "as long as your father is not working." Has five children — very sweet and lovely. Wife very thin and worn.

James Myers had investigated local resources:

> I interviewed the County Welfare Commissioner who in addition to poor relief for the entire county is charged with the duty of enforcing school attendance (this is his main job), care of families of prisoners (which he is unable to attend to, to any extent). . . . His department is not equipped with funds or staff to handle an emergency. He said there are no county or public health nurses, and people are without such services entirely.
>
> I exhausted the possibilities of setting up a local church relief committee. . . . I interviewed local ministers . . . and all agreed that no local church committee could function impartially because of the sharp divisions, the public prejudice, and the influence of the mills in all the churches. The —— pastor at Marion is referred to by the strikers as their "worst enemy."

And, toward the end of the report, there was this note about funds: "The Social Service Commission of the Federal Council of Churches will cooperate energetically in the raising of funds."

This meeting of our Board of Directors was intensely significant. We had fed men, women, and children in many countries of the world, but we had made only slight beginnings in this country. As the social frictions which cause hunger came closer home, the decision was not so easy as it had been when those who needed help were farther away. A few members of the Board had had sad experiences in difficult negotiations with their own laborers. One in particular found it hard to believe that this was an appropriate thing for us to undertake.

However, at the end of a rather long afternoon session, Rufus M. Jones, honorary chairman of the Service Committee, who was presiding, expressed the conviction that there was practically a united concern in the group that such an undertaking should be entered upon. I knew very little about raising money, and I foresaw considerable need over and above what the Federal Council of Churches might be able to solicit. As we walked up the one flight of stairs to my office, one of the Board members who had been most difficult to convince that this was a right move hurried to my side and said, "Thee will need something to start on, and I will write thee a check for a thousand dollars."

The memory of that act of loyalty and encouragement has become for me a symbol of the priceless relationship which I have enjoyed for more than twenty years with the constituents of the American Friends Service Committee.

The financial agreement reached with the Federal Council of Churches in subsequent conferences anticipated relief for at least three months, December 1 to March 1. Estimates were that for relief alone this would cost in the neighborhood of $1000 a week, or a total of $12,000. For these funds the Social Service Commission of the Federal Council would make the major appeal. Our particular commitment was to obtain and pay personnel, supply supervision, and carry overhead expenses. Thus every cent of the money raised for relief could go directly into relief.

The problem of finding the right kind of personnel is always at the very heart of any undertaking. In this instance two Friends, J. Lawrence Lippincott, a farmer from New Jersey, and Frank D. Watson, professor of sociology at Haverford College, were prepared to go to Marion to help us get the project under way. But what should we do for someone to carry the work through the winter? It seemed natural and highly desirable to appeal to North Carolina Friends, with whom we had been in close consultation throughout deliberations on the Marion undertaking. It would be an inestimable advantage to secure a North Carolinian to supervise the project. Word came back that Friends at Winston-Salem were willing to release their minister, Hugh Moore, for this service, and that he would abide by our decision. This was a most auspicious beginning.

I had known Hugh Moore when he was a student at Guilford College, North Carolina. Visiting that institution as a kind of personal counselor, I had watched a love affair developing between Hugh and one of the most charming girls I had seen at any of our colleges. I had followed their later career as a married couple. I knew that as a minister Hugh had been successful in establishing a fine pastoral relation with his people and also in raising funds to build a new Meeting House. There was no question about his being a person of complete integrity and great ingenuity.

Early in November Hugh Moore proceeded to Marion where he worked with Frank Watson and Lawrence Lippincott in organizing relief operations while we at the Service Committee carried on an urgent search for a social worker and a visiting nurse to complete the permanent staff of three which had been decided upon. (Two qualified women were found in time to open operations on schedule.)

Letters from Marion kept us aware of the realities of the situation. The trials of the strikers for rioting were still in session and the atmosphere was one of excitement and tension. Union officials and newspapermen were much in evidence. But it was the people we had undertaken to serve about whom we heard most.

"They just walk right into one's heart, such is the beauty of their spirit in the face of tragedy," wrote one of our representatives; and he continued, "Ultimately the union must come. The spirit calling for it will never die. But the present need is for a labor of love for those wounded and bleeding in body and spirit in this first clash of the economic struggle."

Later there came word of a wonderful Christmas party for the children, for which one of the churches which had expelled the strikers had opened its doors. This was one of the first community moves toward reconciliation.

I decided to go down to get firsthand knowledge of the general situation, for I realized there were many complex peripheral considerations about which I knew little. The Marion mills were not the only industrial trouble spot in North Carolina. There was considerable disturbance in labor circles throughout that state. I wanted to feel the pulse of what was actually taking place, so that we could fulfill our commitments with as wide an awareness as possible. While it was not our function to try to settle the strike or solve labor problems, it seemed to me we should operate in close touch with whatever persons in North Carolina were doing the best kind of thinking along these lines.

Frank Graham was teaching sociology at North Carolina State College. He was only a name to me; I had seen a document published in the press which set forth the nature of the disturbance in the textile mills and expressed the concern of a list of citizens of the country, including Frank Graham, that these matters should be given orderly consideration. So I went to see Frank Graham in his little study and office in Raleigh.

The president of North Carolina University had just resigned to take another job. I knew that Frank Graham's father had been a former president of the University, and early in our conversation I raised the question as to whether he might not be the logical successor. "If there was ever any chance of that," he said, "it was surrendered when I signed that document which you have read. A liberal supporting the cause of labor in North Carolina cannot be elected president of the University of North Carolina."

He then gave me a rich background of understanding in connection with the problems of the textile industry in the South, especially labor's relation to management. He showed a grasp, not only of the immediate, but also of the long-range problems which industrialization of the South had brought about.

This was in vivid contrast to the viewpoint of R. W. Baldwin, manager of the Marion Manufacturing Company, with whom I later had a conference. Mr. Baldwin, whose aunt was chief owner of the company, was a conscientious, practicing churchman. He commuted from Baltimore, spending two or three days each week in Marion. He told me he always made a point of being in Baltimore

Wednesday evenings, so as not to miss prayer meeting. He said he
had tried to be honest and fair in his dealings with his workers.
He could not possibly understand why, when they needed employment so badly, they refused to work for him. He was not so angry
as he was hurt by their attitude. When I tried to explain to him
that in my limited experience I had never seen such inadequate
housing for workers, or such filth in mills anywhere, it seemed to
him incredible that he should be accused of unsatisfactory provision
for his workers.

In Marion, with James Myers and the field staff, I visited the
homes of many of the people who were being fed and clothed. It
was the coldest winter in those parts for twenty years, and there
was much illness. Among the children, pellagra was not uncommon. Most of the worst crowding was due to evictions from company houses. The mills said they were now fully staffed. Workers
had been imported from other towns: this was January, 1930, and
unemployment was spreading like the plague. Some union men had
been re-employed, but about four hundred workers (with their dependents) were left permanently stranded unless they could find
other types of work in the vicinity or move elsewhere.

We saw letters of dismissal which strikers — and even strikers'
nonparticipating wives and children — had received from certain
local churches: "This is to certify that X is a member of the ——
Church and is hereby dismissed from it to unite with any other
church of the same faith and order." One deacon who was also
overseer in a mill answered a woman who asked the reason: "The
union and the nonunion can't associate."

We had come into this Marion situation, not on the "union side,"
but to minister to the needs of union and nonunion people alike,
with a redemptive faith in the oneness of humanity. We were also
concerned for the human beings involved in management. We did
not want our presence there to deepen the bitterness, but to contribute to reconciliation. While we could not claim great achievement in this respect, I believe our insistence on the central value

of the individual did bear fruit. Certainly to the striking men and women who had been cut off by local churches, gradually it began to mean something that our efforts represented the concern of Christian people all over the country.

I visited the little three-room frame house used for clothing distributions and general headquarters for our program. Set up on pillars, this building was amply ventilated by wintry blasts sweeping up through wide spaces between floor boards. I witnessed food distributions at the commissary established in an old store on what was locally known as "Nigger Ridge" — a name which indicates the general spiritual and cultural level at that time in that place.

Each family certified for assistance came twice a week for rations which represented the barest minimum necessities of life — flour, lard, "fat back," dry beans, sweet potatoes. The few families who owned cows turned the milk over to the commissary in exchange for feed for the cows, and the milk was used for children in most urgent need of it. Most of the work of distribution was done by the strikers themselves, under AFSC supervision.

Hugh Moore showed real skill, not only in the purchase and distribution of food, for that was relatively simple, but in a kind of pastoral relationship which he was developing with the people of the community. He was much more than a good administrator; he was a spiritual adviser: one who brought tenderness, humor, and color into a drab and dreary life.*

It is interesting to note how it is always the little personal events which stay in the memory most vividly. While I was in Marion, I witnessed the last rites for "Uncle Joe," and learned something important which I have never forgotten. Uncle Joe was one of the older striking mill workers, and his strength came to an end during that cold hard winter. Like many another worker, he had car-

---

* Later Hugh Moore was to become a colleague in the Philadelphia office of AFSC as interpreter of its program and financial secretary, a post which he has filled with dedication and distinction for twenty years.

ried a small insurance policy which was supposed to take care of the expenses of his funeral. Three hundred dollars.

Three hundred dollars was a fortune under those circumstances. One would have thought that the simplest kind of burial might have sufficed, the savings being used by the family for food and clothing.

But nothing of the kind happened. Uncle Joe had a nice casket, and there was a bountiful supply of food for a sort of wake which accompanied the funeral, and to which most of the community came. The three hundred dollars, enough to have taken care of the family for months, had been completely expended by the time Uncle Joe was buried — in the course of only two or three days.

But the family for a brief moment had achieved a kind of distinction in that community, arising in part out of their very distress. I saw the effects of this on their spirits, and I couldn't help pondering it. Prudence would certainly have dictated another course, but I felt I had learned something valuable. Perhaps sometimes it pays to help satisfy those human cravings which are so often suppressed among people who must live on a subsistence basis and who have little opportunity to emerge from the drab mediocrity of their ordinary lives. Maybe the family of Uncle Joe was right.

We talked with citizens of Marion who knew little or nothing about the mill workers — citizens who supposed that because the mills were running again everything was all right. I was to discover many times during the next twenty years that it is possible to live just around the corner from tragedy and know nothing about it — either through blindness or through willing not to know. I was to realize that most of us partake of this guilt one time or another.

It is of course impossible to be thrown into a situation of this kind and to be satisfied just to feed people. Inevitably, one becomes concerned about solutions to the problems which lie behind the hunger. What could be done in this instance?

After my trip to Marion, I had my first experience in asking other manufacturers in the textile field to contribute money to help support strikers in this mill, which actually for them was a competitor; and my respect for the sense of responsibility among employers was enhanced as I talked with some of these men. It is to be remembered that this was during the early days of a very deep depression. Textiles especially were depressed, and one could understand the difficulty that industries had in giving for a strikers' fund at one of their less well administered mills, when they themselves were struggling against almost incredible odds to keep their plants going. While I was able to collect some money from these men, the most heartening thing was to see their growing resolve that the textile industry should not tolerate a mill which was so backward in its physical accommodations for its workers.

After hearing my story, one of the operators without my knowledge made a visit to the Marion mill, found conditions as I had put them to him, and offered to buy the mill. The offer was rejected, but this was the eventual solution in this instance; the Marion mill was purchased, and its working conditions, housing and sanitary facilities brought up to an improved standard by the new owners.

Everyone sincerely concerned in the Marion situation, including the union leaders, agreed that wholesale relief must be terminated just as quickly as the unemployed families could make other plans. But it wasn't easy. A few men were hired locally in other kinds of jobs. Many finally found work elsewhere, and the relief program paid their moving expenses. But by March first, when our services were scheduled to end, there were all too many families still destitute of resources or plans.

Our staff stayed two weeks into March to help a committee of local union men take over responsibilities for continuing assistance to these families. Arrangements were made with the storekeeper in whose store the union had its headquarters, to handle at a minimum profit such supplies as were most necessary.

The Federal Council of Churches had cause for deep satisfaction in the support which church people gave to this effort. Response from ministers and congregations in far-flung villages and cities was all that was asked and a little more, so that actual cost of relief supplies was borne almost entirely through their contributions.

Early in March, when the major part of the work was being brought to a close, James Myers received a letter from one of the North Carolina union organizers:

DEAR SIR,

May I presume upon your time and patience for a few minutes, as I most earnestly desire that you be acquainted with certain facts . . .

I was raised in a Christian home. My father was raised by Primitive Baptist parents, and he assisted in establishing the first Sunday School in his community. . . . My mother was of the "shouting Methodist" faith. . . . At the age of eleven, I began work in a cotton mill, sweeping floors, $2.40 per week.

As I grew older, I began to watch — pay more strict attention to my Sunday School teacher, and to the various ministers. Arriving at the age of 20, I left my home, and since have attended services at Episcopal, Methodist, and Presbyterian churches. I came to realize that 98 percent of the ministers, regardless of what passage of Scripture they used for the text of their sermon, the sermon was always the same.

I have heard the following sermon many, many times. It is non-Christian-like for employees to organize against their employers, what difference if your wages are insufficient, if ye have the faith ye shall reap your reward in Heaven. How often have I wondered, asked myself this question: Why don't the parson reverse the sermon and preach it for the benefit and welfare of his wealthy clientele, doesn't he care if the rich go to Hell? Is he only interested in the saving of the souls of the poor? How can one teach the Fatherhood of God to a barefoot person, and the Brotherhood of Man to people whose stomachs are empty, and who know their children are hungry, though they have just eaten, there being an insufficient amount of food?

We come now to the year 1929, and intolerable conditions which existed in the cotton mill villages of Marion, N.C.; the strike and the agreement, how its terms were violated by the mill management, with not a single minister or church member of the "uptown churches" interested, and the dismissal from the "village churches" of those who dared assert their God-given and man-made rights, more familiarly known as "constitutional rights." . . .

I had long since lost faith — not in God, for He is the same God of all time, but in those who were preaching and teaching the religion that Christ died that we might live. Thousands were sharing the same opinions. . . .

After the massacre, which I will not dwell upon, we had a visitor, one who was connected with the Federal Council of the Churches of Christ. "Who is he? What's he here for? Just another Psalm-singing Parson investigating, that he may tell his Holy Congregation of the 'evils' of working people wanting decent homes, better food, education for their children. . . . James Myers, Industrial Secretary of the Federal Council of Churches. What's he here for? Trying to assist us in this most trying time. Impossible. He is gone — just as we thought, another gesture, Holy people trying to fool God."

But one day in came those representing the American Friends Service Committee, working in conjunction with the Federal Council of Churches. . . . It was with suspicious minds we watched them. They were church people. It became known that Hugh Moore was a preacher. More suspicion.

What of their job? Oh yes, they did a wonderful job, in administering relief, food, clothing, and medical attention, without sound of trumpet or beat of drum, they have performed a humane service. What else? To a large degree they have restored our faith in the Christian ministry, in the churches. 98 percent of us now believe that there are good Christians still living. . . .

I cannot close this letter without paying tribute to the two members of the AFSC, Hugh Moore and Miss Winifred Wildman, with whom we are better acquainted than others. They are honorable Christians, and very innocent, I will even say ignorant, why, they even believe that a lawyer can be good and worldly wise as well. . . . They are loved and respected by those whom they have come in contact with here.

The following August, a revival meeting was imminent at one of the churches which had dismissed the strikers, and the evangelist insisted that the dismissed members be fully reinstated before the meetings began. This was done in the case of any of the dismissed members who still lived in the community. When I heard this, it seemed to me that if it were not all so serious, so intertwined with the people's physical and spiritual life and death, it would be a grand comedy.

The national depression had been worsening steadily throughout the summer, and our Committee was being drawn into other efforts in connection with the textile industry. We were taking part in mediations, and expecting new calls for relief.

But by the following spring, before we had worked further in any major way in the textile field, it was coal that held the head-lines for unemployment, crisis, and suffering. It was the coal industry that was to be the gateway into our most substantial participation in our country's efforts to meet the challenge of the depression of the '30s.

From the Marion experience we had gained a rich host of new friends. The people of Marion, the mill workers, even the mill operator, who seemed to have so little understanding of the forces with which he was dealing, had continued to maintain an attitude of co-operation with us. If in some cases this attitude was more politic than real, it still meant that relationships were kept open — which in times of crisis is exceedingly important.

Perhaps not least of all, this emergency work in Marion had helped a new secretary functioning within the framework of what might have become a sectarian committee to push his own horizons and those of the Committee further out into some of the problem areas of our country, and to form contacts with the hot vein of human pressures that are called into play in the operation of our industrial structure.

Little did I realize then that twenty years later, when we were collecting gifts in kind for relief abroad after the Second World War, echoes of this experience in North Carolina would be heard as the textile industry came forward with unusual generosity, do-nating nearly two million dollars' worth of beautiful woolen and cotton textiles. I do not mean to imply that our work in Marion had any direct bearing on this later gift, but it had at least supplied a backlog of good will and many points of mutual confidence.

In the perspective of the past twenty years' growth of the labor movement, the now generally recognized right of labor to organize, the more adequate pay for the daily worker, the new sense of responsibility on the part of both labor and management, this early experience in Marion sounds very elementary and primitive; but it constituted a kind of meeting point of economics and mercy which has been characteristic of many activities in which our Committee has participated over these years. And I am more than ever confirmed in my conviction that these two can never be separated in a sound working society.

In the spring of 1930, just after the major part of our work in Marion had drawn to a close, I paid a brief visit to the Soviet Union.

On the train going toward Moscow I saw numerous rural villages with squalid houses for the farmers, the church with its tall steeple still dominating the village architecture.

In Moscow, I visited the Museum of the Godless — happily now, I believe, no longer in existence. There I saw portrayed the various forms of exploitation practiced by the church and the priests. Peasants had been required to support a church whose presence was supposed to be the symbol of mercy and concern for people of the community. However, that church had lost — one may say forfeited — its place in the center of Russian community life. This sad development gave considerable justification for the powerful new government's caricature of the institution.

I also saw the transfer of concern for one's neighbors in the individual community, saw it transferred into a function of the impersonal over-all state. Here was a vivid display of what happens when suffering comes and religion fails. I wondered if something like that were happening to us in the United States. Were we losing the sense of local responsibility? Most of the churches in Marion had not concerned themselves with the mill workers and their plight. The latter lived on the wrong side of the tracks. I suppose it was a burden which the people of Marion could hardly have been expected to bear alone. I was profoundly grateful that church people as a whole had rightly assumed a sense of responsibility in the situation, and were continuing to extend their concern into areas of economic crisis in our country.

But this still left unanswered my question as to the significance of the loss implicit in the breakdown of a sense of personal local responsibility. I could see that as a mill distributes its products to the four corners of the world, so responsibility is spread far and wide. I could see that sudden mass dislocations of workers, the need for regularized provision for people caught in such catastrophes, might of necessity call for state action.

But if this were true, did it not confront the church with a double challenge — to see that it did not neglect its own sense of spiritual and physical ministry to those in distress, and also to undertake with increasing intelligence and conscience to influence the way in which the state carried out its responsibility?

In that year of 1930, these were dimly glimpsed as problems that could not be entirely avoided.

2. *The Coal Fields*

It was a gala afternoon occasion at Bryn Mawr College in the spring of 1931. The M. Carey Thomas Prize of $5000 was being awarded to Jane Addams. Distinguished speakers on the program included Grace Abbott, chief of the United States Children's Bureau.

The ceremonies were followed by a tea for the large throng, among whom was Rufus Jones. In the course of the afternoon, he found himself talking with Grace Abbott.

At the request of President Hoover the Children's Bureau was at that time making a study of the condition of children of unemployed coal miners. Reports coming in from counties under investigation painted a stark picture of what it was meaning to be a child in the coal-mining regions of the Allegheny and Blue Ridge Mountains: grave shortages of food and clothing, inadequate housing, widespread illness which it would soon be too late to cure.

Grace Abbott, always a person of unusual charm, but never forgetting her passion to meet human needs, laid this situation before Rufus Jones. Then, knowing how to be effective, she clinched her argument by saying that President Hoover had suggested that she talk this matter over with Rufus to see whether the American Friends Service Committee might undertake to feed these children.

His imagination began to work at once. When he came to the office the following Monday morning, he was all aglow with this new sense of opportunity that had come to our Committee. I knew little about the bituminous coal fields of this country; I had only vague conceptions of conditions in the industry, the workers' way of life, and the many ramifications which such an adventure would open up.

I did of course know that coal, even before the depression, was a sick industry. It had been clear in earlier years when the Committee worked in the coal fields that the industry was in the grip of a crisis which, though it was intensified in places by individuals' ignorance and selfishness, was basically the result of economic and industrial forces which were as yet but dimly comprehended.

Coal production had become greatly overexpanded in the years directly following the war, and now the depression, coming as it had in the midst of fumbling and sometimes tragic efforts at retrenchment, had thrown the whole industry into complete confusion. About 200,000 miners were more or less permanently out of work through no fault of their own. A large proportion of them not only had never done any other kind of work, but lived in regions where, with the mines shut down, it would have taxed anyone's ingenuity to find ways of making a living for a family. An additional 300,000 miners were employed only spasmodically, and wages had become so depressed they could hardly be dignified by that name any longer. In the frantic competition for survival, prices on coal were slashed below production costs, so that often the best-meaning employers were unable to pay living wages and stay in business. Under these conditions, strikes became pitifully futile.

After conversations among ourselves and correspondence with Grace Abbott, she and Fred C. Croxton, acting chairman of the President's Emergency Committee for Employment, came to Philadelphia and presented the full situation to our Board of Directors, officially requesting that our Committee assume responsibility for a program of child feeding.

It was eventually decided that we should undertake relief operations in selected areas, in the hope of demonstrating what might be done by other groups, governmental or industrial. This idea of "pilot projects" is one which has always appealed to the Service Committee, since in most situations in which emergency action is called for we do not have at our command the resources, in either funds or personnel, to tackle the whole problem. In this instance, in the light of later developments it is interesting to note that we thought in terms of concentrating on "one, and perhaps eventually as many as four" of the neediest mining communities.

Although this was looked upon primarily as a relief undertaking, those of us who had had experience in such enterprises knew from the beginning that it could never be kept fully within the bounds of relief. With half a million miners facing bewildering and often tragic insecurity, it was inevitable that we should become concerned about long-time solutions as well as emergency measures.

President Hoover could be a stern man when occasion called for such an attitude, but when, in the early days of our deliberations concerning this enterprise, Rufus Jones, Henry Tatnall Brown, Lucy Biddle Lewis, and I sat around his table in the White House discussing the prospects, he spoke with a depth of understanding and appreciation which strengthened our confidence in AFSC and in myself as the one who should have considerable administrative responsibility. This was of immeasurable value to me. By no means least of all, he added that he would turn over to us $225,000 remaining from the American Relief Administration Children's Fund, provided we would do our utmost to raise the additional funds necessary, especially making sure that local governments and agencies were giving every assistance possible. Tentatively, we were thinking of the undertaking in terms of about two years' duration.

When I had considered coming to the Service Committee as its executive secretary, I had been told by Wilbur K. Thomas, the retiring executive secretary, for whose judgment I had reason to have high regard, that the total current annual budget of the Committee was somewhat more than $100,000, that the income was shrinking, that soon the overhead was likely to take so large a proportion of the income that services would dwindle and support be difficult to secure.

Yet here was a new single operation calling for several times the amount of our budget. Could we possibly match the amount President Hoover was setting aside? Well, during the first year alone, the public's response to the "universality of destitution" in the coal fields enabled us to carry out a $400,000 program.

Bernard G. Waring, of Philadelphia, accepted the responsibility of general director of this coal-areas work, bringing to the task invaluable business experience and the enthusiasm which was invariably his response to a genuine religious and social challenge. We sought a field director with training in economics and sociology whose interest would be focused primarily on the larger problems of rehabilitation. Homer L. Morris, professor of economics at Fisk University, would be just the person. He had served with the Committee in Germany, Poland, and Russia, and his religious commitment, abilities, and interests were all exactly right. Fisk granted his request for a leave of absence.

The fine working relationship we had enjoyed with the Federal Council of Churches in Marion, North Carolina, now bore fruit of further co-operation in this effort. They contributed personnel to the Coal Committee; and through their official approval of the work and the energetic services of their staff, they greatly augmented funds and clothing collections.

Within five months 40,000 children were being fed. They were in 563 communities scattered from northern Pennsylvania to Tennessee, with a special concentration in western Pennsylvania, West Virginia, and eastern Kentucky. About fifty-five men and women, mostly volunteers, driving secondhand cars which had been procured for this purpose, were daily carrying out their round of services.

Here, for instance, was a great coal vein opened up during the First World War in northern West Virginia, a vein fourteen feet thick, of beautiful bituminous coal, pouring forth its immeasurable wealth; it had helped to make steel, to create steam for all kinds of power plants, including railroads. But now its operations were largely stilled because of the slowing down of the industrial machine. People had endured bad housing and unsanitary conditions as long as wages kept them fed and work was active, but spirits had become bitter and moods threatening when unemployment was robbing them of food and shelter.

Into this scene went two women who had had experience in relief work in Russia after the Revolution — Alice Davis and Nadia Danilevsky. Alice had gone to Russia for the Service Committee in the middle '20s, and there had formed a lasting friendship with Nadia, who belonged to one of the distinguished families of old Russia, a deeply religious and cultured woman who after the Revolution dedicated herself completely to the needs of people in distress. Now further seasoned by nurses' training and professional experience in social work, these two women organized in a masterly way the distribution of food and clothing. They were even successful in setting up an outdoor oven to bake bread for the community, a nursery school to take care of the children, a system of sewage disposal to make sanitary the stream which trickled down through the camp.

The climate of these years is rather easily forgotten in the midst of the inflation in which we are now living. "We arrived at one town just after notice had been posted of the complete closing of the mines," wrote James Myers, who was investigating conditions for the Federal Council of Churches in the fall of 1931:

A deserted village filled with still living people. They stood idly about or sat on the porches of the company houses. There was no place to go — no work to be obtained anywhere. The steep hillsides which rose above the narrow valley hemmed them in. By the most arduous effort some of them had last summer cultivated patches on the almost perpendicular hillsides, and had perhaps a "poke" of corn laid up against the winter. There was a general atmosphere of silence — like a funeral. . . . The mine officials were as concerned as anyone. . . . The Quaker representative explained tactfully to a group gathered for the purpose — the school supervisor, teachers, the local minister, the mine manager, and a group of women (the

"Ladies' Aid"), and members of the Parent-Teachers Association — that the Friends Service Committee would be glad to supply food for a hot lunch to be served in the school each day to such children as might need it. "You've come to the right place," said the school supervisor.

Courage, compassion, rage, and silence were intermingled with the victims' search for a way out.

We went on to Pigeon Roost [read one worker's report]. At the mouth of the creek we spied the most dismal of sheds. We crossed on stepping stones and waded through the mud. A woman poked her head through a paneless window and said, "Come in by the door, my old man is blind." . . . He was a gigantic man, with a mop of thinning blond hair and an apostolic stubble of beard. His mouth was nearly empty of teeth. One eye was stony, and the other one was covered by a dirty patch. He got up when we entered, grabbed for me and caught my arm. "This man," I thought, "is going to be violent." Then I recognized my idea as a relic of dealing with civilized nerves. He meant me no harm. He was eaten to the vitals with a rage against his world, and here was an outsider to hear him. He tapped his once broken legs, tore open his shirt to show caved-in ribs, pulled the patch from his wounded eye. I could not help but see him as a ragged, much too young King Lear; without the dignity of fighting clean death on a winter heath. His anger subdued all of us. He had been a miner, he said, for forty-five years. His bones had been broken in accidents, but the mine companies then had taken care of him and his family. His right eye had gone in a powder blast years ago. He had provided for his family all his life until last May, when a piece of coal lodged in his left eye and his boy had walked him home blinded. There he had sat ever since. He wanted to work, but he never could again. Why did the company doctor refuse to sign his paper for compensation? He was blind, and compensation was the law. He went into a muddled harangue . . . a mass of incomprehensible ideas through which blazed his sense of injustice. There was no answer to give him. He was probably wrong about some of the facts. The company doctor must be presumed innocent of cheating a blind miner. The only reality to me was, the spectacle of a strong man with the sap still in him, spending his rage and his strength, certain to drag out the rest of his days in infinitely slow cooling of that rage, until he should no longer care whether there was food in the shack.

The people in these coal camps were not used to receiving "charity." Often they were literally starving, but more than one father or mother explained to our workers that they had "hated to ask." The roots of the tragedy here were nation-wide, and the responsibility could not have been laid on the local communities alone. As a community leader of Morgantown * put it, Morgantown simply could not be expected to carry the entire burden of relief for thousands of miners brought into the county by coal companies which in turn were owned almost entirely by outside capital.

Banks in these mining regions were closing thick and fast in the fall of 1931. "Last night about eleven o'clock," a letter told us, "Mrs. Runner called us to say that Mr. Leadbeter, the new superintendent of the Crown Mine, was anxious to get in touch with us to ask us to begin feeding at once. He had visited the mine that afternoon, and was so impressed with the seriousness of the situation that he had given as much as he could out of his own pocket and had called upon Mr. Henry of the County Court for help. The Court is absolutely bankrupt at the present time and no taxes are coming in, because of the bank failures. The Council of Social Agencies gave a grocer their last money, a cheque for about $60. The Second National Bank closed its doors before he could cash it, and he does not know whether he will be able to carry even this sum for them. The Salvation Army has lost its funds. The Union has no money. . . . "

* In this chapter, the story of our coal-fields work is told largely in terms of the Morgantown, West Virginia, area, because I personally witnessed developments there more consistently than in other regions. There are equally interesting, and in some cases more intense, stories to be told about other communities. Conditions in Kentucky were particularly grim and challenging.

In publicizing our work, we made a good deal of the point that the resources of states and local communities were exhausted. This was true so far as funds were concerned; it was not true when it came to the co-operation of the people. An agency coming in from the outside, fresh and new to the scene, is helpless unless it can merge its resources with the concerns and desires of the people in the local community.

Furthermore, it would be a grave mistake to picture our program as coming in to interest local people in the miners' plight, and to initiate action. Actually we were coming to help already over-burdened localities. In the Morgantown area, for example, one of the first persons to welcome us was Dr. William E. Brooks, pastor of the First Presbyterian Church in that city and chairman of the County Welfare Board. He was a poet and a scholar. He had a great sense of humor, and a broad feeling of responsibility for local conditions. He and several of the faculty of the University of West Virginia, as well as other local residents and officials, had done wise planning and given sacrificial help long before we arrived. In fact, the Council of Social Agencies they had formed, in an effort to deal with the emergency, was one of the groups which had ap-pealed to the United States Children's Bureau, which in turn had appealed to us.

In any locality, schools and churches were always among the first groups approached. Usually schools were used as feeding centers. Teachers distressed by the lethargy of half-starved children were more than willing to co-operate in every way possible. James Myers, after accompanying a couple of our workers up a narrow "holler" to visit one of the many little isolated one-room schools, reported:

Not soon shall I forget the sight of the schoolroom, its grimy walls brightened with a flock of paper bluebirds made by the children, in its battered windows bright paper Christmas trees. In command of her fifty-one pupils of all ages and grades stood a magnificent woman. Beside her little desk stood a table, on the table an electric stove with a great pan of steaming cocoa which, together with apple-butter sandwiches, constituted the "700 calories" for that day. It was small wonder that, amid her small army of children and her multitude of duties, she failed to hear the plea of a pinched-faced little boy near me. "I'd like," he whispered, "I'd like for to git me another sandwich."

Often mothers of the community helped prepare the food. Men came around to volunteer their assistance in setting up needed facilities.

Some of the coal operators, too, gave valuable assistance. The local owner of a coal mine who lived close to his workers was likely to be especially helpful. It was more difficult to reach those owners whose offices were in distant cities.

We were interested to discover that the Ford Motor Company owned large mines in eastern Kentucky, and that there was real distress in those mines. I took it upon myself to discuss this situation with Edsel Ford. I found him most sympathetic. As we talked, it seemed there were two things that might be done: one was that the company might make a contribution to our work; the other was that they might themselves shoulder responsibility for the special relief required at their mines. They decided upon the latter course, and carried out their program with adequacy and dispatch.

Our relief operations did not always run smoothly. Two of our young women were spending a long, hard day at a school in southern West Virginia, hearing the statements of parents about the number of children in the family, their own status of employment, total income, and any other sources of relief, to make up authentic relief rolls. Politics is always a meaningful topic of conversation in these communities, and for some reason the report got spread abroad that our workers were feeding Republicans only. Men of the neighborhood watched with eagle eye over the shoulders of these women while they took the statistical data of the day. Men don't shave as often when they are unemployed; domestic quarrels thrive; also many of them lean toward hard corn liquor to drown their cares. In the overheated schoolroom, the hot scented breath pouring out of the semiangry group of men huddled about the reiief workers throughout the day was symptomatic of a tenseness of feeling which was ominous, and the women had to close up for the night before the job was finished. Rumors had it that they would never be back, or that they were definitely furnishing relief to persons of one political connection, or the other, but not to both. As they were driving back toward Charleston for the night, a bullet zipped through the windshield and out through the top of their little car. It was a close call, but no one was injured.

The governor and his staff had been most co-operative, and the women relief workers thought it appropriate to report this incident to state officials. The immediate response of the governor was to offer to call out the state militia, but our workers restrained him, saying that any such step would make their work very much more difficult in the local community.

In view of the degree of suffering and insecurity among the people, it is remarkable that this was the only instance of physical violence of any sort toward our workers throughout our entire relief experience in the coal fields, stretching over a period of nearly three years.

However, the workers sometimes found themselves witnesses to violent tragedies. I think of the explosion in a mine up Scotts Run, near Morgantown, West Virginia, which resulted in the death of thirteen men. Some of our field staff were among those who tried heroically, but futilely, to get through to the trapped miners before it was too late.

Eleanor Roosevelt and I were asked to participate in a memorial service for these men. It was held in a high-school building near Scotts Run, and it was an occasion for the expression of the deep grief of an entire community. Coming from the outside, from a protected world, both of us, I think, felt inadequate to express our fellowship with these people in their suffering.

During this period I had relatively little direct contact with the work of distributing food and clothing — only enough to give me a sense of the real tragedy that lay behind what one saw as children eagerly ate their porridge or drank their allowance of milk, or became silent with ecstasy over a pair of secondhand shoes. It was the children who were the designated recipients of a major part of our relief, and it was the children who responded quickly to extra rations. To see them at a picture show put on by the relief program was to marvel at their gaiety and charm. From a radius of several miles they would come, hundreds of them, white and Negro, and crowd onto the floor of a bare barrack, singing lustily until time for the pictures to begin, "Old MacDonald Had a Farm," or "Many a Beau Have I Let Go Because I Wanted Julie."

In Marion, North Carolina, all the textile workers had been white. In the coal fields, we were reaching native white and Negro families, as well as foreign-born. Wherever our program could bring racial and national groups into closer friendship, that we considered a major result, no less important than bread for the hungry.

The immediate tragedy was the continuance of unemployment. Second only to this, economically speaking, was the widespread chronic poverty of some of the states. Obviously, what we were doing was only a stopgap measure. Relief efforts of this sort on a wide scale should be a public responsibility.

I undertook to have talks with governors, with legislators, with county officials, with anyone who might in the normal course of events be the official to take care of these responsibilities. Without exception, everyone was a sympathetic listener. However, at that time, the state of West Virginia had seen its forests denuded largely by companies owned outside of the state, the wealth accruing from the forests transmitted to Philadelphia, New York, and other locations. This activity had left only a very small residue in taxes to help maintain the unemployed workers who had assisted in the process of deforestation. Now the forests were gone, but great veins of coal had been discovered. However, at present most of this coal seemed not to be needed!

Perhaps, after all, we who were collecting money in the larger metropolitan centers for relief work in mining camps were only helping very modestly to return to these regions some of the profits which had been drained away to the cities, leaving impoverished communities behind. As this became clear, it was with good conscience that one thought it right to support public officials in a policy of increasing taxes on exploitation of local resources when so much of the profit from such operations went outside the state.

I later appeared before governors and state legislatures in Pennsylvania, West Virginia, Kentucky, and Illinois, in defense of more adequate provision for state funds to take over the emergency relief work as quickly as possible, realizing that our own efforts must be temporary and instead of relieving the public of its responsibility should stimulate states to act. It was during these days that one saw a new sense of sharing suffering being born. Was this the birth of the Welfare State in our midst? We didn't stop to philosophize much in this emergency. We felt then, and I still feel, a justness in this growing sense that the chief function of the state should be the welfare of its whole citizenry.

The problem of alternative employment under circumstances such as those which prevailed in the early '30s was most difficult. One had a profound respect especially for the smaller coal companies which tried to find outside employment for their workers, even though these smaller companies often were suffering financial losses which endangered their capital structure.

Crown Mine, in northern West Virginia, was a typical illustration. This mine, isolated from other communities, had been closed down, and about fifty-five families were left destitute of any income. We decided to make it a test case, and see what could be done.

Usually coal camps are not in good agricultural country, and Crown Mine was no exception. But something could be done to revive gardening. Clearly, the situation called also for the introduction of crafts.

In the first months, a carpenter and furniture-making shop, a cobbler shop, and sewing classes were established, but the problem of a market for handwork was very difficult, unless some unusual product could be turned out. The mere initiation of new activities was having a revitalizing effect, but we needed a person — or a couple — to give full time to the project, to work with it and help find the key to its success. The leadership called for was the kind which cannot be bogged down by discouragement, for the situation was a depressing one to walk into.

Well do I remember having dinner one evening in the Brooklyn apartment of two young people who had been students of mine when I was a college professor. Also, I had presided at their marriage. They were William and Ruth Simkin. Both were now teaching school in Brooklyn. I knew of their interest in attempting something that involved the use of vivid imagination in the field of social change. So on this occasion I suggested to them that they might join us in West Virginia and see what they could do to develop the Crown Mine experiment. I was delighted when a few days later they said they would like to undertake the venture.

Bill was born in a little village in northern New York and had helped his father, a hardware merchant, in plumbing, carpentry, and all sorts of handy jobs. Both Bill and Ruth seemed to me to have the kind of spirit that would enable them to understand and successfully live with the people in these distraught communities, and in this I was not mistaken.

One of the first things they did, through arrangements with the mine superintendent, was to take an empty company house right at Crown Mine, clean and paint it, and move in, so that they might be part of the community. This was in the spring of 1932, and immediate problems at Crown Mine had to do with seed, seed potatoes, fertilizer, farm placements of a few men, sale of some of the handwork.

But Ruth Simkin wrote: "The thing which goes to my heart most quickly here is the group of boys and girls between 12 and 18. Just old enough to dream and nothing to dream about. They can't afford bus tickets to the high school in Morgantown. I'm sure we can do something to correct this awful condition next winter."

Other letters from Ruth brought glimpses of weaving and other handwork, a library, a playground, clubs, a nursery school with older girls in charge, a community play, and progress in gardening. Meanwhile the search for crafts to make the community self-supporting seemed to point increasingly toward the woodworking development if only it could be put on a more highly skilled basis.

This search diligently carried on led one day about the middle of March to a meeting at the University of West Virginia, sponsored by the University Extension Division — a meeting of persons interested in woodwork and other rehabilitation schemes. It was at this conference that some of our representatives met Tom Skuce, State Extension Forester, and that was an historic meeting.

Tom Skuce was alive to his fingertips with ideas for rehabilitation. He was enthusiastic when he heard about the Crown Mine experiment. He knew exactly the man who could put the furniture-making project on its feet. Tomorrow he would go with Bill Simkin to the far ends of the state to see Bud Godlove.

Bud Godlove, a mountaineer of German extraction, had been making a particular kind of chair most of his life. About 150 miles from Morgantown, in the wilds of the Monongahela National Forest, five generations of his people had been furniture makers. The tradition was that their furniture lasted forever — or practically so; that they had genuine pride of craftsmanship, and that they could always sell as much as they could make.

"He is a real craftsman," Bill Simkin reported after his first visit to Bud Godlove, "a man who would rather not make chairs than make them out of faulty material or in any way less than perfect. His shop is witness to his ingenuity and skill, all of the equipment being homemade. He seems very much interested in the idea of teaching miners in the art of chair-making. I feel he has a very unselfish desire to pass on to someone else the skill he has achieved through years of work. His own boys have not taken the idea of chair-making very seriously, and he seemed to brighten up at the prospect of his work being carried on by others."

A few days later, more of our field staff, including Homer Morris, visited Bud Godlove. They saw chairs made by his family as far back as 1760 and still in use. He had never in his life been more than fifty miles from his home, yet it was said there was hardly a house in the Shenandoah Valley that didn't have in it at least one chair made by him, his father, or his grandfather. He had nothing on paper. All the dimensions and designs were in his head or on a series of measuring sticks with pins driven through at the proper places. One of his secrets was to use native woods, and do his own curing. That meant cheap material. He estimated that the cost of materials in a chair for which he received two dollars was about twenty cents. Homer Morris talked with him in specific terms about coming to Crown Mine for a few months, and at the close of that visit arrangements were fairly definite that he would come.

It is an exciting story for all of us who had a share in the development: how Bud Godlove came and with the men's help immediately set up a lathe and a shaving horse in the old store building which Mr. Leadbeter, the mine superintendent, had made available for the purpose; how the hickory wood which the men had labored so hard to have ready wasn't straight-grain enough to suit Bud Godlove, so the search had to start all over again.

Such were the beginnings of the successful chair industry at Crown Mine. At the outset, seventeen men were candidates for the new training. After all, there was nothing to lose, and there might be something to gain.

At first some of the men were awkward in handling woodworking tools. Their experience had been in tearing loose the works of nature at the face of the coal in the mines. Now they must learn to conserve and shape with precision and skill the precious wood brought in from the scarce timber supply of the

West Virginia hills. Bud Godlove was patient in showing them how to fashion a chair so that the joints tightened as the wood seasoned. He was inexorable in his demand that the thing be done right.

All seventeen men were able to support their families only because Service Committee relief was available. They were receiving very little pay for their efforts in chair-making, but they were learning a new trade. Gradually, this fact alone began to bring a new spirit of hope and accomplishment into the hitherto stricken community. These men might no longer be dependent upon the fate of coal! If they made good enough chairs, the Committee had agreed to do its utmost to find a market for them. It might be that in this way they would finally emerge from the despised dependence upon coal-mine scrip, which was about the only money they had had for years! Could they eventually escape company housing and be able, perhaps, to live the dignified and independent life of which they had dreamed?

At the end of six months, every one of the seventeen men who had worked from the beginning under Bud Godlove's instruction was able to honestly classify himself as at least a hammer-and-saw carpenter, and six eventually became skilled woodworkers. What was more, other men had now joined their ranks.

The little experiment flourished beyond our dreams, and soon outgrew the shop at Crown Mine. Within the first year it was moved to much larger quarters in an old junk shop near the Monongahela River in Morgantown, where it was combined with other craft developments around Morgantown to form the Mountaineer Craftsmen's Co-operative Association. The basic products of this Association were Godlove chairs and cabinet work from Bertha Hill Mine; there were also needlework and weaving, work in pewter, copper, brass, and iron.

The marketing of these products was developed largely through the ingenuity of one energetic and dedicated woman.   Shortly after the craft industries had moved to Morgantown, Edith Maul, a Friend deeply enthusiastic over the workmanship of these men and women, and understanding its meaning to them, loaded a little truck with chairs, tables, and stools, as well as other handwork, and drove from one Quaker gathering to another, especially in the Middle Atlantic and New England states, interesting communities in the whole Crown Mine experiment and particularly in the virtues of the hand-hewn furniture. Throughout the East, notably in Quaker homes, one can today find many pieces of furniture made in that little original shop in Crown Mine, West Virginia, or in the Morgantown junk shop. They are now on their way to becoming family heirlooms, priceless products of beauty and endurance.

Primed by Edith Maul's persistent enthusiastic salesmanship, the demand for the Mountaineer Craftsmen's Co-operative Association products grew rather rapidly, in certain periods outstripping supply. From 1933 through 1936, $43,000 worth of furniture alone was sold. But the true value was human rather than economic. Hope was returning and confidence was rising that men displaced by industry were still capable of creating values and beauty.

Meanwhile, gardening had continued to be one of the most dependable aspects of rehabilitation efforts throughout the coal fields. In Monongalia County, West Virginia, for instance, enthusiastic garden clubs had been formed; church kitchens had been made available for canning purposes; and in 1933, thirty-four clubs had raised and canned $59,453 worth of food in addition to what was eaten fresh. Besides co-operating with the local Council of Social Agencies in these garden enterprises, we had been able to locate a few families on the land, with provisions that enabled them gradually to buy the property.

Some of our craft and farm experiments were less successful than others. Even at their best, none of us claimed that they represented the solution for all unemployed miners. But they had proved false the almost universal claim in those days that coal miners could learn no other skill and could not be interested in trying.

For a voluntary agency such as the American Friends Service Committee, it is quite as important to know when to quit an enterprise as it is to know when to begin, but it is far more difficult to quit. Personal relationships and a vision of new things to be done sometimes tend to cause an agency to stay on too long. In this instance, it was a great satisfaction to find our workers energetically assisting in the development of local organizations, eager to induce township, county, and state to take over.

The sense of public responsibility in the situation developed rather slowly, especially in parts of Kentucky. There the commissioner of public health, Arthur McCormack, came to the rescue, exhibiting fine statesmanship in helping the state to acknowledge and meet its responsibilities, and to profit by the things we had done.

In Logan, West Virginia, in a region notably deficient in health provisions, a health service, financed in the beginning partly by the Service Committee and partly by coal operators, later was taken over by the county, the miners' union, and the coal operators, and still continues under the name of Friends Health Service.

Our Committee finally withdrew from all direct relief operations in the coal fields, leaving plans for federal and state participation, but we brought away with us many lasting friendships, a very precious residue.

During approximately a three-year period, we had received and used in this one enterprise close to a million dollars in money and gifts in kind. More than 150 tons of used clothing had been cleaned, mended, shipped, and distributed. We had utilized well over 150 persons from outside the coal communities, and hundreds of local citizens had participated in actual distributions of food and clothing. Governors, sheriffs, labor organizers, coal operators, steel-company executives, social workers, government officials, ministers, schoolteachers, college professors — all of these I find on the list of those who took a deep and sacrificial interest not only in meeting the physical needs of children during a depression, but also in trying to think through a way in which such calamities might be avoided in the future.

It would be impossible to name the many organizations and individuals who made substantial donations to this work. During the second year, Reconstruction Finance Corporation funds were turned over to us in certain areas at the request of local officials. And in the third year, Federal Emergency Relief money in Kentucky was assigned to us to administer.

By no means least among the values coming to me from the coalfields experience was getting to know the operators who were responsible for the management of a great industry in this country.

Often coal had been discovered in parts of the country where housing and the social institutions necessary for an organized society were practically nonexistent. Coal mining had been developed largely before the general use of automobiles; housing, water supply, shopping centers, all facilities for a community life, had to be provided — a condition which gave operators an abnormal control over workers. There was much serious exploitation. Miners and their families were required to trade at company stores, kept in debt so they couldn't move, often charged higher prices than prevailed in neighboring, nonmining communities. Also the residential communities thus thrown together were located in what were usually extremely unhealthy surroundings. Smoke and dust from the mines, and pollution of streams which ran through the camps, were critical problems.

With the increase in popular use of the automobile, it was growing steadily more possible from the physical viewpoint to go farther afield for both shopping and housing. A pattern for this departure had been worked out in eastern Illinois, a very rich bituminous region, and also in connection with the anthracite mines of central Pennsylvania. But in the bituminous areas of the Allegheny range most miners still lived in the company town.

To some operators, the hold on the miner resulting from his living in a company town was an economic advantage to be clung to. Other operators felt it would be far better for them if they did not have to be involved in housing and facilities for their workers. This whole economic pattern, therefore, was wide open for new thinking and experimentation.

Another factor favorable to experimentation was the large size of the unemployed group in the average coal-mine community. It was obvious that coal mining as a trade was seriously overcrowded.

Diversification of skills, decentralization of workers, subsistence land-plots for families: these were needs which had impressed themselves deeply upon those of us who, coming from the outside, seeing the situation with fresh eyes, had haunted the coal camps for two or three years. And on the whole our views were not looked upon by operators with hostility. Heavily burdened as most of them were with the unforeseen problems of a great general depression, they were the more ready to understand that many kinds of experiments were due to be tried. It turned out to be quite feasible to solicit the co-operation of some of the operators in new kinds of planning.

We of the Service Committee were not the only ones thinking along these lines, and we cannot claim to have taken any significant part in the development of new trends. But after this relief experience in the coal fields we did play a further role in a very interesting self-help housing experiment; and as an administrator of the Federal government's subsistence homestead program, I was privileged to learn firsthand much that has been invaluable to me in later situations.

This chapter would not be complete without some recognition of the present program of the Welfare and Retirement Fund of the United Mine Workers of America. This Fund's reports are heartening human documents to those of us who battled misery beyond description in bituminous regions during the depression, our one million dollars admittedly like the broom trying to sweep back the ocean. Not that the employment services and unemployment benefits for miners can yet be said to be adequate. For instance, there is still no satisfactory provision for orderly movement of workers from camps where coal is exhausted. When, however, we compare the benefits of the program now in operation with our earlier voluntary emergency measures, we have a vivid picture of the kind of social progress which can be chalked up on the credit side of our national ledger for the past twenty years. I think no one outside the industry can appreciate this particular progress more than those of us who remember what the coal fields were like in the early '30s.

But though there is this great advance in general provisions for basic human needs, citizens sensitive to the suffering of their neighbors will do well to remember that no provisions of industry or state can obviate the necessity for human beings' concern, one for the other, on the personal level. This deep instinct of our human life, nurtured by our religious heritage, will still find adequate opportunity for exercise if we stay open to the claims and privileges of our common brotherhood.

Looked at in perspective, these days about which I have been writing seem like a kind of watershed for social forces working in the world, the true proportions of which are only now beginning to be seen. If the sufferings of the early '30s had been taken by more privileged members of our society simply as complaints to be suppressed, what might we not have seen in the way of violence, political upheavals, and a public that grew less and less sensitive to human values! But instead, we had the Senate hearings conducted by Robert LaFollette, tuned to the suffering and agony throughout the country: hearings which resulted in the appropriation of a substantial fund during the latter days of the Hoover Administration, for Federal relief assistance. There was also an awakening of local groups in every region, an exercise of local initiative, ingenuity, and sharing. Then came the dramatic and colorful presentation of the crisis in the early days of the first Roosevelt Administration, and those historic words: "The only thing we have to fear is fear itself."

The American community, setting its hand to the immediate problems of its own survival, little realized it was entering into a type of thinking which would lead eventually to what are now known as the technical assistance programs of the United States and of the United Nations — programs which represent the realization that we should no longer and must no longer disregard poverty, hunger, illiteracy, and illness anywhere in our human family, and that in most places where these are the rule there are also the resources to provide an adequate standard of living, if some assistance can be given in the development of these resources.

This whole idea of technical assistance means the emancipation of peoples enslaved by ignorance and poverty. We of the United States can sit on the lid or we can eagerly help to find orderly ways for the development of the rights of minority peoples and decent provision for those too long denied the necessities of life. All this may seem somewhat unrelated to the coal fields of the '30s, but often the tangible, the near, and the obvious help point the way in larger situations. Suppression of the cries of the '30s could have meant disaster. I believe the same can be said of the world situation today, and that the practice which this country had during the depression in throwing off traditional patterns in order to meet unprecedented emergencies may have prepared us to move in the right direction at the right time in terms of world forces.

3. Government Subsistence Homesteads

JOHN WILKES was discouraged. He stopped by the office Saturday evening on his way home from the coal pit, to receive his pay check. During the past two weeks he had mined slightly more than fifty tons of coal, for which he was paid thirty cents a ton, and he had done a few other odd jobs which would increase his pay a little. But he had a heavy debt at the company store, and there would be other deductions: for insurance, union dues, and the doctor. He wondered how much cash he would have. This is what he saw when he was handed his pay slip:

FOR TWO WEEKS ENDING SEPT. 26, 1931 (2 days a week)

3 hrs. at 40¢ (cleaning up)	$ 1.20
50.75 tons at 30¢	15.22
Total	$16.42

Deductions:

To Company store on account	10.00
Explosives	.94
Insurance	1.50
Smithing	.25
Doctor	.75
Dues [Union]	1.50
Check weighmen	.88
Relief	.50
Total deductions	16.32
BALANCE CREDIT	10¢

He would be able to take home to his wife and children a credit of ten cents as a result of his four days' work in two weeks, which was all the work he had been able to get.

To make matters worse, the mine might not open at all next week. It was certain that it would not open on Monday or Tuesday; beyond that, the boss would let him know.

Winter was coming, the children's shoes and clothing were wearing out, two of the children had not yet been able to buy the textbooks required by the school, even at low secondhand rates, and credit at the company store was close to the exhaustion point. Then there were John's father and mother, with whom John and his wife had been sharing as best they could. But how long could it continue? His father was now well over fifty, and hadn't been able to get work in the mines for three and a half months.

It wouldn't be so bad if John could transfer to another mine where things were better, but he had talked that day to a man from a mine in the rich coal region of southern West Virginia, and his story was the same: short work, poor market for coal, no employment for older men. Only one ray of hope had come through the general gloom. In Washington, they were discussing the possibility of the Federal government's assisting states in public relief. Until now, John Wilkes had always been able to earn a living for his family, and he did not want to be on relief. Nevertheless, his children must eat. He was humiliated, embarrassed, discouraged. Today, when the miners had knocked off work at noon to eat their thick bread-and-butter sandwiches, conversation had lagged. All the men were feeling the same way. In fact, Abe, John's most intimate friend, said that when he checked in last time he found he owed the company forty-one cents.

Throughout these steadily worsening conditions, John and his family were devoted church people. Every Sunday morning they all went to Sunday school and church, and for that brief stretch of time their troubles were vanquished by the somewhat boisterous reaffirmation of the local preacher that if they believed in Jesus

Christ, abstained from drink and swearing, and supported the church, their happiness after this life was assured. Great joy welled up in them in these hours. This joy helped them to bear their burdens. John was at least still employed. He would go back to the mines as soon as there was work, and they would find a way to make out. They would have to find a way. This was in one of the many mining camps near Morgantown, West Virginia.

Alex Mayer, in Bertha Hill Camp not far away, faced a similar problem, but for him there was a bright ray of light. Daniel Houghton of our Committee had established small cabinetwork shops at four mines, including Bertha Hill, and Alex had been among the first to respond to the new opportunity. His father had been a cabinetmaker in Germany, and some of Alex's clearest boyhood memories were of his father's great joy in making wood respond to his skill in handling tools. Now Alex was finding that he too had this skill, as well as great delight in the process.

When in January, 1933, the cabinetwork at Bertha Hill was transferred to larger quarters in Morgantown to be combined with the Godlove chair industry and other crafts into the Mountaineer Craftsmen's Co-operative Association, Alex was one of the craftsmen most concerned with the development; he had a new trade and an opening future.

It was not long after this move that political events began to be of greater interest to both Alex Mayer and John Wilkes. Earlier, President Hoover had succeeded in getting Congress to recognize the Federal government's responsibility toward unemployed workers caught in a network of circumstances over which they had no control, living in states and counties where funds were exhausted; and Congress had appropriated certain funds to help tide the unemployed over this emergency period. Now the Roosevelt Administration was going further. Congress had been asked to make what then seemed large sums of money available for what were called subsistence homesteads.

Hardly had the Subsistence Homestead Act passed Congress

when feverish activity developed concerning its administration. It was only secondarily a relief measure; primarily, it was thought of as the beginning of a decentralization program for workers in industry. It was hoped it might find wide application. The picture was of millions of workers living on small homesteads with some two or three acres of land for gardening or small farming, in some instances keeping a cow or a pig, certainly chickens, in this way having some backlog in case of unemployment. M. L. Wilson was appointed director of the over-all program, and I was made his assistant, with special responsibility for homesteads in mining communities.

Here, then, was my first experience in participating to a very modest degree in government administration. I still continued as secretary of the American Friends Service Committee, but I was liberated by the Committee's Board to give three or four days a week to the subsistence homesteads interest. As I look back upon the experience now, I am profoundly grateful that I did not know how many things one cannot do under government regulations. If I had known all the restrictions, I doubt whether the four homesteads for stranded miners would ever have been built.

There were endless rules about purchasing land, letting contracts, and the circumstances under which local people might or might not be employed. There was extreme sensitiveness on the part of government to charges of entering industry in ways that seemed to compete with private enterprise. These and many other similar considerations, arising from a perfectly legitimate concern of government to protect itself, made the handling of a program such as Subsistence Homesteads complicated, difficult, and expensive. There were interminable delays and never-ending competition between local politicians, most of their efforts exerted for the genuine welfare of their communities, but sometimes only for the sake of patronage and votes.

My administration had to do solely with the transfer of unemployed miners from coal camps to subsistence homesteads where they might find some employment on their own land and where hopefully we might introduce new industries for cash employment. If you go to Westmoreland County, Pennsylvania, today, you will see a thriving community called Norvelt, which was established for unemployed miners under this act. Three others initiated at about the same time were the Arthurdale Subsistence Homestead and the Tygart Valley Subsistence Homestead, both in West Virginia, and the Cumberland Homesteads near Crossville, Tennessee. Both President and Mrs. Roosevelt took a great deal of personal interest in this program.

Soon after Roosevelt entered the White House, Mrs. Roosevelt had expressed a desire to see the living conditions of families in the bituminous coal-mining regions. I had arranged for her and Miss Lorena Hickok to visit some of the mining communities in the neighborhood of Morgantown, West Virginia. This visit had greatly stimulated her interest in the problem, and had some bearing on the fact that the first subsistence homestead was located on the Arthur farm, east and south of Morgantown.

One cold November night in 1933, Mrs. Roosevelt, Louis Howe, the President's confidential secretary, and I boarded the train at Washington for Fairmount, West Virginia. The next morning we were met by some of the Service Committee workers who were still assisting with relief, and taken to the Arthur house, an old mansion on the land recently purchased for the first government subsistence homestead. Here we conferred with architects, builders, and engineers, and before the day was over Louis Howe had called certain manufacturers of prefabricated Cape Cod cottages and ordered fifty houses of various designs to be shipped forthwith to Arthurdale. (It must be admitted that these houses, when they came, proved quite inadequate: they were scantily built, unplastered little summer cottages, and by the time they were made suitable for the rugged climate of West Virginia they were more expensive than the houses later built from native stone.) Louis Howe inspired the group with the anticipation that before Christmas families would be in these houses. It must be pointed out that speed was important. Some demonstration that government could act, even to the disregard of regulations, was called for. We were dealing with human misery, and there was general realization that we must not let regulations, or politicians, or our own fears prevent our acting with promptness and reasonable adequacy.

I had taken pains to see that Alex Mayer, who had now developed into a high-class cabinet craftsman, had a chance to tell his story to Mrs. Roosevelt. I knew that with her interest in cabinet-making she would be genuinely appreciative of what had been accomplished already toward providing alternative employment for unemployed miners. I had hardly dared to expect, however, that this conversation would stimulate the decision to build a properly arranged plant in Arthurdale, to which the handcraft industries, now in the Morgantown junk shop, might be transferred. But this did happen; and Alex became one of the first homesteaders.

That November day on which the houses for Arthurdale were ordered was indeed a memorable one. The county superintendent of schools came in to inquire about plans for education. Local builders appeared, hoping they might find employment. A Congressman expressed his interest in seeing that suitable employees were chosen for the new venture. The nearby University wished to make a record of the progress of this new experiment in relocating mining families. Ministers wondered about church facilities, and the public health officer of the county raised the question as to whether this might be the time to get government aid for additional health equipment for the county. On this day we first heard the proposal of the Upper Monongahela Valley Planning Council, to build a bridge across the Monongahela River which would enable miners to live on land suitable for cultivation even while continuing their employment in the rich coal fields north of Morgantown. The county commissioners were anxious as to whether taking rich land for this government experiment was going to reduce their tax income. Would the government provide compensation in lieu of taxes? And then there were individuals who came with appeals that because of their poverty, unemployment, and hopelessness, they might be considered as homesteaders.

Dramatized before our eyes was the ferment going on in peoples' minds and spirits, the anxiety about the future, a hope that unemployment could be conquered, a dimly seen future wherein new ways of doing things might be uncovered for the welfare of human beings, and measures for this kind of progress placed at the very heart and core of government activity. Most concerned of all were representatives of the United Mine Workers union, who wondered whether the homestead movement was going to take miners out of the union and weaken it, or whether government interest in problems of the industry would stimulate and strengthen the union. What one saw on that November day was the turning point in American concepts of public responsibility for suffering of citizens, wherever they might live and whatever might be their circumstances.

As assistant administrator of the Homestead Act, I could hardly be otherwise than concerned at seeing many prompt, if not hasty, actions being taken by people next to the President — actions which would have to be brought into some kind of order in accordance with the regulations of the Department of the Interior. But at the same time I could not miss the far more fundamental fact that those who had come into positions of high responsibility had a deep sense of commitment to the good of the people, and were ready to take prompt and vigorous action in the present national crisis. In perspective, I am convinced that the efforts made in the crucial early '30s were essential, even if at points misguided or wasteful. They demonstrated government's concern and willingness to act, they gave a new sense of confidence and hope to otherwise discouraged people. It could not have been a very far step, had the suffering gone on, to where acts of violence might have been commonplace as a result of too long suffering.

In the journal I kept during my government service in Washington there is revealed a good deal of activity springing directly out of the psychological search for solutions that was characteristic of the period of the great depression and the early days of the Roosevelt Administration.

When Mrs. Roosevelt had visited the bituminous coal fields of West Virginia, she had been shown around by Alice Davis and Nadia Danilevsky. Early in January of 1934, she invited me to bring Alice and Nadia to visit her in Washington. The two young women were fresh from the administration of relief in the coal camps, and they brought a vivid sense of coal-mine realities to the White House.

Dr. M. L. Wilson and Assistant Secretary of the Interior Oscar Chapman joined us that evening for dinner, and we had a lively discussion with the President and Mrs. Roosevelt about plans that were developing for the use of the Subsistence Homesteads appropriation. I told the President about the Upper Monongahela Valley Planning Council, which had done some excellent thinking on how the whole human aspect of that valley might be quite thoroughly changed by building a bridge across the Monongahela above Morgantown. Dr. Nat Frame, who was the leading spirit in this study, had made a deep impression on me with his presentation of the idea. One can never quite forget how interest and sparkle kindled in the President's face when anything of this sort was suggested. He asked me if I would bring Nat Frame to see him on the following day, which I was able to do.

Being able to bring together people who ought to know each other is one of the rewards of the kind of work in which the Service Committee had been engaged in the coal fields. One's circle of acquaintances and friends expands with amazing rapidity, and because the contacts are made in the interest of constructive solutions, they tend to become permanent points of co-operation.

In West Virginia and Washington, as well as in many other parts of the country, strong convictions for and against the admission of Negroes to the homesteads had been gathering momentum. The problem was not "the Negro" but the tensions that were intensifying around the question. Mrs. Roosevelt had been anxious to give the issue the thorough consideration it warranted. Therefore one day she asked me if I would be willing to invite on her behalf a group of Negroes to the White House for the evening of January 26, 1934.

Those I recall as present on that evening were Mordecai Johnson, president of Howard University; John Hope, president of Atlanta University; Robert R. Moton, president of Tuskegee Institute; Charles S. Johnson, head of the department of social science at Fisk University; Walter White, executive secretary of the National Association for the Advancement of Colored People; and Charles C. Spaulding, president of the North Carolina Mutual Life Insurance Company of Durham. The unrestrained way in which these men unburdened themselves with regard to the predicament of Negroes in the United States, not only in connection with this question of the homesteads but in terms of the over-all deep sense of frustration they felt, was an impressive experience. No one could have entered more fully into the nature of the problem or have expressed more intelligently a desire to find a way to help than did Mrs. Roosevelt. We talked from about eight o'clock until twelve, then the President came in from the Oval Room, where he had been in another meeting, and briefly entered into the spirit of our conference.

By no means do I wish to imply that this meeting solved the problem of race on the homesteads, but it helped considerably; and, what was more, it set before all of us a new standard for understanding and co-operation in the field of race.

"Subsistence Homesteads" was a new term. I don't know who thought it up, but whoever he was he did a good job if his object was to create interest and excite imagination. Every kind of new idea concerning community life that had been brewing in the minds of people over the country finally found its way to the office of Dr. Wilson or myself.

Here was a chance, thought one Henry Creange, to revive the

ancient craft guilds. A Frenchman by birth, he knew a great deal about European life — rather more, I should say, than he knew about American life. He was a fascinating person, and after cultivating Dr. Wilson and myself assiduously for many days he gave a dinner party at the Washington Hotel for everybody in the government who might be interested in the introduction of craft guilds into American life; his idea was that this could be done through the new homestead communities. The dinner was replete with all refinements, including a large, beautifully bound volume, each guest's name printed on it in gold, setting forth his ideas for craft guilds. There were numerous speeches and there was plenty of wine. But Creange's idea, fascinating as it was to contemplate, never took hold.

One day a tall gaunt man came into my office in Washington, slumped down in the chair before my desk, and laid a beautiful drawing on the table. His name I cannot remember, but his story was a vivid one. He wanted to reorganize American life around what he called the "road town idea." His proposal was to build all the housing for people living on farms or subsistence homesteads along a beautifully developed road. This road would make possible all kinds of modern services: adequate shopping centers, telephone, mail, and other public facilities; and from their homes on this road people could move out to their farms of larger or smaller size, thus having the advantages of both town and country. I remember introducing him to Dr. Wilson, and insisting that he also hear the story. Encouraged by our listening ear, this man persisted for weeks, getting his story told to government officials and to other groups in Washington, all interested, but nobody ready to commit himself to the plan, for varying reasons. Perhaps greater frankness on the part of those of us who listened to him might have been a kindness; for in the end this man could not accept the fact that nothing much was going to come of all his labors. One morning the newspapers reported that he had jumped out of the window of his hotel in New York.

Land planners came in with all sorts of novel ideas; psychologists saw in this effort a great chance to analyze, test and retest, and measure the achievements of families selected as against those being helped by run-of-the-mill relief. One plan we received from a brilliant psychologist was of such a nature that no member of our staff could understand the language.

I prized very highly my association with the working staff of our office, most of whom had a great abundance of common sense. Before I had become part of this government effort, M. L. Wilson had been little more than a name to me, associated with the "brain trust" that was dreaming up a scheme for planned use of the world wheat supply. But when we began to work together, we found we had much in common. He also had been brought up in a Middle West farming community; he had been a teacher in the State Agricultural College of Montana, and a wheat farmer in that state; he had been a county agent, deeply immersed in the life and development of rural communities.

M. L. was a born philosopher, and while sometimes one might be a little impatient for his prompt decision on some administrative matter which for the moment seemed of central concern, I learned to appreciate his ability to lean back in his chair and look with philosophic quiet on the longer-term significance of steps we were taking. Later he became Director of Extension in the Department of Agriculture, and there, especially through land-grant colleges, he had a chance to exert enormous influence in connection with the use of Federal educational facilities. Concerned as he was with the economic development of the country, he was yet continually alert to the philosophical, cultural, and spiritual values involved. He seemed always to be in touch with a wide range of people who had this broader interest in the American scene.

Toward the end of our period together, Dr. Wilson one day invited me to come over to the Department of Agriculture to meet George W. Russell, otherwise known as "A.E.," the Irish poet. He was in this country on invitation to share his experiences in the development of co-operatives and a new plan for rural life in Ireland. "A.E.'s" philosophy revolved around the need for quiet reflection, the benefits of the right kind of rural life, and the central value of human personality. To talk with him was a beautiful experience. He had played a great role in Ireland, or, I should say, two roles: one as a poet of distinction, one as a practical social scientist. I have a rich memory of this occasion, and of a later time when he, Lilly Pickett, and I spent an evening in the home of the Wilsons, where "A.E." reminisced over his experiences in Ireland, quoted at length from his own poetry, and shared with us some of his deepest thoughts and feelings. He was to sail in a few days; then go directly from the boat to a nursing home, where he soon died.

He had given us a feeling of participation not simply in the administration of an official Congressional Act, but in a new movement that was abroad — a new expectancy from life — which, though it dealt most immediately with the economic side of citizens' lives, came close to the very heart of deep and abiding longings of people far beyond the group who might ever expect to be homesteaders. Fulfillment of yearnings for a home, for a good life for children, for "community" in the true sense, for creative use of the imagination and intelligence of men and women who had mostly been treated as cogs in a machine: a movement of this kind was glimpsed and felt. If the slow, recreative forces in this direction had not been interrupted by the return of war-stimulated prosperity, the revolution in values which we saw beginning might much more deeply have enriched our national character. For a rebirth of spirit is always more important than an economic revival.

From the beginning there had been a great deal of discussion, among those interested in the subsistence homestead movement, concerning decentralization. This word seemed to furnish the key to America's future development. And we placed much stress on the need for growth of the human spirit, and the fact that rural living provided more favorable conditions for this growth than did urban or congested industrial life.

But now what we see is that with the expansion of industry and the return of full employment centralization has gone on apace. The increasing mechanization of agriculture has materially augmented this process. More adequate social-security provision for the city dweller has also encouraged the move to larger centers. Though I have no doubt that the experiments of the '30s will stand as living examples of the benefits of decentralization, they do not as yet show any appreciable influence in the direction of luring people to the advantages of rural living. It is possible that in more trying times these demonstrations and crusades will have more effect. But I think that not until we place a higher premium on the life of the spirit, and also not until we learn better how to apply modern machines in small units to semirural living, will the movement away from overcrowded centers become an accepted, voluntary part of American life.

But to get back to the development of our specific program: once the construction of the communities was well under way, we had of necessity to consider some of the other, no less vital problems.

There was the perplexing question of how to go about selecting families from among the large number of applicants. Chief among the difficulties was the fact that we wanted to get people who were most likely to make good in the new pattern of life. The government homesteads were being watched eagerly — or skeptically — all over the country. Many were those who said that families not accustomed to bathtubs would use them as coalbins. Such arguments are always greatly overplayed. The settlers' adjustment to new laborsaving devices was the least of our difficulties. We learned that people readily adjust to physical improvements. Mental and spiritual shortages are what cause the lags and breakdowns in an experiment of this kind.

However, besides wanting the new projects to succeed, those of us concerned about the coal miners and their families wanted also to see the most needy families given a chance, and there was some conflict between these two justifiable desires. Here, Mrs. Roosevelt's interest was of enormous value. I went with her on more than one trip to visit home after home in Scotts Run and other coal-mining communities. I saw her sit and talk with a bewildered woman who wanted to make the effort to move to a homestead, but whose intelligence and chances of real accomplishment caused one to have serious doubts. Mrs. Roosevelt held the woman's baby on her lap as she listened carefully to the pitiful tale of her struggle to get along on the pathetically inadequate sums which her husband was able to earn.

We took this problem of selection to the University of West Virginia, located at Morgantown. Here, members of the faculty who were especially interested in the experiment worked out a formula. It was decided that although most of the settlers should be in reasonably robust health, able to work well, and not too old, a small proportion of aged people could be taken. It was interesting to me that the University professors, the local West Virginia communities, and the homesteaders themselves, were all more conservative about accepting families that might present a social security problem than were the representatives of the Federal government. Large families were to be no obstacle to acceptance. Here was an opportunity for children to grow up in surroundings perhaps better than they would ever find elsewhere. Questions were asked concerning domestic relations; while not all people who were having domestic difficulties were excluded, it was thought unwise to have any large proportion of homes in which relationships did not seem stable and permanent. Searching questions were asked about the personal habits of the applicants; it was not the idea that Arthurdale should be a community of saints, but neither did the University committee feel justified in offering the opportunity to persons whose lack of moral character was likely to jeopardize their ability to contribute to the venture and to receive benefit from it. I believe the long-term success of the Arthurdale community speaks well for the basis of selection worked out by the University.

In the summer of 1934 the first homesteading families occupied their new homes in Arthurdale. The little prefabricated summer cottages had been insulated and plastered, and were now deemed adequate for the climate of West Virginia. Hot and cold water had been installed, bathtubs and all, and the resulting homes were both convenient and charming.

I had been told by an administrator of relief for the Federal government that one eighth of the population of the United States was on relief; the figure was one fourth in one of the counties in which we were building a homestead. Essential as this relief was, it was most unhealthy. Here, as the Arthurdale community was opening its life as a neighborhood, we were seeing the beginnings of emergence from relief into self-support and the recovery of dignity. And it was the kind of dignity that comes from an emphasis on the home and the community as well as on individual achievement.

Long before construction of the homes had begun, we were giving serious consideration to the problem of employment opportunities for the homesteaders, over and above their subsistence farm activities. At Arthurdale, we could at least count on the little cabinet industry which was to be transferred from Morgantown. But other businesses that would absorb more people would be essential. As this community became an actuality, we tried a number of experiments, some of them short-lived.

One of our most hopeful ideas was to establish a plant to manufacture post-office boxes. We had discovered that the boxes used in small postoffices throughout the country were made by one concern, whose monopoly of the business enabled them to charge postmasters in little towns what seemed an exorbitant price. The Post Office Department was interested in providing Federal funds for a plant at Arthurdale which would make such boxes, giving employment to the homesteaders and at the same time acting as a healthy con-

trol on the price of this equipment. But the proposal came up
against the power of a strong lobby, Louis Ludlow, a very effective
Congressman from Indianapolis, being promptly on the job to protect the private industry, which was located in his city. He and his
colleagues were so efficient that even though the Post Office Department was strongly in favor of it the project was killed.

A shirt manufacturer was interested in establishing a small
branch of his industry in Arthurdale. But scarcely had the new
plant been put in operation when the manufacturer discovered he
could not find enough markets for the shirts made in the parent
plant alone; so that effort came to an end.

Likewise doomed was an arrangement with a manufacturer of
radio cabinets, who soon found he glutted his market by establishing a new plant.

The men in the Mountaineer Craftsmen's Co-operative Association were continuing to make and sell Godlove chairs, and beautiful dining tables, coffee tables, corner cupboards, and other household pieces for a rare and specialized market. But this enterprise
could use only a very few persons.

A large commercial furniture industry became interested in the
location and in time established itself at Arthurdale. It provided
assembly-line jobs for practically all who wanted them.

Then something happened which I suppose was inevitable. The
MCCA craftsmen could make more money in the mass-production
business than in cabinetwork. They had families to support, children to educate. They decided to accept jobs with the larger company, and try to continue with their cabinetwork in off-hours. But
in time this decision gradually resulted in the dissipation of the
craft enterprise.

One does not begrudge the greater income; in fact, the men had
almost no choice but to take it when it became available. But to see
men who found great joy in producing beautiful handmade furniture abandon it for routine jobs that pay better causes one to ask
pertinent questions about our civilization. We saw the craft born of

necessity, under economic conditions we could not wish back; we saw it carried forward through affection, sensitiveness to beauty, and response to the challenge of thorough workmanship. Now we see the same men on assembly lines. It would seem that our American society is yet far from having solved the problem of the immeasurable loss that comes when human beings' ingenuity and sensitiveness are swallowed up in mass production.

The final propitious turn of events from the economic point of view was the general upswing of business activity which increased the demand for coal, so that some of the men were able to return to full-time employment as miners.

As Arthurdale was being made ready, a study of the homesteaders being accepted (an eventual total of about two hundred families) indicated that there would be more than three hundred children of school age in the community. What was to be done about their education? Both locally and nationally, persons who understood the potentialities of the homesteads felt that here was an opportunity to attempt more creative methods of education than are usually employed in public schools. Many were the dreams which were written out and presented.

Eleanor Roosevelt chaired a small committee which made a study of the situation and possible procedures. Dean William Russell of Teachers College, Columbia University, was early called in to advise. Others who served on the committee, besides myself, were John Dewey, E. E. Agger, representing the Resettlement Administration, Fred J. Kelly of the United States Office of Education, Lucy Sprague Mitchell, and W. Carson Ryan.

The general plan which grew out of initial deliberations was to build a school at government expense, since the county was poor and was thus far receiving no compensation for the land taken over by Arthurdale, and to design an educational program built around the needs of the children and the community as a whole, boldly looking at the problem with fresh eyes and without feeling constrained by traditional educational patterns. However, the school should be a public school, receiving whatever regular support from the county and state it warranted; and it should eventually be turned over to the county. Therefore West Virginia educators must be participants in all the detailed planning, and official sanctions would have to be obtained. Because many of the Arthurdale children would be new in Preston County, available county funds (based on the previous year's attendance) would be less than in ordinary school situations. Mrs. Roosevelt offered to try to raise additional funds through a series of radio broadcasts. This she did, and also we received contributions from a few other interested individuals.

A group of West Virginia educators was asked to draw all the dreams for this school into a specific plan. Elsie Ripley Clapp, principal of the Roger Clark Ballard Memorial School in Jefferson County, Kentucky, was invited to direct the experiment. She immediately spent as much time as possible among the people who would be coming to Arthurdale as homesteaders, and with the committee of local educators. She attended the all-day session of this West Virginia Advisory School Committee, as it was called, when it spelled out paragraph by paragraph what it would recommend for the Arthurdale school. It was ready to endorse as imaginative a program as the national committee had dared dream: a school integrated with the community, serving residents of all ages, its curriculum built around the community's vocational and recreational needs and possibilities: agricultural and animal-husbandry projects, industrial arts and crafts, home care, social and civic enterprises, music, drama, dancing. Nursery school, elementary and high school, and adult education were recognized as the three major divisions of the program as it developed, but interlocking activities made even this classification somewhat arbitrary.

All of these steps were taken with the best intentions in the world, and yet as I look back on it now I think the enthusiasm of a few people who had thought deeply and dreamed long about the possibilities of the right kind of education led in this case to commitments which assumed more experimental-mindedness among the homesteaders than had yet developed.

Nevertheless, great things began happening. It was felt by everyone concerned with the venture that the nursery school was in many ways its most important feature. If the little children could be started off in the right direction, the future of the community would be as nearly assured as human beings could make it. Jessie Stanton, director of the Harriet Johnson Nursery School in New York, came to put this part of the enterprise on its feet. The children's response was thrilling and reassuring. Their education in good health habits gave impetus to the entire community's health program. In time, this nursery school became widely known as a model, both as to building and equipment, and in terms of results with the children. The Mountaineer Craftsmen made a considerable proportion of the equipment.

Projects for the elementary and high-school-age boys and girls tied in with the nursery school and with adult activities. What are usually partitions between age groups became bridges. Dramatics, singing, gardening, canning, poultry raising, handcrafts, business enterprises: all ages either participated or benefited. In the three R's, the learning measured up to state requirements and the sponsors' expectations, and the children had a wonderful time in acquiring it.

On the Arthurdale property stood an old log cabin, which had been built probably no later than 1790. The fourth grade took this log cabin as a project and, as they studied pioneer life, fixed up and furnished the cabin, creating some of the period furnishings themselves: split-log benches, crude tables, a churn, wooden dishes, candle molds and candles, tin lanterns, a wool wheel. They learned to spin and weave. They grew flax and made linen. They visited neighboring mills, and kept notebooks about the making of cloth. They kept accounts. They wrote and presented a play in the cabin — a play of pioneer days.

About half the class had grandparents now living in log cabins, and certainly all had either relatives or friends in such cabins. In the recent economic debacle, there had grown a slight edge of shame at these humble origins. Now, it was pride in log-cabin life which was developing, and the children had a new appreciation of the materials which most of us take for granted in our daily living. Such was the climate in which education was taking place at Arthurdale.

A simple auditorium had been provided for the use of the whole community, for meetings, shows, and other recreation, including folk dancing. As I had been brought up on the theory that all dancing was dangerous to the morals of those participating, it was especially instructive to me to watch the homesteaders and their wives, the young people, and visitors from outside — even including Mrs. Roosevelt on occasion — enjoying themselves dancing in a completely delightful and wholesome fashion.

For two years the school and community thus went along happily. All of us felt that real progress was being made in terms of the children and the entire homestead.

But toward the end of the second year we began to think about turning the school over to state and county direction. In consultation with the West Virginia Advisory School Committee, it was decided that the time had come. This local committee wished to see the school continued as a community school.

It was at this point that those of us who had participated in the adventure began to find out how slow education sometimes is in taking hold. We learned that at least some of the parents, while acquiescing in what was happening, often had not really understood, and feared that their children might not be getting as good an education as children in "regular" schools. Doubtless the economic insecurity which had hounded them during the past few years intensified their desire to be like other communities, and made them suspicious of "experiments." The school was negotiating to be accredited by the state, and this had aroused fears that it wasn't acceptable to state authorities. There was some feeling among the people against having received "citified" treatment, this feeling evidently springing out of the fear that they were now going to find themselves on the short end again.

I suppose that if it had been possible to maintain leadership in recreation and education in the community for a period of years, and if a great deal of thought had been given to interpreting to adults what was being attempted in these efforts to release the human spirit through education and recreation, plus surroundings of adequate, simple, but charming homes, this community might eventually have afforded a striking demonstration of what was possible for a group who had suffered long and severely from unemployment in the company coal town.

But it is difficult to hustle history; it takes time for the educational process to help people grow sufficiently so that the new growth can stand alone. When the time came to turn the school over to the county, certain aspects of the experimental program were kept for the time being: the health work and the nursery school were especially wanted, and those who had been subsidizing the school continued to supplement the budget somewhat, on behalf of the special features that were retained. But in time practically all of the experimental aspects of the school were abandoned, and it became a rather indistinguishable part of the county school system.

I think none of us who took part in the experiment has any regrets at the amount of energy we put into it. It meant a great deal to us and certainly something to the community, especially to those who themselves participated. But the full hopes of our committee's dream were not realized.

It may sound from the discussion so far as if we had no concern regarding the religious life of the homestead, but that is not true; however, we did feel that we should be very careful to respect the wishes of the people in this matter. After local conferences on the question, arrangements were made for a local minister to hold services each Sunday in the auditorium. While this was useful, and a

small number of people responded, it was never possible to get anything like a large community response.

Of course from the beginning the health of the community was
very much in our minds. While the new law was being studied and
interpreted it was found possible to get some assistance from Subsistence Homestead funds to provide health facilities where none
were available. Out of such assistance Arthurdale established a small
clinic, employed a doctor, and developed a public health service
which any community might happily have aspired to. All this
sounds easier than it was. For instance, most doctors don't want to
live and work in a community of this kind. The pay is not large,
and the work is demanding. Nevertheless, the people understood
the health service better than they did the educational opportunities,
and its contributions were perhaps longer-lived than anything else
that was attempted.

Eventually, county health services were made possible on the
homesteads when Congress provided for government compensation
to counties in lieu of taxes (the Federal government cannot pay
taxes to a county).

While all subsistence homesteads were thought of as attacking
our economic problem and were often discussed in terms of a general and desirable trend toward decentralization, many of us had
something even more fundamental than this in mind. We had a
strong feeling that while we had built the façade of abundant production in this country higher and higher until its foundations had
become inadequate to sustain it, we had forgotten that the hearth
where the family gathers and where neighbors are welcomed is at
the very heart of human life. We were trying again to put the welfare of the home and the individuals who live in it in the center of
our national interest. The school, health facilities, the church, adult
education: all of these were very close to the central significance
of the movement as we saw it.

In the beginning, there was considerable opposition to the homesteads from the United Mine Workers. It was said that we were

attempting to wean miners away from the industry, to eliminate them as possible members of the union, and thus to weaken the union.

It was this problem that I took to John L. Lewis. Mr. Lewis recognized the surplus of miners in the industry, and after listening to our story promised to see that the union did not interfere. His promise was kept.

Generally speaking, during the early days of our subsistence homestead program, the press opposed the move. The danger of these communities' becoming wards of the Federal government, second Indian reservations, and even concentration camps, was pointed up without restraint.

It is true that there was a period when these communities were especially favored, and in a dependent relation to government; but from the beginning the plan was to sell the houses to the homesteaders as soon as they could reasonably assume the obligation required. I am now able to report that all of the homes are sold to the families who occupy them, and that there has been very little loss from default on payments. The industries are in the hands of private concerns, schools are a part of the public-school systems of the various counties, and altogether on the material side the homesteads have been more successful than the most hopeful prophet could have predicted. In fact, three out of the four communities with which I was personally associated have returned a modest profit to the government on its investment. This, of course, has been made possible by the recovery of industry, particularly the coal industry, as the depression receded, and more especially, sad to say, as the Second World War enormously increased the demand for coal.

As soon as the four communities for unemployed miners were built and occupied, it seemed to me that my service to the government was no longer needed. However, I remained a consultant for several more years, and during that time watched, often with a good deal of agony, the carrying out of our early creative ideas by

people who had not had the exciting thrill of conceiving and initiating the projects, and who sometimes treated administration of the
communities simply as a job.

One special problem continued to haunt me. It seemed quite abnormal to employ a contractor for these homes for unemployed
people, and to supply so much of the direction and skilled labor
from outside. True, the homesteaders had been employed increasingly in the construction work as Arthurdale had developed. But
why couldn't such a community be a true co-operative enterprise on
the part of those who were to live in it? In the building of a new
community, one very important item is to build community spirit
and interdependence among the settlers as part of the process of
the physical construction. It seemed to me, also, that the government effort had been entirely too expensive in dollars. I felt sure
that a similar community could be built largely by its future occu-
pants, and that a successful demonstration of this kind could be
invaluable as a pattern for other groups to adapt, as they saw fit.

After much helpful consultation with Homer Morris and other
persons who had been close to our earlier rehabilitation experiments
in the coal fields, and who had views similar to my own, I now
proposed to the Board of the American Friends Service Committee
that we should make an effort to build one community ourselves,
and to attempt to do it in ways that would be more or less dupli-
cable by other groups.

4. Penn-Craft

It's a long way from Kansas to New York City. It is still farther from the secluded security of a little Quaker farm community in the Sunflower State to the Board room of the United States Steel Corporation at 61 Broadway, New York. And, also, I am a slow traveler; it had taken me nearly fifty years to make this trip. I had arrived at this particular goal through slow stages during the past few weeks. To Arthur Young, then in charge of industrial relations for that giant corporation, to the late Edward Stettinius, one of its high officials, to Myron C. Taylor, chairman of its Board, I had talked privately about the dream of a new community for coal miners in western Pennsylvania, and in return they had shown a great deal of interest. They can never know how deeply their simple words of understanding during these visits were appreciated.

The Board of the Service Committee had approved our building a community if we could get the money, and, while I had to acknowledge that the steel corporation had provided housing well above the average coal miner's, still I had chosen to put the case to these responsible officials. I had pointed out that it ought to be an experiment in a different kind of community life for coal miners; especially should more attention be given to provision for men who could no longer be used in the industry. The invitation to me to appear before the finance committee of the Board of Directors of the United States Steel Corporation and state my case, accompanying it with my request for $75,000 toward a total of $200,000, may have been only an incident in the heavy business schedule of that committee. To me it came as the supreme opportunity to plead the case of fifty families living in company towns in Fayette County, Pennsylvania, where employment in the mines was at low ebb. It was probably this sense of trying to speak adequately on behalf of others that gave me courage for that (to me) important meeting in the spring of 1936.

I do not remember all of those who were present, but I shall always be grateful for the deep sympathetic understanding of Thomas Lamont, for the enthusiastic support of Edward Stettinius, and the calm reassurance of Myron Taylor. There, too, was Walter S. Gifford, later our ambassador to Great Britain, who seemed to comprehend how deeply I felt the significance of this experiment. And there was J. P. Morgan. I came away wondering whether I had really captured his imagination. I am sure Arthur Young understood my anxiety, for late that evening, after I had returned to my home, he took the pains to call me by telephone to say that the corporation had been glad to grant my full request.

Those who have had experience in raising money will know what I mean when I say that it is an almost incomparable emotion that sweeps over one when after an effort of this sort he finds he has been successful. This, it seemed to me, gave the project sufficient standing so that it would not be too difficult to get the rest of the money. Also, this initial step had been accomplished in what seemed to me to be a right spirit.

One day when Myron Taylor and I were sitting together in his office he revealed to me something of his own inner struggle when he said, "It is not easy to be a kind of Saint Francis and at the same time an effective chairman of a great corporation; and I should like to be both." No remark in the whole experience impressed me more than this, for it gave me fresh realization that we were dealing not just with houses and gardens and roads but with the unconquerable spirit of man yearning to fulfill all his capacities. This applied not only to Myron Taylor, but to the struggling family at Thompson Mine #2 in Fayette County, who would later be settlers in the new community, and to myself.

Myron Taylor was good enough to introduce me to a number of his colleagues in other large corporations who, encouraged by the action of the steel company, made possible the accumulation of the necessary funds. As the experimental community came into being, we reported to contributors on its progress. All of them showed keen interest, but there was never the slightest suggestion of any desire on their part to exercise control.

Anyone driving through Fayette County, Pennsylvania, in 1936, saw mountainsides covered with scrubby timber, a few active coal mines, and many shabby remnants of once prosperous mining communities. Stark rows of dilapidated shacks in lifeless mine "patches" were nearly as grim as the faces of a once industrious population, now unemployed. In the fall of '36, we received from one of our workers the following Fayette County statistics:

> Number of cases on direct relief
> Permanent 1,450
> Temporary 1,200   Total 2,650
> Number of cases on WPA   Total 7,800
>
> Grand Total 10,450
> These two items represent more than 40,000
> persons, or 20 per cent of the population.

It was a situation not different in kind from that in many another county, but Fayette was among those most acutely stricken because of the highly specialized one-industry economy which had been developed with the intensive exploitation of coal.

Yet there had been a time when Fayette County was thought of as good farming country. We asked Homer Morris and Errol Peckham, with their practiced eyes for locating projects, to do their best to locate good farm land in this county within reasonable distance of suitable roads, and, if possible, so situated that inhabitants of the new community might find employment in mining in case the mines should return to full activity.

I thought I knew something about the history of Friends in America, but I was ignorant of one phase of it which was soon to become quite interesting to us. As early as the decade before the Revolutionary War, Friends from northern Virginia, Maryland, eastern Pennsylvania, and New Jersey were taking part in the migratory movement that was peopling western Pennsylvania — a movement motivated largely by a spirit of adventure and desire for economic betterment. A number of migrating Friends from Hopewell Monthly Meeting in Virginia halted in their trek in the Redstone area of the Monongahela Valley, in what is now Fayette County, Pennsylvania, and across the river at Westland, in what is now Washington County. They farmed, and they were resourceful in utilizing the water power so plentiful in that region. Sawmills, gristmills, a woolen mill, even a paper mill, were built and operated successfully. There was a little smelting of iron quite early in the history of these communities. That there was coal in the hills everyone knew, and occasionally some of it was gathered or dug out, by both Indians and white settlers. By the early 1800's an increasing number of "furnaces" and "coal banks" were presaging the great industrial development soon to take place.

In the years between the Revolutionary War and the turn of the century, Friends' meetings for worship grew rather rapidly in this region, until by 1793 two Monthly Meetings — Westland and Redstone — had been established, one on each side of the river. In 1797 Baltimore Yearly Meeting granted these Friends permission to set up Redstone Quarterly Meeting, which by 1800 included at least eleven Friends Meetings.

Meanwhile, another Friends' migration was well under way, from sections in which slavery prevailed. Friends had become increasingly sensitized to the evils of slavery, and as individual Quaker families in the South freed their slaves they found themselves out of favor with their neighbors and also unable to compete economically. Seeking a place in which to set up a new life, it was natural they should gravitate toward the pioneer Friends' settlements in western Pennsylvania. So the Redstone area became host to at least two considerable Friends' migrations.

But from 1787 on, a further call was in the air. The Northwest Territory was open for settlement, with slavery forever barred from its wide fertile lands. Within a few years, westward migration from the whole Eastern Seaboard became a broad stream, and Redstone Quarterly Meeting in western Pennsylvania found its membership in a continuous state of flux. Large numbers of Friends were coming in from the East and South, especially from slave-economy states; but large numbers were also answering the call of the rich Ohio River Valley.

At best, Friends Meetings had had little time to take root in the Monongahela Valley. Now the loss of some of their most reliable members to the westward migration, the barrenness of the inner life of a good many of these pioneer Friends Meetings, and the influx of thousands of migrants from the East whose religion and culture were at sharp variance with Friends' disciplines: all these factors doubtless had something to do with the breakdown of morals and morale in the Friends groups in western Pennsylvania around the turn of the century, although in the same period many rural Meetings suffered somewhat the same fate, partly for lack of adequately vigorous intellectual and recreational life.

In the various minutes of Redstone Monthly Meeting between 1793 and 1811, there were recorded 146 cases of marriage contrary to discipline, which in most cases meant the marriage of a Friend with a non-Friend, the ceremony being performed outside the Meeting, often by a member of the "hireling ministry." Of the offenders, 104 were disowned by the Meeting; the rest, perhaps actually less sturdy in their inner conscience, expressed penitence for their offense and were permitted to retain membership. During that same period, the same Meeting found no less than forty persons guilty of fornication or adultery. Although these Friends had escaped the dilemma of living in the midst of a slave economy, they were finding forces at work here in Pennsylvania with which they could cope even less well.

Finally, the lure of rich level lands to the west plus the hope of escaping those worldly forces which were now decimating their spiritual community resulted in a steadily increasing movement of Quakers on to Ohio and Indiana, until by the middle of the nineteenth century Friends had ceased to be more than a small scattered remnant in the Redstone region of the Monongahela Valley.

Imagine, then, our surprise when we discovered that the Craft family farm, which had been selected as the site for our new self-help housing project, was actually in the very heart of what had once been a heavily populated Quaker community! Only one woman could be found in that region whose ancestry went back to the once prosperous Redstone Monthly Meeting. Most of the local inhabitants hardly knew that Quakers existed. But here we were coming back in an effort, not to establish a Quaker community, but to provide a new opportunity for another group of Americans who had been caught in a network of social forces which they had been unable to master.

The community we had envisioned on this two-hundred-acre farm which the Committee purchased in April, 1937, was made up of fifty families, each with at least one and a half acres of land and a substantial, attractive house. The houses were to be built by the homesteaders themselves — all unemployed or at least partially unemployed coal miners. On their own places they would be able to raise some of their food, keep chickens, maybe pigs or a cow. And about half the original farm, or a hundred acres, would be operated as a commercial farm by the manager of the project, the purpose of this being to produce commodities for cash sale to homesteaders at near-to-cost prices, and to provide farm employment and training for homesteaders. (Later this farm was leased to one of the homesteaders.)

Experience at Arthurdale had indicated that there were many pitfalls in the employment end of a homestead development. We were determined that whatever industry came into the Fayette County project should be with the consent and understanding of the homesteaders, and should as nearly as possible be a natural growth, not an artificial mushroom affair. We were not looking for a chance for someone to make high profits out of the homesteaders' labors; neither did we want an industry that had to be subsidized.

We were fortunate in securing Henry Regnery to work with us on this problem. He had made a study of the subsistence homestead movement in Germany, and was now working on a thesis in this general area of interest at Harvard University.

Fortunately, school facilities were available within reasonable distance of the property, and the same was true of churches.

It would be hard to convey the quality of anticipation and faith which went into the planning and building of Penn-Craft, as this community came to be called. (The name paid tribute to William Penn, Quaker founder of the state in which the project was located, at the same time carrying forward the name of the Craft family from whom we had purchased the farm.) It must be remembered that the enterprise was designed and largely carried out in a period in which our national economy had all but collapsed, and people were thinking seriously in terms of new patterns of living which would make them less dependent on business "cycles." Whole counties were in a condition of complete economic ruin, hundreds of thousands of unemployed workers had no background of experience or training for anything besides the one job they had been doing and had now lost. Here we had two hundred acres of beautiful rolling farmland where, with the experience of government subsistence homesteads behind us, we and fifty homesteading families were free to work out to the best of our ability what we believed could be done by people with low incomes if they would only pool their labor and dreams. We had no government restrictions, no limitations except the recalcitrant aspects of human nature, with which one must always reckon, and the framework of national and international trouble, which in one form or another would be with us for a long time to come. In other words, we had as much freedom to work out our ideas as people can well ask for, at least in this stage of human development.

The financial arrangement provided for a loan of $2000 to each family, for the purchase of land, lumber, and other supplies. The rest of the cost would be in terms of their own labor. The $2000 was to be repaid at the rate of $10 a month, which would include principal and interest at two per cent, thus enabling a family to amortize the entire loan in twenty years. Taxes and insurance were additional.

The task of selecting fifty families out of more than 250 applicants was a puzzling and exciting challenge. Errol Peckham spent many months in the community in a kind of pastoral relation to the people, learning to know them and making an effort to find out which families would be most likely to take full advantage of the opportunity. Part of the initial work of clearing the land, digging ditches for water mains, and building roads, was done at regular pay rates by men of the families applying, and some of these eliminated themselves, finding they had a distaste for so much work of this kind. Most of the men who with their families were finally selected were thirty-five to forty-five years old, and all were unemployed or partially unemployed miners. They represented a cross section of the coal-mining population of that part of Pennsylvania: Croatian, Slovak, Welsh, Polish, Rumanian, English, Russian, Syrian, Italian, German; and of native Americans, we had both white and Negro families, and one of Indian lineage. As groups of homesteaders were selected, they drew lots for the order in which they might choose their locations.

Early in 1937 David W. Day, who had been manager of the government homestead in Westmoreland County, Pennsylvania, for three years, was employed by the Committee as general manager of Penn-Craft, and he and his family moved onto the farm. Errol Peckham would remain in charge of selection of homesteaders and concern himself with many of the personal problems that were bound to arise.

In one of his early letters to the Philadelphia office, David Day reported:

> There has come to us this week from three of the first six homesteaders the suggestion that they would like to build a good poultry house on their lot, in its permanent location, and move into it while building their home. For those who do not have cars it is particularly perplexing to know how, in every spare half-day, they can make the most of that time unless they live on the land. The more we have discussed the idea here the more we find ourselves thinking that something of that sort must be done if the courage and morale of the group is to be preserved during the long pull. I have made a hasty, but I believe a safe estimate of the material cost of a 20 × 40 poultry house of the Pennsylvania State College type, adding to it roof and sidewall insulation on the inside, using novelty siding and T & G material all the way through. The house would be set on concrete foundation and floor, making a permanent and valuable building for poultry later. The materials, in carload lot, can be purchased for a maximum of $350. . . . A 20 × 40 poultry house will give them as much, if not more space than most of them have in their present houses. . . . We see the additional value of the opportunity to live with the people as a community during the building period. . . . Any decision on this matter must be made promptly because gardens are involved.

This plan was carried out, and the poultry houses were so well built that even recently some of them have been temporarily occupied by young couples while they sought permanent dwellings.

It must be admitted that in the beginning skepticism and even jibes from people of that general vicinity found echoes in the form of questions deep in the homesteaders' own minds and hearts. Could they ever really build their own homes? Would they actually some day own these nice-looking houses, the plans for which they were choosing and modifying to suit their particular circumstances and tastes? "All this free work! Do you really believe you'll have anything out of it in the end?" Such taunts came out of complete lack of experience in any form of co-operative undertaking. Not that what we were trying was basically new. It was more or less the way our country was built in the first years after the coming of English settlers; it is a technique still used to some extent in farming areas where labor-swapping makes up for paucity of cash. But to an industrial population it was new.

In the early days of the project the homesteaders who were not working part-time in the mines were employed by the Works Progress Administration. All were earning enough to take care of their families' minimum requirements, though no more. The WPA required only about thirty hours a week. So in the beginning most of the men had a good deal of free time to devote to their houses.

In the first place, of course, they had to be taught the necessary skills — especially carpentry and stone masonry. One skilled carpenter and one skilled mason were employed to initiate the work and give the men adequate instruction. People looking at the houses today find it hard to believe that they were built almost entirely by "amateurs." I do not mean to imply that the homesteaders became expert workmen all at once, but the incentive was about the strongest a man can have, and it was impressive to see how quickly these miners were building good sturdy homes, even if some of the skillful touches of professional builders might be lacking.

Large-scale public housing developments had not yet got under way, and it had been an architect's paradise to be able to dream out cottages suitable for this new kind of settlement. We had had five house plans drawn up, as good basic designs for the various-sized homes which would be erected at Penn-Craft. But it was to be expected that the homesteaders would have their ideas also, and, as we had anticipated, their changes and modifications of the original plans have resulted in no two houses being alike. It was important that they should participate in the planning as well as the construction of their homes.

On this old Craft farm was a plentiful supply of beautiful sandstone. Not only was it early decided to build the houses largely of blocks of this native stone, but also quantities of it were ground into sand for the mortar. Lumber was purchased in odd widths and lengths — which are cheaper — and in a carpenter shop, set up in the old hay shed, homesteaders turned these odd-size pieces into standard-size window frames, doorjambs, interior trim, and other parts of building construction. Most decisions and choices were made in light of the fact that the homestead families had almost no money but plenty of time. To use 1½-inch-wide flooring would have been economically wasteful in most instances because of labor costs. But David Day and the homesteaders found boards of this size cheap at the mills, and they decided to put in the extra labor, thus getting superior hardwood floors at low cost.

Under David Day's leadership, the homesteaders organized themselves into crews to work on each other's homes. A unique system of bookkeeping was developed, the medium of exchange being credit hours rather than dollars. At the end of each day a homesteader filled in a timecard showing where he had labored and how many hours. This was charged against the man on whose property he had worked. Labor was swapped on a straight time basis, regardless of a man's efficiency or the type of labor performed.

But there was plenty of pressure for efficiency, for these were the men's own homes, and as miners they had long since learned to be frank with each other. It was interesting and revealing to note the kind of discipline that developed in the working crews. The constant urge to do a good job, to be accurate, to get on with the work, came not from an employer or a union or a boss, but from the man who looked forward to living in the house. It was he who was anxious to make sure that the windows would go up and down, and that the house stood square with the world.

I must say that to a very considerable extent this phase of the project in particular demonstrated what so many of us believe about the right adjustment between man's nature and labor. It was hard work, it seemed in some cases to be dragging on forever, there was grumbling aplenty, some lack of responsibility, it was not all roses; but the motivation held, it came from within, it carried practically all the families through to the day when they proudly took possession of their own attractive, comfortable homes, each finished house representing about 3500 man-hours of labor. Furthermore, the cooperative nature of the enterprise consolidated the modest means and abilities of these families into an achievement far greater than they would have believed they had talents for. Gradually, one saw it bearing fruit in a new sense of independence and interdependence, of individual dignity, integrity, and worth.

It must be added that, once a house was completed and the family moved in, pride of ownership of this work of their own hands went so deep that a threat to it was the same as a threat to their very being.

At the time of this writing, it is particularly gratifying to be able to record that several of the houses have been completely paid for long ahead of time, and that there is only negligible delinquency. Each home is an attractive stone house, five or six rooms being the average size, with basement, modern kitchen and bath, central heating, hardwood floors, at least one and a half acres of land, with poultry, fruit trees, and garden plots — these outdoor developments varying considerably according to the individual family's preferences and tastes. This is a far cry from the grim coal-blackened little shack without water or electricity which used to be home to these families. And the people have wrought the change largely with their own energies. This, it seems to me, is the important point. These families do not, and have no call to, feel dependents or wards of anybody. Hence the human relations that have developed between them and the rest of us who have participated one way or another are rich with mutual regard and appreciation.

The first basement excavations were made in the fall of 1937, and it was two years before the first five stone houses were occupied. By the end of the third year, twenty families were in their homes;

it was two more years before the last of the fifty families were in. In part the project was slowed down during these latter years by the rise of employment opportunities, which the men could not afford to forego; then especially by the war, which drained off a good part of the younger workers for the duration.

On recommendation of Henry Regnery and after exhaustive research on his part, a knitting mill to manufacture sweaters was installed. We were taking a long chance when we encouraged the homesteaders, who had been learning by building their own homes, to join together in constructing a factory as a community enterprise. Suppose the venture failed?

As a matter of fact, it did undergo severe difficulties, due largely to the war, and some basic changes eventually had to be made. It had been anticipated that to train new workers in a highly competitive field would mean a lean period in the beginning. For this we were prepared. But with the outbreak of war, shortage of raw materials became an increasingly formidable problem.

Henry Regnery had stayed at Penn-Craft to see the business under way. Later he found a man who knew the skill of making beautiful sweaters, to come as manager. This man, Louis Gallet, had learned the trade in Vienna. His successful Austrian experience transferred to the little community of Penn-Craft proved an invaluable boon. And both he and his wife were interested not only in the success of the industry but in the all-round development of the community itself.

In the beginning, a separate nonprofit corporation had been organized to carry responsibility for the mill, which in its initial period employed approximately thirty workers, and turned out around 125 dozen sweaters a week. This, together with the farm, did a great deal toward solving the employment problem of so small a community.

The recovery of coal production during the war took many of the men back to the mines. The sweater factory then employed mostly women. In fact, it finally had to bring in women from outside the homestead to make up its full quota of workers. This had a healthy effect, for it helped Penn-Craft emerge from being a special kind of community without much relation to its neighbors.

In 1943–1944 the knitting mill became a private enterprise, Louis Gallet paying for the building and buying the business. At the time of this writing he has finished paying for these assets and is full owner of the mill, which during the 1952 fiscal year employed an average of eighty-seven persons and turned out 13,313 dozen sweaters, providing Penn-Craft with a payroll of $194,842.51.

A true co-operative store, started in a barn during the project's first year, was later moved to a stone building erected by the homesteaders for that purpose. It is now serving a considerable area beyond the boundaries of Penn-Craft, and thus has become another important link between Penn-Craft and the surrounding neighborhood, since most of its customers soon become members of the co-operative. This store now employs seven persons, has 341 frozen-food lockers, does about $150,000 business a year, and yields some $4000 a year in dividends and refunds to its members.

It is easy to be enthusiastic about the idea of growing one's own vegetables; it is less a matter for enthusiasm when one learns what hard work is required to bring back into production soil that has lain idle for a long time. Not all the settlers have been equally assiduous in cultivating the soil, but the over-all result has been a large food production and growing enjoyment of the resulting independence.

The old red brick farmhouse on the two-hundred-acre farm was from the beginning used by the settlers for parties, meetings, entertainments, a clinic, and other community enterprises. Its functions continued to multiply, and now, largely through the efforts of the families themselves, this building and the grounds adjoining it are being made into a modern community center, with a variety of recreational facilities for young and old.

As the young people of Penn-Craft have grown up and married, many of them have discovered that its way of life has a great at-

traction for them. It was largely the desire of this younger generation to live in or near the homestead which encouraged the Committee to take the funds that had been repaid, to purchase additional
land adjoining the first site, and to begin the establishment of a
second homestead unit there. On this farm of 165 acres the emphasis
is on development of the land as a source of cash income. Each
homesteader's plot is about ten acres, and the land is being worked
with an eye to building the soil. Many of the cinder-block homes
have been completed, and as this is written others are under construction. These new homesteaders will be able to share many of
the advantages and facilities of the original development.

It takes time and thought and devotion to build from such an
assemblage of families a true community. People who have moved
about from one coal camp to another, living in rented houses
owned by the companies, find it difficult to develop real community
feeling. Besides, miners are in the nature of their trade somewhat
individualistic.

On this social-spiritual side of the undertaking, I saw demonstrated, even more than I had in the government homestead program, the power of example. Errol Peckham, brought up on an
Iowa farm, trained for the ministry, and dedicated to the recovery
of the values of community life, had not only come in to help select
homesteaders but had become a homesteader himself, developing a
Farm Bureau Insurance business at Penn-Craft and until his death
in 1948 serving as a kind of unofficial pastor whose spirit and life
exercised a tremendous influence. It was he who was so convinced
of the value of the co-operative idea for the store that he gave literally months of his labor, sometimes without very much help from
other people, getting the building ready for business. It was his
strong lead, based on deep conviction, that bore its fruit in helping
homesteaders to understand the significance of the co-operative nature of the enterprise. And I am afraid it was to some extent over-
work in this heavy physical job which caused Errol's all-too-early
death. I think he would say he discovered that deep spiritual and

human values can be purchased only at the price of suffering and sometimes even death. His wife, Mary Peckham, fulfilled much the same function in the community until she removed to California in 1952.

David Day, when he was no longer fully employed as manager, found occupation nearby, and he and his wife, Olive Day, still live as unofficial counselors among the people with whom they have worked since 1937. The permanence of the relationships formed in the building of this community does, it seems to me, signify something important about the way the job was done.

It is difficult to appraise results in terms of that all-important dimension, quality of life. One is too aware of all that remains yet to be achieved in this respect to try to make a success story out of present accomplishments. Yet those of us who have watched the experiment and worked with the people from the beginning have seen a deep and gratifying growth among them of a sense of independence, of integrity, and of hope.

There will be those who are concerned because no Quaker Meeting was established at Penn-Craft and no attempt made to proselytize. It must be said in all candor that the problem of religion in a community of this sort is a difficult one. A vital, real contact with a church and a personal religious spirit are both essential to the building of such a community. Surrounded as the farm was with churches, all needing more members and support, it did not seem appropriate to try to have any kind of church on the property. A community Sunday school which was started did not prove successful. Yet the attachment of members of this community to a variety of churches has tended to make religion a divisive rather than a uniting factor. This problem remains unsolved. The Friends who took part in launching the enterprise were clear that they must exert no pressure on any settler to ally himself with the Society of Friends as a kind of compensation for the privileges made available through the Service Committee's efforts.

However, the contagion of a dedicated life is immeasurable, and

Penn-Craft has felt the impact of such lives. Who knows but that in the long run this kind of individual contribution is more vital than anything else that can be done in the realm of the spirit?

The enterprise has had a good deal of publicity, and has inspired groups of widely different backgrounds to undertake similar developments. From the beginning, part of the Service Committee's intent was to make the findings of this venture available to others wishing to adapt the idea to their own needs. Such service has been extended to a group of veterans in Lorain, Ohio; to Flanner House, a Negro community center in Indianapolis; and to a slum-clearance and redevelopment project in Philadelphia for which the Committee has also assumed managerial responsibility.

Throughout the experiment, it has been our conviction that any development of this sort should have as little subsidy as was feasible in order to make it go. We decided that the education of men in new skills might well be considered a donation. In the case of Penn-Craft, management also was furnished without being assessed against the property. This, of course, was an abnormal subsidy. Also, the interest rate of two per cent is lower than could be expected if money were secured from ordinary sources. In Lorain, Ohio, however, the funds have been secured from banking sources; and the Philadelphia project has been financed through a bank mortgage insured by the Federal Housing Administration, the necessary down payments being made in the form of self-help labor of the future occupant owners.

One hopes that these achievements may be found to have a still wider application in the future. Full employment at high wages lessens the felt urgency of such developments, but some of the big industries have investigated the possibility of using this self-help homestead plan if and when employment begins to drop. Both unions and management have noted the fact that it is an area in which co-operation between management and labor might be developed to a high degree.

While one does not pray for a depression or other national calamity, one does wonder whether the time may not come when the experience, the inward yearnings, and the qualities of spirit developed at Penn-Craft are more highly prized than they are at present.

We had entered into this effort determined to work *with* homesteaders, and to do our best to see that both they and we understood each step as it was taken. Time alone, I suppose, will tell how penetrating was our success. Perhaps the clearest evidence of achievement is that, although for some time now there has been no paid management at Penn-Craft, it has continued to grow as a community in its ability to conduct its own affairs. I think it would be fair to say, also, it has grown in its belief that a job of this kind can be done with integrity — without paternalism and without being directed to the benefit of someone or some agency outside.

What, people frequently ask, has all of this to do with development of the religious life? That, after all, is the purpose of the church. And especially why does a Quaker organization get involved in housing and community development? This is an appropriate question to raise. If such developments are purely external to the central meaning and purpose of life, then there may be a justifiable query as to the appropriateness of such efforts.

If we went as "experts" to "show people a better way to live" we would probably fail. We serve in these physical jobs of reconstruction in the faith that we, together with those among whom we work, are children of a common Father, who has implanted His own image and spirit in each of us. And together we seek to give that image release in work together for the common good.

I I
Nobody's Nothings

A little five-year-old boy, who had been bombed out of his home and evacuated to the country, said: "Now I am nobody's nothing." It is worth very much to help these "nobody's nothings" to discover that somebody cares, and that somebody with a face and a heart comes to save them from hopelessness and despair.

— RUFUS M. JONES, in the foreword to the 1943 Annual Report of the American Friends Service Committee

1. Europe, 1930 and 1934

Probably everyone who knows anything about the work of the American Friends Service Committee knows that Europe was the first scene of its activities. The story begins in 1917, when, in spite of pledges of neutrality and promises of President Wilson to keep us out of war, there we were in the midst of it. Thousands of Quaker boys who had never seriously faced the conflict between their religious beliefs and the demands of the state for military service now had to make a decision. Many found themselves under the stern and unpopular necessity to choose against participation in war. But most of these urgently desired to dedicate their lives as unreservedly as did those who went into battle. It seemed clear that alternatives in the form of service opportunities were called for.

Under the leadership of Rufus M. Jones, a representative group of American Friends met in Philadelphia just twenty-four days after war was declared, to consider how the Society of Friends in the United States might help provide such service opportunities. Out of the deliberations of this group, the American Friends Service Committee emerged. The minutes of the first meeting carry a brief declaration of purpose: "We are united in expressing our love for our country and our desire to serve her loyally. We offer ourselves to the Government of the United States in any constructive work in which we can conscientiously serve humanity."

As a first step, and after consultation with the government and the Red Cross, one hundred young men, carefully selected from a large group of applicants on the basis of religious motivation, ability, and health, were admitted to a training course at Haverford College. After a short period of preparation for overseas reconstruction work, they sailed in late summer for France. A precedent for such activity had already been set by British Friends who had organized for relief immediately after the outbreak of war in 1914. Now, as the new American Committee was entering the scene, arrangements were made for close co-operation between the two groups.

The story of the opening up of war-torn France through reconstruction services under the general umbrella of the American Red Cross has been ably told elsewhere.* At the peak of that program, our Committee had almost six hundred men and women in French towns and rural areas, distributing food and clothing, beds, utensils, and farm animals, planting trees (25,000 in the Verdun region alone, most of them fruit trees), caring for refugee children, setting up hospitals, repairing and rebuilding houses — all, of course, alongside the French people themselves. United States Army dumps in France were purchased at extremely low prices and the materials utilized directly or sold for cash to invest in reconstruction. By the end of 1919 Friends in France had assisted more than 46,000 families.

Equally well known, I believe, is the fact that shortly after the signing of the armistice the Service Committee accepted Herbert Hoover's invitation to undertake child feeding in Germany. Financed chiefly by the American Relief Administration, then by Americans of German descent, and later through General Henry T. Allen's special committee, this program, in which thousands of German men and women co-operated with a small group of American and British workers, fed around a million German children a day during critical periods in 1920–1922, and again in 1924. This service to the late enemy led our representatives into almost every

---

* See, for example, *A Service of Love in War Time,* by Rufus M. Jones (Macmillan, 1920); *Quakers in Action,* by Lester M. Jones (Macmillan, 1929); *Swords Into Ploughshares,* by Mary Hoxie Jones (Macmillan, 1937).

part of Germany and into the affection and inner sanctuary of a great many German individuals and homes.

In Austria child-feeding operations in the early 1920's assumed such proportions that at one time the Friends' Unit was the largest milk distributor in Vienna.

Serbia, Poland, and Russia had early presented some of the gravest recovery problems. In these areas immediately following the war, the rise of typhus was so swift and deadly that for a time it seemed it might sweep over the whole of Europe. Friends' units in each of these countries developed unsurpassed devotion to their particular assignments, perhaps in part due to the grimness of the struggle.

AFSC workers had gone to join British Quakers in Russia as early as 1917. One report in 1918 informed our Committee that the Quaker group was the only outside relief mission functioning in Russia, others having withdrawn because of the peculiar difficulties of that period. Between 1917 and 1930, at several different times of deep crisis, British and American Quakers in Russia identified themselves unreservedly with the Russian people in their desperate battle against starvation and disease. War, drought, and blockade were responsible for indescribable tragedies.

A letter from Buzuluk in the fall of 1921 reported:

Though our work here has increased, the famine has increased at a much greater rate. The death-rate from hunger has risen. . . . The number of people seen dead in the streets of Buzuluk is greater than ever, and yesterday at the meeting with the Ispolkom we were told that the reason why the volost [district] of Oosmanovskaya had not sent to our warehouse for the supplies for their kitchens was because the whole of the famine committee had either died or were ill from typhus. The man who brought the message to Buzuluk is in bed with a high temperature and will probably be unable to take our supplies to his starving volost. . . .We received a telegram last night from Finch who is at Alekseevka that the people in that vicinity are too feeble to bury their dead and that corpses are being thrown into sheds instead of being buried.

It is *absolutely essential* that we increase the amount of feeding very considerably; otherwise the 50,000 we are feeding at present (which we hope to extend by 50% with the arrival of new supplies) will simply be 50,000 orphans stranded without anyone to take care of them.

This was the process by which it had come about that in the postwar world hundreds of men and women, Quaker and non-Quaker, were working under the red and black star of the American Friends Service Committee in numerous countries. The personal attachments which had been formed, the consciousness that war had planted dangerous seeds of bitterness, plus a sense of the enrichment which may come to anyone involved in a close association between people of the various nations, prompted individuals in many countries to urge continuation of the Quaker units after emergency relief operations ended.

Carl Heath, the distinguished secretary of Friends Service Council in London, caught the vision, and spoke with great clarity and conviction of "Quaker Embassies" in many of the leading capitals and tension spots of the world. His presentation was certainly in part responsible for the eventual development of Quaker International Centers. If another major conflict were to be prevented, people must be brought together and learn to understand each other; it seemed necessary that such meetings should be in a climate not only of friendliness but of spiritual concern. It was hoped that various permanent Quaker centers in Europe might be staffed with personnel drawn from Great Britain and America as well as from the countries in which they were located, but they were not to be centers for proselytizing from other churches to build up a Society of Friends. They were, rather, to represent the cohesive quality in human life, seeking in the spirit of religion to draw together, in understanding, people whose countries tended toward misunderstanding or even war with one another. The American Friends Service Committee and the Friends Service Council of London joined hands in this development.

It was inevitable that the meetings for worship in connection with these centers would in time involve some people of the countries in which they were located. However, as the years have passed, the distinctly small growth of Continental Friends' groups, while valuable in itself, has, I should think, indicated that Quakerism's influence in European countries for the most part will not be reflected in terms of people becoming members of the Religious Society of Friends. This does not mean that the Society may not have a place of dignity, significance, and character in the life of many of these countries. But it may best fulfill its mission simply through being the medium of bringing people together on a deeper level of the life of the spirit than that on which conflicts arise.

These International Centers formed the major part of the foreign program of the American Friends Service Committee when I became its executive secretary in 1929. Naturally, I was eager to visit them as soon as possible. Also I wanted to become acquainted with the British counterpart of our Committee — the Friends Service Council of London.

This opportunity came in the spring of 1930.

One of my most memorable experiences on that trip had to do with a student-club meeting at our Quaker Center in Berlin, during which there was a prolonged and heated discussion, especially between Polish and German students, concerning the Polish Corridor. Furthermore, the German students were deeply disturbed by many other provisions of the Versailles Treaty. This discussion, I remember, irked me considerably. True, the treaty was not a perfect settlement; but I saw no probability of its being altered, and I did see great possibilities for the young people of Germany, if they would only take hold of them. In fact, it seemed to me that the tendency indefinitely to argue about their troubles was perhaps the chief obstacle in their way. I found many persons in Germany and elsewhere who had achieved creative patterns for their lives even under the existing imperfect treaties, and I'm afraid I was not very sympathetic with the viewpoint of impatient youth.

In retrospect, I can see a good many limitations to my under-standing at that time. The significance of national pride, the impor-tance of equality in national standing, the sense of hurt on the part of a generation of young Germans who were held responsible, but actually bore no real responsibility, for the First World War: all this was difficult for me fully to understand, and looking back now I think it was probably more difficult for many Americans who had not had the opportunity of being associated with Germans in Ger-many.

Friends' work in Geneva was being carried largely by two Eng-lish Quakers, Bertram and Irene Pickard, who served in this capacity for almost fourteen years. Here our regular International Center provided a place for Friends' meetings for worship, an office for work with the League of Nations and other international organizations, and an international student hostel. Bertram Pickard was secretary of the organization made up of all nongovernmental agencies at the League of Nations. He has followed this interest ever since, and is at present employed by the United Nations as liaison officer between UN and the hundred or so nongovern-mental organizations now recognized by UN.

Throughout Europe in 1930, Quaker Centers were tending to concentrate on work with students. In Paris, groups from the Sorbonne found in the nearby Quaker Center a hospitable place in which to get acquainted across national barriers. This Center had to guard itself to some extent against becoming a loafing place for the "perpetual student" who above all things loved to sip his coffee and discuss endlessly subjects which had little relevance to the element of personal and social responsibility. But here also I at-tended a spirited student meeting in which oppression in Indo-China was the subject. In addition to the student work of this Cen-ter, French Friends, especially Henry van Etten, were developing a new sense of responsibility for French prisons and the treatment of prisoners.

A large student club which met regularly in the Vienna Center

represented all religious and political persuasions — Jewish, Protestant, Catholic; and Christian Socialist, Social Democrat, and German Nationalist. This did not seem especially noteworthy until one
learned how intense were the antagonisms being bridged. I was
told that nowhere else in Vienna could such a fellowship develop.
Not long before, some Jewish medical students had been attacked
by Nationalist students at the University, and many wounded.

In Moscow, which I visited briefly with Gilbert MacMaster, our
faithful representative in Germany, the hope of continued peace
and greatly improved standards of living loomed high. The people
were cynical about religion, not too much interested in help from
the West, and confident of their future. I felt I was seeing what
had been a slumbering youth rising to feel the full vigor of his
inherent strength and eager to go his way pretty much under his
own steam. At this time, there was still the remnant of a thriving
Moscow Quaker Center, which had been maintained during relief
operations in the USSR. But it was becoming increasingly difficult
to be useful there under the growing restrictions, and a few months
later this Center was closed.

Toward the end of this all-too-short overseas journey, I spent
some time in England, especially in London where I attended sessions of London Yearly Meeting of Friends. The principal subject
was India. Rabindranath Tagore, the distinguished Indian poet,
who at that time was giving the Hibbert Lectures at Oxford, had
asked for the privilege and was invited to speak at one of the
sessions. The doors had to be closed to all non-Friends, and even so
the house was packed. It was a colorful and memorable occasion
when the long-bearded, blue-velvet-robed prophet appeared and
gave an address in classic English full of feeling of the urge for independence, eloquent in his plea for an interdependence built on
India and England as equals. There followed a very electric session,
for English Friends were not all of one mind on the question of
India. However, in the course of the next couple of days, the Yearly
Meeting did draft a minute to the Prime Minister and the Secretary

of State for India, which in a remarkable way reconciled and lifted widely divergent points of view to a higher level of united concern.

In all the countries I visited, the issues of the next decade were shaping up clearly, but whether we would have the spirit and imagination to deal with them creatively, or let them lead us into war, was still an open question.

That fall, not long after my return to Philadelphia, the Service Committee sponsored Rabindranath Tagore's visit to the United States on behalf of his "World University" at Santiniketan, India. I had helped complete the arrangements when I was in London.

Now I met him and his party on the boat, and went with them to an apartment in uptown New York where he was to live. It was one of those exciting high moments of life, and Tagore responded partly with appreciation but also with trepidation. A limousine with driver had been furnished to bring him from the dock, and a motor escort squealed its way the full distance from lower Manhattan to the upper Seventies.

At the apartment, we were met by newspaper reporters and photographers and movie cameramen. Tagore was rebellious and wholly unwilling to co-operate. I began to discover that, saintly as he was, he was also able to be very positive and vigorous in expressing his disapproval. I tried to explain to him that, since he was hoping to place his cause before the American public, it seemed unwise to completely antagonize both the press and the moving-picture industry. Finally we were able to organize an orderly press conference, and also an opportunity for him to be properly photographed for the newsreels.

He was in the United States about a month. During that time I traveled with him occasionally, though Amiya Chakravarty, his secretary, and Harry Timbres of our Committee, who was to work with him in India, were his more constant escorts. It was like handling a piece of delicate glass to take care of this aged saint.

His last public appearance in this country was in a theater in

New York in a joint program with the well-known interpretive dancer, Ruth St. Denis. To see this bronze-skinned prophet with long white beard and flowing white robe sitting in a kind of throne chair on the platform, surrounded by children, and reading his poetry, first in his native tongue and then in English, was a sight which I am sure no one who saw it would ever forget.

While this whole episode was a kind of peripheral development, it marked one of the Service Committee's most direct contacts with India up to that time.

Meanwhile, conditions in our own country were claiming the greater part of the Service Committee's energies, and I soon became immersed in efforts to help meet emergencies in the coal fields. Nevertheless, newspapers and personal communications from Europe kept us increasingly aware of the rapidly deepening gloom over there. Mention of fear that there would be open persecution of Jews in Germany gave way, in 1933, to grim and bitter stories of the reality.

By the spring of 1934, it seemed desirable that I should revisit England and Europe. For the Committee I was to explore whether we could do anything to help prevent the barbaric treatment of Jews and to assist the immigration of those who were so fortunate as to be able to go to the United States or elsewhere. Also, as an administrator of our government homesteads, I wanted to study European resettlement schemes, for in this matter Germany and Austria especially were far ahead of the United States.

At this time we dimly realized that a mild form of social revolution was under way in the United States. In more violent form, it was also under way in Europe. Seen in perspective, that trip to Europe in the spring of 1934 was obviously one of our Committee's earlier attempts to find its place in a world in revolution. This time Lilly Pickett accompanied me.

Our first stop was in Paris. We had not fully realized the deep human tragedy of the refugees from Hitler Germany. Our little

International Center in Paris, co-operating with other concerned agencies through the *Entr'aide,* reported some four thousand refugee families in France still trying to get along in makeshift fashion while they sought permanent relocation.

Even now, I can see the lines of physical suffering and mental agony in the faces of these people forcibly away from home; and I can recall that the appearance of persons fresh from America brought a ray of hope. I tried talking with some of the refugees. I found them asking assistance which I could not at all promise because of the difficulties of immigration regulations and resettlement in our country. These interviews impressed upon me the importance of more rapid and thorough planning on the part of agencies in America who were concerned with this new wave of immigration from Germany. The Jewish Joint Distribution Committee, with which we had co-operated in Europe after the First World War and more recently in New York, had an office in Paris, and I talked with its agents there. These Paris conversations were really the beginning of a much closer relationship in America.

While France had done a great deal toward taking care of the German refugees who had so early crossed her borders, the rise of the Hitler regime in Germany had once again paralyzed her with fear of the future. Weakened by the last war, France now seemingly placed great hope in the "impregnable" Maginot Line. I have always wondered whether her dependence on her large army and physical defenses, though it lulled her with a certain surface sense of security, did not at the same time augment a deep subconscious feeling that her real security was in jeopardy.

Austria made one want to both laugh with joy and weep. Traditional fervor over learning and music and the other arts, eager quest for spiritual freedom and for the emancipation of the intellect, were wonderful to behold. We went to the opera one night, and although Austrians were poor and the middle class largely gone the auditorium was packed. We were told it was always so, though opera went on for ten and a half months of the year. Economically the country had almost collapsed. Yet here were the young people pursuing music, painting, philosophy, and science as if they had court patronage, like the favored few of old.

Politically the Austrians were active and alert; they could hardly have been otherwise. They lived alongside Germany with whom they shared a common culture and a common language, and the Nazis were now in complete control in Germany. Moreover, in February, 1934 — just three months before our visit — Dollfuss had crushed Socialist opposition to his authoritarian regime within Austria. He was violently anti-Nazi, but nevertheless was a dictator.

We were surprised when confronted with the extent of the Vienna Center's relief operations in this time of internal crisis in Austria. During the February fighting, thousands of Austrians had been seized and imprisoned, or killed in the wild shooting, or even executed. Others, more fortunate, only lost their jobs. A large proportion of those needing outside assistance were the families of Social Democrats. The small Center staff, plus a few relief workers called from other points, had been supervising aid to as many as eight thousand families, with funds to the extent of $150,000 supplied by the International Federation of Trade Unions. A volunteer staff of about two hundred Austrian youth were helping with distributions.

Later that year, after the attempted Nazi *Putsch* in July, the Vienna Center was approached concerning the need of families of Nazis who had been seized and imprisoned or killed. Some of these families were suffering acutely. In Philadelphia the question arose as to the rightness of feeding families of Nazis. Shying away from the project a little bit myself, I recall Rufus Jones's feeling a real sense of vigorous concern that we should not let our objection to the prisoners' Nazi views prevent our taking care of their families if that was humanly possible. Members of the Vienna staff were ready to undertake this work exactly as they had cared for victims of the February fighting — on the basis of need without reference to religious or political affiliation. But in the case of the earlier work, the International Federation of Trade Unions had supplied large sums of money. There were no such international nongovernmental sources of funds for relief of Nazi families, and there was a clear feeling that we could not take assistance from available German sources. Between the search for funds and the new Schuschnigg government's more drastic policy toward Nazis, this project of feeding Nazi families did not develop in any major way.

There was a great deal of ferment about religion in Austria at the time of our visit. Dollfuss was a devout Catholic. While we were in Vienna it was announced that 30,000 Austrians had joined the Catholic Church within two months. This religious revival centering in the Catholic Church had its roots in political revolution and did not necessarily indicate a growth of confidence in the way of life which transforms the spirits of men.

One evening I was asked to speak to a group of men and women in Vienna about the Quaker view of the religious life. But I was warned that if I used the words "Christ" or "God" I was likely to get a vigorous reaction against what I had to say because of the wide differences in interpretation of the meaning of those central realities of the Christian faith. I can testify that to observe this caution puts strict limits on one who is accustomed to use those words freely, and to whom they have rich meaning. But I have never talked to a group in which I felt more deeply the search for something real and genuine and abiding.

Carrying responsibility for the Vienna Center work were Headley and Elizabeth Horsnaill of Friends Service Council and Emma Cadbury of our Committee. All had been there since the 1920's. Superb in their work and in the quality of their lives, they were deeply loved and respected by the thousands of people who flowed through the Center.

It was a revealing experience to go with Emma Cadbury after a long day and late evening at the Center to her apartment a few blocks away. We walked up a small back street, and then she pulled out a huge key, unlocking an iron gate into an inner court, then another key to open the big front door to her house, a third key to open the door to the hall of her apartment, and a fourth key to the apartment itself. Trusting soul that she was, these keys seemed to us a kind of symbol of the political, economic, and spiritual instability of Austria.

But there were constructive forces at work in the country, also. Austria had been famous for its interesting housing. As early as 1921–1922 Friends had loaned a considerable sum of money to a co-operative building association in Austria for a new housing development which provided small holdings of about a quarter of an acre of land per one-family home. This small experiment was one of the precursors of the Austrian government's development of public housing, in which the emphasis gradually shifted from small land holdings to city apartments, culminating in the construction of the famous Vienna apartment houses which became the scene of bloody fighting in February, 1934. Now the Dollfuss government was interested in resettling workers in small homes close to industrial employment yet with enough land so they could cultivate it for a part of their subsistence. I had the interesting experience of hearing a glowing description of these government plans from a politician, and then visiting one of the projects he had described, talking with the residents and the nonpolitical local director. Actually, far more fundamental things were being done than the politician had pictured. His description of the external development had been pretty heavily overdrawn and empty of meaning, but one could see, when one visited a little house and talked with the mother and children, that they had real respect, if not affection, for the man who was directing the enterprise on the local level: a very important ingredient in any community development. And when I talked with this man himself, there in the midst of the new community of 425 homes and small landholdings, I felt in him something of the love and intelligence of a Woolman or Penn.

Every inch of ground was being used. Most of the householders had one or two pigs, and those pigs were washed every day and their shelter kept almost as clean as the family's own housing. Every bit of waste from the household was used as fertilizer. I have never seen as complete and thorough a job of using everything possible as we saw in those developments. And I have rarely seen more resourcefulness in the presence of political and economic insecurity, more feeling in the people of independence of what might happen in the political world.

We decided to stop in Dresden on our way from Vienna to Berlin, simply to see the Sistine Madonna; we had never seen that historic painting. We shall probably never quite lose the wonder of the experience of sitting quietly — the only people in the room — looking at that great representation of the painter's idea of Mary. It was calming and reassuring to the spirit; something of the eternal significance of life had passed from the painter's soul into the pigment of the picture.

But the realities of immediate life were not far off. As we emerged from the gallery, a Nazi parade was just about to pass. We had heard the story of a fellow American who, when a parade went by, had not lifted his hand in a "Heil Hitler," and the consequence had been that he was pretty brutally beaten up. With this in mind, Lilly Pickett and I ducked into a back alley to avoid an incident, or, to be more exact, to avoid a threat to ourselves when we too failed to heil the Führer.

That evening found us in Berlin. What a change had come over our Center there! In 1930 it had been the scene of student-group discussions of the Versailles Treaty. Now there was an almost constant flow of people, mostly Jewish, anxious and troubled because threats had come to them from their neighbors, from the police, through mysterious notes, or perhaps just through the general climate which they knew spelled doom. They wanted to ask about possibilities of United States immigration. We had taken our privileges of American citizenship pretty much for granted all our lives, and had assumed they came without money and without price, but here we began to understand what a precious possession was ours, highly coveted by a growing number of uncertain citizens of Germany.

I wanted particularly to talk with someone of the Jewish community of Berlin who knew what was happening to the spiritual life of Jews, due to the oppression which had come upon them. It was arranged that I should meet the distinguished leading rabbi of Berlin, Dr. Leo Baeck.

He objected to coming to our Center because he thought his presence there might mark it as a Jewish hideout, so we met in a room surrounded by black curtains in the middle of the American Women's Club in Berlin. There he told me of his experience as rabbi of a large and wealthy synagogue, where ordinarily his congregation had been perhaps fifty or sixty souls. He said that now he often had to hold four services on Saturday to accommodate the crowds. He said that his obligations as a rabbi had never been so satisfactory to him as at present. Chiefly, he read some of the great Psalms of consolation. These brought to his congregation a sense of fellowship with their forebears who had suffered similar tragedies. He said his constant theme was "Let no drop of bitterness enter your hearts, to defile them." He told me that often, after the congregation dispersed, hoodlums would throw stones at them. Of course, the people realized this was what they might face each time they left the great, beautiful synagogue — which was later burned.

He spoke to me of a recent celebration in the synagogue at Worms, which was marking its 900th year of consecutive service. He pointed out that Jews were in what is now Germany before the time of Christ, that they loved Germany, and wanted to stay. During the past year about ten per cent of the German Jewish income had gone into establishing four hundred private schools for children who were no longer wanted in public schools. Also, the Jewish community was retaining Jewish lawyers, doctors, and other professional men who had lost most of their practice, as locksmiths, repairmen, and the like, trying to absorb and take care of the problem among themselves.

Four years later, when the suffering in Germany had reached proportions we all know about but cannot well comprehend, I raised the question with Dr. Baeck as to whether he should not migrate to the United States. He said he would have no difficulty doing that if he so desired, but that he had decided to stay by his people in Germany as long as he could minister to them in any way. In fact, a number of times I came across this sentiment among the Jewish leadership in Berlin and in Germany generally. It has always reminded me of the accusation made against Jesus: "He saved others, himself he could not save."

I was to meet Dr. Baeck many years later in New York, after he and his family had spent four years in Dachau, where he had seen three members of his family die.

He told me then that unspeakable though his personal griefs were, and perhaps partly because of them, as a rabbi he had found the richest experiences of his life in Dachau. There after the lights were out at night, people would gather in the great corridors in the darkness of the prison to listen to him preach a sermon or give a lecture on their cultural and religious heritage. During the day, part of the time he volunteered as a horse to help pull the plows. He was a husky man and more able to do this than the less physically stalwart prisoners. The rest of the time he spent going from cell to cell, reminding people who had come to be called by numbers instead of names that they were not numbers but persons, they were the children of God and precious to Him.

My inquiry as to what was happening to the spiritual life of the Jews went on through the years. It embraced the tragic picture of the great majority of those who were caught in the vicious network of racial and religious fanaticism, six million being killed or dying in the process of being exiled, millions of others showing phenomenal capacity for endurance, a small minority within the minority triumphing spiritually over Nazi political power, coming out not only unembittered but with richer spiritual gifts for all who came in contact with them. An ancient Hebrew prophet described how "one should chase a thousand, and two put ten thousand to flight." In Rabbi Baeck, through his strength of character and the depth of his religious faith, one saw this vision of the possibilities of the strength of one inspired man fulfilled in our day. I suppose one can say that the persecution of Jews in Germany brought a great revival of cultural consciousness, of nationalism, and of inherent ability to endure; but to a few it brought to the fore the enormous prophetic resources which are possible to men and women dedicated to the historic and ever-present realities of a religious faith rooted in an eternal God and expressing itself in daily conduct.

While the question as to what the Service Committee could do in relation to this tragic persecution became the dominant consideration of our stay in Germany, we had also come to learn what we could about government housing projects comparable to those with which I was working in the Subsistence Homesteads Division of our government. Totalitarian governments, which demand subservience and obedience from subjects, must also give some quick and easily understood results to those on whom they make such demands. This was true in Germany. During my visit in 1930 I had been impressed by the number of small holdings in the suburbs of cities, where very productive vegetable gardens had been developed. Now, this desire to cultivate the land and supplement the family budget had been recognized by the Nazi government, and it was establishing small holdings for workers on a large scale. Visiting some of the projects near Berlin, I saw for myself that the Germans were ahead of us in these matters. They had done a more scientific job of planning than we had, they built better and cheaper, and although frequently the houses were all virtually identical the planting had been so varied that the effect was most pleasing.

Also, Nazi educational plans were more thoroughly organized than ours. Of course what they were teaching included not only information about how and when to plant, cultivate, and harvest, but also much Nazi party propaganda. However, I learned a good deal about the way in which educational material as well as house planning and layout might be more fully perfected.

I talked with a number of men and women in these new developments in the spring of 1934, especially women in their homes. I am sure that very few of them at that time had any real conception of the amount of political bondage they had assumed or of the anguish that was going on in the Jewish communities.

The grip of Nazi ideology on young Germans came home to us in another experience one day. A few years previously Dr. X, a distinguished German international lawyer, had been a guest in our home near Philadelphia. He and his wife, a German-American woman of some wealth, had invited us to visit them at Braunschweig, and we were happy to accept. We arrived just in time for coffee. Father, mother, and three of the four sons were present. After the first joy of reunion, we heard sad tidings. Dr. X had recently defended two Jews against what was obviously a travesty against justice and decency, and for this he had now lost his right to practice law in Germany. He and his wife were bewildered. Their old friends were shunning them as though they were lepers.

Then, in the midst of our coffee, the fourth son came in from somewhere, dressed in Nazi uniform, clicked his heels, heiled Hitler, and refused to greet the American guests in English. He could speak English perfectly but disdained to do so, promptly commenting that if we wanted to talk to him, we could do it in his language. Deeply chagrined by their son's conduct, the father and mother remonstrated, but he was a loyal member of the Nazi party. Something imperial, not to say Messianic, had taken hold of this youth and many others like him, due to their new political affiliation. They were a superior race. Here was a manifestation of that spirit — in what had been a lovely, harmonious German home. Recently it has been my privilege to help this young man, now quite changed, to find work. We were never to see those parents again. The mother died of cancer, and the father, unable to endure the violent changes that were taking place in his country, threw himself in front of a train and was killed.

The middle of May found us in England and in the Rhondda Valley in Wales, where we were particularly interested in seeing what was known as the "Allotments Scheme," a subsistence land-plot development for unemployed miners initiated by some English Friends, and now receiving attention and assistance from several agencies, including government. Workshops, garden and craft instruction, clubs for reclamation and recreation, health and welfare programs, were integral aspects of the new communities, which, as in Germany and far more than in the United States, were thought of as a new way of life.

We noted that the educational effort was without political propaganda, and that it had more of a cultural emphasis than in either Germany or the United States. There was even a margin of attention to the development of the fine arts, and later we were presented with a beautiful little wooden statue of Saint Francis carved by an unemployed coal miner who was working one of the allotments and had begun to find a new plan for his life and a completely new set of interests.

England had felt the depression earlier than the United States, and her system of the dole was thoroughly organized. While it gave one a sense of satisfaction to see the wider distribution of such supplies as were available, one could not escape the normal reaction of an American in wondering whether this kind of provision of security did not take away from initiative. The British government so far showed little experimental-mindedness, remaining relatively cautious and fearful, seemingly casual and dull in its human interest and ventures, though there was a sense of the long-term nature of the economic problem it faced — more so than in the United States.

While it had not yet been recognized in governmental acts to any considerable degree, we felt that we were seeing the passing of the age of privilege and disparity between the income of the upper and the lower brackets. In fact, even in the countries controlled by totalitarian governments, the economic equalitarian emphasis was strong. Whether the change was being compelled by dictatorship or would be worked out voluntarily through orderly procedure, as in England, the direction everywhere was unmistakable. And one realized that the deep forces at work might end in war.

We did not in this year of 1934 foresee that Spain would be the scene of our Committee's next major involvement in the European dilemma. We could not anticipate that a bitter Spanish civil war would interpose itself between the situation we had just witnessed in Central Europe and its culminating explosion in a second world war. Yet so it was to be, and deep down it was all one pattern, a world in revolution but unsure of its star.

2. *Spain*

It was not until Spain burst into flames in 1936 that we of the American Friends Service Committee fully faced the fact that the days of war relief were not over, as we had hoped. Until then, there had always been the open chance that a way or ways through Europe's dangerous tensions could be found, leading into solutions instead of into further destructiveness. Even after the Spanish explosion, it took us a little time to come to the point of active participation.

All over the world at all times there is so much suffering, that it becomes a perpetual task for an organization such as our Committee to weigh each need in relation to its own basic commitments, resources, and character. For human beings in distress, this kind of delay is intolerable. I can only say that if we leaped to answer each call as it came, without careful consideration, we would find ourselves in the predicament of not being able to follow through on our beginnings, and there is great cruelty in ineffectiveness of that kind. Like other similar groups — or like individuals — we must make our specific decisions the best we can in the midst of insoluble dilemmas. We were at this time assuming heavy responsibilities in connection with the Penn-Craft development in western Pennsylvania, and our Centers in Paris, Berlin, and Vienna were deeply involved with the victims of Germany's and Austria's internal troubles. Would it not be better to concentrate on tasks to which we were already committed than attempt to take on more?

Calls from Spain soon echoed with acute suffering. English Quakers from the scene wrote to Friends Service Council in London and to our Committee, of the shocking homelessness and misery of throngs of children who themselves were "neither Nationalist nor Loyalist." They appealed for a Friends relief mission to these children. We sought more facts and advice. But children who aren't eating sicken and die swiftly. An English Quaker living in Spain wrote, "We had expected something more from Friends."

It was, indeed, the kind of emergency which falls within AFSC's special field of concern. Other agencies are better set up to meet natural calamities. We seek to supply missions of service and reconciliation in the midst of man's inhumanity to man.

Within Spain there was generous, spontaneous, unorganized aid to the great tides of refugees washing in and out of cities in the first back-and-forth of battle. Spanish Loyalist organizations were establishing children's colonies. The International Red Cross was protesting the bombings, bringing medical assistance, arranging for exchange of prisoners of war and hostages; two English partisan organizations were already at work on relief, the pro-Loyalist Spanish Medical Aid Committee and the pro-Nationalist Committee of Cardinal Hinsley, Archbishop of Westminster.

Friends Service Council of London, having received vivid firsthand reports from men and women arriving from Spain, decided in November of 1936 to enter into child-feeding operations, and wrote our Committee to that effect. They joined with the Save the Children Fund, the English branch of the Save the Children International Union, in an appeal to the English people for contributions; and on Christmas Day, 1936, SCIU and Friends Service Council opened a joint Spanish relief program by giving hot milk to a small group of children in Barcelona. Their first major project was serving hot cocoa to refugees as they poured into the Barcelona railroad station.

Meanwhile we in Philadelphia were also receiving some firsthand accounts of the evacuation of Madrid and the tragic need of perhaps a hundred thousand women and children. We were strongly encouraged by Spanish representatives, with whom we conferred in this country, to undertake a nonpartisan relief mission for the children of Spain. Among those with whom I had helpful conversations were Fernando de los Ríos, Spanish ambassador to the United States, Señora de Palencia, Spanish minister to Sweden, who was in this country briefly; and Salvador de Madariaga, former Spanish ambassador to the United States and permanent delegate from Spain to the League of Nations from 1931 to the summer of 1936. Also, American Red Cross officials strongly approved our organizing a relief mission; they gave us to understand that their organization did not expect to enter into the task directly but would give every facility at its command to help, if we would shoulder the responsibility. (This it did to a very generous extent as the program got under way; during 1938 and 1939, gifts in kind received through the Red Cross were valued at more than a half million dollars.)

Sylvester Jones, who had been a missionary in Cuba and was now a businessman in Chicago, agreed to go on our behalf to survey the needs of children on both sides of the fighting line. He visited refugee children's colonies throughout Loyalist territory, entered Madrid during the siege, and later visited Burgos, the Nationalist headquarters. He found 150,000 refugee children in Loyalist Spain in desperate need of food and medical aid, and on the Nationalist side 30,000 war orphans in similar straits. He was struck by the zeal with which the Spanish people were exerting themselves on the children's behalf, but they could not possibly meet the need. He saw the beginning of the work of British Friends. He cabled us concerning the extent and urgency of the need as he investigated the different areas, and early in February returned to Philadelphia. We were ready to act upon receiving his report.

In both England and the United States, feeling ran high concerning political issues involved in the Spanish Civil War. Most American liberals' sympathies were with the Republican government *

---

* As in common parlance, the terms *Republican* and *Loyalist* are used interchangeably in this chapter.

which had been attacked by General Franco and his Fascist troops. General Catholic opinion in this country was with Franco, though there were Catholics who felt otherwise. This sharp division of public opinion made the solicitation of funds doubly difficult throughout the Spanish operation.

We would be attacked at one time because our relief was going entirely to children on the Republican side of the line; a few weeks later, however, liberals would be attacking us because we insisted on feeding children in what had come to be Franco territory. We might be feeding the very same children.

This did not necessarily mean that our Committee's representatives in Spain did not have their own political convictions. I think we have never functioned in a situation in which our workers' personal feelings ran stronger. But so far as feeding children was concerned, it was essential to maintain above all a concern for them, which meant political neutrality in administering the program. This called for highly developed personal discipline.

Part of the difficulty in raising funds for this work could have been eliminated had we been able to take advantage of the willingness of energetic young American Communists to solicit contributions on our behalf. In fact, they did raise some money for our use, by street meetings and other devices which we have not commonly employed. But we discovered that although the collection of funds was made possible because of the appeal of the innocent Spanish children and also partly because the solicitors were able to say that our Commitee was the distributing agency, these meetings were quite political in character, and no small proportion of the money thus raised was used for political purposes in this country. We therefore found it necessary to refuse their funds. Decisions of this kind are not easy when one is aware of the critical need of little children. In this respect perhaps no relief group is completely consistent, or able to be sure it has done the right thing. The more tender the conscience in these matters, the less dogmatic does one become. At the same time, one cannot accept funds raised in the name of impartial relief when he is conscious that a proportion has been deducted for political purposes.

Especially in the case of this bitter Spanish conflict were the decisions difficult. Our modern world had experienced no war so fraught with cruelty, intense hatreds, and ruthless prolongation of terror and misery. A time came when it seemed the whole civilized world was rising up to say *No* to the monstrous suffering. A special Committee on Spain, established within the framework of the Service Committee to direct the Spanish relief program, drew its membership not only from our group, but also from the Mennonite Church, the Church of the Brethren, and the Federal Council of Churches. In addition to these, many other religious, peace, and social organizations in the United States made generous contributions of money, time, and ideas. A group of prominent business and society people in New York organized the Spanish Child Welfare Association, to raise money for the undertaking. Later, under President Roosevelt's direction, a Committee for Impartial Civilian Relief in Spain was set up.

There was closest co-operation with the International Commission for the Assistance of Child Refugees in Spain. This commission, established in December, 1937, through the initiative of English Friends, was designed to receive gifts from governments and allot them to nonpartisan distributing agencies. Judge Michael Hansson, president of the Nansen International Office for Refugees, became president of the International Commission, and within the first year of its operations Howard Kershner, arriving in Europe as field director for our Committee in Spain, was made director of the Commission as well. Organizations collaborating with the Commission included Friends Service Council, American Friends Service Committee, Save the Children International Union, and *Service Civil International*. The two Quaker organizations carried a large share of the responsibility for actual distribution.

Gifts in kind, as well as money, came from many governments and organizations. One gift alone, channeled through our Com-

mittee, consisted of 60,000 barrels of flour from the American Red
Cross. The wheat for this flour was surplus wheat made available
by the Federal Surplus Commodities Corporation. Costs of milling
and transportation to the seaboard were paid by the Red Cross,
ocean transportation to France was furnished free of charge by the
United States Maritime Commission, and the two Spanish governments provided the additional transportation to Spain. Shortly after
this transaction, Canada contributed a shipment of dried fish valued
at $10,000, and Brazil gave 10,000 sacks of coffee. The Scandinavian
countries shipped milk, cod liver oil, and clothing. Coal was sent
from South Wales. In all, twenty-four countries contributed vital
commodities.

As early as January, 1937, the League of Nations Commission
reported more than one million refugees in Loyalist territory. In
1938 the number was estimated at three million. Our workers wrote
back about roads filled with hordes of refugees. "A sight that will
go down in history, unparalleled," wrote one woman. Little did she
know this was only a beginning of long and harried experience of
humanity uprooted through political upheaval — a chaos which was
to become an outstanding characteristic of our generation.

To be a refugee is a tragic thing! [another worker wrote]
He may be compared to a plant which has been violently uprooted, but instead of being properly transplanted, is simply
"heeled under" with thousands of others, and left until things
right themselves somehow. We cannot transplant him, so that
he can take root again, but we can give him some nourishment
and perhaps keep his roots from withering and dying altogether, so that when the war is over, his suffering will not have
been too great and he can fit in again to a normal life. I cannot
picture to you his sufferings, but I hope you can get something
of the feelings that he must have. . . .
You read the story of Malaga, how the population fled as
the city was being bombed, and the bombing planes followed
them along the way, killing many and terrifying them all.
They were eight to ten days on the road without food or shel-

ter. If they had tried to take anything with them most of it was dropped on the way, and they were left with the clothes they were wearing and nothing more. And then we must remember that they have been without soap for a long time, and I find myself marveling that the children's faces and hands are clean as they come in for their chocolate. How do they do it? Some of the children come in creeping along as if they were afraid of the whole world, but others are much more normal and make enough noise to make up for the quiet ones. One little girl starts feeding her younger brother and waits for another cup to come for her. One child empties hers into another cup she brought with her and tries to take it out, and almost weeps when she is stopped, because her mother is sick and she wants to take it to her. She says her mother cries all the time because she lost the baby brother on the way from Malaga. The child was assured that other cups of chocolate would be taken to the sick people, and then she sat down and enjoyed hers as much as any of them. It seems hard to keep account of the number of children fed. . . .

This was from Republican Spain. And from a worker in the north, in Nationalist territory, came equally tender word of the children: "We found Oviedo children scattered in temporary and permanent orphanages for seventy miles around. Others still huddle amid the ruins. One of our experiences that most tugged at our heartstrings was that of giving out forty blankets to 652 children. Several of the little ones who did not get blankets walked up to them and felt them; one child patted the blankets and then walked outside into the night cold. . . . "

On both sides, Spanish men and women gave unreservedly of their energies and skills in an effort to save the children from hardship beyond their strength to bear. In Nationalist territory, we worked in close co-operation with the Spanish Red Cross and Auxilio Social, the official welfare agency of the Nationalist government. The larger part of our program was in Loyalist territory because of the enormous concentration of refugees in that dwindling area. There we co-operated with Spanish Republican government officials and organizations, the confusion of the hundreds of thousands of extra people in those parts posing a particularly acute problem. Three children's hospitals — in Murcia, Alicante, and Almería — were eventually among our Committee's special responsibilities. These hospitals had been established largely through the initiative and work of English Friends, and they continued to be staffed by English nurses.

"Last night I was at the hospital for supper with the two perfectly grand English nurses there," wrote one of our representatives. "After we had eaten they slipped into the room where the babies are, to look at one who they didn't think would last the night. It was dying of starvation."

And from another hospital: "As for the beanbags [sent from the United States among other toys for the children's hospitals], this very day Irene and I just finished opening them up to get enough beans for soup. None of our orders has come and we are short."

There were projects to bring groups of Spanish children to America, to England, to France. Some of them were actually brought out of Spain during the war; and of course in the war's final weeks when a half-million Spaniards fled into France and North Africa, large groups of children were included in the mass exodus.

"It was a moving sight to see the four to five hundred children crowded like ants into the landing-barge, waving, singing, and shouting. . . . They looked to me terribly thin. . . . One boy had a dog. . . . They showed a gay courage. I never thought to be so moved as I was by the first boatload," wrote one of the Quaker workers who received the first batch of Basque children in France.

The largest part of the exodus was over the Pyrenees into France. At first civilians filled the passes; then what was left of the retreating army of the Spanish Republic marched through — "outfought but not broken," reported *Life* magazine on February 20, 1939, in connection with a striking pictorial spread showing segments of both armies, but featuring the refugees — men, women, and children dragging their way through the snow of the mountains, where many fell dead from exhaustion and cold.

A Friends' unit which had established itself in the north of Catalonia, after the Nationalist march on Barcelona in January, managed to move into France ahead of the bewildered refugees. This unit, by daily trips back over the frontier, by setting up canteens along the way and providing trucks for the sick and wounded, eased the rigors of the grim trek.

In the then unparalleled emergency, French authorities improvised enormous camps for the Spaniards. More Quaker relief workers came from Spain. And the International Commission suddenly found itself working in two countries.

This is how it came about that the relief program in Spain led into refugee work in France; and from that time on there was no retreating from the growing responsibilities that faced us in France.

Relief operations in Spain itself came to an end in due course after the Nationalists' victory, as they assumed all responsibility for the country's welfare. We had some difficulties about confiscation of supplies, but in the end restitution was made, and we withdrew, leaving the work in the hands of Auxilio Social. Six new mobile medical clinics bearing on their sides the inscription A GIFT FROM THE QUAKERS AND THE INTERNATIONAL COMMISSION would for a long time to come be touring the provinces of Spain, accompanied by Spanish doctors and nurses, bringing medical aid to children in the most remote villages.

The three-year emergency relief program in which we had participated (1937–1939) had provided milk clinics for infants, public dining rooms for refugee children, children's colonies, children's hospitals, extra rations for mothers and old people, and clothing distributions. At the peak of these services — in February, 1939 — gifts from thousands of individuals and groups and from various governments through the International Commission had enabled Quaker workers to supply at least one meal daily to about 350,000 persons.

Donations received by our AFSC special Committee on Spain

had totaled well over a million dollars, more than three fourths of this amount being in gifts in kind from co-operating organizations and American business firms.

A total of twenty-seven men and women had gone from the United States to serve with our Committee in Spain, some of them joint appointees, representing also the Church of the Brethren, the Mennonite Church, or the American Unitarian Association. Friends Service Council had sent twenty-five workers, and in addition had appointed fourteen others on our behalf.

Now, for the time being, we would no longer be in relief work in Spain. But because of all the circumstances we would continue to be associated with large groups of the Spanish refugees.

Individual Spanish leaders who were deeply devoted to their country but forced to flee and take up lives of hiding, and eventually to seek permanent sanctuary in foreign countries because they had been politically allied with the Republican cause, are today eloquent testimony to the continuing tragedy of Spain. In the United States, in Mexico, and in certain capitals of Europe, I have talked with these fugitives, many of them extraordinarily fine men and women of great literary or political genius who long to use their gifts for their own country's welfare.

But for the most part, such outstanding leaders have at least found positions of usefulness elsewhere. More tragic has been the fate of the large number of less notable Republican sympathizers who failed to find permanent sanctuary soon enough after their arrival in France, and were caught up in France's own sudden peril a few months later as the Second World War was declared and a million French citizens were evacuated from their homes. The Spaniards had no government legally responsible for them. As winter came on, the cold, hunger, and illness in the camps was indescribable. Service Committee representatives joined men and women from Friends Service Council and the International Commission in bringing blankets, clothing, milk, and medical aid. Emigration plans were worked out for a few, but by and large the closing in of the Second World War was effectively trapping most of the Spanish refugees who were still in France.

By the following spring, the spring of 1940, three and a half million fleeing French civilians were clogging all avenues leading south — and what now was to become of the 200,000 Spaniards who remained within France's borders out of the half-million who had been swept across from Spain the preceding spring? Quickly these Spaniards in France were to become the forgotten victims.

Their morale was remarkable, considering all the circumstances. They had pride, self-respect, and intelligence, and our workers' reports consistently stressed their fine caliber. "You were dead right about the Spaniards," wrote one of our representatives upon his arrival in France somewhat later. "They are a grand lot, and very difficult, and inspiring, and lots of fun."

"Do not let anyone forget that the problem of the Spanish refugees, especially the children and the mutilated, is an obligation which we cannot shirk," wrote Howard Kershner in the summer of 1940. "We are now the only organization interested in or working for these people." This was after the separate armistice between France and Germany had necessitated the evacuation of the British staff, and our Committee had had to assume full administrative and financial responsibility.

Even during hostilities in Spain, self-help workshops had been established for refugees in Loyalist territory, to enable them to do sewing and cobbling, to make rope-soled sandals when there was no leather, to do everything possible for themselves. In France, this rehabilitative aspect of the program was expanded, and, as the shops were made more professional, they began to afford retraining experiences for amputees and others who for various reasons could not expect to return to their previous trades and professions. Sewing, tailoring, cobbling, carpentry, and electrical skills were taught. The response was most rewarding. Some of the people became highly proficient in fields brand-new to them. One group of men learned to make artificial limbs, and by 1942 this little industry had developed remarkably. A report written in 1942 describes it:

> Perhaps the most important of these self-help projects is the *atelier* for making artificial arms and legs at Montauban. This was founded by a group of clever Spanish workmen, most of whom had lost a limb during the war in Spain. The Quakers have supplied machinery and tools and have directed the work of this shop for nearly two years. Some ingenious improvements have been made for artificial limbs. The output of this little shop is given to French, Spanish, or other mutilated men, and many of them have now become self-supporting. The devotion and industry of this group of Spanish workers has had a widespread and socially beneficial effect. Plans have been made for expanding output, but the difficulty of obtaining raw materials is limiting production.

With warm devotion our representatives maintained work with these Spanish refugees until severance of diplomatic relations between France and the United States in November, 1942, forced us to withdraw entirely from France, leaving what resources we could in the hands of a small group of European workers. It was not until after the liberation of France in 1944 that we, along with British Friends, were able to resume participation.

From then until 1949, when the project was turned over to the International YMCA, we were privileged to continue with the vocational training of Spanish refugees. And the reports we received in Philadelphia did not cease to sing their praises. "Their courage is very moving. One must hear them singing their Spanish songs to appreciate the full pathos of their situation. They have but one wish — to go home."

The whole story of this Spanish refugee group is one of the most moving of all we have touched. And it has not yet been resolved. No flag has gone up, no bells have rung, as in Spain at the end of the Civil War, as throughout Europe at the end of the Second World War, to announce to these people the end of their emergency. Many of them — notably the mutilated and the aging — have even to this day found no satisfactory way to live their lives, and continue to suffer acutely.

Alleviating touches in this tragic history come on the level of personal contact, in the creative meeting of individuals. A French peasant family opening its home to a refugee child, to an old woman, even to a whole family: such unpublicized personal acts of sharing, and they have occurred many times over, give one glimpses of qualities in French life which we miss when we look only at the gay life of Paris, or the intellectual life of the Sorbonne, or the political life of French government leadership. These individual solutions are beautiful life-threads running through an otherwise grim tapestry. They are the kind of revelation of richness in the human spirit by which our field workers live, and because of which they greatly treasure their periods of overseas service.

One often hears it said that "war settles nothing." Certainly it did not relieve Spain's poverty, or her inequitable distribution of wealth, or her lack of regard for civil liberties. All these evils have been intensified by the civil calamity. The tidal waves of human misery did bring out in certain individuals a holy capacity to suffer and to serve, but in most people they left an entrenched bitterness which has not been relieved by the passing of the years. And there seems no doubt that this Spanish war and its temporary achievements encouraged Hitler's adventure in Poland in 1939. It is reflections like this that lead one to consider bolder adventures — not to attempt the futile task of overcoming evil with evil, but to match evil with an effective, vigorous form of good. Our present-day recognition of Spain politically and our attempt to use her as a military ally are morally dubious adventures, having no reference to her inner tragedy and deeper need.

3. *The Climate of Doom*

Wᴴɪʟᴇ the Spanish Civil War was at its height — in late summer of 1938 — Lilly Pickett and I made another trip to Europe. Much had taken place in the four years since our previous journey. In the United States a reasonable degree of economic well-being had returned. I had withdrawn from government service, except as a consultant, when the relocation of unemployed coal miners was no longer a pressing need.

But my appointment schedule and that of many other individuals in the United States had begun to indicate a wider context in which we must work. It carried notations of meetings of the Jewish Joint Distribution Committee, the Co-ordinating Committee for German Refugees, the American Christian Committee for German Refugees, the Committee on Spain, the Spanish Child Welfare Association, the American Red Cross. It noted appointments with a German Jewish family seeking to migrate, a German musician seeking to stay in this country, a former secretary of the German Medical Association who was now a refugee, a Jewish woman whose non-Jewish fiancé was imprisoned in Germany because of her. Other events recorded were an interview with the Japanese ambassador in Washington concerning the Japanese invasion of China, meetings on the problems of stateless persons, and the Service Committee's decision to establish a receiving hostel for refugees near Philadelphia.

In terms of newspaper headlines, since we had visited Europe in 1934, Ethiopia had been seized by Fascist Italy; China had been invaded by Japan and was in great distress; Spain was being rent asunder by civil war; the League of Nations had lost all vestiges of prestige because of its ineffectiveness in these situations; France was wracked by acute economic and political tensions closely linked with the Spanish Civil War; Austria had collapsed under an almost casual occupation by Nazi troops; the fate of Czechoslovakia was trembling in the balance; and England was frightened. Could it be that we were seeing a repetition of the Thirty Years War? Were we in a genuine period of revolution? If so, how were persons and organizations dedicated to good will to behave in such times?

Our first stop on this trip was in London. It was August, and usually life in England is lax in August. We were astonished now at the intensity of activity. Cabinet officials who usually take a vacation that time of year were hard at work. Ambassadors were holding sober conferences. Friends returning from Germany spoke most gravely. Friends House in London was seeing a flood of refugees from Germany every day. I visited the Jewish refugee headquarters, and they reported handling three hundred cases daily, each case extremely difficult, calling for emigration somewhere . . . where?

Lilly Pickett and I stayed in London to attend Friends Service Council and Meeting for Sufferings on September 1 and 2. Both were weighty occasions, almost entirely overtaken by the unprecedented relief needs: Spain, German refugees, China. American and British Friends had at this time decided to join in a relief and Friends Center development in Shanghai.

On this visit in England, we found the British government extensively engaged in subsidizing new industries in economically distressed areas. To see a Conservative government going so far in socialistic schemes was astonishing, especially since only four years before I had been impressed by the government's apathy in economic matters. I was especially interested to find the Allotments Scheme for helping unemployed miners now substantially subsidized by the British Treasury. Sir George Gillett, with whom I talked about this co-operation between government and private agencies, spoke with real appreciation of the experimental, pioneering work of the Allotments Committee. I began to wonder whether our fear of government and private groups working together wasn't a bit doctrinaire. After all, both existed for the public good. Perhaps we could learn something from this British experience.

On our way from England to Germany we stopped in Holland. We found that Friends here were working out with the government a plan for receiving a small number of children who must leave Germany, to give them a period of training and adjustment while permanent emigration plans could be arranged. American and British Friends were asked to join in this work, which we did in small measure. Holland seemed remarkably quiet and peaceful, much less fearful of air raids and war than England.

We spent a day at the International Friends School at Eerde, Ommen, which we had visited in 1934. Here in the midst of rural Holland, in the spacious old Eerde Castle with its moat and a beautiful, belligerent swan who would not allow the children to come near the water if he could help it, Friends in 1934 had only just begun to gather in a few children whose parents, mostly Jewish, wanted to get them out of Germany. Now, in 1938, still to all appearances the most untroubled spot on earth, this castle-school had 120 students, four fifths of them refugees. The day before our visit, a little Jewish boy had arrived from Germany, and while we were there word came of his father's suicide.

Though pupils at Eerde spent only mornings on academic studies, afternoons being devoted to work in shops and on the land, they were able to conform to entrance requirements for English universities in the usual time. There was a remarkable wholesomeness, a creative balance, in the kind of life they led.

From Holland we entered Germany, where we immediately found ourselves in the midst of tremendous activity. Trains were crowded, streets were thronged. New suburbs were being built, new factories constructed, industries were running full time and over. There was no unemployment now. Hitler had taken care of that. In fact, there was a severe shortage of men because so many had

been taken to the western border to rebuild forts destroyed by order
of the Versailles Treaty. One draft alone had taken 300,000 men.
We sensed anxiety everywhere because of memory of war days and
the fear of war with Czechoslovakia. People were watching each
issue of the press and each radio broadcast for news.

A visit to our Berlin Center now was a very different experience
from anything we had known before. Every day a long line of
people with heart-rending tales of woe waited to talk with some
member of our staff about the possibility of migration to the
United States. A new office had been set up to take care of these
rapidly growing lines of distraught human beings.

The most difficult problem of our workers was to keep alive within themselves that spiritual poise and adequacy for which the
crowds of people reached desperately. Where it seemed at all possible to work out plans for emigration or other practical assistance,
that procedure was started — but more often than not it required a
very long period of time to complete any arrangements. It was
during the weeks and months of waiting, it was during the
time without beginning or end in which most of the people
seemed to be living, that the resources of the human spirit were
taxed to their utmost, and the need for great reserves made
plain.

I remember sitting in a quiet Quaker Meeting one Sunday morning in our Center on Prinz Louis Ferdinandstrasse and listening to
the screaming voice of Goebbels (from a loud-speaker outside)
pouring forth a venomous attack on all Jews and calling upon the
churches to have nothing to do with them. It was difficult to fix
our minds on the eternal verities as we sat in worship with these
screams dinning into our ears. To hear the "still small voice" in
the midst of such human thunder is an art of the prophets which
requires cultivation. But we did finally become more deeply conscious of the very great need to find practical ways of expressing our
belief in the value of human beings, no matter who they were or in
what circumstances. This included a concern for the bitter spirit of

the persecutors. Had not John Woolman been concerned for the slave-owner as well as for the slave?

The next day I was able to have an interview with one of the high-ranking officials of the Nazi government, and talked frankly with him of what lay in my heart, not only as to what was happening to the Jew, but what was happening to the German. I told him I wanted to see Hitler.

His answer was that Hitler was a tyrant, was not quite normal, that certainly he would pay no attention to our protests if we were able to get to him, that such an effort might result in every vestige of our work being thrown out of Germany, and possibly even vengeance being taken on German Quakers, of whom there were perhaps three hundred.

Having heard it commonly reported that all German officials spoke in the fear that dictaphones were transcribing what they said, I was apprehensive for this man who had been so frank with me, but no harm came to him because of it. I didn't press the case further officially, except to have a conversation with the American ambassador in Berlin, who seemed to me very casual in his concern about what was happening to Germany. I felt that if he was reporting to the State Department and the President in the terms in which he spoke to me, he was by no means reflecting the tragedy which was so rapidly gaining momentum.

On the other hand, the American consul general in Berlin, Raymond Geist, was nearly overwhelmed by the tides of woe. The day we visited him in the large consular office, we found it literally swarming with people, and that, he told us, was a comparatively quiet day. He said that the preceding Saturday three thousand people had applied for visas for America, and all had heartbreaking tales of absolute desperation.

It is difficult to recapture a sense of the amount of tension under which people in Berlin lived during those days. I remember vividly one evening at the Center when, after a brief meeting for worship, Lilly Pickett and I joined the staff members in profound question-

ing as to what our contribution could be, not only to German Friends
— which was perhaps our most fundamental responsibility in this
hour — but also to the possible staying of the forces of hate and
violence. As the hour approached when the Berlin-to-London train
was due to leave, one of our English colleagues suddenly rose and
said that he had decided the thing he ought to do was to take that
train for home. He feared that war was imminent, as of that day
or the next. No one felt critical of him. We later learned that he
just barely got onto the running board of the train as it left,
crowded full of people who were of the same mind. This was not
long before the Munich pact, and although the German papers
were carrying none of the details of negotiations, the fever pitch of
their denunciations of Czechoslovakia and Beneš, plus the prevalence of war equipment on trains and highways, kept the population
in a jittery state. Add to this imminence of war the quite apparent
determination by now to rid Germany of Jews, the ever-present
threat of the state police toward all opposition, the tendency of
people to whisper when they said anything that might be used to
incriminate them — and you have an atmosphere in which tension
and danger were driven right through one's skin.

Yet there were outstanding Jews still choosing of their own free
will to remain there, in order to do all they could for the thousands
of less well known Jewish men, women, and children who had
no choice.

There was a woman, a teacher — I shall never forget the anxiety
on her face when she came to the Center to talk with me. She ran
a small private school to which Jews and non-Jews alike had come,
but she had watched the gradual withdrawal of all the non-Jewish
children. She did not know how much longer she and the school
would remain unmolested. Raising the question as to whether she
should move her school to some other part of Europe or to America
before it was too late, deeply searching for wisdom in her anxiety,
laboring under a sense of mission to these children she loved, this
Jewish woman who had always been devoted to Germany found

herself slowly but surely being crowded into a corner and made a citizen of the ghetto. She eventually decided to stay on as long as she could be of any service to her group of children, even at the risk of her own life. (She did eventually find sanctuary in America when no longer able to carry on her school.)

Our hearts went out in agony over the suffering of these people. We were seeing also the corrosion, deformity, and subjection of thousands of Germans, and this was equally destructive of the inner resources of the life and spirit.

I talked one evening with a group of young Germans who had formerly been in America as work students employed in American industry. I had met a few of them at that time. Now, when I told them frankly what I saw happening to the Jewish community in Germany, and to the Germans also, most of them maintained that I was entirely incorrect in my observations, and that while a few Jews might be suffering unduly, and this they regretted, for the most part there was no danger of widespread persecution. Only if there were provocative acts by Jews themselves would they suffer. They assured me further that the Führer would see to it that there was no war.

I remember particularly the story told me by one of these young men who sat next to me at dinner. He had a wife and two children, he had undergone a long period of unemployment, and was almost desperate. Then along came the new regime, business began to pick up, and he was able to get a new foothold in his own field, dairying. Now he was supporting his family and pursuing work for which he was trained and which he felt was useful. He was not a member of the Nazi party, but he was clearly of the mind that it had been a necessary thing for Germany, in order to revitalize the economy.

I talked most frankly with these fellows who, on the whole, were very friendly toward the United States. They had not only worked and studied here, but they had learned how to hitchhike, several of them having crossed the continent that way, and they thought it was a wonderful country. Evidently part of their hope was that perhaps Germany could be a prosperous, up-and-coming country like the United States! It was largely without avail that I called attention to the significance of Nazi methods: persecution of Jews, emasculation of labor unions, general suppression of free thinking, and an attitude of self-assurance and boastfulness which, while it seemed to be evidence of assurance, was more likely evidence of inward insecurity.

Nearly fifteen years have gone by since that evening in Berlin. A terrible war, which defeated Hitler's regime, has come and gone. As I recall those conversations, I feel like reminding myself that we are seeing demonstrated before our eyes a fact of life which in theory at least I have always believed to be true — that if you solve a problem by violence, as we attempted to do, the very spirit which was in those whom you defeat has to be watched or it will get into you. When one reads of the violation of civil rights in our own country now, and has the experience of having haunted and frightened victims coming to see him to pour out their fears, as has happened to me in these days at the beginning of the second half of our century, one realizes how dangerous it is for us to criticize the violation of civil rights among others and assume that we are immune from the same danger. We kill an enemy to get rid of a manifestation of the wicked spirit in him. How can we avoid that spirit's hopping out of him into us? That is one of the central dangers of the use of force and violence.

But we also met non-Jewish Germans who understood what was happening and opposed it effectively within the radius of their own influence. There was Dr. Wilhelm Mensching, a long-time friend of our family. This pastor of a state church in a little village in western Germany was a dedicated, free spirit. Much beloved by his parishioners, deeply troubled during these years, he had consistently refused to take the oath to Hitler, and would continue to refuse. He and his wife and four children were as beautiful a family both in appearance and spirit as I have ever known. They believed they might be forced to leave their home and community at any time. Doubtless the loyalty of their parishioners had saved them thus far, but they were being constantly harried by government and church officials. With remarkable vitality they maintained their testimony to their faith, and continued to employ a Jewish doctor and to keep their house available as a refuge for Jews when needed.

We were to learn after the war how some of our own small Quaker group in Germany suffered concentration camp for the crime of giving assistance to their Jewish neighbors. And we find there were little cells of Catholic clergy, Orders of Brothers, Protestant ministers, laymen of all faiths, who refused to bow to the domination of the Nazis and whose testimony to truth enriched their spirits. Some lost their lives and some survived. It may be that in people like this there is the seed of a new spirit and life, not only for Germany but for all of us. The early Christian Church had a way of putting it: "The blood of the martyrs is the seed of the Church."

Before we left Germany for Czechoslovakia, German Friends drafted a most touching message to Czechoslovakian Friends, which we carried in person. German radios were hourly booming out threats toward Czechoslovakia, but we saw no reason to change our plans. It was our belief that calmness and devotion to normal duty might in itself be a contribution in such a fearful and nervous time.

In fact, we took a two-hour extra period which we found we had before train time to go to the Berlin Zoo — the best zoo we had ever seen. Crowds of people were there, all very quiet, unexcited, and no doubt finding some relaxation, as we did, in the very unconcern of the monkeys and other animals.

We stopped over night at Breslau and stayed in a hotel near the station, since we must leave for the border quite early in the morning. All night soldiers marched past the hotel, and at six the next morning, when we awoke from a short snatch of sleep, it was to hear and see cavalry and tanks proceeding toward the border. Crowds of people were along the streets, but there was no enthusiasm. It was as though they said in dejection, "Must we go through with a useless war again?"

At first our train took us through beautiful farmlands, men, women, and children out digging potatoes or getting in the hay, hastening the harvest before the crisis should break, the women dressed in full gathered skirts and basques, with bright-colored handkerchiefs over their heads.

Then at Glatz, Germany, all who wanted to go farther were transferred to busses. Over rocky roads we jiggled and jostled to Rengersdorf, where a funny little pony train of two coaches awaited us. Now the number of passengers dwindled to about a dozen. We were not headed in a popular direction. There in Rengersdorf we sat on the tracks to let two trains coming out of Czechoslovakia pass us. They proved to be fairly long trains, well loaded, mostly with women and children, Sudeten Germans fleeing to the Fatherland. They were greeted at this station by a huge welcoming crowd. The children at the open train windows were all shouting and laughing, each waving a little Nazi flag, giving every appearance of a gala picnic occasion. A somber German businessman sitting opposite us smiled and waved to the children, then turned to us and said in very broken English, "Children do us good. They don't know the troubles." Later we passed other trainloads of German refugees, and always at the German stations they were met by great cheering crowds.

Our little train took us on to Mittelwalde, where again we had to disembark, and this time only Lilly Pickett and I were going farther. We entered a quite spacious waiting room in the station, and found ourselves the only travelers there. It was very strange. A lone soldier-boy was on guard. We told him we were going to Prague. "We aren't supposed to like those people," he said, with a trace of a smile on his face.

After about an hour's wait, a little train consisting of an engine and one coach came backing in from across the Czech border, and a very handsomely uniformed Czech official came into the station to check our passports and escort us to the coach, where about a dozen similarly uniformed officers awaited us. We were the only passengers.

Thus in slow stages and with great to-do we finally reached the Czech border and began to ride through Czech farm country where the sun shone just as brightly as on the German fields, and where crowds of people in the same type of peasant costume were likewise digging potatoes and raking and loading hay, in the same effort to get the work done before full mobilization.

After we were out of the "trouble zone" we were once more transferred, this time onto a real honest-to-goodness train which carried us to Prague. And that evening saw us reunited with friends.

We had learned to love Prague on our previous trip to Europe; we had found there a fresh breath of air, a concern on the part of President Masaryk and his government for the meanings of life, instead of merely for "a place in the sun." And the Quaker group in Prague had endeared itself to us.

Now, as we sat with this same group on the roof of a Prague apartment house that evening, the sense of a happily developing future had given way to near-certainty on their part that there would be war. Every time an airplane passed over, our host watched carefully. Although the Munich agreement had not yet been signed, Chamberlain had made his first trip to see Hitler, and Czechoslovakians felt betrayed. Radio broadcasts hourly brought news of developments together with the caution to remain calm.

We entered into a period of silent worship, after which I read the message of German Friends. I spoke as I had in Berlin of the "Family of God" conception of life so prominent in early Christianity. There was a spirit of deep worship and prayer throughout our meeting. One Prague Friend spoke of their nation's sad disillusionment at being deserted by France and England, but said he believed in the love and concern of German and English and French Friends, even so.

We didn't have time to meet many people in Prague, but the next day we did visit the Social Welfare Department of the government and also Alice Masaryk, daughter of the former President, who was head of the Czech Red Cross. Friends had been carrying on some child feeding in the Sudeten area, and we wanted to confer directly with the groups through whom the work had been done. Alice Masaryk quite obviously partook of the courageous and statesmanlike spirit of her father. We found her not at all hopeless, though with a clear feeling of the ominousness of the situation. There was even a certain gaiety about her as she said to us in parting, "Shall we all be blown up in this strange world? Well, even so, I go on fighting for the health and pure mind of my people — let come what will."

We went on to Vienna that day, September 21. As we waited for our train at the Prague station, two trainloads of Germans (Social Democrats) and Czech refugees from Sudetenland came in: old men and women, and wives and children — hundreds of them with a few articles packed on their backs, now and again a dog, a beautiful quilt, or whatever they most prized. There was no brass band to meet them. As they walked along the platform, peasants leaving their homes and for the first time being in the city, fearing they would never again see their farms, they almost all wept. It was impossible to view it calmly. It was so unnecessary and so brutal. They were led by guides to the great public stadium, where they were being provided at public expense with beds of a kind and food, awaiting transfer to a colony in the country or to some farm home near Prague.

A few German refugees from Czechoslovakia were on the train with us on the way to Vienna, and were met at the Vienna station by a crowd of Brown Shirts who gave them coffee and sandwiches.

Tensions in Vienna were as extreme as in Prague. The day after our arrival, Chamberlain flew to Godesberg for his second meeting with Hitler, and Vienna initiated blackouts. An evening or so later, we were having dinner in an Austrian home, and a number of times during the evening our host excused himself and went to the roof to see whether the plane flying over might be Russian. He was convinced that the USSR had massed thousands of planes just over the Czech border, and that they might arrive any minute.

I might add that this Viennese host of ours later became a Nazi army official and participated in the occupation of Paris, where he attended the French Quaker Meeting, much to the distress of the others in the group!

No. 16 Singerstrasse had been the home of our Vienna Quaker Center since the First World War. There in an old castle, the winding stone stairway of sixty-seven steps (Lilly Pickett counted them) might have told a tragic tale. For years the Center had been hoping to emerge from relief work, but had never been able to do so. Now, since the *Anschluss,* throngs of jobless and maltreated "non-Aryans" were crowding its doors for assistance and advice. The staff had been increased in an effort to meet the responsibility, but the strain on the workers had become almost unbearable. Emma Cadbury was at this time largely responsible for the over-all direction. For fourteen years she had carried on work of amazing dimensions, much of it under severe stresses and strains.

Here, as in other European Centers, we found that attendance at the regular Quaker meetings for worship had greatly increased over the past four years. For many individuals, the chaos of hate, fear, and suffering had accentuated the need for periods of quiet in which they could unite with others in rediscovering and renewing the inmost sources of calm and strength. I spoke in the Vienna Friends Meeting on Sunday morning, and felt coming to me from the group strangely deep yearnings for words of truth and sincerity, words of comfort and courage. In that hour I wished more than ever that I could speak German. But under such circumstances one's attitude perhaps speaks louder than his words.

We left Vienna at 7.30 the morning of September 26. As we drove away from the Center, at least 150 persons were already in line to get their numbers for interviews the following week. By

9.30 when the Center doors opened, it would be three or four hundred. We left with heavy spirits. To Friends as well as to thousands of others it was clear that circumstances and events were daily taking the measure of our stature, and we seemed very small alongside the mountain of need and opportunity, and very casual in thought when up against final realities. As a man said so well to one of our Vienna staff that week: "The police say the Danube is available to us [suicide], and you say there's a good God. How can I find Him?"

Along the Danube for sixty miles or more were heavily armed troops, pontoons at every bridge, ready to be thrown across in case the bridge was blasted, and miles of tanks and guns concealed only by thin disguises of brush or canvas covers.

On our previous trip we had passed through Innsbruck, in the very midst of the Alps, and had wanted to stop but couldn't. We arrived there now at five o'clock in the evening and decided we would stop and spend the night, so as to drink in the beauty of the surroundings and be able to take our journey on to Geneva by daylight.

And that night came Hitler's famous speech in which he fairly shrieked that he would have his Sudetenland by October first. All over Innsbruck were loud-speakers, clusters of people gathered around each. Bus drivers stopped their busses to hear. We moved slowly about from group to group to see what happened. In Berlin, in the Sport Palast where he was speaking, loud cheers interrupted the Führer. Not a word, not a whisper came from the listeners in Innsbruck.

We left Innsbruck September 27. As we rode through the awe-inspiring Alps, the pall of almost certain war hung over us.

Gilbert and Marga MacMaster, who had served in our Berlin Center, now lived in Basle, and we spent an evening and night there. All over Switzerland complete blackouts were rigidly enforced, so we sat in near-darkness while we talked that evening.

France had ordered general mobilization the day before, and Basle was tense.

The next day we found Geneva even more so. The American consul had issued letters urging all American citizens to leave at once. After some hesitation, we decided to move forward our departure by one day, leaving Thursday the 29th instead of Friday the 30th.

Plans for a general public meeting at which I was to speak were changed to plans for a meeting for prayer and worship. It was a profitable time for us all.

The evening of the 28th it was announced that Hitler, Mussolini, Chamberlain, and Daladier were to meet in Munich the next day.

We took the night train to Paris on the 29th. During the night our engine broke down and we sat for three hours in one spot. It was the very night the Munich settlement came, and I confess that until I got out and found what was wrong I wondered whether we had been sidetracked to let troops pass.

We spent only a few hours in Paris between trains. As we went to the boat train for London, we were held up by a terrific traffic jam and general milling about and excitement. Daladier was coming back from Munich bringing peace! Everywhere there was a sudden burst of gaiety and relief.

When we arrived in London, we found Hyde Park and other parks, once beautiful swards of green, now dug up into rows on rows of ditches designed to house people against air raids. For days, every train out of London had been packed with people fleeing what they were sure was imminent air attack. We arrived just in time to see the outburst of praise of Chamberlain's peace.

When one returns from a visit of this sort, it is not an easy matter to decide what are one's responsibilities. We came back to the United States with a sense of impending doom. We were sure things would grow worse for the Jews and nonconformists in Germany, and we could see nothing to stop the drift toward war.

Shortly after our return, I had a conversation with President Roosevelt. After talking with him about some of our experiences in Berlin, Vienna, and Prague, I said I wished it might have been he who was sitting across the table from Hitler instead of Chamberlain. Was it possible that he might yet have a talk with Hitler face to face? He then told me that he had considered trying to arrange such a conference, both of them traveling to the Azores. But at the moment he was more concerned about building up a strong United States air force. I reminded him that Hitler had said he was prepared to discuss disarmament, and that, even though it might not be said sincerely, the German people thought it was and were themselves in deep dread of another war. It seemed to me that one of the very best ways to give them a chance of expression would be to take seriously the statement of their leader. The President agreed with this in principle.

It was reassuring to see his imaginative mind feeling around for steps which he himself might initiate. However, then as now, I questioned in my innermost mind and heart whether one can with one hand prepare the instruments of war and with the other hand the instruments of peace. That was the effort in 1938, and it is the effort as these words are being written. In time it produces a split personality in our national life.

This conference with the President was on the 9th of November, and the 10th was the Day of Broken Glass in Germany — a terrific shock to the world outside and to millions within Germany. Obviously, in order that it should seem to happen spontaneously, it had been most carefully planned. We learned that thousands of German shops, mostly Jewish, in hundreds of communities had their windows broken, their goods stolen or despoiled; and many people were injured or killed.

While further terrible news of this day was reaching our country, Paul Baerwald, chairman of the American Jewish Joint Distribution Committee, called our Committee to inform us that not only had Jewish shops been wrecked, but the large Jewish feeding centers had been shut down and Jews were being denied permission to buy at Gentile shops; there was danger of mass starvation. He raised the question as to whether our Committee might open feeding centers.

After consulting Vienna and Berlin by cable, we decided to discuss this matter with the German ambassador in Washington and with our own State Department. It seemed to us that the first step would be a visit of a few American Friends to Germany, to determine what could be done.

In our conference with the German ambassador, he indicated that it would not be difficult to get permission to enter Germany to discuss this problem. Further, he thought we might investigate whether some plans could be made for orderly emigration. This was particularly on our minds.

We consulted the State Department. They not only encouraged us to work out a feeding project, but with all speed to send the proposed delegation.

Not long afterward, Rufus M. Jones, D. Robert Yarnall, and George A. Walton were on the boat on their way to Germany. This development had taken place rapidly and quietly. It seemed important that there be no publicity whatsoever.

Imagine, then, our shock one morning, while they were still at sea, to find a big headline across the front page of the *Philadelphia Record*:

FRIENDS' SOCIETY SENDS MISSION
TO INTERCEDE FOR GERMAN JEWS

The story which followed was what a reporter had been able to make out of Rufus Jones's replies when he reached the latter by radio-telephone in mid-ocean. Part of the story was accurate, part was extravagant, and the whole thing was what we didn't want. It caused great consternation in our Philadelphia office. It probably taught us that it is almost impossible to avoid publicity entirely, and that in the future it might be better to make orderly provision for some kind of official release.

We were afraid the publicity as given might handicap the mission in its efforts, but such did not seem to be the case, though Goebbels's paper did come out with an editorial ridiculing the "Three Wise Men":

> Surely these three Quaker figures are wise men who, no doubt, this time, too, hail from the East, or at least regard it as their spiritual home. We hope they will make themselves known when they are here. Then we will know, you see, when to begin to quake — quake duly before the Quakers from the U.S.A. Don't expect us to take them seriously. We can't help it, we must laugh, even if in this case it is ever so honorable a sect.

There were answering editorials in this country. The *Chicago Daily News* published quite a piece called "Dr. Goebbels's Joke," in which it rehearsed the story of our Committee's feeding German children after the First World War, quoted Goebbels's editorial, and concluded, "That is a good joke, is it not, about the warlike and iron-willed Nazis knowing when to quake before the gentle Quaker pacifists who fed them in their hour of need? Yes, a very good joke. Ha, ha, ha! Ha, ha, ha — ha — ha — ha — "

Our delegation found the agony of suffering even greater than they had expected. Jews said to them, "Don't put food and hunger first. For the love of God, get us out!"

English Friends had come to explore what they could do, and a small conference group was immediately set up in Berlin.

Every attempt to approach the problem directly through what would seem to be the obvious German government departments ended in failure. No door could be opened. Finally it became clear that only by first getting the Gestapo's permission could any progress be made. So the group decided to try to see the Gestapo. Rufus Jones later told the story this way:

> The Monday after our decision was reached we went in the morning to the office of the American Consul-General, Raymond

Geist. If ever there was a good man, he was one. We told him that we had to visit the chiefs of the Gestapo and that we knew of nobody but himself who could make the visit possible. He said, "I will do what a man can." After trying to telephone, which we already knew always failed to get any response, he put on his hat and went into the storm that was raging that day in Berlin — said to have been the worst storm and lowest temperature for eighty years. In about half an hour we were summoned. We leaped into a taxi and drove to the huge buildings. Six black-shirted soldiers with helmets and muskets escorted us to the great iron doors which opened and let us into the ominous building. It is gone now. Nobody will ever see it again. We were given tickets and were told that we did not need them to get in but we should need them to get out!

We went through seven corridors, each one opening into an uncovered square, and then climbed five flights of stairs to a top room where Raymond Geist met us and said, "I have done it. Two chief officers of the Gestapo have been delegated to hear your plans and to get a decision on your project." The chief of the Gestapo at this time was Heydrich, nicknamed "The Hangman," who was later assassinated in Czechoslovakia. He was in the next room and we could see him through the window. But our first task was to convince the two hard-faced, iron-natured men assigned to us.

The delegation laid before the two men of the Gestapo a document prepared the night before by Rufus Jones, in which he had set forth the history of Friends' service in Germany, and Friends' desire now to bring another service of healing to all who suffered. It said, in part: "We came to Germany at the time of the blockade, organized and directed the feeding of German children, reaching at the peak no less than a million two hundred thousand children per day. . . . We have come now in the same spirit. . . ."

Rufus Jones's account continues:

They read the document slowly, carefully, and thoughtfully. It plainly *reached* them and we noted a softening effect on their faces, which needed to be softened. Then followed a prolonged conference in which we presented our plans and pleaded our cause, answering many questions. Finally the leader said: "We are now withdrawing to consult with the Chief Heydrich and in about twenty-five minutes we shall report the decision."

During this awesome period we bowed our heads and entered upon a time of deep, quiet meditation and prayer. . . .

The two men returned at the announced time and the leader said, "Everything you have asked for is granted." I said, "That is splendid. We should like to have the report in writing." "No," the leader said, "the Gestapo does not give its decisions in writing." "What will be the evidence, then," I asked, "that this decision has been made?" "Every word," he said, "that has been spoken in this room has been recorded by a mechanism and this decision will be in the record." We were glad then that we had kept the period of hush and quiet and had uttered no words for the record! The leader then said, "I shall telegraph tonight to every police station in Germany that the Quakers are given full permission to investigate the sufferings of Jews and to bring such relief as they see necessary."

As Rufus Jones goes on to say, it is unlikely that this message was ever sent.

Nevertheless, it must be pointed out that the visit did have certain tangible results for a while. Workers in our Berlin Center found they had a new freedom in making emigration arrangements for Jewish families, and in bringing relief. This short reprieve meant the difference between life and death to some families, at least.

But the rest of the record is all too well known: how the tides of violence closed in, finally engulfing all organized succor to the persecuted within Germany, leaving as lights in this night of doom only those courageous individual deeds which we now know never ceased to take place.

4. The Full Tide of the Homeless

ON November 16, 1938, six days after the Day of Broken Glass in Germany, a group of us meeting in Rufus Jones's home in Haverford set up a special refugee division of the Foreign Service Section of AFSC.

But the Service Committee had been engaged in refugee work long before this. Not only had its European staff members been involved, but a growing demand on the Philadelphia office had been met as well as possible. A good many individual cases had come to us through Hertha Kraus, herself from Germany and now associate professor of social economy at Bryn Mawr College. In Germany she had been prominently connected with AFSC child feeding after the First World War, and it was natural that she should turn to us as appeals from refugees came to her — first a thin stream, but, because she did her best to help, an increasingly formidable number.

On March 12 of 1938 had come the Austrian *Anschluss*. A few days later, Joseph Hyman of the Jewish Joint Distribution Committee told me they had word that five thousand Jews had left Vienna and were simply on the roads somewhere; also there was a great wave of suicides. It was almost impossible for a Jew to send a cable out of Vienna, so we offered to get what information we could.

On March 18 our Committee received a letter from the International Red Cross in Shanghai, asking whether we would undertake a refugee relief service there.

The world was breaking loose in so many places that it was

difficult to know how to think about one's responsibilities. Nevertheless, we knew it was important in such a time not to become simply paralyzed by the quantity of the need.

On March 21 I met with a combined Catholic and Jewish group in New York about the plight of their people in Vienna.

Shortly thereafter, by letter and cable Emma Cadbury and other workers began indicating money needs, but the overwhelming cry was for affidavits and the location of relatives. Emma Cadbury wrote:

> May I pass on a request from the American Consul that American telephone books should be sent to them? (American Consulate, Vienna.) He says that people come and pore over them looking for possible relatives, and their Brooklyn book is already worn out. Old books are perfectly good for this purpose, and from any city. Perhaps you can advertise this need. . . . Is there any committee which could be applied to for persons who do not have relatives in a position to give them affidavits? . . . There is great need for full information about the work and possibilities of all American committees for refugees.

As summer came on, cables and letters were even more urgent.

> The situation here has become infinitely more acute. . . .
> The following are people whom we could recommend, but who do not have affidavits. . . .
> We have just had our cases analyzed according to religions, and we find that over one-third of the total are Roman Catholics. . . .
> ATTEMPT EXPEDITE AFFIDAVIT FOR H. FAMILY. MOST URGENT.

Our Committee was securing some affidavits, and turning other cases over to Catholic, Protestant, and Jewish organizations. All religious groups were affected.

"The Jews are being smashed against a wall," wrote an AFSC worker from Berlin shortly after Lilly Pickett and I returned to the United States that fall. "It is an agonizing spectacle. We have troubles, but when one is talking with people who calmly drop all money, friends, past life, and desperately struggle to go to China, Chile, the Chaco, Australia, or anywhere else to start life afresh, one has a strange feeling of the magnitude of their scale of struggle.... On October 18 all Jewish doctors cease to have patients by law (they can tend Jews but not officially). Jewish dentists follow soon thereafter. Apartments cannot be rented to Jews, and after the turn of the year they will be dispossessed."

Again: "The behavior of Dr. X on the day of his arrest is of the unpublished heroism. He had patients to serve, whom he had promised to see. He asked the Secret Police if he could meet these engagements. They agreed, provided he be back at a certain hour, which he was, to be taken by them. . . . "

In the total European tragedy of many millions uprooted and persecuted, the service which our European workers could render was indeed relatively small. Yet in proportion to the size of the staffs it was sometimes surprisingly large, because we had been in those countries a long time, were trusted as having no purpose except to be of help, and also our international contacts and channels were the result of more than twenty years' consistent work. It would be hard to exaggerate the advantage of this kind of long-time contact in such an hour of crisis. A worker finds he can call on a wide variety of strong and useful persons and organizations, not through any virtue of his own, but because of what those who have preceded him have built up in the way of confidence. This is an experience which in turn gives one a sense of the greatest possible responsibility to his on-going organization.

We had discovered on our European trip that one of the blocks to emigration was lack of sufficient staff at the consular offices to handle the growing number of applications for visas. Now I raised the question with the State Department in Washington as to the possibility of their adding to the staffs in order to expedite issuance of visas. They said this was not feasible at the time, because the budget had not provided for it. I therefore offered to recruit a number of trustworthy young men who spoke German fluently, and to see that their salaries and other expenses were taken care of while they worked in American consular offices in Europe to help clear up this bottleneck. My boldness in making the proposal sprang partly from the fact that a Jewish friend of mine had said she would contribute generously to make such a scheme possible. But the Assistant Secretary to whom I made the offer reminded me that the State Department could run its own affairs, and that if it desired to add to its consular staffs it could and would go to Congress and ask for an appropriation to do so. It was a hard blow.

It was in September, 1939, that the outbreak of war between Great Britain, France, and Germany started the evacuation of French citizens, and forced British Friends to withdraw from Quaker Centers in Germany and Austria. During this year, additional Quaker International Centers were established in Frankfurt, Amsterdam, Copenhagen, and Shanghai. Small groups of Friends in these cities formed the nuclei for the Centers. British and American Friends contributed support and assistance. In all of these places the waters were rising, the waters of homelessness, need, and grief. "We need centers of quiet as never before," was the burden of many a worker's letter in that year, bearing witness to valiant efforts to carry out commitments in the midst of intolerable happenings.

Since Jews, Protestants, and Catholics were all making efforts to service communicants of their own groups especially, many of the refugees who came to us were persons with no close religious ties, or families in which the members were of different faiths. By the very nature of the situation, a major portion of those we assisted were Jews. Perhaps they were members of a "mixed" family, perhaps their first relief contact in Europe had been with Quakers — for any number of reasons they might be with us instead of with a Jewish organization. We tried always to respect the desires of the individual, understanding that the Jewish agencies were doing a phenomenal job in volume and in quality, and only wanting to supplement where it seemed that our services would be particularly welcome.

In time, we chose as a special focus for our efforts the problems of refugee teachers, scholars, and other professional groups. The Unitarian Service Committee concentrated on aid to political refugees. But as in the division into religious classifications, these categories were only loosely applied, set up for the purpose of preventing overlapping of effort, but not to be observed at the expense of human considerations.

Although our Committee's refugee work in Europe often included "relief," in this country we did not provide financial relief, except in rare cases, but only such services as affidavit and other migration assistance, temporary hostel-shelter, orientation and training programs, job counseling and placement, location of friends and relatives — personal services which can mean so much in a time of large distress if they are handled in a warm, human way. The personal equation was what we tried to keep uppermost, and I think by and large we succeeded in this, because of the caliber of the individuals on our refugee staff.

Relatively our refugee services in the United States were small. Maurice R. Davie, in his report, *Refugees in America,** mentioning the work of the American Christian Committee for Refugees, the Catholic Committee for Refugees, and the Refugee Division of the American Friends Service Committee, the three major Christian agencies offering general services to refugees in this country, points out that expenditures of the National Refugee Service, which focused the efforts of a large part of the Jewish community, exceeded two million dollars each year between 1939 and 1942, reaching a peak of three and a half million in 1940, while the combined expenditures of the three Christian organizations totaled only between $300,000 and $400,000 a year during the same period. This puts our American services in their proper setting. Refugees taking advantage of opportunities in our Quaker hostels or training pro-

* Harper and Brothers, New York, 1947.

grams were often receiving maintenance from one of the organizations established to provide financial relief.

All of this meant that we of the American Friends Service Committee found ourselves working in ever-increasing co-operation with Jewish groups in the United States. Scores of warm, heartening memories come back to me, of occasions along the way of this growing closeness.

Back as early as 1936, Rabbi Philip S. Bernstein of Rochester and I planned a twenty-four-hour conference of about a dozen Friends and as many Jews, in the thought that we should come to know each others' cultural and religious backgrounds more intimately. This group met in a hotel in Asbury Park, New Jersey, on November 17 and 18 of that year, for two half-days of rare fellowship. The afternoon of the 17th, the Jews laid before us the significant points of their history, their divisions into groups, and their aspirations and prophetic outlook on life. It was extremely interesting and stimulating. Then, that evening, Friends did the same thing, with Rufus Jones taking the lead. And the experience of fellowship and discussion was carried over to the next day, when especially the meaning of the prophetic outlook and the interpretation of pacifism in terms of immediate problems were given thoughtful consideration. I think all of us felt that this experience should be repeated, and that we should take even longer for it the next time. But it never worked out in quite the way we hoped.

However, constant contacts did develop between Jewish groups and ourselves over matters of more urgent concern. It was through a suggestion from the American Jewish Joint Distribution Committee, in the first place, that our delegation went to Germany after the Day of Broken Glass. And upon that delegation's return, several of us were invited to talk with Jewish groups on various occasions — sometimes around a dinner table, sometimes at larger meetings.

As American Jews shouldered an ever-increasing load of responsibility for refugees, and were thus compelled to raise large sums of money, I traveled to Chicago, St. Louis, Toronto, and many other cities, speaking at great gatherings of Jews who were concerned to help their coreligionists in Germany. I was invited to give a lecture at the Jewish Theological Seminary in New York as a part of (President) Rabbi Louis Finkelstein's attempt to bring Jews, Catholics, and Protestants together in a search for basic religious unity.

Then there was the huge meeting in Detroit of all the Jewish welfare agencies throughout the country. The evening session was held in a very large synagogue, and the two speakers, besides myself, were Chaim Weizmann, the great British chemist, later president of Israel, and Solomon Lowenstein.

I have never heard a more impressive orator than Chaim Weizmann on that occasion. The eloquence lay partly in the speaker, but quite as much in the open and prepared minds of those who listened, who were anxious to have an established home somewhere in the world for any Jews who wanted to avail themselves of such a home. Here was the man who had championed that cause for many years, and the people's hearts opened to his words in a way I shall never forget.

I attended a staff meeting of the American Jewish Joint Distribution Committee in New York, where Joseph Hyman, executive director, told us that as they saw the curtain of darkness come down they instructed all their groups in Europe to make any commitments they needed to during the next six months on behalf of JDC, and that these commitments would certainly be honored some time in some way. This was in December, 1941, just as the United States was entering the war. It was a great venture of faith on the part of JDC, but typical of the kind of thing Jews over and over again were able and willing to undertake on behalf of their own people.

And these are only a few of literally scores of occasions that come to my mind. I have almost consistently happy memories of the very frequent association of Jewish and Quaker groups. While there was a worldly quality of exuberance and outward fellowship that was more expressive in Jewish groups than among Quakers, there was also a most profound dedication, the willingness to give generously, an emotional commitment to help their brethren, and many times a spiritual yearning for a deeper quality of religious life that was most significant for me. I shall never again be quite the same because of these experiences. I can still see an elderly orthodox rabbi with a long flowing beard, coming in to talk with me about bringing Jewish theological students out of Poland to study in this country — and, as he left my office, raising his hand in benediction, asking God's blessing upon me.

One day back in 1938 on the occasion of our visit to the Vienna Center, I had been dictating some letters to the young Viennese girl who was serving as my secretary, when suddenly she stopped at the end of a letter, and with a blush of timidity asked, "Could I say something to you?" "Of course," I answered, and she told me how for the first time a sense of insecurity was creeping up on her own family. I had just learned that her mother was part Jewish, which brought the family under the inhuman provisions of the Nürnberg Laws.

Two days later Lilly Pickett and I were having dinner with this family. The father was a highly respected and prosperous lawyer. He had practiced in several major cities of Europe, and was a widely read and cultured man. He had a hobby of collecting antique rugs. His wife taught piano, and was a musician of recognized gifts and attainments in composition and performance. As we entered the drawing room, we saw two beautiful grand pianos. It was a home of a modest degree of wealth, genuine refinement, and considerable comfort. A son, younger than the girl, a vigorous youth, seemed to have no inkling of what lay ahead for the family, but the daughter, watching the daily flow of refugees through our Center and hearing their stories, had sensed that their own persecution was inevitable.

That evening we discussed what might be done, and whether they could come to the United States. A lawyer trained for practice in Austria would have no recognition in his profession in America. Could the mother go through the mental and nervous anguish which probably lay ahead, and still retain enough buoyancy to begin over again as a teacher of music? Both she and her husband were in middle age. The children seemed the real hope. They would be able to transfer their lives almost intact. The boy knew some English, and the girl had stenographic training in English. This would be useful anywhere. I advised beginning at this point, and expecting a rather large share of the responsibility for the transfer to be carried by the children.

It was our privilege at a considerably later time to welcome this family into our home near Philadelphia, where they lived for some months while looking for a permanent place. It was a good deal of a shock to see them when they came to us — a bewildered father, having lost the chance to pursue his profession, the mother forgetful and continually anxious. She would touch our piano and wander about as though in a constant daze.

It was very different with the children. The girl was immediately busy in a job as stenographer. Through her energy and skill she made a place for herself in her new country, married happily, and is a well-adjusted, useful American citizen. The boy quickly perfected his English in American schools, found his way into a job, married a charming American girl, and almost completely escaped any disastrous effects of the transfer.

For all its tragedy, this has been one of the less difficult transitions made by people who for racial or political reasons were forced to leave Europe and resettle in lands to which they were unaccustomed.

Our Committee encountered strong opposition to the immigration of refugees in 1938 and 1939, the chief reason being fear: fear that our country would soon be "flooded with refugees," "flooded with Jews," and that the newcomers would swell the ranks of the unemployed, or, worse, take jobs from native Americans. Affidavits of support had to be given each refugee before he could immigrate, but this did not mean he was not in some respects a charge on the general resources of the country if he had to be supported by some loyal individual who had become his friend. The Service Committee decided that only facts were any proper answer to this fear, so we set about making a careful, objective study of German refugees in relation to the United States, as of the end of 1938.

We discovered that under our current immigration laws 153,774 immigrants could be admitted anually, of whom 83,574 were assigned to Great Britain and Ireland, countries which in the year ending June 30, 1938, used only 4551 of their total. With this small number coming from these two countries, immigration was in effect limited to approximately 75,000 annually.

For the six-year period, July 1, 1932, through June 30, 1938, roughly corresponding to the years of the Nazi regime in Germany, 4487 more aliens had departed from than were admitted to the United States. During these six years, the total immigration quota allowance had been 922,644 persons, and only 241,962 had entered.

For the year ending June 30, 1938, the year of the largest refugee immigration up to that time, there was a net immigration into this country for permanent residence of only 42,685. In 1929, the net immigration figure had been 210,475; and in 1924, 630,107.

Among the refugees currently seeking admission to the United States from Germany were some of the finest, most intelligent representatives of democratic Germany — conspicuous champions of liberalism, democracy, and international co-operation, persons gifted in science and the arts. They would greatly enrich the culture of any country lucky enough to extend them hospitality. Their exit from Germany would be part of the tragic impoverishment of that country's human resources which the Nazis were methodically enforcing.

A large proportion of the potential refugees were businessmen, manufacturers, and tradesmen. Some of them would bring new skills and new businesses into our country, and not only they but their wives and children would be new consumers. In England, the

British Home Office had recently reported to Parliament that eleven thousand German immigrants coming into Great Britain had provided work for fifteen thousand workers. In certain cases, whole industries had been transferred to England, and had helped take up the slack of the British unemployed. No one could guarantee that the refugees would create more work in this country than they needed to maintain themselves, but the experience in England seemed pertinent.

In terms of religious classification, which should not be relevant in the United States, except that it demonstrated to the anti-Semitic that you didn't have to be a Jew to find the Nazi regime unbearable, about one third of all refugees from Germany in 1938 were Christians, and among those still urgently seeking migration from Germany the proportion was higher.

The pamphlet in which we published our findings, called "Refugee Facts," was given wide circulation, especially to the press, and I think helped correct misinformation and perhaps had some influence on public opinion's acceptance of the refugee as an asset rather than a liability.

However, it seemed to me that the truly patriotic American should recognize more fully than was commonly the case that not only should we receive the refugee because he was an asset, but we should receive him because he needed the kind of welcome and hospitality which we could furnish. We who have been blessed by the riches of this great continent far beyond our deserts find our own spirits shriveling and our sense of appreciation weakening when we refuse to share this abundance with those in greater need. It has always seemed to me unfortunate and unwise, as well as a denial of the central meaning of our Christian faith, that we consistently refuse to take our share of the lame, the halt, and the blind among the refugees whom someone must care for. I realize the necessity of protecting our country against communicable disease: that I would take for granted. But I think we ought to bear our part of the burden of the world's suffering as represented by those uprooted people who probably never again can be self-supporting but will always have to be a charge on someone.

By the time AFSC services to individual refugees had come to a virtual close in 1950, more than 50,000 requests for help had been followed up in varying degrees, depending upon opportunities and our ability to serve. Many a thin file of initial correspondence with a family was cut short by advancing battle lines, and the case closed perforce — sometimes permanently, sometimes to be reopened months or years later. In certain instances, literally volumes of correspondence and memoranda in connection with only one family testify to the years required to get its problems brought to a satisfactory conclusion.

In 1939 our Quaker receiving hostel in Bryn Mawr, just outside Philadelphia, was accommodating small groups of newly arrived refugees for short periods, until more permanent plans could be worked out. In that year also, through the co-operation of Iowa Friends, a hostel and placement center which received refugees for longer periods of preparation was established in the old Scattergood School near West Branch, Iowa. Later a spacious homestead in Richmond, Indiana, was lent for similar purposes. Also through the generosity of its owners, a beautiful estate near Nyack, New York (Sky Island Hostel) was open as a vacation spot for the newcomers for several summers.

One of the most harrowing problems in Europe was the refugee who was under great pressure to emigrate because he must get out of the country or run the risk of being sent immediately to a concentration camp, yet whose case would be investigated for immigration to the United States only at some vague future time when the consul could get around to it. Therefore it was a great boon that Cuba was willing to accept such persons for temporary residence. This is how it happened that we established a temporary refugee hostel in Cuba, in co-operation with the Church of the Brethren and the American Jewish Joint Distribution Committee.

An AFSC Co-operative College Workshop at Haverford, Pennsylvania, received refugee scholars for orientation courses, and aided them in finding opportunities for study, observation, and teaching; a number of summer seminars performed somewhat the same function. Like Quaker hostels, these workshops and seminars were experiments in co-operative living, in which Americans and refugees alike participated in the necessary everyday chores as well as in language study and other intellectual pursuits. Now it was discovered that many Europeans of the professional classes had not learned to use their hands. Dishwashing was something new; gardening as well. These people's circumstances made one realize afresh what a tremendous asset it is to learn to use one's hands in the growing process of education.

At a later date, our Committee established Powell House in New York City, in response to refugees' desire to have a way and a place in New York to become better acquainted with new and old Americans. Here classes and recreational programs supplied numerous opportunities for such personal contacts. The Committee's regional offices across the country, aided by hundreds of devoted volunteers, made similar efforts to give personal content and meaning to the many refugee services they carried on.

In May, 1940, the invasion of Holland, Belgium, Luxembourg, and France unloosed the war in its full dimensions. That spring, after many months of difficulties and delays, the Non-Sectarian Committee was established in this country, to bring refugee children to the United States. Among its backers were Marion Kenworthy, Justine Wise Polier, and Louis Weiss. I had taken a great interest in this effort, for we at the Service Committee were kept vividly aware of the homelessness and helplessness of many thousands of children in Europe, living in camps and colonies, orphans or the children of parents whose fate was unknown, or the children of men and women being loaded into freight cars for "destination unknown" who begged that their children be saved the fate of accompanying them. One of the Non-Sectarian group's initial aims had been to sponsor special legislation calling for the admission of a maximum of 20,000 refugee children of all faiths under the age of fourteen, outside quota restrictions. The bill embodying this proposal had been known as the Wagner-Rogers Bill. This was back in 1939, before the Non-Sectarian Committee was officially established.

There were prolonged hearings, and day after day people of distinction from many walks of life testified in favor of the bill. Questions raised by members of the Congressional Committee, however, kept us in doubt as to whether the bill would ever get out of committee. Were we sure these children would not become a public charge? Would they not add to the already shockingly large criminal element in our country? Did we not already have a larger number of orphan children in the United States than we could properly take care of? Why should we be called upon to shoulder this burden? Why shouldn't other countries do it? Why must it always be the United States?

Then one morning Rabbi Stephen S. Wise came to testify. I can hear his voice yet as he began. "As I awoke from my slumber this morning I turned in my Bible to the Forty-sixth Psalm, and I read it, and thought of these hearings.

" 'God is our refuge and strength,
        A very present help in trouble.
    Therefore will we not fear, though the earth
            do change,
    And though the mountains be moved into the
            heart of the seas;
    Though the waters thereof roar and foam,
    Though the mountains shake at the swelling
            thereof.

    There is a river, the streams whereof make
            glad the city of God,
    The holiest dwelling-place of the Most High.

God is in the midst of her, she shall not be
    moved.
God shall help her, at the approach of morning.
Nations were in tumult, kingdoms were moved;
He uttered His voice, the earth melted.
The Lord of hosts is with us;
The God of Jacob is our high tower.' "

When in that great resonant voice of his he had finished quot-
ing the Pslam, first in Hebrew and then in English, there was
hardly a dry eye among the visitors at the hearing. Then, in his
most eloquent vein, he pleaded for the admission of these children.

The facts and the logic, the eloquence and the fervor, seemed
to me all on the side of the bill, but those of us who supported it
plugged away in vain. The bill never came out of committee.

By mid-June of 1940 the "Battle of Britain" was imminent. There
was a sudden quickening of interest in and sympathy for the
English people, especially the children. I was asked to request
Mrs. Roosevelt to call together leaders of various groups who were
thinking in terms of rescuing children, to see whether some con-
certed effort might not be undertaken. The founders of the Non-
Sectarian Committee were extremely interested in the possibilities
of such a joint movement. Mrs. Roosevelt agreed, and on June 19
the meeting was held and arrangements made for setting up the
United States Committee for the Care of European Children. This
organization was to be responsible for bringing large numbers of
children to the United States for temporary residence during the
bombings. I was asked to serve on its executive committee. At this
time, I was also acting on the executive committees of the National
Refugee Service (Jewish) and the American Christian Committee
for German Refugees (Protestant). While it meant a very active
life, it was a great advantage to be in close touch with these various
services. It gave one an over-all knowledge of plans, and aided some-

what in the Service Committee's effort to intelligently supplement the larger programs.

The staff set up by the newly formed United States Committee was completely swamped with offers of volunteer service, homes for adoption, and all sorts of co-operation.

Within a short time about 850 British children were brought over, and a very good job was done in receiving and placing them. Then the British government clamped down on the exodus.

After this the United States Committee devoted itself almost entirely to the problem of the children of the Continent. In co-operation with the American Friends Service Committee and the European-Jewish Children's Aid, it helped bring several hundred Continental children to the United States, and more were ready to come when the fortunes of war stopped them in the very midst of preparations for sailing.

To go ahead of our story a bit, in order to follow this work of the United States Committee, we might look at one or two of the messages which came to our Philadelphia office concerning child emigrés from Marseille. AFSC workers were co-operating in Europe, the United States Committee carrying responsibility for the children in this country. The following letter arrived ahead of the group of children it introduced:

Marseille, May 9, 1942

Re United States Committee children. I am sending you a short biographical statement of each child, which I hope may be helpful to the Committee in giving them some background on the children. I am sorry that these histories are not as complete and full as I could have wished. It is very difficult to gather information from parents scattered around in internment camps. For the children without parents in France our indications are necessarily scanty. You will note the dates which are recurrent: February 1939, the Spaniards struggling across the Pyrenees in the bitter cold and snow, with defeat and despair in their hearts; May 1940, the mass exodus from Belgium as a whole population fled before the invasion; October 1940, the forced transports of the Jews from the Baden and

Palatinate area, with families driven out of their homes on a few hours' notice, allowed to take none of their belongings, packed into freight cars and shipped off to France where thousands of them were placed in the Camp de Gurs, which had not been prepared to receive them. You will be well able to supply the descriptive details which are not emphasized in each history. And the camps! You may see a statement such as "The child spent six months in the Camp de Gurs, and was then transferred to Rivesaltes where he spent a year before being liberated." The statement is bald and unadorned, but I cannot describe in each case the mud at Gurs, and the cold wooden barracks without windows where people stay huddled all day in their beds, too cold and hungry to get up, nor the bleak glaring barrenness of Rivesaltes, treeless, grassless, stretching for kilometres, a monotony of stony earth and gray cement barracks, and biting dust-filled wind. . . . I would like to see the children dressed decently, really cleaned up and properly groomed; I think on the whole they would be an attractive-looking bunch — or maybe that's just because I'm fond of them.

And in late summer of that year, again from Marseille:

August 18, 1942

Re United States Committee children. Your cable announcing the safe arrival in New York of the children who sailed on the Nyassa was delayed and did not reach us until August 10th. That same day we sent out reassuring letters to all the parents, but I am afraid the news reached us too late to be a comfort to many of the Jewish parents. Four of our letters sent to the Camp de Gurs have just been returned to us with the notation, *"parti sans laisser addresse,"* and I imagine we will be receiving others back too. The four which just came back were addressed to the parents of A, B, C, D. . . . I do not know just what policy the Committee may feel it wise to adopt in the matter of informing the children. For the time being it is only the Jewish ones that are affected, and not the Spanish. I am very very glad for each child that we got off — I only wish it could have been several times as large a number.

During the years represented by these efforts, these small successes and enormous disappointments, some of our Service Committee's best energies had gone into presenting our viewpoint concerning refugees to the United States government, to international agencies, and to the American people. Throughout our nation, either expressed or implied, ran the hunger to answer violence with a better way.

"Here it is," was the theme of our plea. "A great continent opening its doors and its hearts to those who flee violence, especially to the children — who would not flock to such leadership? How could it fail to fire the imagination of the world if it were done on a bold enough scale? How could such a world-wide movement as it could become fail in the end to isolate evil, leave it stranded for lack of disciples. . . . In the end, the real victory will go where the hearts of the people turn. . . . " But we did not have much success.

It was on June 17, 1940, that France's request for a separate armistice with Germany necessitated the withdrawal of the entire British staff of thirty from the Quaker program in France. Other workers, including Americans, were still able to carry on in both occupied and unoccupied areas, permission being received to cross back and forth from one zone to the other. It was estimated by responsible officials that between eight and ten million refugees were at this time in southern France. Even after the repatriation of large numbers of French civilians, there remained probably not less than five million refugees in that area, including Spanish Loyalists, Czechs, Belgians, Poles, and Germans. In one group of camps alone, 40,000 Belgian boys were stranded.

After the United States entered the war in December, 1941, doors closed all over the world, and with finality, for thousands of refugees midway in their plans for escape. And in the second week of November, 1942, the severing of diplomatic relations between France and the United States left perhaps eighty to ninety per cent of all persons seeking to emigrate from Europe completely trapped.

Hardly had Pearl Harbor become a landmark in history when a cry arose on our own American West Coast that the large Japanese and Japanese-American population in that part of the country was a threat to our national security. Local propaganda to this effect finally reached such a pitch that General DeWitt, who was in charge of security for the West Coast, by proclamation established Military Areas One and Two, taking in the West Coast states, and ordered the relocation of all persons of Japanese ancestry living in those areas. The general outline of what occurred is common knowledge: how the people were required to leave their homes for assembly centers where they remained until they could be transferred to relocation centers outside Military Areas One and Two — mostly in unpopulated, arid regions; and how they then gradually moved out into new jobs and homes — or, later, back into their old communities — as arrangements could be made and their loyalty to the United States government cleared.

This meant the uprooting of more than 110,000 people who had thought of themselves as loyal residents or citizens, many of whom were owners of homes and businesses, or students in schools and colleges, and very few if any of whom had anticipated any such fate coming to them. Approximately two thirds were American-born and therefore American citizens.

The Northern California Committee on Fair Play for Citizens and Aliens of Japanese Ancestry became intensely active. So did other regional, national, community, and church organizations, including the Federal Council of Churches. Other minorities rose to champion the civil rights of the evacuees — a most healthy manifestation. The National Association for the Advancement of Colored People was among the national organizations alert to the significance of the mass evacuation. West Coast Friends' groups, including AFSC regional offices, were joining hands with innumerable other groups and individuals when they sought to bring emergency aid and comfort to their neighbors of Japanese ancestry who were so suddenly and shockingly uprooted. Businesses and homes, built up over many years, had to be left behind with no time for adequate transferral or other arrangements.

It is extremely easy for us to say that the German people, for instance, even under threat of physical violence, shouldn't have allowed their government to do what it did. But we of the United States, under no intimidating threats and with a long history of individual freedom, did not stop this forced evacuation which took place over a number of months and subjected many thousands of loyal citizens not only to bewilderment and the misery of barren, crowded barracks but to large, permanent financial losses in the form of hard-earned businesses and properties; sudden amputation of plans and hopes; disillusionment about their citizenship in America. If we ask ourselves why we did not stop it, and listen to the reasons we start to put forth, perhaps we may understand why similar questions asked of Germans about "stopping Hitler" are in reality too vague and inadequate to be helpful.

In the ten hastily constructed relocation centers the usual distribution of evacuees was one family to a compartment twenty by twenty-four feet. This meant that as many as six or seven persons sometimes occupied such a unit, grandparents, parents, children — with the barracks walls on either side so thin that the noises of the adjoining families also were part of their intimate environment. And there was little for the people to do. On the whole, these were individuals with above-average habits of industry and enterprise — adults and young people who had made a great deal out of their opportunities in the United States.

It was highly important, once the initial deed had been accomplished, to get the camps emptied with as much dispatch as possible. The government appreciated this fact.

Sitting at lunch in the Cosmos Club in Washington one day, I was approached by Milton Eisenhower, who had been asked to head a War Relocation Authority. He raised the question as to whether the American Friends Service Committee might be of assistance in connection with some aspects of the undertaking.

As it turned out, he left this post for other government service shortly after the pattern for the Authority's work had been laid down, and was succeeded by Dillon Myer. During the entire period of the existence of the War Relocation Authority, we had the most cordial relationships with Dillon Myer and his staff, and were able to co-operate in their very difficult task in a number of ways.

In the first place, we gave some jobs to evacuees, and helped a number of others to find jobs. In this effort, Friends across the country were most helpful, especially those connected with our regional offices on the West Coast and in the Midwest. We also opened an office in Hawaii to carry on the same kind of service. And Quaker relocation hostels in Cincinnati, Des Moines, Chicago, Los Angeles, and Pasadena provided a few weeks' housing for a total of some three to four thousand evacuees while they looked for jobs and permanent housing. Also these hostels were centers where they could meet old friends, and where precious new friendships were formed. These friendships have become part of the texture of our on-going American life.

The Federal Council of Churches, through the Committee on Resettlement of Japanese Americans, demonstrated exceedingly effective leadership in the organization of community advisory committees to work with the War Relocation Authority's resettlement offices. These community committees usually included representatives from the Churches, YMCA and YWCA, AFSC International Institutes, and other religious and social agencies.

Our Committee's contribution in connection with the whole problem was so intertwined with the work of the Federal Council and other organizations that it would be impossible to make a separate story of it. What we did had more the dimensions of "token" participation than of a major role — except in the case of the National Japanese American Student Relocation Council, of which we were a member agency.

This Council was a voluntary association of a number of concerned educational and religious organizations, to facilitate and administer the transfer of college students from relocation centers to inland colleges.

Few undertakings have ever been more completely satisfactory to me. About four thousand young people were aided in locating in more than six hundred colleges in various parts of the country, many of them never returning to the West Coast. Almost all of these students did very well academically, a high proportion winning special honors, and so far as I know there were no disciplinary cases among them. Also they proved to be excellent "ambassadors" for the over-all Japanese-American population, quickly making a place for themselves in terms of friendship and citizenship in the various college communities. One wonders whether a similar group from any other segment of our population would have shown such a high degree of achievement.

As the records of those held in the relocation centers were scrutinized preparatory to their leaving, it was a great satisfaction to learn that extremely few cases of disloyalty to the United States were uncovered. This applied to both Issei and Nisei.

It is a credit to the relocation officials that they took a firm stand for closing the camps as soon as possible. Relocation camps have a way of tending to perpetuate themselves. Some of the older Japanese people were reluctant to go out, because they feared American hostility. Dillon Myer, however, insisted that our government must not get into the business of running camps, and that the centers should be closed as promptly as possible, and, where necessary, the people aided in getting on their own feet again.

When they had been taken from the West Coast, many of the internees had simply left homes and businesses behind, or sold at a great loss — for all too many buyers were willing to take advantage of their necessity. Now, as they returned, there was little left on which to start over. Those who had been renters of homes had no homes to return to, and often were up against restrictive covenants when they tried to rent other places. Business clients had been lost. Vandalism was responsible for much wanton destruction of the considerable property owned by this group. I remember hearing the story of a florist who returned to California to find the several thousand small panes of glass in his greenhouse systematically broken out. Each pane had required a separate blow of a brick or stone. And each reinstalled pane represented a separate operation, which this man performed with his own hands, before he could even start the culture of his beloved flowers again. Then there was the father of a young woman who came to work in our Philadelphia office; over the years, through much hard work and intelligent management, he had built up a thriving dairy business in Oregon. His children were grown, he was in his late sixties and about ready to begin taking life a little easier, when war came and he was arrested before satisfactory provisions for leaving the business could be made. His family followed soon after. When the whole experience was over, both dairy equipment and customers were so scattered that he wasn't able to pick up again, and at the age of seventy he went to work as a dishwasher. These stories are not unique. The losses were enormous, and many times during the war as I talked with Japanese-Americans and learned what was happening to them I couldn't help wondering what we were fighting the war for, if the spirit that we were supposed to be fighting against had taken such possession of us at home. Thus far, our government has made only a small and inadequate start in compensating these people for the loss they suffered.

However, it is a tribute to the residents of many communities on the West Coast that the returning Japanese and Japanese-American families were often given a warm and helpful welcome by their neighbors, who frequently had looked after their property and kept precious possessions safe for their return. Though the total experience seems to have been quite unnecessary and a grave blot on the history of the United States, and though the injustice and immeasurable personal tragedies must not be underestimated in our memories, I think it is fair to say that in many instances one of the ultimate results was a strengthening of the spiritual bond between the people of Japanese ancestry living in our country and other Americans. Insofar as this is true, it may be attributed to the Relocation Authority's sincere desire to do as human a job as possible under the circumstances with which it was saddled, to the warm neighborliness which grew in many communities on the West Coast and elsewhere when they realized exactly what had happened, and, above all, to the extraordinary self-discipline and maturity which the internees themselves exhibited.

The world-wide problem of dispossessed millions has not yet come to an end. As these lines are being written, the way is somewhat open to serve in Korea, where we see another huge volume of human agony — some eight million displaced people, away from home and with no homes to which to return. In the Middle East more than three quarters of a million Arabs are homeless.

In Europe, incredible though it seems, the end of the Second World War brought the dislodging of additional millions! The agreements reached by Great Britain, the Soviet Union, and the United States at Potsdam provided that people of German ethnic origin living in Poland, Czechoslovakia, and Hungary could be required to migrate into Germany, there to become part of the responsibility of the German economy and social structure. One wonders whether the men who signed that agreement understood what they were doing. What it actually meant — after nations not named in the agreement had followed suit in expelling their populations of German ancestry — was that twelve million people, mostly hard-working small farmers and craftsmen, were uprooted from the places where their families had lived for generations, and were forced, even in the midst of winter, to leave behind most of their possessions and a self-contained pattern of life to become in some respects the most difficult tax on truncated and partitioned Germany. Nine million of these "expellees" came to West Germany. It must be realized that hundreds of thousands of them are still living in makeshift camps and barracks, and that millions lack jobs and decent housing, their woeful condition not only laying waste their own well-being but affecting that of the world as well.

All this has been in addition to the problems of "displaced persons," people of non-German origin, most of whom were victims of Nazi persecution and at the end of the war found themselves stranded in Germany or other Axis-controlled nations, far from home and often with no home to return to. By the end of 1945, UNRRA had repatriated several million of these persons. Later, in connection with the International Refugee Organization's program of resettlement, our Committee took a modest part, co-operating with Church World Service in finding homes and jobs for displaced persons in the United States, especially among the Society of Friends. More recently, it has been possible to co-operate in the resettlement of a few expellees, but as things now stand it seems probable that most of the expellees must find their future within Germany.

Overseas we have participated in the effort to bring social and personal services to those still living in mass quarters, above all else striving to give them a sense of our concern, interest, and companionship.

It is outside the scope of this chapter to try to trace the international efforts on behalf of refugees, such as those of the Intergovernmental Committee on Refugees, UNRRA, the International Refugee Organization, and now the UN Office of High Commissioner for Refugees and the Intergovernmental Committee for European Migration. Such over-all efforts are indispensable, and must be further perfected, for the UN High Commissioner's Office does not now have the resources required for the job that needs to be done, and the Intergovernmental Committee for European Migration, operating on a modest scale, is a controversial undertaking, having been set up outside of the United Nations.

But even if international machinery is perfected, how are we to overcome the results of having reduced millions of individuals and families into the terrible anonymity of "mass"? Great as is the need for food and shelter and clothing and jobs, the yearning to be considered with a sense of respect and dignity, the desire for affection and fellowship, go deeper. Insofar as we have dealt with refugees in the mass and caused them to lose the sense of individual worth, we have cheapened the whole society of our time. But with millions dislodged all at once — the world figure now is said to be between thirty and sixty million — how are they to be dealt with on the personal level? It is simply impossible to have war, to upset the orderly processes of society, without this devastating, dehumanizing effect. Insofar as we handle people in mass, either as refugees or as soldiers, we threaten that inner sanctuary of the individual.

In no small degree our political acts since the war have partaken of this general nature. We fought to rid the world of totalitarianism, especially of German and Japanese militarism, and now in our extremity we turn about, and, in spite of having encouraged Japan to renounce war forever, we ask for the right to have naval bases and air fields in her territory, concessions for army camps, whatever we think we need — even to the point of asking the Japanese to rearm. This again makes the individual Japanese feel that he is not considered for his inherent worth, but only as an instrument for our protection. Likewise in Germany we fail to eliminate militarism, and, on the contrary, urge rearmament so that the German may protect us from the Russian. Every moment we continue this kind of behavior, the dignity goes out of the human being. Not only does it take away from the Japanese and the German, but in the eyes of much of the world these days we are thought of as a people who have no regard for the dignity of man.

And the spirit which creates soldiers instead of individuals, and refugees instead of individuals, has often made its way into our own hearts and lives. While it has been the privilege of many of us in the United States to serve the needs of those so unfortunate as to be refugees, and in that serving to find enrichment of our own souls and spirits, we have also the more delicate task of seeing that, in the increasingly depersonalized society in which we live, we nourish the power to serve in the simplest daily relationships of community and neighborhood, not allowing the corroding effect of mass to attack us, but remembering that each person, whatever his color, religion, or nationality, is a potential brother and one in whom the eternal God has invested the immeasurable riches of His Divine Presence. Surely this kind of individual affection and concern for those most immediately around us, whoever they may be, is the central vocation of Christians of all time.

The abiding, hopeful note about all of this is that modest, but honest and whole, expressions of concern and good will almost always touch and transform human relationships. In saying this, I am not disregarding the facts of present-day life, the mass-mindedness and materialism of modern society, the name-calling and vindictiveness in the United Nations. And I ask myself and my friends the question, How deep is our own sense of penitence, how earnest is our search for healing ways of dealing with those who suspect us? To what extent am I responsible for the continuation of this spirit of fear and bitterness, how deeply am I willing to sacrifice to partake in the healing ministry of service, whatever may be the race, nationality, political or religious persuasion of the man who for the moment thinks of me as his enemy? The secret of achievement here lies not in great political decisions, but in the human heart and within the will and decision of each individual — being thus in a sense a Divine Calling to all men, but especially to those of us who are inheritors of the transforming Christian faith. While we have planned so much in the way of techniques and organizations, and planned because we felt we were doing what was best, still all too often in our own conduct we have shown little of that personal affection and concern which is the first step toward a redeemed humanity.

5. The Blockade

In June, 1940, the extension of the British blockade to include France posed increasingly severe problems for those of us trying to feed refugees and other victims of the war, especially children, in France.

Back in February of that year, English Friends had delegated two of their number — Karlin Capper-Johnson and Frank Pollard — to come to America to confer with American Friends regarding the possibility of an international group of Friends getting together in Geneva, Switzerland, to further strengthen unity among Friends, to study how channels of international communication might be kept open in wartime, and to confer as to what Friends might do to help end the war and build the peace. It was thought that, since America was still officially neutral, American Friends might have a special opportunity.

It was agreed that such a conference should be held, and the Service Committee selected E. Raymond Wilson of the AFSC Peace Section, and Errol T. Elliott, minister of the First Friends Church of Indianapolis, for this mission.

The actual meeting in Geneva the last week of April was disappointing, since not only was it impossible for German and Scandinavian Friends to be there, which we had known, but also French and English Friends were unable to come. The two English delegates were denied exit permits from England.

However, our delegates' visits with small groups of Friends in Switzerland, France, and England were exceedingly helpful. On their way to Geneva they had stopped in Rome, where they had called on American Ambassador William Phillips, asking what in his opinion was the most useful service which groups like the Society of Friends might perform in such an hour. He had replied, in effect: "Keep open the channels of communication as best you can when so many doors are being closed. Now the world is ruled by ideas and concepts of physical force. Some day that must change. You must keep alive the hope and faith in a better way and a better world."

Meanwhile, I had been having very disturbing conversations with officials in Washington. Just after the German attack on Norway and Denmark early in April, one of them told me that a number of persons in the government were rapidly drifting to the opinion that the German nation must be completely crushed if there was to be any hope of a lasting peace. He himself felt that for us to enter into military participation would be fatal to our influence at the peace table. I was in agreement with this, and he encouraged me to talk with some of the Senators and Congressmen who were firmly opposed to our country's drift into war.

Jerry Voorhis was then in Congress, and I found he shared our concern. But all of us knew it wasn't enough just to say, "We must stay out of war." We knew the drift was inevitable unless the American people were presented with an alternative which would tap their energies, their imagination, and their faith. I argued that large-scale assistance to the victims of war could afford an outlet for our idealism and energy, if it were done not along "conformist" lines but with new and venturesome faith and boldness.

It was in this spring of 1940 that an incident occurred which proved rather embarrassing to me, though it was also interesting. When I had returned from Germany in 1938, I had spoken with President Roosevelt about strengthening our embassy in Germany. It seemed to me that the ambassador was taking too lightly the seriousness of the situation in Germany and the possibility that it might eventually involve the United States in war. My appeal was for the President to consider placing the ablest representation pos-

sible in the German embassy, in view of the very critical relationships that were developing.

To my amazement he turned to me and said that he was thinking
of appointing me as ambassador — which was the kind of jest of
which the President was capable. I said that of course he didn't
really mean that; and I reiterated that I was concerned about choosing the most distinguished American in terms of this particular
undertaking. He said that seriously he had given thought to the
possibility of capitalizing on the long-standing reputation of Friends
in Germany due to their relief work after the First World War, and
that he had not spoken in jest. I reminded him that I would have to
carry too many handicaps for the idea to be given serious consideration.

After that, I dismissed the matter from my mind.

Imagine, then, my embarrassment in the early spring of 1940
when, walking onto a platform to speak before a large audience in
Los Angeles, I was handed a column by Drew Pearson and
Robert S. Allen, reporting the possibility of my appointment.

If the matter was ever carried any further by the President, I
never heard anything about it. I'm sure that the State Department
would have come down strongly on my incapacity to handle the
undertaking. And in this case, I should have had to agree with
them.

When the Nazis invaded the Low Countries and France in May,
1940, British Friends were already engaged in extensive work
among refugees of many nationalities in France, in collaboration
with the International Commission for the Assistance of Child
Refugees. Quickly they improvised additional feeding centers,
shelters, special services for the sick, the old, and the children.
Edith Pye, an English Quaker, broadcasting to America from Paris
on June 8, made an eloquent appeal:

> Our funds are now being used by our delegates in fifteen
> departments. . . . The French official services are doing mag-
> nificent work, but it is obvious that where you get an average

of 37,000 refugees pouring through a town each day, the problem of seeing that they are fed and sheltered leaves room for every kind of help that is co-operative in spirit. . . . Practically none of them have any clothing but what they stand up in. Other needs are milk for infants, beds and bedding for the sick.

The American Red Cross had made immediate grants to this emergency service.

Meanwhile, Howard Kershner of our Committee, who was director of the International Commission, had come to the United States seeking more American help, and had received the following cable from Paul Reynaud, Premier of France:

THANK YOU FOR THE REPORTS WHICH YOU HAVE BEEN GOOD ENOUGH TO SEND ME ON THE IMPORTANT WORK ACCOMPLISHED BY THE INTERNATIONAL COMMISSION IN THE EXISTING TRAGIC CIRCUMSTANCES. THE RECEPTION OF MILLIONS OF REFUGEES OF ALL NATIONALITIES ON THE SOIL OF FRANCE, THE EFFORT TO SHELTER THEM FROM THE HORRORS OF WAR, TO NOURISH THEM AND TO CARE FOR THEM, HAS PLACED UPON US AN ENORMOUS BURDEN AND RESPONSIBILITY. WE ARE VERY GRATEFUL TO ALL THOSE WHO WISH TO HELP US, AND I ASK YOU TO INTERPRET TO ALL CONTRIBUTORS IN ENGLAND, AMERICA, AND OTHER NATIONS OUR DEEP APPRECIATION OF THEIR GENEROUS COLLABORATION. PLEASE APPEAL IMMEDIATELY FOR THE GREATEST POSSIBLE FINANCIAL SUPPORT OF YOUR COMMISSION WHICH GIVES VERY VALUABLE HELP TO THE AUTHORITIES RESPONSIBLE FOR THE CARE OF THE UNFORTUNATE REFUGEES.

AFSC participation increased rapidly from this time on. Urgent conferences were held between our group, the Red Cross, the American Jewish Joint Distribution Committee, Protestant and Catholic agencies, concerning the possibility of a combined nation-wide appeal for foreign relief funds. While this co-operative effort never came about, there was considerable interdependence in actual meeting of the situation.*

* By the end of 1940, money channeled through us by the Red Cross totaled about $100,000. Other grants included, in approximate figures, $10,000 from the American

From every direction now we began receiving appeals to engage in large-scale relief undertakings — in Finland, Poland, Norway, Holland, Belgium, France, and among refugees in Germany and Italy. There seemed to be a feeling that because of our reputation for "neutrality" we ought to be able to go anywhere and do anything. Unfortunately, such was not the case.

Concerning the central and southern departments of France, where millions of refugees had congregated, urgent cables and letters began arriving daily as soon as lines of communication were open. Howard Kershner, returning to France, cabled from Madrid on July 7, 1940, through our State Department:

CANNOT QUAKERS AND RED CROSS COLLABORATE FURTHER LARGE SHIP-
MENTS THERE. BRITISH AMBASSADOR HERE ASKING HIS GOVERNMENT
FOR BLOCKADE EXEMPTION. SEEKING ALSO GERMAN ITALIAN APPROVAL.
SUGGEST YOU DO SAME THERE. ACCOUNTANT STENOGRAPHERS ABLE
PERSONNEL NEEDED. SPANISH TRANSIT VISAS BY RAIL LISBON MADRID
BARCELONA SATISFACTORY BUT NO STOPOVERS PERMITTED. LEAVING FOR
FRANCE TUESDAY. MOST NEEDED COMMODITIES FLOUR MILK MEAT CHOCO-
LATE OIL SOAP. WILL REVISE AFTER REACHING FRANCE. . . . CABLE ADDRESS
AMERICAN CONSUL MARSEILLE.

Another AFSC representative wrote from Toulouse, France, on July 14:

The food situation is exactly, or even worse than Hoover said it would be. . . . One of the great problems is the condition of 40,000 Belgian boys between the ages of 15 and 22, who were evacuated by their government as they had not yet been mobilized. They are mostly in one department, housed in camps, garages, barns, etc. . . . They are hungry all of the time.

Jewish Joint Distribution Committee, $5000 from the American Christian Committee for Refugees, $30,000 through the Committee on Foreign Relief Appeals in the Churches, $8000 from the Mennonite Central Committee, $60,000 from the International Commission for the Assistance of Child Refugees, $60,000 through the Co-ordinating Council for French Relief. In 1940, our income for refugee and relief services alone totaled just under one million dollars.

... They are becoming a social menace. ... The army is all over the place, being demobilized. ... To give you some idea of the quantities of food we have to deal in to feed these hordes of people, you might be interested in our reports for this month. 25 tons of soap, 10,000 kilos milk powder, 25 tons sugar, 50 tons rice, 20 tons olive oil, 60 tons white beans, 400 cases black raisins, 10,000 cases condensed milk, 20 tons macaroni, 15 tons lentils, but no meat or nuts. ... There are infinite problems of transportation including the shortage of gasoline. ... We have distributed this much food with no red tape.

Other messages from Howard Kershner and his coworkers arrived daily:

Toulouse, July 13. Margaret Frawley came from Bordeaux last night. She has shown remarkable initiative and courage in dealing with a very difficult situation. All of the English contingent left more than three weeks ago, and she has very ably headed up the work since then. She has permission to circulate freely in both zones and has also obtained such permission for me. I am going with her soon to Bordeaux and consult the German authorities concerning our work in the occupied area. ...

Toulouse, July 21. ... Our emergency work is now taking two million francs a month. We are only touching the most difficult spots and could efficiently use many times that amount. We are still buying some food at the port of Marseille. It comes from Greece and other Mediterranean ports, but the importers at Marseille do not believe that these sources will remain open long.

Toulouse, August 7. The $90,000 is for sardines from Portugal, particularly valuable now because they are packed in oil, rice coming from Egypt, and milk from Switzerland.

Marseille, August 29. CAN BUY LISBON THOUSAND TONS SUGAR DELIVERED FRENCH BORDER FOR HUNDRED THOUSAND DOLLARS. CAN BUY SWITZERLAND THREE THOUSAND CASES CONDENSED MILK MONTHLY. CABLE ADVICE BOTH PROPOSITIONS.

Marseille, September 4. MILK FOR CHILDREN FRANCE NEXT SIX MONTHS CAN SAVE THOUSANDS LIVES. NORMAL SUPPLIES HOLLAND NORTHERN FRANCE CUT OFF. OUR DELIVERY FOUR CARLOADS TOTALING NINETY-SIX THOUSAND CANS SWISS CONDENSED DISTRIBUTED FROM

TOULOUSE HAS FED TWENTY-FIVE THOUSAND CHILDREN IN HUNDRED
CITIES VILLAGES ELEVEN DEPARTMENTS. FEEDING CHILDREN ON
REFUGEE TRAINS LEAVING TOULOUSE. HUNDRED FORTY-FOUR THOU-
SAND ADDITIONAL CANS COMING SEPTEMBER. SAME QUANTITY
ORDERED FOR OCTOBER. URGENT NEED FINANCIAL SUPPORT AND
AMERICAN MILK IF SWISS SUPPLY FAILS.

Marseille, September, 1940. It is heart-breaking to be charged
with the responsibilities of deciding who shall eat and who shall
go hungry, who shall have clothing and who shall have none.
Dispensing charity in France today means exercising the power
of life or death over one's fellows. How does one do it and
retain his sanity?

The British blockade against France was tightening, and the
United States government tended to support Britain's position.

During the entire summer and fall of 1940, there was a great deal
of public discussion in the United States concerning the advisability
of feeding children in what were called "the democratic countries
of Europe." Ex-President Hoover strongly supported the move to
feed, and had created an organization to promote this point of view.
In addition to our Committee's fundamental conviction in this
direction, letters from our staff in France were pointing out that
the people of France and the Low Countries were victims of
Nazism, that this was the hour when they most needed our friendship and assistance, and that whichever course we took they would
never forget.

On August 8 and 9, on our way to Cape Cod for a two
weeks' vacation, our family stopped at Hyde Park for a visit with
Mrs. Roosevelt. Harry Hopkins was also there, and at breakfast
on the 9th our whole group had a rather animated discussion concerning the merits and demerits of feeding French mothers and
children. Harry was opposing feeding, because it would relieve
Hitler of responsibility and actually might assist him in his war
effort. I had seen a good deal of Harry when he was making ardent
pleas for the underprivileged of the United States during our own
depression, and this opposition to feeding in France seemed to me

a new role on his part. It was as if political expediency had overcome the natural human impulse which heretofore he had always
represented to me. It was quite clear that the drift in the United
States was taking this turn, and that President Roosevelt's attitude
was shaping up in this direction.

Mrs. Roosevelt, of course, was in a very difficult position; but she
said she would be willing to see even German children fed if they
needed it.

So far, the Service Committee had been able to carry on considerable relief work in Vichy France. Early in September, a letter
came from Marshal Pétain, head of the Vichy state, encouraging us,
along with other agencies, to continue and if possible increase relief
services. A French lawyer brought the letter in person to us, and
was taking a somewhat similar one to President Roosevelt. In spite
of the British blockade, the door was still not completely closed for
continued agitation to get food into France, Belgium, and Holland.
In fact, two days before this messenger's visit, our Committee had
decided to try to proceed with relief in unoccupied France at the
rate of $50,000 per month, concentrating on license permission to
export that much in food and funds.

On September 12 James G. Vail, secretary of our Foreign
Service Section, joined me in conferring with Norman Davis and
Ernest Swift of the American Red Cross concerning the possibility
of our uniting in an effort to secure British blockade exemption.
We agreed to approach the President later, but meanwhile I was to
talk with William Bullitt, our ambassador to France, and to Robert
Murphy, his counselor. This I did on September 17, and Mr.
Bullitt ordered a cable sent to the American embassy in France, asking whether they had any evidence of food's being extracted from
unoccupied France by the Nazis. I agreed to ask Howard Kershner
for the same information. If we turned up no evidence of such
activities on the part of Germany, Mr. Bullitt offered to go to the
President and specifically ask him to request Mr. Churchill to allow
relief ships to go through the blockade.

Many individuals with whom I talked during these months shared my view that our country's function in the international emergency should be one of assistance to its victims and leadership into peace. Letters and cables from France intimated that our failure to feed France was causing it to drift, almost by necessity, more and more into German hands. Even from the political point of view, it seemed to many Americans and Englishmen that the refusal to feed was unwise. As long as this debate continued, there was a chance. I was spending a good deal of time speaking at large public gatherings, and taking part in radio broadcasts, urging our Committee's point of view, that starvation of children was a weapon we had no right to use, and further, that no brave new world could be built by a generation whose childhood had been starved and left without kindness and mercy.

Members of the Service Committee remembered going into Germany during the blockade between the First World War armistice and the signing of the Versailles Treaty. Rickets, pellagra, and diseases of the bone which resulted from malnutrition, were widely prevalent. Our efforts — and those of other groups, for we were not the only ones engaged in the task of feeding — prevented large-scale starvation, but the cankerous effects of undernourishment left their permanent scars on literally millions of German children. It seemed to us clear that although the blockade of Germany at that time had been effective in the short view (it did help force Germany to sign a treaty which she signed unwillingly), in the long run it had contributed no small portion of the bitterness which festered in the German people until Hitler picked it up into his program of revenge.

We also remembered that during the administration of Belgian relief in 1914 and after, the British and French governments advanced about 100 million dollars each toward the relief of Belgium, which was then German-occupied territory. At that time, it was considered both the humanitarian response and a good investment in friendship.

We could not imagine that large-scale starvation, occurring as the result of a blockade, could be accompanied by a deepening sense of human worth and a growth of the spirit of concern for our fellows, and these are basic to the survival of any kind of civilization. We felt that if children especially were allowed to starve to death in Europe, deliberately, while we were embarrassed by food surpluses, they would not die alone, but would drag down with them into spiritual bondage those of us who participated in causing their death.

British leadership was adamant on the question of the blockade, and our own leadership understood the British position so well that little pressure was brought to bear to change it. Great Britain was fighting not only to maintain her traditional position of dominance over Europe; she might be said by now to be fighting for her very national existence. Her position was that to allow food to go past her blockade even into unoccupied territory would be to assist the Nazis in their job of feeding the peoples they were absorbing, and it might even lend enough comfort to the bewildered peoples to prevent their rising up in revolt. Terrible as the suffering was, a rigid blockade was thought to be the best instrument of shortening the war, thereby in the long run reducing the total suffering more than if there were alleviation of hunger now.

We of the Service Committee were by no means untouched by these arguments. In such a time, there is almost bound to be terrific conflict in one's mind. But if one pictured himself the parent of children who were starving, with the possibility of food's coming through the blockade for them, it seemed difficult to think of insisting that the blockade be maintained rigidly, right down to the children, on the far chance that feeding them might help the oppressor. But the contrary position could be stated eloquently; and if the conflict was acute for us, it was far more so, I am sure, for people of the countries directly concerned.

My own final answer was that it is never to the advantage of anybody to starve children. We should get food to them, at the same time opposing with every nonviolent means the extraction of food from their countries by the Nazi occupation.

It is not uncommon for this kind of issue to arise when one has his mind centered on relief operations. To my way of thinking, the great danger is that we may accept too readily the demands of the governments "on our side," and find ourselves participating in the infliction of long-time wounds for the sake of some immediate goal. Is not the only escape from this dilemma to do both things at once: to be completely frank and strong in our position with the oppressors, and also to insist on saving children with food?

On the wall of my office I have for years kept a picture sent me by a friend — a picture which is synthetic, but nevertheless highly suggestive in hours of inner conflict. It portrays Hitler and Gandhi sitting facing each other, each in characteristic pose. Pondering that picture always helps me in my effort to discover where truth lies. It suggests to me as direct an approach as possible to individuals responsible for the violation of rights of human beings, on the other hand keeping intact in one's soul the spirit of penitence, truth, and love. If one does this, he will be quite as concerned for the spirit of the oppressor as for the needs of the oppressed.

One day while we were working for modification of the blockade, I had a very searching conference with John Winant, then director of the International Labor Office in Geneva, who was in the United States on a visit. He asked me whether I felt our country had any other recourse under present circumstances than to use force. I answered that often international affairs are allowed to reach a stage where the use of violence becomes inevitable, and I feared we were fast approaching that time. However, I as a pacifist who had tried to do my bit to prevent affairs reaching such a stage, would not now desert my belief in pacifism and go over to force. I was determined to try every possible means of preventing affairs from coming to that inevitable point. I did not believe that the war would settle anything, and I did believe that if war came, we should still be alert to promote those ends which could use humanity's energies creatively — which is the only effective alternative to destructiveness, as we learn very quickly when dealing with young children.

To this Winant heartily agreed. He said that the ILO had held two conferences with the various American states concerning settlement of refugees and that the Latin American states were very much interested in holding a third one, which he was authorized to call at any time. If there could be a re-training experience preceding their going for settlement to Latin American states, and if the United States could be induced to furnish capital, then a conference at which this announcement was made, might be of extremely significant value.

He shared my conviction that we must make every effort to respond to the crisis creatively, in dimensions as large and human as the destruction was large and insane.

One day at lunch with Jean Despres of Coty Company, and Louis Francis Closon, commercial attaché of the French embassy, I discussed with them whether it would be possible to divert $50,000 per month from French funds in this country for French relief. They said it would be quite possible provided the United States Treasury Department would release the funds. This I agreed to try to help bring about.

I interceded with Arthur Sulzberger, owner of the *New York Times,* concerning the *Times's* policy on relief in France. He said the *Times* would support such relief if adequate guarantees could be given that it would not even indirectly feed the German economic-military machine, and if British approval could be secured.

In November I spoke to a meeting of about 150 ministers in New York, along with Herbert Agar, Henry P. Van Dusen, Henry Sloane Coffin, and others, on the desirability of feeding children in the German-occupied countries. It was obvious that I was terribly outnumbered by brilliant and able people. I believe I was the only speaker who upheld feeding. Yet there was considerable sympathy in the audience for my point of view, that if we had food, and could get it in, we shared deeply the responsibility for any fate which came to these children.

We were developing a plan to send a Christmas food ship to France. We discussed this proposal with President Roosevelt and found him willing to support it if a British navicert could be obtained. He offered to request funds for buying enough supplies to fill the ship out of the fifty million dollars set aside by Congress for foreign relief, and encouraged the idea of a ship large enough to have its mercy cargo divided between the children of Spain and the children of France. He gave me a letter to Norman Davis asking him to discuss the project with me.

Norman Davis had a good deal of hesitation about the plan. He doubted whether the British would grant a navicert for the ship, but was willing to make a try. In very few quarters did I find the kind of enthusiasm which could have made the cause of the children a rallying point for non-military-minded people everywhere. To me it was sufficient challenge to the imagination and spirit to have mobilized all right-minded people, but the persons who shared my viewpoint were diminishing in number.

James Vail and I visited the State Department, to follow up on the French embassy's willingness to allocate French funds in this country for French relief. We found that our government's policy was now definitely against releasing any funds from French dollars in this country except to support consular and diplomatic offices in this hemisphere.

By December 20, the proposed Christmas Ship had not yet been approved by Britain. We of the AFSC were greatly distressed, particularly because if it did not sail, we did not know how we should have milk after January 15 for the 30,000 children we were now helping feed in southern France. For the time being, at least, our supply of Swiss milk had been cut off. President Roosevelt felt a commitment to this Christmas Ship project, and, after hearing our story again, called the Red Cross to encourage every possible effort on their part. They insisted they had done everything they could.

I then asked the President whether he would call up Prime Minister Churchill and request him to let the ship pass, but he did not commit himself that he would make this call.

It was difficult for our representatives in France to reply authoritatively to our question as to whether Germany was now taking food out of the "free" zone. For some time we had been thinking of the desirability of perhaps two American Friends' visiting Germany in the interest of (1) making unofficial explorations concerning possibilities of bringing the war to a close, (2) finding out whether food was being taken from the western countries into Germany, and (3) interceding for the children of the western countries. I told President Roosevelt of our thinking, and he warmly encouraged such a visit.

James Vail and I then went to the German embassy to discuss the matter with Ambassador Thomsen, who agreed to authorize the issuance of visas for such a visit.

Pursuant to this, it was decided by our Board of Directors to send Harold Evans and James Vail to Germany, Robert Yarnall and Henry Cadbury to England. The latter visit was in the interest of exploring what help American Friends might give British Friends, and discussing with the British government the possibility of modification of the blockade to the extent of allowing food to go in from America to feed children in Holland, Belgium, and France.

On January 3, 1941, James Vail and I talked with Breckinridge Long, Assistant Secretary of State, about this entire proposal, and it received his warm approval. We also talked with Mary Craig McGeachy, who was in charge of the information section of the British embassy. Though she took a quite firm stand on the proposition that any food which went in tended to help the Germans demonstrate their "new social order," she yet saw the importance of the delegation's going to Germany, and hoped we would lay heavily upon the Germans their responsibility for feeding. She thought that if they would agree to match what we took in, pound for pound and calorie for calorie, that would go far toward persuading the British government to relax the blockade.

Our two delegations left for Germany and England respectively on January 11, 1941.

Meanwhile the British government had decided to relax the blockade to permit the passage of a limited number of American Red Cross ships carrying American supplies to the children of unoccupied France. The first such ship finally sailed on January 25, with 6000 tons of cargo, half for unoccupied France and half for Spain. AFSC representatives in Europe absorbed some of the distribution responsibility. The second ship, which sailed March 17, carried as part of its cargo children's clothing to the value of $25,000, as the gift of the Service Committee to the American Red Cross.

In March Robert Yarnall and Henry Cadbury returned from England. They had had a long and patient session with Hugh Dalton, Minister of Economic Warfare, and had found no willingness to allow feeding in occupied territories, no matter what might be the condition of life under which the children there must live. They had shared firsthand the conditions in England which lay behind this firmness. They had seen the English people's sufferings and the heroic way in which they were meeting them. They recommended that AFSC contribute a minimum of $10,000 monthly to British Friends' emergency relief work in England. We did contribute $10,000 per month for a considerable period of time, funds well used by British Friends for social welfare services in badly bombed areas, and in their program of some eighty hostels for evacuated old people, mothers with children, and unaccompanied children.

James Vail and Harold Evans returned from their visit to Germany later that month. They reported severe shortages of food in Spain, unoccupied France, occupied France and Belgium — the three areas being named in order of severity (occupied France and Belgium forming one area). It had been difficult to get the facts concerning transfer of food. There was transfer both ways, from Germany to western countries, and from western countries to Germany, but whether the rate of exchange was a fair one it was not possible to find out. French wheat was flowing into Germany. Was the compensation received in terms of German commodities adequate? There was doubt, but the doubt could not be proved. Of course there was no opposition on the part of Germany to food's being shipped in for the children of Holland, Belgium, and occupied France. The Nazi government was even willing for us to send in American personnel to supervise the distribution. However, this would have to be done under eventual and final inspection of the Occupation. That would not be easy. No clear case could be made, therefore, as a guarantee to contributors or the British government that in the occupied areas food would always reach its intended destination, that it would never be used in other ways. We of the Service Committee felt that the effort should be made, and the risk taken. But public sentiment was such that it was exceedingly doubtful whether the job could be undertaken.

The French ambassador told me one day that he was in the position of sitting on top of a pile of gold which had accumulated here while his people starved at home. He offered us a million dollars to be used for the purchase of food anywhere in the world, provided we could get permission from the British government to ship it, probably through Lisbon, to Vichy France. He mentioned food then obtainable in the Argentine, and French ships already there, waiting to be commanded. Such action of course would necessitate unfreezing French funds in this country through co-operation of the State Department. It was interesting that the French ambassador had no objection if food thus purchased by French funds were used in occupied as well as unoccupied France. He had received communications from his government indicating acute and widespread suffering throughout western Europe, even to the point of near-starvation already, and he urged us to get at least a token shipment in to Belgium and both zones of France.

After this we had another session with Assistant Secretary of State Adolf Berle, who said that if proper transportation facilities could be secured and we were able to get a British navicert, he thought it was appropriate that we should address a request to the Secretary of State to allow this transaction. In order to make certain that the Secretary of State had substantial backing, I discussed the matter with the President, who agreed that he would support the Secretary of State in such a transaction, if we obtained British approval.

On April 4, Mr. Berle told us that the State Department was willing to grant the special request we had made that $50,000 of French government funds in this country be unfrozen for our use in purchasing food and clothing in Lisbon, providing we could secure a British navicert for these materials.

On April 10, Frank Aydelotte and I paid a visit to Lord Halifax, then British ambassador to the United States, in regard to (1) getting the $50,000 worth of commodities released in Lisbon, (2) securing a navicert for food going directly to occupied territory.

We found Halifax to be a true aristocrat, a devout Christian, and above all a devoted administrator for the British government. As a Christian, he confessed himself moved by the suffering of children, no matter whose children they were. But he was appointed to carry out British government policy. He said that getting the food released from Portugal would be extremely difficult. As for a navicert for food for occupied territory, that would be in definite contradiction to British government policy. He was compelled by his obligation in representing His Majesty's government to take government's view of the situation. All of this was said at a delightful tea on the terrace of one of the most charming embassies in Washington. It was a pretty final blow to our hopes.

The history of our efforts to get food to the children of Europe during the remaining months before we had to withdraw from France is largely a story of frustration. In this period, no agency was able to do anything substantial for the children of the occupied territories.

Even feeding the children of unoccupied France remained a battle to the very end. French groups in this country were pressing for permission to take more aid. Anne Morgan and those associated with her were deeply disturbed that the whole French nation was being undermined in health and general resistance. Like our Committee, she was receiving reports that made it hard to sleep nights — reports, for instance, of the abandonment of physical education in schools because the children fainted when required to exert themselves.

We had been able to build up our program in unoccupied France to the extent of giving supplementary food to about 50,000 children daily for twenty weeks in 1941. Response from the children was poignant: "Dear American friends, I thank you for sending vitamin candies. I think the other ship will soon come because we are hungry." "Dear American friends, I have eaten chick peas for a whole week and feel very satisfied about it."

In the fall of that year there was enforced curtailment of the program. One worker wrote of the process of selecting those who would continue to receive milk:

While this sad little choice is being made, the other children come forward and ask eagerly, "May we not have milk also?" And looking down on what is often a small thin face, the answer is made as cheerfully as possible, "Why, *no! You* are *well!* The Doctor has ordered it for the sick ones. You must be thankful that you don't need it!"

By the beginning of 1942 we were able to resume child feeding on a larger scale. From the field came word: "We are now engaged in sending out *légumes secs* to start feeding 84,000 children in the public schools of the eleven most needy Departments." Reports told also of 100,000 children receiving special vitamin doses for seven weeks; of regular food distributions to some seven thousand persons in internment camps; and of the interesting development of self-help workshops among the Spanish refugees in particular.

There were continuous clothing distributions. Earlier, one of our workers had written, "Can't you send more warm clothing? By no stretch of the imagination can Hitler be aided by putting a warm coat on a shivering child."

In the early part of 1942, a staff of fifteen Americans and about 150 Europeans were sharing the responsibilities of this emergency service in unoccupied France. The greater part of the financial support was non-Quaker, coming from religious and philanthropic organizations in this country, from individuals rich and poor, and from France herself. A financial report from our unit in France carried this memorandum: "It will be noted that during the eleven months covered by this financial statement, funds received from Secours National, the official French relief agency, exceeded the income from all other sources."

Eight AFSC representatives stayed in France through the break in diplomatic relations between that country and the United States the second week in November, and were interned by the Germans at Baden-Baden. They left our relief work in France in the hands of a small international group of workers.

I cannot close this chapter without noting a conversation I had with Jerry Voorhis in the late spring of '41, when we were attempting to rouse the people of the United States to this country's unparalleled opportunity to respond to the need of the victims of war. Jerry said at that time that he found serious-minded Congressmen much disturbed because, although they could see the necessity for stopping Hitler, they saw no light beyond that. There was no great new day called for by what we were doing — *that* seemed to be left exclusively to Mr. Hitler to propose. He said that his own constituency had raised this question with him, and he seemed to have no answer.

This was what many of us felt so keenly during those days: that while Germany was proposing a new order, we — Britain and our-selves — were simply setting out to defend an old one. We did not want the order Germany outlined, but we did need to project one of our own. That was the challenge we were failing to meet. In terms of Toynbee's theory of challenge and response, the challenge was present, but the response was not forthcoming.

6. Relief and Rehabilitation: Europe

As the Nazis were pushed back across France in the latter part of 1944, and that country was opened up for relief and reconstruction, the threads of our Committee's participation were picked up almost where we had been forced to lay them down, but with a grim chapter having intervened. News releases told the story in terms of statistics:

Lyon, Oct. 26, 1944 (JTA). Fifteen thousand Jewish children — half of those living in France before the war — were killed or deported during the German occupation, officials of OSE, Jewish Health Society, told the Jewish Telegraphic Agency correspondent today. About 13,000 were killed or deported from the occupied zone, while 2000 met a similar fate in the so-called Vichy area. . . .

Throughout the occupation the OSE cared for 6000 children, . . . and lost only 80 of these to the Gestapo, but 28 OSE workers, both Jewish and non-Jewish, were captured by the Gestapo and either shot or deported. The OSE, the officials said, also sent 1500 children to Switzerland.

Aroused French public opinion, as manifested by the courageous denunciations of the deportation of children by Cardinal Gerlier, Archbishop Salièges of Toulouse, and Pastor Boegner, head of the French Protestant Church, was directly responsible for saving about 1400 children in 1942. As a result of protests by these religious leaders, 600 children at the Rivesaltes camp, who were awaiting deportation with their parents, 400 at the Gurs camp, and about 400 at Les Milles camp near Marseille, were released. The parents were deported. . . .

Of the 15,000 children who remain, at least half lost their parents through death or deportation.

Helga Holbek, a Danish Quaker worker who had remained in France throughout the occupation, toured Normandy to survey needs in that newly liberated area. She sent her report to London and Philadelphia:

. . . . A few roads have been cleared through the masses of ruins. Here and there a small board is seen giving the new address, and people shivering under the ceaseless drizzle search about in the hope of still recovering a few things, since it must not be forgotten that these ruins represent for many all their worldly possessions.

Housing. In all towns, from 20% to 90% of the houses are destroyed, and practically all the rest damaged, especially the roofs. . . . Every room, every attic, every hovel is filled to the last square inch with people sleeping anywhere: on the floor, on the tables, on billiard tables, without bedding or blankets.

Blankets. At Le Havre alone, more than twenty thousand people are sleeping on the floor without a single blanket.

Le Havre. Out of 18,000 houses, 14,000 have been destroyed, 11,000 completely; 140 hectares completely razed; total of 40,000 persons bombed out; 8000 killed. The Chef du Cabinet du Préfet appears to be struggling tenaciously to help the city. . . . With a score of lorries and fuel, he would be able to solve nearly all the urgent questions: repair material, heating, and food supplies. For example, fruit is going bad in the country for lack of transport.

He asks for heavy oil for fishing vessels which at present cannot go out, and coal to restart the water and gas services.

He asks us to take steps in England to obtain a few small coasting steamers of 200–300 tons.

At Le Havre, one finds bitterness, and deep sorrow and disappointment. There was never any complaint about 136 previous [Allied] bombings. They were recognized as a military necessity. But the last one was different: nothing to explain it. . . .

"Secours Social" is working desperately. Its stock of furniture, blankets, bedsteads, utensils, etc., is already exhausted. Distribution of clothes has only so far reached the 2000th family out of the 11,000 families bombed out.

These are only excerpts from Helga Holbek's long report. The total number of French persons displaced at this time was estimated at seven million.

On November 18, Edith Pye, in Paris for the British Quakers, wrote back to London: ". . . . The Jewish refugees who had been interned by the Germans but not yet deported were released in August. . . . The plight of the Spanish refugees is now much worse. . . . There are 30,000 Polish refugees in northern France, 50% being children and a very few men."

Margaret Frawley and I were the first AFSC representatives to re-enter France direct from Philadelphia in the wake of liberation. This we did on November 26, 1944, after a long wait in London for the necessary permissions.

Edith Pye, Roger Wilson, and William Fraser of Friends Relief Service of London were already in Paris, as were David Blickenstaff who had been representing our Committee in Madrid and Kendall Kimberland from our Algiers office. Those who had maintained relief services in southern France throughout the occupation had come from Marseille, Perpignan, Toulouse, and Montauban, to join the Paris Center staff in welcoming English and American Friends, and to confer about future program. They were a valiant and weary group, in nationality French, Dutch, Danish, Norwegian, Irish, and Latvian! Margaret Frawley caught some of the emotional quality of the reunion in a letter to the Philadelphia office:

There was Henry van Etten's excited voice on the telephone Monday night when we announced our arrival, and the warm welcome they gave us — Henry, Marcelle, and Albert — when they came to fetch us Tuesday morning. All our friends were waiting for us when we came to the upstairs room of Guy de la Brosse: Helga, Mary, Toot, Ima, Eleanor, Helene, Nora and Fred, and David just arrived from Madrid. Seeing them all together, knowing how all of us had anticipated this meeting when the curtain should lift a little, the coming together was almost more than any of us could bear. It is strange for our friends to speak English again after these years, for these last years it was hardly safe to speak English. They are weary, more tired than one may guess on a first quick impression. . . .

All of them have felt our love and support during this time of separation and have waited eagerly for our coming, working in tragedy in the expectation that we would come to help not France alone but Europe.

Paris, cold and hungry, is lovely, but civilians walk more slowly than of old, for human energy runs low. The book stalls along the Seine are open and the luxury shops offer fine merchandise which no one has coupons or money to buy. I took three of our friends to dinner the other evening, a simple place with oil cloth on the tables — soup, meat and one vegetable and cheese — the price was twelve dollars. There is, of course, no heat in any of the buildings, nor any prospect of any this winter. These days we have been here are mild for November and early December, but it will be hard as the winter wears on. Yet in the North life is indescribably more difficult and in other parts of Europe it is worse.

It is good to come and may the others follow quickly.

We learned of heroic and resourceful efforts that had maintained relief for children in southern France and served Jewish and other political deportees in every way that could be devised. We learned of the hiding and feeding of Jews. We listened to firsthand accounts of the Battle of Marseille. We heard about the arrival in Toulouse of a shipment from Switzerland. A member of the unit from Toulouse told us: "Suddenly there appeared two armed German soldiers in the office. My first thought was, 'Ah, now it is our turn.' But they simply came to ask 'if we expected a carload of sugar and tomato sauce from Germany?' Sure, said we, and realized it was the sugar announced a couple of months before from Switzerland, and which we had given up all hope of seeing." Also there was the miracle of the arrival of ten tons of Danish bacon, a gift from Danish people in France: "The energetic young Attaché at the Danish Legation met the lard at the border, and insisted so long that he managed to get the freight car attached to a passenger train, and brought it safely through France down to the South. . . . The children hadn't been growing at all. Some who had gained no weight in two years showed improvement within six months when fed the bacon. It was like watering a parched flower." *

We heard about the imprisonment and physical suffering of members of the Paris Center staff.

We felt that the Quaker relief program in France now should look to this group for guidance; that we of America, especially, should go in as helpers, letting them take the lead. They were the seasoned ones; they knew what most needed to be done.

Representatives of other foreign private relief agencies felt the same way. On invitation from Paul B. Anderson, some of us then in Paris from such agencies came together December 1, to get acquainted with each other and to explore avenues of co-operation. The group consisted of Paul Anderson, representing the American Council of Voluntary Agencies for Foreign Service, the Church Committee on Overseas Relief, the American YMCA, and American Relief for France; Joseph J. Schwartz of the Joint Distribution Committee; Henry Amiel from War Relief Services of the National Catholic Welfare Conference; Roland Elliott of World Student Relief; Edith Pye, Friends Relief Service (British); and Margaret Frawley and myself from the American Friends Service Committee.

We exchanged information on need, availability of supplies, and international regulations. In Normany, where food was plentiful in certain sections, the desperate needs were for transport, shelter, and blankets. The Service Committee had already shipped clothing, and UNRRA (United Nations Relief and Rehabilitation Administration) was making clothing collections through the churches. We agreed to take immediate action to get blankets.

In the southern half of France, the great need was for food. Our workers reported exhausted supplies and undersized, undernourished, pretubercular or tubercular children. Some of us had avenues through which we could get minimum amounts of food into France

* This and the preceding quotation are from workers' written reports.

quickly. For example, the Service Committee had money in Lisbon for purchases in Spain.

There was much discussion of UNRRA, for private agencies' relationship to this United Nations effort was not yet clear.

In the United States we had seen the development of an agency within the State Department, called the Office of Foreign Relief and Rehabilitation Operations, designed to administer public funds for foreign relief. It was understood when this agency came into being that if a United Nations agency developed, OFRRO would merge its efforts with those of other countries in the UN organization. Now this merger had taken place, and all private agencies were somewhat concerned as to their relation to the new international effort. I had many friends active in its administration. In working with Jewish agencies I had come to know Herbert Lehman, who was its director. Philip Jessup, well known to our Committee, had been in charge of the selection of OFRRO personnel, much of which was carried over into UNRRA; Allen Bonnell, one of our own group, was among its administrators. Altogether, we at AFSC had great confidence in the motivation, intelligence, and wisdom of those who were responsible for this undertaking.

Nevertheless, there was some concern on the part of voluntary agencies in the beginning, lest UNRRA pre-empt their special fields of interest, fields in which they had worked in their own way, distributing funds as seemed to them best. A large international agency could not be expected to administer its functions exactly as we in private groups would like to see it done.

UNRRA had an enormous undertaking, really beyond the capacity of any human instrument to accomplish. Its personnel problem was infinitely more complicated than that of private agencies. The latter could call on persons schooled in their own traditions and willing to give dedicated service with little or no compensation. UNRRA must quickly build up a staff representing a wide range of national groups, giving them at least a minimum degree of financial security.

From time to time I have heard a great deal of criticism of UNRRA and of those who administered it. I am sure they had great difficulties with political influence, dishonest personnel, efforts to exploit, and outright stealing. No doubt there was some incompetence. But knowing the size and complexity of their job, the dispatch with which it had to be executed, the nervous tension in countries which had long endured violence, hunger, and cold, I have felt that this international service of relief and reconstruction was carried out with about as much competence as could reasonably be expected.

Certainly, as time went on, the relations between UNRRA, particularly its over-all administrators, and our own Committee, were most cordial. Early in 1944 we lent an AFSC team to UNRRA for refugee work in Egypt, Greece, and Yugoslavia. In the late summer of 1945, before AFSC as such had entrance to Germany, part of this team served in Germany in UNRRA's refugee and displaced-persons program. We carried out reconstruction projects in China with the aid of UNRRA funds and equipment. We co-operated in its reconstruction program in Italy. One had to recognize that relief and reconstruction needs over the world were of such volume that they could only begin to be met by government funds and international administration. I am glad that the American Friends Service Committee tried to give every possible assistance to UNRRA, and looked with consideration and understanding on its delicate problems in international relationships. For instance, in UNRRA both contributing and receiving countries sat on the same board. Ideally, this was fine. But it is inconceivable that there should not be some sense of priority in influence on the part of the giver as compared with the recipient. This is not ideal, but it is a fact; it came up, and it had to be dealt with.

One hopes, of course, that the world will not again require relief on this enormous scale. If such should be the case, however, the experience of UNRRA in working out some of its problems will be invaluable. Even in programs of technical assistance and general welfare between nations, this body of experience has great value as a guide and a warning of where the danger points are.

It is beyond the scope of this volume to try to give anything like a thorough account of the American Friends Service Committee's postwar relief activities, which in terms of budget so far surpassed anything we had attempted in recent years that sometimes it was as if it were happening in spite of us.

However, the number of persons we had working in Europe and Asia did not begin to match the numbers in Europe in the wake of the First World War, when during one period the Committee had almost six hundred men and women in France alone! For as World War II receded, it was clear that the pattern of relief following World War I would not apply this time. For one thing, UNRRA had at its command large funds from governmental sources, and would be expected to carry the major relief responsibilities. In addition to this, during the past twenty-five years there had been a marked growth in sensitivity to relief needs on the part of many American groups. The Catholic Church, the Protestant Church, and organized labor were deeply concerned and were prepared to raise voluntary funds for relief in many parts of the world. Moreover, in Germany the war had been fought through to an unconditional surrender. While this was looked upon with favor by many people, it soon became clear that the reverse side of this shield was that the Allies became unconditionally responsible for the maintenance of life and welfare in Germany. The occupying forces therefore assumed heavy responsibility for feeding. All this was in considerable contrast to the First World War relief period, when AFSC was asked by the American Relief Administration to handle the distribution of food to children throughout Germany.

In order to see that the voluntary efforts in America were coordinated, President Roosevelt had created what was called The President's War Relief Control Board. Each voluntary agency doing work abroad was required to be licensed by this Board. Fortunately, the administration of the Board was carried out by men of broad sympathies, who understood the significance and character of the voluntary contribution.

In the cases of Germany and Japan, all private American agencies were required to distribute their material assistance through a single co-ordinated channel, and at first the number of workers sent from the United States was limited to the minimum needed for over-all administration. In Germany, the co-ordinated channel was known as CRALOG (Council of Relief Agencies Licensed to Operate in Germany).

Besides the more thorough government regulation of relief agencies after World War II as compared with World War I, the increased number of such agencies seemed to call for greater voluntary co-ordination of their efforts. This situation led to the establishment of the American Council of Voluntary Agencies for Foreign Service, a voluntary association of more than fifty organizations. Dr. Joseph P. Chamberlain, professor of public law at Columbia University, became the first chairman of this group, and remained in that capacity until his death in 1951. I served during most of that time as vice-chairman, later as acting chairman. Especially during the earlier days of acute emergency, the fellowship which developed among those of us who were uniting our efforts to meet the need was both a strength and a delight. As the programs of the various agencies have changed with the changing character of the need, it has not been so easy to maintain this helpful fellowship, but the Council does continue to co-ordinate information and provide opportunity for joint planning among agencies.

It is almost inevitable that, among the general public, interest in foreign relief lags after the first period of acute distress. Yet the political and social structure of the world was more completely devastated by the Second World War than by the First, and relief problems have persisted into the present, requiring an ever-increasing amount of interpretation if the necessary funds are to be secured.

In addition to this natural lag of interest, there is, I think, a vague realization in most of our minds that prolonged giving of relief

constitutes an abnormal relationship, and while it is healthy to respond quickly and generously to an emergency it is not healthy for
America to be in possession of such a preponderant part of the
world's goods that she must forever be the donor. This in itself is
likely to do damage to relationships between people. Who has not
felt that we Americans suffer from the fact that we are the rich
people of the world?

This situation leads our Committee into an ever-deepening concern that everything possible shall be done to prevent further wars,
and to make sure that we Americans shall not come to think of ourselves as better than others because it is we who give and they who
receive. We have a strong feeling that in the administration of relief we have often received enormous benefits for ourselves, and
these benefits partake of that permanent, spiritual quality which
transforms life. We realize the necessity to continue relief as long
as there is acute suffering, but we want to be sure it is recognized
as essentially a spiritual interchange, and that it is always accompanied by a frame of mind which enables us to learn from those to
whom we give.

But I have strayed from my on-going story.

In Germany in the immediate postwar period, AFSC had two
representatives on CRALOG, helping supervise the distribution of
American voluntary relief supplies. Beyond this, we were able to
move in only slowly with those more personal services which we
consider our greater strength. However, by 1947, when our work
with the German people was most extensive, representing more
than two million dollars for the two years 1946–1947, we had some
fifty representatives within Germany.

Other units which brought the Committee's total overseas per-
sonnel to around two hundred in 1947, included, notably, groups in
Austria, Finland, France, Hungary, Italy, Poland, China, and India.
For the fiscal year ending September 30, 1947, our expenditures for
foreign service, including gifts in kind and the regular Quaker
Center work, totaled close to seven million dollars — a rather star-

tling figure to some of us who had become acquainted with the Committee when its combined foreign and domestic budget was not much over $100,000.

Yet the whole meaning of what we did still lay in the individual. It is a curious fact — one of those paradoxes of the mathematics of the spirit — that the hunger of a million persons, far from meaning more to me than the hunger of one, actually means less. It means less, not on the intellectual level, but in terms of my ability to respond to it wholly, with feeling and action. This is a commonplace, but it is something which any agency carrying relief from those who have to those who need must constantly be realizing afresh. A glance at the statistics given above may be interesting, but the significance of our work lies elsewhere, and is quite otherwise comprehended.

In the winter of 1946–1947, most of us could not readily take in the statement that Europe's basic *emergency* needs added up to 583 million dollars. But any of us could realize, if we took the trouble to do so, how we would feel if we had to send our children off to school barefoot in a land where winter snows were heavy, with temperatures hovering around zero. And 400,000 children in Poland that winter were trying to go to school with no shoes on their feet. When they walked into the snow with rags tied around their feet, they went out from unheated shelter — sometimes only a dugout — many of them carrying diseases in their underweight bodies. Tuberculosis was becoming a commonplace. In one province alone, Kielce, 146,000 persons were still living in hollows dug out of the rubble of their destroyed homes. We did not need the statistics on the subnormal size of babies being born to tell us that all this violation of our common humanity would be visited on the coming generation — the generation on which the hope of Europe rested.

From France came word, "The need is a very subtle one here. In many places, food supplies now would be barely sufficient if bodies were well and strong to begin with. But there is a growth in tuberculosis due to the sustained period of undernourishment, which cannot be checked except by using large quantities of the more highly nutritive foods, and these we don't have."

A doctor from Germany outlined for us at the Service Committee a carefully worked out plan for segregating and treating tuberculosis cases in Germany. But he added, "It is an absolutely futile gesture unless we can get the proper food, not only for all these patients, but for those who are on the verge."

A book published about this time, Robert Neumann's *Children of Vienna,** illumined the meaning of Europeans' preoccupation with food. One of a group of waifs living in an underground hideout was discussing the mystery of calories. He pondered the fact that in a concentration camp you died of 800 calories; in Vienna you died of 1100. Yet Americans were reported to eat as many as 6000 a day and live. It was strange. Americans must be the only people immune to calories.

In that winter, when the depth of the deprivations in Europe and Asia had been fully revealed, the meaning for us in the United States lay largely in connection with our own superabundance, for we were dumping potatoes and projecting plans for curtailing agricultural production.

These were the months during which UNRRA was closing out its program. Other international machinery — notably the International Refugee Organization — would not be fully functioning for a considerable time. Into this gap voluntary relief agencies had to step at once if a suffering world was not to know yet greater physical privation, a higher death toll, and a deeper anguish of spirit. It was impossible to overemphasize the urgency of the situation. Adults and children, whose vitality had been depleted through the years of shortages, could not muster strength to make-do or muddle through until new measures were operating in some future time. If the pipe line dried up now, for many it would never flow again.

In the early spring of 1947, an UNRRA worker with a mission supplying food to some 300,000 children in Minsk telephoned me,

* E. P. Dutton and Company, New York, 1947.

pleading for the very lives of these children. He said there was no question of their wriggling through somehow until new plans were in effect. Without immediate interim relief, they would not be there to benefit from future measures.

This was the kind of pressure, backed up by our knowledge of American abundance, which caused us to become involved in such large relief operations in 1946–1947.

Yet always, underneath, one's mind and spirit were grappling with the problem along broader, more far-reaching lines.

Now, at the time of this writing, we have seen the rise of the Food and Agriculture Organization and the World Health Organization, both agencies of the United Nations. We have glimpsed what might be done to right the imbalance among nations through planning for increased production, especially in those parts of the world which chronically suffer from food deficits, at the same time working to eliminate epidemics and establish new public health services. Valuable as may be the relationships which develop between those who suffer shortages and those who share their relative abundance, how much greater may be the fellowship among people who are able to be self-supporting and who enjoy good health. There will always be need for human charity and its attendant spiritual fellowship, particularly in emergencies, but the volume of such need at present could be greatly reduced, and we cannot continue to be satisfied simply with distributions from the wealthy to the poor, when benefits might be much more substantially and healthily shared through co-operative planning and effort. Dumped surpluses of food in America and hunger in other parts of the world breed an infection of bitterness. This we cannot continue to countenance and at the same time build healthy international relationships.

Nevertheless, it is with a sense of deep gratitude that one is able to report the responsiveness of Americans to critical overseas needs after the war. Money poured into our Committee. In relation to our size, it was phenomenal. In the first six months of 1946 we received as much as had been received in all of 1945.

Large support for certain of the overseas programs came from groups in this country whose national origin or ancestry went back to the country being served. German-Americans supported the bulk of the German program; Japanese-Americans, most of whom had been evacuated during the war and had themselves suffered critical loss and hardship, contributed a high percentage of the funds given specifically for Japan; two groups of Finnish extraction, with differing political slants, raised most of the funds for Finland.

In 1946–1947 we were sending large amounts of food, clothing, and medical supplies into most of the war-devastated countries of Europe. In some of these countries we were picking up threads of fellowship formed in the days of AFSC relief missions in the wake of World War I. In other regions the fellowship was new. Finland was new, and the associations there were heart-warming. Hungary was new to us, and Quaker food and clothing distributions bore fruit of warm friendships between Committee representatives and Hungarians of all shades of political belief. One couple returning from this mission told us, "As in so many countries now, group fears group . . . and all fear the future. Our presence — after they were convinced that we had no political ax to grind — had a healing, releasing effect."

Germany, Austria, Poland, France — in these countries, memories of World War I relief were still vivid. Into each we sent supplies and small units of workers. The problems in Germany were particularly difficult, due to that country's division into four zones of occupation, so it was no longer an economic unit — this with cities smashed and the economy in ruins. Then, to greater confound confusion, there were the displaced persons, and ten to twelve million expellees pouring in from eastern Europe.

In Germany, Poland, and France, our co-operation with Friends Relief Service (British) was especially close.*

The visible rehabilitation which is taking place in those being

---

* For an account of the work of Friends Relief Service, see *Quaker Relief*, by Roger C. Wilson (Allen and Unwin Limited, 1952).

reached is the ray of hope in any postwar emergency relief operation. And this rehabilitation occurs not only in those being fed and clothed, but in the many who come in to assist, to be of help even while they are among the suffering. As one worker wrote of a distribution in Marseille:

> The clothes and shoes that are distributed, much needed though they may be, are not the most important services given here. The twenty or so women who work on the clothes are not so many factory hands. As you look at their faces, you will see on many the marks of suffering. Each one has had her own troubles and difficulties to face, and all have found this work a haven of refuge. Some have nowhere else to go for support, and others come for a time and then pass on strengthened and refreshed. Here they are, young and old, busily engaged in work that will meet the need of others; their own burdens grow less as they help their fellows. There is a sense of peace about them now. "We are like a big family," says Madame B. "When one of us has good news we are all happy and laugh together, and when there is bad news then we all share the sorrow; each one helps the other."

This is the very heart of what our Committee tries to accomplish: this kind of personal relationship which grows out of some of our services, the coming together of bewildered people in warmth of affection, the links formed, too, in the act of contributing pennies or dollars or shoes, or time and talents, the vast net enveloping the earth, woven often of the smallest of threads, but woven for all time. It is a saving net in times of emergency; in ordinary times it has sturdy, workaday functions. It imparts a peculiar feeling of security to those who have become part of it — not necessarily security against physical cataclysm, but what might be called the security of the fellowship of the weavers.

Not only have we carried aid to both sides in terms of the battle lines of the Second World War, but we have also made every effort to transform the "iron curtain" into a bridge. In Poland, Anglo-American Quaker services of major proportions extending over a period of several years were fruitful in terms of both material relief and relationships formed. The same was true in Hungary for the time we were there. In both Poland and Hungary, however, as the Communists gained in power, many of those who had been employed or self-employed became the unfortunates, while others, who had been on relief, were now better taken care of. In both countries we were told that, much as they appreciated what we had done, they were now happy to say that our services were no longer required because the people we had been helping were on their own feet, due to successful rehabilitation measures of the new government. This was largely true; however, what we knew to be equally true was that many of those who had been able to support themselves before, especially as property owners or public officials, were now out of favor, must keep in hiding, and must of all things not find themselves in association with Westerners. More than once we knew that tragedy of this kind was going on, yet were helpless to assist because our very presence would have endangered the security of those needing help. When our workers left Budapest, where they had had most happy relations with the people of Hungary, they were seen off at the railway station by large numbers of persons whose honest expression of affection was accompanied by tears at seeing the departure of the last vestige of nongovernmental connection between themselves and the West. The same was more or less true in Poland. To be present and watch the curtain go down is a heart-rending experience.

We have made some efforts in relation to the USSR directly. One day not long after Friends Service Council and AFSC had received the 1947 Nobel Peace Prize, two representatives of Amtorg, the Russian trading corporation, came to see me, saying they had come to receive our gift. At first I was somewhat puzzled. Then it dawned on me that, not many days before, I had announced in a speech at Yale University that we were going to use the $20,000 which was our share of the Prize to attempt to improve Soviet-American relations. As these visitors were talking, I wondered whether their superiors had inferred from that statement that we planned to give these funds to the USSR. This had not entered our calculations.

However, there was another possibility, which was also known to Amtorg. For some time we had been seeking a way in which the people of the United States could send a token of friendship to the people of the USSR. We had been interested in the fact that as word of this got around small contributions came from all over the country, mostly in one- and five-dollar bills, as an expression of the American people's desire to see something done to bridge the gulf between them and the Russian people. We had been trying to find an effective way to use these gifts.

Now I asked the Amtorg representatives what material needs in the Soviet Union they were unable to meet. They said that tuberculosis was the greatest health scourge in the USSR, that they were conquering it but were hindered because of lack of the new drug, streptomycin. They had doctors who knew how to administer the drug, but were not able to purchase it in the United States, the only country in which it was available in considerable quantities.

Shortly after this, our Committee decided to take the contributions earmarked for American-Soviet friendship, amounting to about $25,000 in all, to purchase streptomycin for distribution in the USSR through the Russian Red Cross. Happily, the plan was approved by our own government and accepted by the government of the USSR. The streptomycin was sent, and we received a cable of appreciation from the Russian Red Cross, informing us that the gift had been distributed among children in tuberculosis hospitals and sanatoria.

In addition to this, some of our postwar relief shipments to Germany included food and medical supplies for the Russian zone, distributed through the International Red Cross.

Thus here and there, as way opens, and of necessity in small measure, the American Friends Service Committee continues to try to utilize food, clothing, medical supplies, and personnel at its dis-

posal, to dissipate fear and mistrust, after the manner of those acts
in history which seem to us most redemptive, and in the knowledge
of an instruction written long ago: "Perfect love casteth out fear."

But though the Service Committee has made its name, if I may
use that phrase, in works of relief, it has no love for the necessity
of relief. It is always all eagerness to get on with the task, to get
beyond relief into the more far-reaching openings for reconstruction and rehabilitation. In most regions despoiled by war, ways to
make a living have been removed from the picture. Fishermen no
longer have boats, factory workers no longer have factories to work
in, small business owners have lost their businesses, artisans have
lost their tools, doctors their instruments, truckmen their trucks,
farmers' fields are still planted with live mines (in Normandy
alone at the close of the war, some 50,000 acres were sown with
live mines). And the housewives have no homes for all the productive things they used to do there.

For those confronting the task on the first day of "freedom," it
looks simply insurmountable. Yet a start has to be made.

It may seem incredible that in face of such overwhelming destruction as World War II left across Europe, a small organization
like ours would think it could do anything about rebuilding. Here,
as always, if our efforts are to be judged by quantity, it is true we
can do practically nothing. But there is an interesting further fact
which we have discovered. As everyone knows, most European
countries have the skills, the knowledge, the ability, to do the job
themselves. The wherewithal may be lacking, but in that case why
not just send the wherewithal? In large measure, this is the correct
answer, but it isn't quite the whole story.

For instance, take Italy. Two members of our Committee went
to Italy in 1944 to serve with the Intergovernmental Committee on
Refugees. Members of the Friends Ambulance Unit — a group of
British Friends — were also working there.

In the course of their services, the two Friends' groups learned that transportation was one of the greatest needs in the mountain villages of Chieti Province in east central Italy, where destruction had been nearly complete. In many cases, the homes of the villagers — what was left of their homes — were high up the mountainside, and the only sources of tile and mortar needed to rebuild them were down in the valley. There was no means of transport to bring materials to these remote places. Also no money.

During the latter half of 1945, the two Friends' groups co-operated in a transport service in this province, starting with five men and three trucks. The unit grew to a dozen men, with six trucks. In five small villages, a plan was worked out.

Firewood was available in the hills for the cutting. Villagers cut it for sale. Quaker trucks began hauling it down to the kilns thirty miles away, there exchanging it for tile and mortar, which they brought back up the mountain to the little villages. With this help, between two and three hundred families were able to provide themselves shelter before winter set in. This meant about one thousand persons. Is there any use in doing such a small job in the midst of vast need?

Most persons would answer Yes, if only for the sake of the one thousand persons. But the significance of the small start was greater. Once a family had made a beginning, there was release of creative energies hitherto deadened by hopelessness. This was contagious. Our workers found that the upsurge of morale in these villages was out of all proportion to the size of the unit's actual contribution. By January, 1946, the service had proved so beneficial that other forces rushed to its support. UNRRA, impressed by the villagers' enthusiastic work, offered two hundred trucks, plus gasoline and oil, and became the over-all supervising agency. Most regions did not have firewood to sell. Various other arrangements were substituted. Ways were found to make more use of available Italian government aid. Earlier, this government had passed legislation designed to help people rebuild their homes, but low morale and lack of confidence in anyone's integrity had resulted in small response.

Now Italian volunteers and Italian paid workers joined augmented transport units of men from Friends Ambulance Unit, *Service Civil International,* Brethren Service Committee, and American Friends Service Committee. By the fall of 1946, seven thousand rooms were reported rebuilt in one month. This was hardly a small project. And it had not been envisioned by any one of the organizations participating, but had simply grown from the observations of several young men who thought it might be a good thing to undertake. By 1947 the whole enterprise was largely in the hands of CASAS, a semiofficial Italian welfare organization formed with the co-operation of interested agencies, chiefly UNRRA, and we had worked ourselves out of a job, which is what we like to do.

A second type of rehabilitation effort on the part of AFSC was initiated in Finland. Not only had Finland undergone destruction within her borders, but she had lost a valuable piece of territory to Russia, and had been called upon to receive thousands of people who had formerly lived in Karelia and who left it when it was taken over by the USSR.

We had done some relief work in this situation, but our representatives felt that a further contribution could be made if a skilled and imaginative person were sent to survey Finnish resources. We were able to secure Arthur E. Morgan, formerly president of Antioch College and chairman of the Tennessee Valley Authority, a conservation engineer and a man with a high quality of imagination and a real dedication to service, to go on this mission, accompanied by his wife, Lucy Morgan. Although he was not able to stay in Finland to supervise the undertakings which he proposed, and most of them were carried out, if at all, by the Finns themselves rather than by AFSC, I think we look upon this venture as one of our more effective services to Finland. Especially because of Arthur Morgan's world-wide reputation for his work with TVA, he was warmly received by the Finnish government and citizens alike. He studied small businesses in Finland, as well as undeveloped potentials, and made recommendations as to how production costs could be reduced and standards raised to meet the stiff competition of world markets. To the Finnish people's courage, capacity for endurance, and willingness to work hard, he added his wide knowledge and experience in industrial processes as he had worked them out in his own business and in studies at Antioch College.

Perhaps a little further removed from primary relief and rehabilitation measures is the project which has now come to be known as School Affiliation. There had been a good deal of exchange of letters and gifts between individual children of various countries, but to my knowledge no scheme of well-rounded affiliation of whole schools in the United States with similar schools abroad had yet been worked out.

Then one day Alfred E. Stearns, formerly headmaster of Phillips Academy at Andover, Massachusetts, came to my office to talk of his dream of close affiliation between schools. He had started to sponsor such a plan, but found it was beyond his capacity to finance or manage. After considerable investigation, our Committee decided that this could be an extremely valuable enterprise, and that if Dr. Stearns was prepared to give some counsel and assistance AFSC would assume responsibility for the development.

At first, when schools in this country began to correspond with schools in France and Germany,* and to inquire as to needs, the answers came back: "pencils, crayons, books, clothing, food." But as time went on, the exchange began to include art work and ideas. Friendships grew. Finally, pupils and teachers themselves began to exchange places for one-year periods. More recently, a summer work camp in Europe has been the means of bringing together pupils from affiliated schools in various countries.

The entire project has required a great deal of careful supervision and stimulation; but especially as it has become a means for establishing living personal contacts, as in the exchange of pupils and teachers, it has resulted in an enrichment of the whole school life.

* The project is especially alive in France and Germany; it includes a few schools in Holland, Italy, and Japan.

One other example of services beyond the direct relief stage should be cited. As soon as the war was over, our Committee felt a particular urgency to establish services in Germany which would enable German and American personnel to work together on community rehabilitation. Probably no country was more ravaged in spirit: there was not only the suffering of war and military defeat, there had been also evil's fanatic possession of Hitler and of a large part of the soul of the German people. We of America were not without our responsibility, too, in this holocaust. In a way more profound than can be articulated, what had occurred in Germany — the very depth of the degradation of man — was the work of us all, and we felt that co-operation growing out of this recognition was the only way to healing.

We found an expression for this impulse through establishment of what we called neighborhood centers. As one of our workers described the project: "In Germany's destroyed cities, let neighborhood centers spring up, gifts of America physically, but German and American in planning and operation. Let these centers be places of rich human relationship where all classes and groups meet and work together, a neighborhood Tree of Life in the reconstruction and rebirth of Germany."

The first news of actual construction of these centers to reach the American public was a dispatch from Dana Adams Schmidt to the *New York Times*:

Frankfurt-on-the-Main, Germany, February 13 [1947]. So far as anyone knows, nothing very nice has happened for a long time to the people who live four and five to a room in the half-smashed houses on the Rohmerplatz in Bockenheim.

But early this morning three young members of the American Friends Service Committee and five young Germans broke ground in a corner of the Rohmerplatz for a neighborhood center designed to help them.

Because their factories have no coal, many of the workmen in this part of Frankfurt's "Lower East Side" have not worked for a month. Most of them were still in bed keeping warm

when Richmond Miller, Jr., of Philadelphia and Lewis Berg
of Bremen, Indiana, began breaking the frozen earth today
with a pneumatic drill. The five Germans recruited from an
air-raid shelter devoted to homeless juveniles followed up with
shovels.

To the puzzled crowd that soon gathered, Mrs. Nancy
Good, of New York, said this was to be the first of five centers the Quakers would set up here, in Darmstadt, Cologne,
Freiburg, and the British sector of Berlin. She added that barracks from Sweden had arrived and none would be deprived
of precious space.

The idea is to help the people to help themselves and one
another. There will be equipment to repair shoes, including
leather, washing machines with soap, sewing kits, and a warm
place for people of the neighborhood, especially young people,
to meet.

In the work of constructing this center, youth groups of all
political and religious persuasions were brought together. This in
itself was an inestimable contribution in a situation where fear
and mistrust between groups were the rule.

Elmore McKee, on our staff in Germany at the time, sent a
story of the opening:

> Fair weather, the songs of children, and a rousing welcome
> from the neighborhood characterized the "Frankfurt opening."
> Over 1500 persons — mostly children and young people —
> streamed into the Rohmerplatz, thronged the large hall of
> the new homelike Quaker barracks for the official celebration,
> then took over the improvised stage and outdoor seats for a
> song-fest that lasted long into the night.
>
> Over the doorway were German words saying: "This is your
> neighborhood home; use it; enjoy it; give to it your best." In
> prophecy of what this "supplement to their home" was going
> to mean to the bombed-out people of the workers' district of
> Bockenheim, the people took their new *"Nachbarschaftsheim"*
> to their hearts on opening day. . . .
>
> In the large hall, every seat and foot of standing room taken,
> the Neighborhood House was formally opened at 5.30 P.M. with
> songs by neighborhood children, and speeches. In the audience

were official representatives of Frankfurt University and the University of Stockholm, of the Catholic and Protestant Churches, and of OMGUS * Youth Division.

The official part of the program was over by seven. . . . There was handshaking, inspection, and much photography. Then some refreshments before the happy spontaneity of the second half. . . . Outside a temporary stage had been built. Instrumental music, group dancing, and songs by a neighborhood choir were part of the evening program that took its natural course for several hours. The audience sang too. It was eleven when the last people left.

All is not gala celebration in such a center, but the vision out of which these neighborhood centers were conceived and launched was a good, sound vision. They have released deep veins of trust and co-operation, they have afforded inestimable practical helps to people bombed out of homes and facilities. In 1947, to have warm rooms, facilities and materials for shoe and clothing repair, laundry, and carpentry, meant something to the people of Frankfurt which we of America cannot comprehend. And to have these within friendly walls, along with playrooms for children, and music and books, often brought deep healing for the spirit.

Mittelhof, the neighborhood center in Berlin, housed in what used to be a private estate, has had a peculiar opportunity to see the fruits of this kind of effort ripening in the midst of acute strife. Alice Shaffer of our Committee, writing from Mittelhof during the blockade in 1948, reported:

One cannot say that Mittelhof life is other than vigorous, for there are few places where more human needs and strivings are kept in such constant movement before one's eyes and in one's spirit day and night, every day of the week. Part of it is Berlin itself, part is due to the release it seems to give those who come and who need to feel we are here, not in theory but in practice; it is one of the finest ways to share by example the essence of what we call democracy and to create an atmosphere where such can develop and thrive. . . .

* Office of Military Government for Germany (U.S.).

German staff members usually feel lost when they first begin work here because of such decentralized responsibility and different atmosphere. Guests notice it; before they are here a day they come up and say, "What an atmosphere you have here, that we haven't seen or felt for years."

People here, in all Germany, but I can speak especially for Berlin, are in a pretty neurotic state in addition to their tired condition, general uncertainty, and hopelessness. They are so unaware of things outside of themselves or Berlin — especially of the world beyond, and therefore they do not see themselves in relation to it. I don't mean there are not exceptions. . . .

It is hard for the young people to think of individuals first and not identify people with a party and therefore react first politically. No matter what we are discussing, if the names of persons are being suggested, the next comment is, "He's SPD" or "SED" or something else. . . . As an American, one is more apt to react to a person as a person; they insist you can't do that and only foolish Americans would suggest it.

This letter goes on to mention the friendly co-operation of occupation personnel, the frequent visits of two young Catholic social workers from the Russian sector of Berlin, the busy activity of the sewing rooms, shoe shop, carpenter shop, children's rooms, library, office, and kitchen; and the inconveniences of the blockade. In closing, it stresses the gratifying response of youth to the methods of democracy as practiced in the center.

Mittelhof and Frankfurt are examples. I might as well have chosen Freiburg, Darmstadt, Cologne, or St. Nazaire in France, or Toyama Heights in Japan, or any one of several others. Eleven neighborhood centers in Europe, three in Japan, and one in Israel, now represent this type of effort, two of ten in Germany being sponsored by Friends Service Council (British). Also, of our regular International Centers, those in Calcutta, India, and Dacca, East Pakistan, fulfill many of the functions of a neighborhood center. Naturally, services change with changing conditions, and vary in accordance with local needs. The centers near universities specialize in services to students; where there are crowds of unabsorbed refugees, these are the focus. In each instance, the immediate community supplies the problems, and the aim is co-operation of all elements of the local population in the creation of a new society based on goals common to all.

This is enough mention of rehabilitation projects in Europe to suggest the kind of approach the Service Committee makes. What interests me especially is the freshness of pattern, the creative spirit which is often engendered in the midst of utmost desolation of rubble and hopelessness.

Social workers, church groups, many agencies and individuals are continuously at work in an effort to reconstruct society. But as long as the already established patterns hold together to a certain extent, changes are most difficult to effect. When, however, a catastrophe such as the last war in Europe breaks down the whole structure of society, people are often willing to begin new practices and enter into new relationships which would have been almost unthinkable to them under former circumstances.

Early Christians envisioned a society in which respect for the individual was not contingent upon whether he was Greek or Jew, rich or poor, educated or uneducated. But most churches find the full application of this gospel very difficult. All too often the church becomes the institution of the privileged.

In time of catastrophe, however, public officials, clergy, intellectuals, management and workers in industry, often can be drawn together in the common good. It is in these efforts that one begins to see the kind of fellowship which could prevail within the very differences that characterize our society. For when the spirits of men and women are thus kindled around a common effort at self-help and co-operation, they come into a new free appreciation of the loving Spirit in our midst, and the society that springs up is the one for which we all yearn.

Must we have the destruction of war or other disaster to bring this about?

How can we sufficiently open our hearts and minds to make it a reality, here, now, in whatever form of society we find ourselves?

7. *Relief and Rehabilitation: Asia*

CHINA

THE Friends Ambulance Unit which sprang into colorful and dashing existence with the coming of the Second World War has been looked upon with some question by both English and American Friends. It was not an official organ of the Society of Friends; for that matter, neither is the American Friends Service Committee. Both organizations have been independent of any legal denominational connection.

During the First World War a Friends Ambulance Unit (British) had done yeoman service, but a good deal of its work had been carried on in such close contact with armies that it had seemed to some Friends an inadequate demonstration of pacifists' unwillingness to participate in war and of their desire to associate with only the constructive. The FAU which came into being in England in 1939 was in the same tradition. Those who watched its career first in Finland and Norway, then in England and the Middle East, recognized that it had vitality, idealism, dedication, and unusual skill. An organization of high-spirited young men, it pioneered in opening up opportunities for service which more cautious official bodies had not even dreamed of. Its financial support in those early days came chiefly from individual Friends in England, but from the beginning the control of the Unit was largely in the hands of the young men who were its members.

For years the devastating war of Japan against China had been going on, and it was natural that, as the Nazi occupation of most of

Europe made service there impossible, FAU members should turn their attention to ravaged and disease-ridden China. There was no difficulty in getting volunteers for this most difficult service. The young British conscientious objectors, and later the Americans, wanted nothing so much as to demonstrate their willingness to run risks for their convictions, comparable to the risks of men in the armed forces. But the problem of financing a unit in China was something else again.

It was with this aspect of the undertaking particularly in mind that Christopher Sharman, a young Englishman and a member of FAU, paid a visit to our office in Philadelphia in February, 1941. He hoped we would participate in terms of personnel, but especially that we would find it possible to give financial assistance.

Our Committee had had little experience in China. It was a long way off, and there were what seemed to us immense obligations already on our shoulders. Yet the intense need was there, and the voices of young men wanting to take part in such an enterprise were full of vitality. After extensive consultations it seemed quite clear to us that we should enter into this venture with the Friends Ambulance Unit.

A little later, Dr. Robert B. McClure, of Toronto, who was going out to China to direct the work, visited our offices on behalf of the enterprise. This young surgeon, born in China of missionary parents and educated in Canada, had earned his expenses through college by working as a stevedore and a barber, and had returned to China to establish a hospital of his own. Then the war had interrupted. His enthusiasm, his medical skill, and his wide knowledge of China, greatly strengthened our confidence in the mission.

Meanwhile, under the leadership of Henry R. Luce of the *Time-Life-Fortune* group of magazines, Americans who were traditionally and currently interested in China were joining forces under the banner of "United China Relief." Our Committee was invited to participate, and having been assured that it was not to be a "hate Japan" campaign we decided to become a member agency. In this connection, Christopher Sharman gave a considerable amount of time to interpreting the FAU to communities throughout the United States. The results of the over-all campaign in this as well as succeeding years were so satisfactory that UCR funds became one of the chief sources of income for FAU in China.

The pioneer work of initiating the China branch of FAU, which was known as the China Convoy, had been done by British members of FAU before any of our men entered the field. Because the great seaboard gateways to China were closed by the Japanese, the most urgent need in the beginning was to get supplies to certain of the hard-pressed inland Chinese cities, such as Chungking, Chengtu, Kweiyang, and Kunming. Medical supplies, as well as doctors and nurses, were desperately needed. The only open land route into this part of China from the outside world was through Rangoon, Burma. From Rangoon supplies could be shipped by rail as far as Lashio; but from there on they must be hauled over the twisting, hazardous mountain route known as the Burma Road. This transportation job was the first one taken on by the China Convoy.

In China, four organizations were already in the field collecting and distributing imported medical supplies; these were the Army Medical Administration (Chinese), the Chinese Red Cross, the National Health Administration (Chinese), and the International Red Cross Committee, which changed its name to International Relief Committee. FAU became closely affiliated with the latter three. Particularly its trucks and its five doctors, in these early days, were eagerly welcomed and used to the utmost.

It was in July, 1941, that the first FAU men arrived in Rangoon. I shall not attempt to tell the story of the opening chapter of this China work. Suffice it to say that the experience was in part a ragged and unhappy one. As yet there was little conception of what the major undertaking of the Unit should be, or just how the program could ever achieve organization and unity. The enthusiasm of the young conscientious objector was now up against sprawling chaos and illimitable suffering. It is to the great credit of the Unit that it did find its own inner balance and organization through extraordinary expenditure of physical and nervous energy, even while it was carrying out hazardous services under bewildering conditions.

Christopher Sharman, who had gone from the United States to China for about five months' service, returned to assist again in the raising of funds, and he gave us a most vivid picture of the prodigious job of transportation which the FAU had been doing — the Burma Road infested with thieves, bandits, bogus and legitimate tax collectors, with everything except filling stations, garages, and mechanics. The road was relatively new, but it was said that already 1500 trucks had gone off it into the abyss, and hundreds of others were simply standing along the way because they had broken down and needed unobtainable repairs. The steep grade and rough surface called for second or low gear most of the way.

There came a night on which there was a last loading of trucks on the docks at Rangoon as the Japanese closed in, and then for a few weeks the task was to rush supplies from Lashio into China, and to retreat with the Chinese army. Some members of the Friends Unit ended up in China, others took part in a grim jungle retreat into India.*

By the summer of 1942, the fall of Burma had made the Burma Road only a memory. The experience had left a deep mark on Unit members. They were charged with an intense and increasing sense of mission, but they had taken part in a grueling retreat, they had lost eleven of their precious trucks, and liquid fuel from now on would be practically unobtainable. Whatever future the work had lay within China. The men who had retreated into India began flying back over the hump to Kunming, and by late autumn the Unit was largely reassembled in China. Gradually its work for

* The story of the China Convoy is dramatically related by A. Tegla Davies, a member of FAU, in his book, *Friends Ambulance Unit*, Allen and Unwin Limited, 1947. My own necessarily sketchy outline draws on his account as well as on the voluminous correspondence which passed between our Philadelphia office and "the China boys."

the future was laid out, in two distinct sections: Transport, and Mobile Medical Teams.

Now the long pull was beginning. Now the Unit was toughening in its power to "take it." Two casualties had to be accepted. Typhus was the villain. John Briggs and Douglas Hardy, both Englishmen, died within two days of each other. Several Unit members suffered injuries. We received this report:

Tom and Ron had broken down two miles from a village and walked there to get their evening meal. On their way back to the truck after supper they were accosted by six men armed with what they took to be sticks. They brushed them aside, and were walking on towards the truck when something made Tom look around, just in time to duck and put up his arm to protect his head from a terrific downward blow. The weapons were swords, and the blow went halfway through Tom's forearm. As defensive weapons they had only their water-bottles, but they wielded these to such good effect that the bandits eventually ran off. Tom got a nasty cut on his other arm, and Ron had a pretty deep gash in his left arm. They had to spend the night in a roadmender's hut, and got a lift to Pichieh the next day. Tom's wound was right through the ulna and had cut two arteries, so he lost a good deal of blood; it was a good thing they had had first-aid training and knew their pressure points.

But, even as in the armed services, the real trial for the spirits of the men lay not so much in danger and death as in the long delays and frustrations, the irritating shortages, the days when they wondered what they were doing out there.

The China Convoy of FAU was not a soft berth. This was one of the facts I tried to bring home to United States government officials during the months of our effort to obtain permission for American conscientious objectors who were in Civilian Public Service camps to serve with FAU in China or in other foreign countries.

All through the early part of 1942 I had frequent conferences with the State Department on behalf of such permission. In March, Sumner Welles, Undersecretary of State, told me that because the problems of transportation to England were so acute and because China had been virtually cut off by the fall of Rangoon the Department did not feel it was feasible to grant us permission to send relief units to either of these countries. We had also suggested using CPS men in Mexico, in some of our Committee's work projects there. But the State Department seemed to feel that the sight of conscientious objectors from the United States might play into the hands of Nazi propagandists in Latin America.

By midsummer, however, these negotiations with the State Department took a somewhat more hopeful turn. In July I was able to present to Sumner Welles a letter from the Chinese ambassador, Hu Shih, urging an increase of the Friends Ambulance Unit by sending some Americans, and letters from Lauchlin Currie and Owen Lattimore, both of whom knew a great deal about China, urging such support from America. This interview happened to come at a time when it was obvious that we as a government were most anxious to support China, and Sumner Welles said that the letters were more hopeful than anything that had been presented previously, and he would let me know by the end of that week. But there was no favorable action.

Pressing the matter again in the fall, I learned from Sumner Welles that part of the trouble was a matter of divided authority. The State Department felt it had no authority over drafted men, and Civilian Public Service men were drafted. Yet they were not in the army; therefore the army could not release them for service abroad. I asked whether, if the Surgeon General of the army would endorse a sanitation unit for China, the State Department would approve their going. Sumner Welles replied that if the Surgeon General would write a letter to the State Department saying he considered such a unit helpful to the war effort, the State Department would approve.

This presented another problem. Were we as pacifists to accept terms which required the work of the unit to be "helpful to the war effort"? At the end of October, 1942, I wrote in my journal that while Sumner Welles's attitude had been consistently friendly I felt that our average in accomplishment with him in the last few months was very low.

At about this time we received a somewhat pressing invitation from British Friends to send at least seventy Americans to join the FAU in China. Our Foreign Service Executive Committee, and also our Board of Directors, felt that because of China's necessity and British Friends' great desire to have our participation we should not stand on phraseology and refuse to go because the State Department used the phrase "helpful to the war effort." It was therefore decided that we should proceed along the lines indicated by Sumner Welles.

Toward the end of November, when we had had no success in getting the suggested letter from the Surgeon General, I told Lauchlin Currie of our desire to increase the Friends Ambulance Unit staff by about seventy persons, drawn mostly from our CPS camps. He felt that the best way to get permission was to obtain a letter from the Chinese embassy saying that such a unit would be welcome in China, then to write President Roosevelt, sending him the ambassador's letter, explaining that the State Department would be willing to have the men go, provided the army opened the way, and asking him to request the army to give the appropriate notice. Lauchlin Currie was prepared to discuss the matter with the President and to support it with the War Department if necessary.

Meanwhile the President was setting up within the State Department the Office of Foreign Relief and Rehabilitation Operations, with Governor Lehman of New York as its director. Late in December I had an interview with Governor Lehman, and found him most interested though he was not fully informed on the problems involved. I told him that British Friends had asked for seventy Americans in the China Convoy, but that only seven had thus far been able to go, with seven others preparing to join them presently. These were men who for one reason or another did not come under the jurisdiction of the draft. I also pointed out that about 5000 men were at that time in CPS camps, 1500 of them in Friends' camps, some of them doing work of genuine importance, but innumerable others languishing in relative inaction, completely frustrated in their desire to serve their country and humanity.

In mid-January, 1943, Rufus Jones and I had an interview with Secretary of War Stimson, who was well acquainted with Friends' work and felt completely convinced that the men in CPS camps should be used in relief and reconstruction work. In fact, he thought it the most appropriate service they could render. We told him he might expect to hear from the President as to the possibility of the army's sanctioning the project, and he agreed to co-operate.

Meanwhile, the Chinese ambassador had written a letter warmly welcoming the larger group of American FAU members to China, and I forwarded this with a letter of my own to President Roosevelt. On February 16 I received the President's reply, as follows:

February 13, 1943

My Dear Mr. Pickett

I am conscious of the benevolent work of the Society of Friends and have read with interest the narrative report on the activities of the Friends Ambulance Unit in China. I approve your request to obtain seventy volunteers from civilian work camps for medical relief, sanitation, and public-health work in China, and I have taken the matter up with the Secretary of War. He tells me that he has discussed this matter with you and that at his request the National Director of Selective Service has agreed to cooperate with you in securing the volunteers you desire and in procuring passports for them.

It is understood that these volunteers will function under the auspices of the Society of Friends and will not, while so engaged, become an active part of the armed forces of the United States or other nation.

I suggest that you contact the Director of Selective Service, General Lewis B. Hershey, for further information and assistance in your undertaking.

Very sincerely yours,
Franklin D. Roosevelt

This, surely, was the turning point. It looked like clear sailing, and we proceeded to choose eight men out of those who had volunteered, to spearhead the larger flow of American personnel to China. They were to go as soon as transportation was available. Also, the AFSC Board of Directors now approved a six-months' training program for two hundred men (one hundred at a time) for overseas work, and appropriated $100,000 for this purpose. The training school was to be at Earlham College in Indiana. It seemed as though the eager desire of CPS men to serve might at last be fulfilled in a way somewhat commensurate with their abilities and spirit.

In June, when the first eight recruits were en route to China and the training course at Earlham was opening, a Southern Congressman introduced a rider to an army appropriations bill which would prevent CPS men's leaving the country for any purpose. This seemed such manifestly cruel and punitive legislation that at first we did not expect it to pass. But we miscalculated public temper. Much of the war fever of hatred was turned vigorously against young men to whom Selective Service had granted conscientious-objector status. The bill with its rider passed in spite of all that could be done by the opposition. Seven of the eight men en route to China had to be notified when they reached South Africa to return as soon as possible to the United States and to Civilian Public Service camps. Because the eighth man was not within Selective Service jurisdiction, he was free to continue on his way.

However, it never pays to let one's plans be too much controlled by hasty and ill-advised legislation, and we went forward with our training program, hoping that eventually — even after the men were released from their obligation under the draft, if not before — those who were prepared could proceed to China. This did actually happen in a number of cases. But as long as the war lasted no CPS man was able to serve in the China Convoy.

Meanwhile, in anticipation of our sending a considerable number of men to China, John Rich, a member of our staff and administratively responsible for AFSC work in China at that time, had gone to see the FAU in action and to help plan for our more active participation. This step in itself seems to have brought a good deal of encouragement to the China Convoy, which was having a hard go of it and felt terribly cut off from England and America. John Rich spent several months not only visiting the FAU in China and India, but participating in the work and entering with great enthusiasm and deep sympathy into the life of the men in the field. It was largely through his encouragement that we assumed rather heavy responsibilities in India shortly after his return. Also, though it was not possible to send drafted men to the China Convoy, we did succeed in finding some men who were free to go. By the end of 1943, out of the Convoy's total membership of about a hundred, there were seventeen Americans, two Canadians, and about twelve Chinese.

Five international mobile medical teams were formed by the Convoy during this period, most of their work being in co-operation with the Chinese Red Cross or the British Red Cross. A typical unit consisted of about eight persons: two doctors, two nurses, an administrator, a laboratory technician, a quartermaster, and a handyman. Such units tried to travel light, but at best laboratory equipment was a difficult load in a terrain so rough that often trucks had to be abandoned in favor of mule caravans. They followed close behind battle lines; they became small self-contained units, mixtures of British, United States, Canadian, and Chinese personnel, functioning in the remotest interior, sometimes cut off from communication with the outside world for weeks or even months.

Our operating theatre was an old cabin [wrote one Unit member], where a log fire burned in one corner and beside it a Yunnanese villager squatted on his heels, smoked his pipe, poked an occasional stick into the embers, and carried on a conversation with the old woman who owned the place. Nearby lay two patients on the straw, one with a dressed head-wound and the other our abdominal man. A soldier brought hot water and washed the place around the wound, and as soon as the patient was lifted on the table Doris and Margaret began the anaesthetic. Quentin and John donned their gowns and masks, and in the light of torches and a blazing fire it began. Curious faces peered from outside while the rain rattled on the leaves of nearby trees and splattered on the roof. One is conscious only of two pairs of hands moving methodically in the bright ring of torchlight, of instruments appearing and disappearing, the click of haemostats, and the snip of scissors. Slowly the great gap in the stomach begins to close as the needle works its way along the edges of the flesh. Quentin says the last words of the performance, "That does it," and everyone loosens up; now we don't have to hurry so much.

It will be noted that by this time women had been admitted to the China Convoy. The men had struggled over this problem; in the beginning they had liked being a man's organization, and had feared the admission of women would tone down the vitality of the way FAU functioned in China. But there were jobs for which they definitely needed women, and at last the barriers fell. Throughout the China experience, women members of the Unit carried their part with as much strength and hardihood as the men, and by their performance wiped out any preconceived ideas as to women's lesser power to meet rugged physical demands.

Sometimes a deserted temple was the scene of a unit's emergency work. One report informed us that after the death of a certain Chinese patient an autopsy seemed called for. The unit was sufficiently acquainted with the superstitions of the immediate community to realize that an autopsy might well be misunderstood by the villagers.

Therefore [the report continued], the body was taken to an unused temple, high on a knob of a hill, and after the local bedtime, we, internees, nurses, and doctors, found our way up tiny steep steps built for women with bound feet, inside the courtyard wall and into the small one-room temple. There we lighted candles on the altar; even lit a stick of temple-incense to mask the odor; held flashlights over the doctor's shoulder, and bent closely over the body on the floor. The midline incision was made and the repugnant odor of death permeated the room. It was considered safe to open the door and, upon doing so, a flood of fresh air and full moonlight was let in. White-gowned and masked figures watched while the doctor examined the internal organs for signs of abnormalities. In the shadows of the walls stood grotesque stone gods. . . .

Fiscal problems became nearly insurmountable. The persistent upward spiral of inflation in China in these years carried expenses almost out of sight. The following prices, quoted in terms of American currency in the late summer of 1943, give an idea of the cost of upkeep on a truck:

1 set piston rings	$500.00
1 headlight bulb	10.00
1 spark plug	45.00
1 pound grease	25.00
1 gallon gas	25.00
1 nail, 2½″	.10

With spare parts practically nonexistent and, when they were at last located, prohibitively expensive, it was no wonder that the mere task of keeping a truck on the road turned out to be an almost monumental undertaking. The spirit of experimentation spread throughout the Unit. Sometimes one good truck could be made out of several wrecks.

The longest trip made by FAU trucks in an effort to keep the mobile medical units in operation was to the oil wells in Suchow on the edge of the Gobi Desert. This was a journey of more than three thousand miles, and it took between three and four months. In Tegla Davies' words, "[Leaving Kweiyang, the convoy was] to deliver medical supplies to Paoki and Sian and as far north as Lanchow, and then drive on along the Old Silk Road, past the Great Wall, across the fringes of the Gobi Desert, and to the oasis city of

Suchow." Lennig Sweet, visiting the China Convoy for United China Relief, wrote enthusiastically of this transport work:

> Three trucks were soon leaving on a three-months trip to bring low-grade gasoline back from the Northwest. They carry 22 drums to the truck and use half the load on the trip, but the remainder is enough to keep 15 charcoal burners * running 6 months by giving them just enough for a shot in the arm (or rather, carburetor) to get over the hills. . . . Life on the road is really rugged. Drivers sleep on their loads and live off the country on trips lasting from five days to a month. Nursing the old charcoal burners over the hills (in one place 72 hairpin turns) is no easy job.

By the time the war ended in 1945, the China Convoy had about 140 members. A report as of the beginning of 1946 named 18 Americans, 26 Chinese, 71 British, 18 Canadians, and 6 New Zealanders. Throughout the project, the presence of Chinese members on the teams had been exceedingly important to the other Unit members, and to the communities served. A visit on the part of Dr. McClure to his native Canada had resulted in a substantial grant to the program by the Canadian Red Cross, and the addition of a number of Canadian recruits. The major continuous support for the program had come from two sources: United China Relief and British Foreign Office grants-in-aid.

It was responsibly estimated that during the war at least 90 per cent of the drugs and other medical supplies which arrived in West China for civilian use were transported by the FAU China Convoy.

Six FAU members had lost their lives in China or en route.

Now China's travail of war was over — at least so we thought; and Friends' work began to shift away from services just behind battle lines with the Chinese Red Cross to helping rehabilitate missionary hospitals. During 1945, a gift of thirty-five trucks from the American Red Cross brought the Unit's transport section up

---

* Charcoal-burning trucks were a grimy but resourceful answer to the gasoline shortage.

to sixty trucks in operation. Medical teams went out on special missions to combat cholera, malaria, leprosy, and the widely prevalent epidemic disease, kala-azar. Other Unit members became "medical mechanics" — restoring heating, lighting, water-plants, and X-ray facilities in places where medical teams were at work. Terribly devastated Honan Province in central China was selected as an area for a co-ordinated project of rehabilitation, the Unit proposing to help that province get on its feet through renewed hospital services, agricultural and industrial rehabilitation, and education. All this was envisioned as a long-range program, and as FAU, which was a wartime emergency organization, prepared to dissolve, it was thought wise to transfer leadership in the China work to the American Friends Service Committee. This was done in 1946, and the program was carried forward, with British, New Zealand, Canadian, Chinese, and American members participating, under the name of Friends Service Unit, China.

However, our vision of a peacetime development was not to be fulfilled, for the internal war between Communist and Nationalist armies was already giving new shape to the problems which confronted men and women of FSU. On principle it was their desire, as it has always been that of AFSC, to serve on both sides of the conflict.

Early in 1946 a truck convoy had delivered medical supplies to the Communist capital of Yenan, but it was December before way was opened for a Quaker unit to work behind Communist lines. With the support of General George C. Marshall and the American ambassador, John Leighton Stuart, an FSU medical team was flown to Yenan by two United States Army transport planes. The team consisted of two doctors, one theater nurse, one ward nurse, an X-ray technician, and a laboratory technician; 7500 pounds of drugs and medical equipment accompanied them.

Preceding this move, a reconnaisance team had made a study of conditions in this Communist-held territory. They had visited an experimental farm where the yield per acre of millet, corn, and cabbage had been built up to many times the average for China. They had found a newspaper called "The Emancipation Daily," a publication housed in caves lined with thousands of small stone Buddhas. They had visited the Communist Supreme Court, a prison, and a nursery school — all housed in caves. They had discovered that medical supplies in Yenan were woefully meager. The International Peace Hospital had one main building with operating room, while the wards were all in caves. The Communists were attempting to put forward a public-health program, emphasizing antiepidemic work. They were making their own vaccines, but were considerably hampered by lack of equipment.

The nearby Northwest Medical College had more than two hundred students who were taking one and a half years of academic study plus an additional year in the hospital. Seventeen per cent of them were women. The students maintained themselves by spinning, building, and food production. English medical books were translated and mimeographed for their use. Our mission noted that one of the three honor students had been an illiterate shepherd in 1936. The motto on the wall of this Medical College read "Serve the people," and, in keeping with this, doctors had no private practice. All medical services were public and free.

This exploratory mission had found that malaria, dysentery, kala-azar, typhoid, and tuberculosis were prevalent. They had secured from the Communists a list of drugs and equipment which were urgently needed, but the list was incomplete and far too modest, indicating perhaps that the Communists did not really believe anything would come of it.

We had realized that time was of the essence, for at any moment it might become impossible to cross the Communist-Nationalist lines. The American Red Cross in China, which had already allocated all its current supplies, canceled allocations and offered anything our unit wanted. UNRRA materials were secured within a few hours. Goods came from the International Relief Committee, and six buyers from the China Welfare Fund, Madame Sun's committee, went all over Shanghai purchasing items requested by the Communists which could not be secured from relief sources. The British consul sent a hundred pounds of textbooks. The final list of supplies taken in was five pages long. It represented hundreds of thousands of dollars' worth of equipment, including seven microscopes, case after case of penicillin, and laboratory and operating equipment. The team made its air-borne entrance into Yenan equipped with an indomitable spirit and a fair supply of medications and other equipment.

As the war in China deepened, it became increasingly difficult to hear from this team. After Yenan was captured — an empty city — by Nationalist troops in March, 1947, we had to assume that the team had retreated with the Communists to the hills. Not until May did a wireless message reach us, relayed through Shanghai: "TEAM SAFE AND WELL IN NORTH SHENSI. DO NOT WORRY."

The next word came in October, through a Canadian member of the team who arrived at the Friends Service Unit headquarters in Shanghai after a two-month trek by mule, horse, and donkey. He reported that the International Peace Hospital staff had been forced to move six or seven times since the evacuation of Yenan, that the group was now permanently located "somewhere in North Shensi," that all members of the team were safe and well, carrying on under severe handicaps, but devoted to their work. "The patients in the hospital lie on straw strewn over the floor or on k'angs — raised platforms which can be heated in the winter," he reported. "The operating room is a cave, with a large opening at the front to let light in, with whitewashed walls and hung with a protective ceiling cloth. A few cabinets put together serve as the operating table, and a few boxes make instrument stands."

Margaret Stanley, a volunteer nurse from Iowa, told a graphic story of the experience after she was back in the United States. For some three months after she crossed into Communist territory, she and the rest of the Quaker team took part in a 400-mile trek as International Peace Hospital Number One became a mobile rear unit just behind shifting battle lines. Carefully trained as she was in nursing, American style, she was greatly impressed by the fact that people could learn medicine and become good doctors without a campus and fine buildings, with little equipment and few textbooks. Although she wore the same suit from October to May, washed her clothes in streams, always slept in a sleeping-bag, and counted it a lucky day when she did not have to delouse herself, she insisted that she enjoyed the experience and did not have a hard time. She said, "Americans keep asking me how I could get along without a daily bath and hot coffee. You just don't miss such nonessentials when you are doing something you care about."

The second major service carried on by Friends in China after the beginning of the civil war was the rehabilitation program in Honan Province, centering in Chungmou. One of the interesting facts about this project was that it was in closely contested territory, which passed from Nationalist to Communist hands, or vice versa, five times while our unit was there. The work continued relatively undisturbed through each political and military change.

Through self-help methods, the village of Chungmou, 99 per cent destroyed by war and flood, was largely restored. In the first place, bricks were needed if the town was to be rebuilt, and under the Unit's direction two kilns were constructed and began to turn out bricks for village buildings. Workshops were erected, and in these new headquarters the program was extended to include a machine shop, a foundry, a blacksmith shop, a garage, and industrial and textile co-operatives. Spinning and weaving took on new dimensions in Chungmou. The village water supply had to be carried from the muddy Yellow River, so with a drill, lent by UNRRA, FSU drilled wells, and the new machine shop made well-pumps, which were sold to villagers at cost; these were exceedingly popular. Farmers' co-operatives grew gradually. The Unit opened two schools and two medical clinics. Then, as a kind of crowning feature, a new small hospital was erected, its buildings being designed by Cho Ting-li, a Unit member with architectural training. This

Friends Hospital, operated by the Unit, charged no fees for its services, but patients who could afford to contribute were encouraged to do so. Often their donations took the form of chickens, eggs, wheat, rice, and other commodities. Because of the frequency with which Chungmou was "liberated," first by one side, then by the other, battle casualties kept this hospital one of the busiest points of the entire Honan Province development. It sometimes happened that a Kuomintang soldier and a Communist soldier were lying side by side. In the beginning, considerable funds and equipment for the projects in Chungmou were donated by UNRRA and CNRRA (Chinese National Relief and Rehabilitation Administration).

In northern Honan Province, kala-azar is an ever-present disease, 95 per cent fatal if untreated. It is spread by the bite of a minute sand fly, and in villages throughout this sandy area anywhere up to five per cent of the population may be affected at any one time. Usually about three fourths of the victims are children under the age of twelve. Fortunately, most cases can be cured by a simple series of injections.

Soon after the end of the Japanese war, the Friends Unit and public health authorities in the counties most heavily affected mapped out a joint campaign to clear these areas of kala-azar through the persistent efforts of several mobile medical teams. It was believed that in this way the cycle of infection could be broken and the disease stamped out.

Unfortunately, because of the civil war emergency, FSU teams were the only ones able to proceed with the work. And even in the limited areas where they operated, military activities prevented their treating every case, which was an important part of the plan. Nevertheless, their efforts did drastically reduce the incidence of kala-azar in a number of counties, saving perhaps eight thousand lives in the course of a four-year campaign.

A genuine "social and technical assistance" project was worked out on a small scale. Hospitals which the Unit had helped rehabilitate found it hard to keep their equipment in good repair because of lack of qualified "medical mechanics." About a dozen Senior Middle School (high school) graduates, in whom the hospitals had enough confidence to help sponsor them, were received into FSU for a year, to live and work with the teams. They learned how to care for generators, sterilizing plants, X-ray machines, and other hospital equipment. Then they went back to the hospitals to assume responsibility for this phase of the work, and FSU took in another group. Finally the project was turned over to the Institute of Hospital Technology at Hankow, FSU lending personnel to get things under way.

Transport had been a function of Friends' work in China since 1941, and in West China a fleet of fifteen FSU trucks continued to distribute medical supplies arriving in Chungking to remote hospitals throughout that region.

Thus in the midst of the hurly-burly of civil war, sometimes behind Nationalist lines, sometimes with the Communists, FSU members found it possible to maintain working relations with the Chinese people regardless of their political alignment. Lewis Hoskins, who is now executive secretary of the American Friends Service Committee, was a member of FSU in China from November, 1945, to November, 1948, and in 1948 made two extended trips from his base in Shanghai into Communist territory to carry on negotiations concerning continuance of the work. Later he reported that both Communists and Nationalists were treating the Quaker units with respect.

But the problems of communication and transportation across Nationalist-Communist lines were to become increasingly severe. Unit headquarters at Shanghai were not finding it easy to dispatch reinforcements and much-needed supplies to Chungmou.

Then in February, 1949, came the battle of Hsuchow, perhaps the largest and most destructive battle of China's civil war. I well remember when the first report of the inspection team came to my desk. It was one of the most hair-raising documents I have ever read from a battlefield. Neither Communist nor Nationalist armies had any adequate medical facilities for war on this scale, and it was from the Chung Yuan (Communist) government that FSU in Chungmou received a request to send an emergency medical team to the battlefield area to take care of wounded civilians and Nationalist soldiers.

Medical Team 24 was dispatched to the scene immediately. Nine months later, at the end of October, 1949, three members of that team wrote a report:

Rain, mud, and wind redoubled the feeling of desolation and horror which the sight of half-buried bodies and scraps of clothing aroused in us. Damaged vehicles were everywhere, sprawling useless reminders. Some of the villages were razed to the ground, leaving mere mounds on the plain. Others were so devastated that we felt they must surely be deserted, but no, a dog would bark, or a baby cry. In half-shattered houses we found children huddled together for warmth, some of them ill with pneumonia and many with smallpox. There were old festering wounds bound in dirty ill-smelling rags. We first of all gave smallpox vaccinations to everyone in the afflicted villages, and later on to the people in the surrounding villages. This happily scotched the outbreak. We then started mass inoculations against cholera and typhoid. The wells were contaminated grossly. We impressed upon the people that every drop of water must be boiled before they drank, advice which was readily taken. . . .

The circumstances under which we worked will not seem believable. . . . The operating room was a hut with a straw ceiling and a mud floor. . . . We rigged up an intravenous set for giving our home-made saline, the bottle hanging by a bandage network on a pole that an available bystander would be charged to hold erect.

We distilled water over an outside fire of kaoliang stalks, weighed out salt powder and filtered the saline for hours through a slow-dripping filter. . . .

One four-year-old child was brought in gasping painfully for breath. The back of his throat was covered with a white membrane. We gave him diphtheria antitoxin and made up a steam apparatus by draping blankets over a foot cradle and put him inside with kettles of hot water. The effect was high in steam if not in oxygen. It helped for a while but when he became exhausted with his laboured breathing we shifted him to the operating room and did a tracheotomy. We had no tracheotomy tube so we cut up some rubber tubing and sewed it in place. For the next few nights we took turns watching him. After a week we were able to take out our makeshift tube and he was again able to breathe normally.

Aside from the emergency work we had regular clinics seeing several hundred patients per day; most of them had never had any medical attention in their lives before. . . .

Flies were thick everywhere. We tried D.D.T. in the operating room, but that only caused the flies to drop dead into the incision instead of flying in under their own steam, which seemed a doubtful advantage. To try to treat the endless flood of cases without trying to stop the cause seemed a hopeless job.

Throughout our whole stay in this area we have worked in close co-operation with the local Communist government, who have given us every kind of help and encouragement. When our six months emergency term was nearly completed they asked us to stay on an additional three months. Since the work was still heavy, we were glad to stay. They have sent us students who, though mostly very young, learned very quickly, and soon were a great help with routine jobs. We could not have accomplished nearly as much without them. They're planning to carry on a clinic after we leave, so the work will not come to a complete end.

Total number of patients seen during the nine months — 35,433.

By mid-1950, the only Friends' enterprise in Chungmou was the little hospital, which had been expanded from twenty-five to forty beds. It served a large rural area from which patients came day and night, often by oxcart, and its out-patient clinic took care of about 120 patients daily.

The Friends Service Unit still provided one mobile kala-azar team, but in this direction its most significant achievement lay in the fact that provincial health authorities had now organized such teams, Friends supplying the drugs and initial training. In many phases of the program, this kind of transfer was taking place, the new Chinese government assuming responsibility and the FSU withdrawing.

There came a period of great difficulty. In order to go from one village to another, it was necessary for a team to have a license. Partly because of lack of civil servants and insufficient organization in local government, it was extremely hard to obtain these licenses. Was the difficulty also a quiet way of asking us to go home? We could not be sure.

However, after the final conquest of practically the whole of China by the Communist army, and as fanatical enthusiasm and zeal over the new government mounted, the very presence of Americans became anathema. Now Chinese who associated with Americans were marked as American-lovers; their status in their own communities was thereby threatened, possibly even their safety. We have had that experience before; we know it is not the result of any one person's act, but the fruit of a complex set of historical events; in any case, it must be faced as a reality, and when developments reach such a stage it is quite possible that the only thing left to do is go home.

By September, 1950, it seemed that this fateful stage had been reached. When General Wu and his associates came to present the Chinese Communist case to the United Nations at Lake Success that fall, I had a brief conversation with him and one or two of his associates about the possibility of licenses being issued to our workers. This question was outside their authority, but they gave me the name of a person with whom I might correspond. It was my old friend Y. T. Wu, who had lived in our home many years ago and was now general secretary of the YMCA for China. He, they said, was chairman of the Party committee having to do with religious affairs.

I wrote to Y. T. Wu, but did not receive a reply. I have been somewhat saddened to see accounts of his denunciation of people with whom he has associated in times past, to read the names of distinguished Americans who have given of their life and vitality to bring the best they knew to China, now held up to ridicule and denunciation by their Chinese friends. But back of all this I know there is a long history of relations between the West and the East, between America and China, some happy, fortunate, and beneficial, but some exploitive and tragic. In the economy of time and through the spirit of God, one has faith that friendships formed between China and the West will be re-established.

It is to be hoped that final judgments and acrimonious decisions will not be arrived at during this time when feeling runs high and tempers are hot. I should think that a spirit of penitence for allowing such poverty and disease to continue so long in China while we have enjoyed so many advantages is a much healthier frame of mind than to think in terms of bitterness and denunciation.

This entire nine-year development in China was one of the most difficult undertakings which Friends' units have ever faced. It was far more self-organizing than our efforts in other parts of the world. It is a signal tribute to the intelligence, dedication, and quality of life of the members of the Unit that in the midst of civil war and the rise of strong anti-Western feeling they so conducted themselves that one feels sure that in the course of time these happy contacts can again be established.

China is proud, strongly nationalist, extremely eager to be accorded a place of dignity and independence in the modern world. The overemphasis on national pride at the present time will have to run its course. We know of no member of our Unit who has come away from his experiences in China, with all the hardship he had to endure — the privations, the hard work, and in the end the misunderstanding on the part of Chinese because he was Western — who does not still have a deep sense of affection for the Chinese, a belief in their future, and a yearning to get back into warm and friendly touch with the people with whom he worked in that great country.

JAPAN

It was a big day in my eight-year-old life when my sister Minnie Pickett left Kansas to go to Japan as a missionary. One of my most vivid childhood memories is of riding in the wagon sitting on one of her big trunks as we took her to town, to put her on the train for this long journey.

She was a voluminous letter writer, and she was charmed and fascinated by Japan and the Japanese. From her we received vivid pictures of the life of what seemed to me a fantastically different world from the one I knew.

She had been concerned about my handwriting before she left home, and now she sent me a copybook containing lines of model penmanship, which I was to copy over and over, eventually submitting my work to her inspection. She also kept me inspired to think in terms of further education. I suppose it was her influence more than any other that caused me to pursue what is called higher education.

When she returned to America after five years, it was to be married to Gilbert Bowles; and later the two of them went to Japan to spend forty-five more years in active service. Through their letters and periodic visits to the United States, I learned of the Japanese people's deep capacity for friendship, and their facility in the arts, scholarship, manufacturing — in fact in every avenue of modern culture. Also through the growing interest of Gilbert Bowles I learned something of the political life of Japan.

But when he was in the United States on furlough in 1924, it was at first difficult for me to understand his tremendous sense of urgency about the need to defeat the Japanese exclusion clause of the Immigration Act which was then pending in Congress.

In 1907, during Theodore Roosevelt's Administration, Japan and the United States had entered into a so-called "Gentleman's Agreement," Japan undertaking to stop the migration of Japanese laborers to this country in exchange for assurances that the United

States would make no open discrimination against her people. This agreement followed close on a flare-up of conflict over a proposal to segregate Asians in the San Francisco public schools.

But a few years later California passed a law prohibiting aliens who were ineligible for citizenship from owning land in that state; and in successive years various state laws on the West Coast further circumscribed real-estate privileges of the Japanese and other Orientals. In 1922, the United States Supreme Court handed down a decision in a test case, to the effect that Japanese were not eligible for naturalization in the United States; and in 1923, it declared constitutional the anti-alien land laws of Pacific Coast states. This meant that some fifty thousand owners of land, mostly in California, suffered severe loss.

In 1923 came the terrible earthquake in Japan. A spontaneous outpouring of sympathy in the United States prompted the Red Cross and other American agencies, including AFSC, to send assistance to the stricken country. For this Japan was abundantly grateful, but the widespread exchange of friendliness between the two nations was only a temporary reprieve in the over-all picture of increasing antagonism, and by 1924, when our Congress established new immigration quotas, the Japanese people were among those denied immigration to the United States, even on the quota basis.

From 1908 to 1923, the total number of Japanese admitted to the Continental United States had exceeded the number who departed by only 8681. Clearly, the Gentleman's Agreement had worked in this respect. Furthermore, Japan's immigration quota, had she not been excluded from the general provisions of the Act of 1924, would have been only 146 persons per year. Both President Coolidge and the State Department made appeals against the discriminatory clause, requesting at least a postponement of Congressional action, but to no avail.

That legislative act of 1924 was one of the factors behind Pearl Harbor in 1941, for the exclusion clause played into the hands of militarists in Japan, enabling them to build up a conception of the United States as the arch-monster and enemy of the Japanese people.

Our country's counter attack included the dropping of atomic bombs on Hiroshima and Nagasaki. Thus Pearl Harbor, an act of intransigent, militarist Japan, was answered by a similar blow from the hard side of American life. And Japan was left impoverished, devastated, her trade reduced, her land possessions truncated, and until May, 1952, her sovereignty surrendered. One is conscious that Pearl Harbor did not represent the deepest and best in Japanese life. I believe it is equally true that neither the exclusion clause of 1924 nor the use of atomic bombs in 1945 represented the deepest and best of the United States' attitude toward Japan.

Since the conclusion of the Second World War there has been a growth of sympathy and understanding between the two countries that is almost without precedent as between late enemies. The act of the Emperor in asking that an American woman come to Japan to teach his son the English language was a gesture of great import. Seldom has one seen the conquered express eagerness to have the language of the conqueror taught to the imperial heir so quickly after a bitter war. Elizabeth Gray Vining, who undertook this service, was an emissary of good will, opening "windows" for the Crown Prince and the rest of the royal family in a way which may in the long run prove as significant, in the opposite direction, as the Immigration Act of 1924.

It was in this climate of a certain amount of penitence on both sides — penitence for the Act of 1924 and the bombs of 1945, penitence on the part of the Japanese for Pearl Harbor — that the door swung wide open for people who wished to take help to Japan after the termination of hostilities.

Esther B. Rhoads, who had taught at the Friends Girls' School in Tokyo for many years, had spent the greater part of the war period living and working in the relocation centers for Japanese and Japanese-Americans in this country. She spoke the Japanese language fluently, had a husky physique, and a deep-seated affection for the people of Japan. Also she had a great deal of common sense and business ability. It was most fortunate that she was able to return to Japan in 1946 to explore possibilities for our Committee's participation in the work of postwar relief in that country as a member agency of LARA (Licensed Agencies for Relief in Asia). This organization was a union of some dozen private agencies to form a single distribution channel for voluntary relief to Japan. As in Germany, the occupation required that private agencies thus combine in order to simplify negotiations and distributions. In certain respects, this made for efficiency. But it placed severe limitations on the use of American personnel, which from our Committee's viewpoint is a very important part of any relief undertaking. It was fortunate for our Committee, and I am sure for LARA also, that Esther Rhoads was one of the three LARA representatives in Japan during the initial period of relief. The other two were Dr. Ernest Bott of Church World Service and Father M. McKillop of the National Catholic Welfare Conference.

One of Esther Rhoads's early letters from Japan to the Philadelphia office brought word of the small group of Japanese Friends:

> The Quaker groups in Japan are scattered and much of their property has been destroyed, but the spirit of groups and individuals is the same — earnest, sincere, and deeply affectionate. Somehow after five years of war, relationships are touched with the miraculous.
>
> There is first of all the miracle of endurance. It is not just that there is almost no fuel, that water has to be carried where formerly it flowed from the faucet, or that food is insufficient and can only be obtained by spending hours in long lines. There is the endurance that it takes to wait for news of close relatives who are caught abroad. . . .
>
> But in spite of all the frustrations one is constantly impressed with the hope of Friends in the future. Mr. Nakamura feels the challenge of his community to such an extent that he has withdrawn from most of his Tokyo responsibilities in order to devote his "remaining years" to religious work in Tsuchiura,

without the interruptions which are inevitable when one is away from one's own Meeting a great deal. . . .

But the greatest miracle of all is the miracle of forgiveness. Almost everyone who calls at the Friends Center has lost some member of the family, his home, or was perhaps himself injured in one of the air raids. They greet us from America with deep affection. There is Mrs. Kusuda who gave up her work to stay with her aged father and stepmother. On the terrible night of May 25 when hundreds of American planes rained fire on the city, she and her parents were separated as they fled through the smoke of the burning city. Next morning she found their bodies not far apart; alone in the world, she attended to final rites, and has gone to an orphanage to help care for children who lost their parents as she lost hers. There is no trace of bitterness.

I talked with atomic bomb victims in Hiroshima. Somehow all these people have the gift of forgiveness. If they blame anything for the tragedies through which they have passed, it is *war* and not Americans. Considering the methods we used, we are hardly entitled to get off so easily, but perhaps the Oriental has a saner sense of values, and does not find it necessary to continue hating.

Of general conditions in Japan, Esther Rhoads wrote:

The picture is as described in the letters we have had, hurrying crowds carrying bundles, transportation horribly overcrowded, with separate cars for GI's and friends. People are neat but poorly clad. . . . I have seen trainloads of repatriates coming in, weary and dazed. . . .

I feel that I move in three worlds: (1) the burned-out districts with desperate need of everything, housing very poor and terribly crowded, (2) unburned sections — shabby but with lovely green trees even though yards are filled entirely with vegetables, (3) the American world of downtown Tokyo with people well fed in army mess, young people tearing around in jeeps, Red Cross entertainments, movies, parades on July 4th, etc.

To the Japanese people, both LARA and the occupation meant

America. In terms of the usual military occupation, the one in Japan is said to have excelled in integrity and discipline. But LARA, though it functioned in close co-operation with occupying authorities, sought a relationship of brotherhood which can hardly be attained by occupying armies.

It is to LARA's great credit, and especially to the credit of its representatives in Japan, that gradually it reached the Japanese people on a level different from that of military occupation. "We work *with* Japanese," Esther Rhoads reported, "while the army works over or above. We *go to* Japanese officials; they have to go to the army. We work in cold offices, and the Japanese government is getting us fuel as a free gift. U.S. offices *require* fuel, and black coal-smoke pours out of U.S.-used buildings and settles on fireless homes round about. Several officials have said that LARA is the one real demonstration of U.S. Christian democracy."

Many of the larger cities of Japan were 80 per cent destroyed. Twenty-one million persons were estimated to have lost their homes. Living costs had risen 350 per cent. In all too many areas, daily rations were just along the edge of starvation. This was in the fall of 1946, and Elizabeth Gray Vining, having arrived in Tokyo to take up her duties as tutor to the Crown Prince, wrote back to the Service Committee in Philadelphia:

At meeting for worship one Sunday, I could see through the window women washing sweet potatoes and laying them out to dry in the sun on the concrete steps that are all that is left of the Friends Meetinghouse. Sweet potatoes keep better that way — and sweet potatoes were just about all they had to eat. A man was squatting on his heels scrubbing the rust off a square of old iron, to use it to patch the shack he is building out of scraps, to live in. In the street women were doing their washing in wooden tubs. They could get water from the main there. It was cold, and they had no soap.

The devastation from the incendiary bombs covers acres and miles. People have cleaned up the debris very well, and have planted little vegetable patches among the piles of stone and the remains of stone foundations and the rusted piles of twisted iron and tin. Little shacks built out of wood, if people are lucky, or of old iron and tin, are going up everywhere. There will be no way to keep them warm this winter, for fuel is scarce and there is no charcoal ration.

Letters from LARA representatives continued to emphasize the need in specific terms:

> Starch bulk is what the people need. I have struck a number of places with no ration (rice, wheat, etc.) for weeks. One can't keep going on the leaves of turnips.
> The 15 to 1 exchange we get is artificial. Actual buying price is often nearer 200 to 1. An oven made out of an oil can costs up to 600 yen — flimsy tin things hardly worth $2.00. Teachers' basic salary is still low, but with extras a mature high-school teacher may get 400 to 500 yen a month.
> Cloth by the yard is just not seen in the stores. There are hands here to do the sewing, but we need warm materials *and we need them now.*
> At the orphanage the children were too well-behaved. They were almost lifeless. They stared at us with old faces. We saw quite a number who were too undernourished to do anything but sit. The resignation of a half-starved child is awful.
> Isn't there *anything* that can be done to get relief supplies off from San Francisco?

There is perhaps never an acute relief situation in which this kind of desperate urgency does not color the appeals of the workers. People are starving. What is the delay?

But shipments did finally begin to arrive:

> You will all be eager for a report of progress. The SS Howard Stansbury arrived on Saturday, November 30th (1946) at 5 p.m., so we can say our first shipment arrived in November. Unloading began that night. . . . Father McKillop has worked closely with the Army officials concerned. He has done a grand job on procedures and in obtaining the use of two excellent warehouses. . . . As the goods were unloaded they were checked by

8th Army, by Ministry of Welfare, and by the warehousing company. We ourselves spot-checked and found the records accurate.

And a little later:

We are still hoping that Americans working for the Occupation will be able to contribute substantial sums and buy the cookies and doughnuts for the holiday season. . . . The Mennonite flour arrived safely yesterday and will start the nest egg for our January distributions. . . . The cold weather is upon us and we are more than ever impressed with the need not only for big garments like suits and coats, but little things like hats, socks, and gloves. It snowed this morning and it is raw and cold. My jeep is in the garage, so I am more conscious of the needs of the people in the streets than when I bounce quickly by on four wheels.

Distributions of LARA supplies were made through religious and welfare organizations, schools, orphanages, and other institutions. The gratitude which poured back to the member agencies in the United States was embarrassing, and the unconscious irony of many of the children's thank-you letters lingered in one's memory. For example:

After supper we each took a piece of candy. It has been years since I tasted anything sweet, and I thought I had forgotten the taste. But it was entirely delicious. Thinking happily of your kindness we rolled the candy about in our mouths. We were all smiling, and we thanked God.

The thing that I miss most, is play. There is nothing now but the radio.

Christianity is the only thing that can save society now. My father is always saying that, and I think so too. I know I must more deeply examine my own heart, and repent.

KAZUYO HOSOYA
(fifth grade in the Mito Girls' School,
a third generation Friend)

Or this:

DEAR GRANDFATHER LARA:

How is everyone in America? I am very well and spending every day very cheerfully so please do not worry. In the middle of December we received many delicious sweets. It was such a treat that I peeked in through a hole which was on the cover of the box. I was so happy that I took hold of the box and danced around all over the house. The candy was very very good. When I leave it in my mouth, the color changes. First it was white and then it became green, and then it became sort of orange, and then it became yellow. Every day we are eating the food that LARA has given us and every mealtime I give thanks to everyone in America for the food they have given us.

We will study hard and try to become good people. I did not know that the people in America were as kind as this. The principal told us many stories and we believe that everyone is as kind as Esther Rhoads. When I heard about this it made me feel very happy. From now on we will try to live more happily. How is the weather over there? It is very cold here. However, we do not mind that, but we will do our best to study hard and make ourselves healthy and strong and also to try to make it a good Japan. Will everyone in America please take care of themselves?

Goodbye.

MATSUYE (Third Grade)

What kind of reply could Grandfather LARA make to such children? Grandfather himself was at this time composed of the Brethren Service Committee, Church World Service, Labor League for Human Rights (AFL), Lutheran World Relief, Mennonite Central Committee, National CIO Community Services Committee, Salvation Army, War Relief Services of the National Catholic Welfare Conference, YMCA International Committee, YWCA National Board, and the American Friends Service Committee. During the first two and a half years of his life, Grandfather LARA had shipped something over seventeen million pounds of food, clothing, and medical supplies to Japan, valued at about five million dollars. But this gave him no feeling of being Santa Claus or even bountiful Grandfather. What kind of reply was America to make to these children?

As of the time of this writing, LARA contributions to Japan have totaled more than ten million dollars. Most of the supplies have been shipped from the United States or other Western countries. For a time, United States surplus commodities were a major source of supply. Since the withdrawal of these commodities from the free list in December, 1950, and the cancellation of free ocean freight on relief shipments to Japan the following month, private grants have helped maintain necessary shipments.

It should be especially noted that over the years occupation personnel made very generous gifts to the program, and in specific cases threw themselves into the LARA work with as much commitment as official LARA representatives.

During 1951 the number and size of projects were greatly reduced. At present, emphasis is placed on milk for babies, extra rations for TB patients and for university students with a tendency toward TB, and clothing distributions to orphanages: services still urgently needed and representing a healing fellowship between the peoples of America and Japan.

As the way has opened for more representatives of AFSC to go to Japan, we have picked up the threads of community services with longer-range goals, mostly in the form of neighborhood centers.

The Setagaya center and nursery are located within an area called Setagaya-go, a refugee community in the outskirts of Tokyo. Here about nine thousand Japanese, bombed out or repatriated from Manchuria, Korea, and China, live in long low sheds and two-story barracks that once housed Japanese army personnel, or in small two- and four-unit dwellings put up by the city of Tokyo since the war. Most of the adults work in factories that are virtual "sweatshops," or on city day-labor jobs, many women working alongside men on Tokyo road repairs, sewer maintenance, and public construction. A small number of the residents of this community are teachers or office workers. In general, living conditions in Seta-gaya-go are dreary, with poor facilities and sanitation, a low level of education, and the kind of discontent and lethargy which come of a depressed mode of life. Here the Friends' nursery cares for young children of mothers who work out, and the neighborhood center provides community recreation and classes, so that gradually out of the ugliness and seeming hopelessness the lives of some of the people are beginning to take on fresh meaning.

The neighborhood center in Toyama Heights, Tokyo, is quite another matter. Toyama Heights is a new housing project of about a thousand one-family homes with simple but modern conveniences. On the whole, its residents are persons with considerable ability and initiative. Classes, clubs, and play groups are under the direc-tion of able Japanese volunteers. This center may be thought of as providing an outlet for the creative gifts of the people of the com-munity it serves.

The gradual growth of the Japanese Friends' group in Mito has been taking place since before 1900, and in 1931 the Japan Yearly Meeting of Friends recognized Mito Monthly Meeting. After the war, with their Meeting House wrecked and 80 per cent of their city flattened, Mito Friends began the difficult task of restoring the Meeting House, and called on the American Friends Service Com-mittee for aid in developing a neighborhood center. Esther Rhoads, visiting Mito in 1951, reported to us:

> I stopped for a minute at the new neighborhood center which has been built behind the Meeting House there. It is a well-built, attractive, sunny addition which will make the place very useful to the community. Right now the main Meeting room is being used by the city on weekdays for one of their kinder-gartens, and as we arrived quite unexpectedly it was good to see how well ordered and neat the whole kindergarten seemed to be. The children were very cute indeed.

In all three neighborhood centers, both Japanese and Western workers are giving dedicated and enthusiastic leadership. About ten Western workers are now participating.

In the healing processes between nations, nothing is more valuable than simple direct contact between individuals. It has been a great satisfaction during this postwar period to find a number of mature American Friends who are eager to establish relations with the Japanese people on this basis. Thomas and Eliza Foulke, the former an active lawyer in the Philadelphia community, spent a year in Japan and were especially involved in the setting up of Toyama Heights Community Center. Henry and Edith Perry of Boston followed with eight or nine months of family visiting, and Howard and May Taylor, farmers from New Jersey, spent a year coming to know and love the Japanese people by serving with them. Passmore and Anna Elkinton, the former just retiring from his Philadelphia business, have spent six months in similar service. Hugh and Elizabeth Borton (the former the assistant director of the East Asian Institute of Columbia University), who had already given a term of service in Japan, returned for a year of study and service. And Howard and Anna Brinton of Pendle Hill School have now gone for a two-year period, to share their spirit, their scholarship, and their outstanding interest in the Far East with Japanese Friends.

It is in the tradition of the Society of Friends for men and women to move about the world this way on the basis of concern to be useful and helpful in any kind of service they may be able to carry out. Usually after some time they come home so enriched in spirit and interest that they feel they have received far more than they have contributed.

It has not been all one-way. There has been a flow of Japanese coming to this country, who have lived in our homes, shared in our educational enterprises, worshiped with us, and coming to know us in all our weaknesses and shortcomings as well as our strengths, still love us.

*   *   *

INDIA

Until the early days of United States participation in World War II, India had been thought of by the American Friends Service Committee as largely the interest of Friends Service Council. Over the years missions had been established in the central provinces by the Friends' Foreign Mission Association of Great Britain, and later these had been absorbed by Friends Service Council. On this side of the Atlantic, we had not participated in Indian life to any major extent.

In the spring of 1942, with Burma and Malaya in Japanese hands, Horace Alexander, who had long had a deep interest in India, left his position at Woodbrooke School, near Birmingham, England, to lead a small section of FAU in India, the purpose being to teach Indians how to protect themselves in case of air raids. At that time it was anticipated that India would be attacked by Japan, and that Calcutta would be one of the most vulnerable points.

Happily, the attack never came in any major proportions. But an even more destructive calamity did descend upon India, due largely to the war, and in time the FAU found itself doing a job it had not expected.

On the night of October 15–16, 1942, a great cyclone, rainstorm, and tidal wave swept over Midnapore. It left in its wake about 15,000 people dead, 200,000 head of cattle destroyed, hundreds of villages wrecked, a million tons of ripening crops washed out, the soil ruined for a long time to come by saline deposits, and wells made worse than useless by salt and carcasses. The small FAU section was on hand, alongside Indian organizations and government emergency aid.

It might have been possible for India to absorb this catastrophe without widespread famine, had it not been for the war, which meanwhile had resulted in the cutting off of almost two million tons of India's usual annual imports of rice when Burma, Indo-China, and Thailand had fallen to the Japanese. To add a further complication, the Japanese conquest of the Netherlands East Indies had deprived the Indian people of their main source of quinine.

Then when actual invasion of India had seemed imminent, small boats — especially fishing boats — had been removed from the coastal regions, large numbers of them destroyed and the fishermen paid nominal sums, which they quickly had to spend for food to keep themselves alive. But their continuing source of food and income had vanished with their boats.

At the same time, greatly augmented Indian armed forces, as well as English and American troops, were drawing on the country for a certain amount of commodities, and some food was being exported from India to Allied forces in the Middle East.

Transportation within India was breaking down under the strains of abnormal wartime shipments, and inflation was gaining momentum. Panic over inflation and the cutting off of rice imports caused frantic purchasing and hoarding, which led to greater inflation. Thus in a dizzy, tragic spiral, India found herself in the midst of a famine so appalling that the Western world could hardly grasp the facts when they began to leak out through an iron curtain of resistance to publicity for the situation. By October, 1943, the Associated Press was able to report from New Delhi that 100,000 persons were dying weekly in Bengal alone; and in February, 1944, the *Toronto Star* published findings of the anthropological department of Calcutta University, to the effect that the number dead in India since the beginning of the famine — over and above the normal death rate — was in the neighborhood of three and a half million.

The small FAU group in India had continued to work on flood relief through the winter of 1942–1943, intending to gradually taper off in the spring. But by spring the specter of famine was stalking the land, and by midsummer the roads into Calcutta were streaming with people from country places where food supplies were exhausted. Surely, they thought, in a city like Calcutta they could find something to eat. But the emergency was too big for Calcutta.

In the summer of 1943 John F. Rich of our Committee visited

India on his way home from China. It was as a result of this visit
that our Committee was roused to a sense of responsibility and a
desire to participate with FAU, whose small unit had organized its
own canteens and was co-operating with the Indian Red Cross in
milk distributions as well as carrying out relief assignments for the
Bengal government. We arranged to ship 20,000 cases of evaporated
milk as at least a gesture of concern and co-operation. But we did
not see how AFSC could undertake the raising of funds on anything like the scale that was indicated.

However, as is often the case, we soon found we were not alone.
We discovered that Pearl Buck and Richard J. Walsh had taken
the initiative in setting up an India Famine Relief Committee, with
a broad base of moral support from political liberals, churches, and
organized labor. This committee was already registered with the
President's War Relief Control Board and had raised certain small
relief funds. Now it was presenting the case of India to the National
War Fund, pointing out the appropriateness of making India a
recipient of NWF assistance.

It seemed to me important that there should be agreement, both
in India and in this country, on some one American agency through
which American relief could be channeled to India. The directors
of the India Famine Relief Committee felt the same way. Early in
January, 1944, at the call of Charles P. Taft of the President's War
Relief Control Board, I participated in a meeting with representatives of the Foreign Economic Administration, the State Department, the American Red Cross, the National War Fund, and the
India Famine Relief Committee, at which time consideration was
given to the problem of raising funds for India and the question
of who should distribute such funds. The IFRC had cabled American representatives in India through our State Department, to find
out what American relief agency would be most acceptable to the
Indian people as a whole, including the various political and religious
groups. Now cables had been received from the American diplomatic mission in India and from Arthur Moore, outstanding Eng-

lish journalist in Bengal, suggesting that FAU, AFSC, and the Indian Red Cross should jointly administer all American relief in Bengal, and that AFSC should be the official contact in the United States. The American Red Cross at this time had sent more than $57,000 worth of milk and medicines, but did not anticipate dispatching any staff and would send additional supplies only if requested to do so by the Indian Red Cross.

There was full agreement among the members of this group meeting in Washington that the American Friends Service Committee should become the distributing agency for American relief for India, and that the India Famine Relief Committee should continue to carry the case for India to the American people and the National War Fund. At this meeting it was indicated that British War Relief, the NWF agency concerned with relief throughout the British Empire, which at that time included India, would be willing to set aside $200,000 immediately, and that the AFL and CIO would probably appropriate $100,000 for India out of their earmarked portions of the National War Fund. (These allocations were actually made within a few weeks.) With these prospects, I agreed to recommend to the Service Committee that we undertake the responsibility for distribution.

This was the beginning of a very difficult job, for in comparison with the large public awareness of the needs of battle-torn countries, Americans' knowledge of conditions in India was slight. This situation was aggravated by the fact that powerful interests in this country wished to play down the distress in India, evidently in the thought that it reflected on Great Britain. As a matter of fact, this particular crisis in India was more an American than a British responsibility, stemming as it did largely from America's war with Japan, and for this reason we felt not only justified in carrying our appeal to the National War Fund and the American people, but obligated to do so.

We soon discovered that there were anti-British groups in this country who were all too ready to use the Indian situation against

Britain. And neither our Committee nor the India Famine Relief Committee wanted this kind of publicity.

However, in spite of the difficulties, we learned that on the part of those who did understand the need there was strong commitment, and in the course of the undertaking innumerable satisfying and healthy relationships developed between our Committee and a wide range of co-operating individuals and organizations.

The over-all project was a good illustration of the way in which from time to time British ' and American Quaker initiative have aided and abetted each other. It was far better that the operation in India should have been started by British Friends. India was still dependent upon Great Britain administratively. Most Friends warmly supported the move for independence on the part of India, and felt it was long overdue. It was perhaps with some sense of compensation for the delay in independence, together with a deeper sense of affection and confidence, that British Quakers had taken the lead. But also in this country it was heartening, as we began to interpret the situation, to find many Americans who sensed that relief for India was not just an effort to keep people alive, but was in addition a gesture of confidence in a country struggling toward independence, a country which, even lacking independence, had produced Gandhi and Tagore and a cultural and spiritual quality of life which meant a great deal for the whole world.

During the first year of this venture, appropriations from the National War Fund totaled $650,000, more than half of which was contributed by the Labor League for Human Rights (AFL) and the CIO National War Relief Committee. But in the fall of 1944, just after James Vail of our Committee returned from a visit to India with a fervent plea for continuation of American relief, the National War Fund decided that India was not an appropriate beneficiary of its funds.

At this point the Service Committee was faced with the choice of abandoning a vital job it had started or seeking new sources of financial assistance. The India Famine Relief Committee did not wish to become a large-scale fund-raising organization, and AFSC felt it could not well add such a sizable responsibility to its regular fund-raising activities. Therefore at this time a group of persons who were vigorously concerned for the continuing program decided to organize a new agency to raise the necessary funds, and American Relief for India, Inc., was established, with the following officers and Board:

Rufus M. Jones, honorary chairman	William Phillips, vice-president
Henry F. Grady, chairman	Guy Emerson, treasurer
J. Edgar Rhoads, president	Gilbert F. White, secretary
Frank Aydelotte	Henry R. Luce
William Green	George Z. Medalie
David Hinshaw	Philip Murray
John Haynes Holmes	Victor F. Ridder
M. Albert Linton	Sumner Welles

This agency did the job of keeping the emergency program going for another year, after which the Service Committee was able to assume financial responsibility for the continuing work, which by that time was greatly reduced in volume.

In the beginning, this India program consisted mostly of milk canteens and other emergency food distributions. To watch an emaciated child fill out into normal plumpness, and a prematurely old but small face regain a spirit of mischief, is the reward wherever hungry children are fed. The heaviest burden of this relief fell on the British and Indian people and their governments. The government of Bengal and the Indian Red Cross were particularly active. The Quaker program supplemented these larger efforts, sometimes pooling its resources with theirs.

In 1944, 150,000 young children and nursing and expectant mothers were receiving milk through canteens staffed by voluntary workers. As America's contribution to this, more than eight hundred tons of evaporated and powdered milk were shipped from the

United States, plus millions of tablets of atabrine, sulfa drugs, and vitamins. Almost two hundred governmental and private agencies in India were used as distribution channels, representing 4500 specific outlets, such as schools, orphanages, hospitals, and religious centers. The private agencies included Hindu and Moslem societies, and Catholic and Protestant missions. AFSC personnel joined an expanded British Quaker group in these early efforts to turn the tide of the terrible aftermath of famine.

Then the long-term works were begun: rehabilitation centers were opened for widows and orphans, where they could learn to make their living through crafts. Some of these were expanded into small industrial centers or village factories, for the Indian people have many skills, and both raw materials and markets were available. Cash and someone to bring all the elements together often worked wonders in energizing a local economy.

Money was lent to skilled artisans whose tools had been sacrificed during the famine, sometimes for only a day's ration of rice, and to fishermen to buy fishing nets and boats, or materials and tools for constructing them. Weaving, mat-making, jute spinning, needlework, and cane work were given considerable boosts. The government itself became interested in the vigor of these developments, and made loans for the purchase of materials.

Small demonstrations of village rehabilitation were undertaken, and various co-operatives were organized under Quaker Unit leadership. In an agricultural co-operative, farmers pooled their land in the interest of improved methods and equipment; a fishermen's co-operative, involving between three and four thousand persons in thirty fishing villages, made possible more advantageous marketing of the daily catch; a weavers' co-operative was established in the interest of equitable distribution of yarn supplies and for marketing of the cloth.

The year 1945 saw most of the emergency aspects of the work come to a close, but in 1946 another famine was narrowly averted by the government of India through an extensive food procurement program. At this time the Service Committee received grants from that government totaling $2,321,400 for the purchase of milk, cereals, and vitamins for India.

It is a great temptation to quote at length from letters and reports which came from India as August 15, 1947, the day of independence, approached. There were increasing opportunities for missions of reconciliation; throughout India the sense of excitement and anticipation was mingled with apprehension, resentments, and fear. But I shall pass over these, to quote from a letter written by a Unit member in Calcutta on August 20:

DEAR FRIENDS, JAI HIND:
This letter comes to you with the salute which is on everyone's lips at the moment in India. JAI HIND. It means glory to India, victory to India, long live India, or something like that. . . . It is really one of the most exciting things that ever happened, and the first time in history, with the exception of the Philippines, when a conquered country obtained its freedom without bloodshed — or very much, at least.

Ever since we have been in Calcutta the city has been tense and jittery and subject to frequent disturbances and incidents: a city almost on the verge of civil war. This is true of all of India in varying degrees.

The Unit has been working in two of the most seriously affected riot areas — Noakali and Bihar, as well as in Calcutta. The outlook was depressing, and we were all prepared for further trouble. The choice of August 15 as the day of the official transfer of power seemed particularly unfortunate for Calcutta, because exactly one year ago on August 16 the great "Calcutta Killing" began. At that time, the Moslems had the upper hand in the government and controlled the police force, and the Hindus took a bad beating. They were all set for revenge, and rumors were abroad that both groups had large stores of guns and ammunition. . . . We were brushing up on our first aid and getting out the stretchers.

On Saturday, Horace Alexander (ex-Unit leader, now British Quaker Ambassador-at-large) went to Bihar to talk to Gandhi about things, as he often does. (He says he is one of Gandhi's several thousand "best friends.") Gandhi was on his way to Calcutta, and Horace rode with him in his special third-class train.

While Gandhi was here, staying in his ashram about ten miles out of town, Horace was with him. As you probably know, it is Gandhi's custom to hold a prayer meeting every evening about sundown, where he and his followers hold a sort of inter-communal religious service. Following this, he talks to the people about the affairs of the day. Many thousands of people attend these meetings daily, and of course we were among them.

. . . . Before I knew what was happening, we were conducted to the little raised platform on which the Old Man himself sits, and were seated on the floor. Just at that moment, he came walking down the path leaning on his grandchildren, walked past us and sat down on his cushion placed on a sort of low table. Beside him, standing on the platform, a man was talking into the microphone. The crowd began to applaud when Gandhi came in, but the man at the mike stopped them. He then began to sing a lovely thing which was a Hindu Veda of some sort. Then he chanted a bit from the Koran, and sang something else to the accompaniment of a sort of Indian violin. It was very lovely. Then they all chanted something. . . .

Then the mike was placed in front of Gandhi, and he began to speak in a very soft, gentle voice, just as though he was talking to one person. He talked for about ten minutes, in Hindustani, which most of these folks don't understand. They sat like statues and listened, though. Then a Bengali professor translated, and that was the end of that. No cheering, or shouting of slogans, no expression whatever on the faces of the crowds, except that of rather intense listening. . . . Well, I didn't know what he said, except that he used the words Hindu-Moslem frequently, so I could guess.

Later . . . while we walked, one of our Bengali friends told us what Gandhi had said. Someone had asked him how he planned to celebrate Independence Day, and he said that he thought it would be a day of fasting for him, and he would give his food to the poor. He didn't urge others to follow this, but he did urge Hindus to invite Moslems to join in their celebrations, and vice versa. Then he said that Suhrawardy, the

Moslem Prime Minister of Bengal whose official duties end on the 15th when the Congress takes over, had come to see him to urge him to stay in Calcutta to try to end the communal strife. Gandhi had planned to go to Noakali to be there on the 15th. He told Mr. S. that he would stay if he, Mr. S., would come and live in the affected areas of Calcutta with him, and talk to the people to try to persuade them to stop this killing. He proposed that they share a house in one of the worst areas, receive callers together, *eat* together, do everything together. S. had informed him just before the meeting that he would accept the invitation, and they would begin tomorrow. That was all, but believe me it was momentous. S. had been prime minister during all these disturbances, including the Great Killing, and was accused by many of instigating the trouble for political reasons.

We all thought it a very exciting announcement. The next day a house was found for them in one of the worst Moslem areas, where no Hindu had dared set foot for months. Some of us took Horace there that night about sundown, and had quite a job getting through the crowd surrounding the place. To our surprise, we found the people shouting, "Gandhi, go back!" and looking menacing. . . .

The next morning, August 15th . . . we discovered that the city had been decorated overnight. Archways of green leaves were everywhere, and countless national flags displayed. People were milling about on the streets, crowded into trucks, busses, and streetcars, tearing all over town shouting, "Jai Hind."

People began to report that all over town Hindus and Moslems were going around *together* celebrating. In areas where no Hindu dared to go the day before, Hindus were calling on Moslems. Moslems were doing the same. They invited each other into their temples and mosques. Unheard-of scandal. We rode around later in the day and it was true. Even in the "danger zones" people were mixing freely, having a wonderful time shouting themselves hoarse. We were invited to a special celebration that afternoon by an Indian organization called the Relief Welfare Ambulance Corps, started during the last riots. It is located in a Hindu area, and they told us that the evening before, the Moslems had come in and offered to help them decorate. When we asked what had happened, and how come all this love, they simply said it was a miracle. Some said it was Gandhi.

As everyone knows, bloodshed was to follow close on this outburst of harmony and rejoicing, for it was one of those momentary previews of the kingdom of love which come easily and go easily; only in Gandhi and in those who, like him, had lived through the personal disciplines of brotherhood, had it come to stay.

When rioting again broke out in Calcutta, Friends Unit members took the initiative in starting a joint reconciliation project, in which they and representatives of the Indian National Ambulance Corps and the Indian Red Cross obtained permission to live together in a house on Bagmari Road in northeastern Calcutta, a district which had been 70 per cent Moslem, and from which Hindu families had fled. Gradually the presence of this one small group gave some refugees courage to return to their homes, and probably did a good deal to make the return safe. In a time of almost universal panic, it is surprising how much can be accomplished by only a handful of people who have overcome fear.

But it was in the Punjab that the greatest need arose, and during the last months of 1947 as riots and rumors brought the displacement of millions in East and West Punjab, the Friends Unit, strongly encouraged by Nehru and Gandhi, diverted approximately a third of its members to this region and mobilized other workers to help. It was an incredible tragedy that was pictured in Friends Service Unit reports:

Oct. 20, 1947. Arriving in Delhi on Sept. 23rd, I found that the FSU had already established a Welfare Tent in Purana Qila. In this old fort, 65,000 or more Moslem refugees were living.

Oct., 1947, Amritsar, East Punjab. Things were as bad as they could be, and yet the rains at the end of last month made it go one more still. Lacs of people were on the march taking their buffaloes, bullocks, goats, etc., with them — continuous rain for three days washed away parts of the river embankment, the road sank, and the river just swept the people, their scanty goods and animals, away. I drove 30 miles through it, taking nine hours, and saw dead bodies lying everywhere.

Nov. 5, 1947. Some things are changing in the Punjab very rapidly. The paper reports that 30,000 Moslems per day are crossing the border into West Punjab. Probably at least that many non-Moslems are crossing into East Punjab. Many of the non-Moslems who arrive are now being concentrated in a few very large refugee camps; one north of Delhi about 70 miles has about 200,000 and may reach 500,000 soon.

At this time, five FSU teams of several members each were distributed as follows: Team 1, four persons, transporting medical supplies from the Pakistan government and working in Moslem camp; Team 2, three or four persons, same from India government and working in Hindu camp; Team 3, in Lahore, working in refugee hospital and tracing missing persons; Team 4, at a gigantic non-Moslem camp 70 miles north of Delhi; Team 5, at Delhi for administrative work and help in relief at the railroad station.

Gradually over the ensuing months the emergency subsided, the immediate problems of the uprooted being resolved through death, through resettlement, or in many cases through return to their old homes. But the basic dilemma of the great country — which was now two countries — remained yet to be dealt with: it consisted of poverty, disease, lack of the kind of education and skills which would enable the people of India and Pakistan to participate creatively in the modern world.

Now a new day moves in this great subcontinent. I can remember no time in the past when Christian churches were not being appealed to, to raise money for starving Indians or Chinese. I suppose we became somewhat hardened to it. Now there is a great effort on the part of India and Pakistan to lift themselves to the level of self-support. The two governments are laying plans and appropriating funds within their capacity, and our government is awakening to the significance of these peoples' taking their place in the family of nations on a basis of independence and equality.

It was with all this in mind that the Service Committee in the spring of 1951 decided to send two emissaries to India and Pakistan, to see whether it might be feasible for us to aid in the technical development that is taking hold in these countries. It had been suggested that we discuss with the State Department the possibility of obtaining Point Four funds for such work. In following up this suggestion we had found that a mutually satisfactory arrangement of this kind might be made. However, we wanted first to make sure that we would not thereby become instruments of American imperialism in the eyes of the Indian and Pakistan people. Also we needed to know where and how we could be of assistance, provided we were welcome. It seemed important to discuss the whole matter very freely in the local communities where we might have projects, as well as with officials of the two governments. Willis Weatherford, economist, and Kay Beach, agriculturist, undertook this exploratory mission, the latter having spent considerable time in our unit in China, the former having been a commissioner for us in Europe.

They found there was no objection in these countries to our using American government funds, provided we had full freedom in the selection and control of personnel. Therefore we proceeded with the plan, and on our mission's recommendation have established a project in the state of Orissa in India.

Here the central government of India is constructing a dam which will provide irrigation for 100,000 acres of land and produce about 24,000 kilowatts of hydroelectric energy by 1954. This government was anxious that we should initiate a project which would include basic education, health services, and improved agricultural methods in this region. The plan calls for Indian as well as Western workers on the AFSC staff, and, in addition, for every Western technician an Indian "understudy." The idea is to turn the project over completely to Indian direction in a few years. In addition to this, we are co-operating with British Friends in an expansion of activities which they have developed over the years in the central provinces. Here, centered in Rasulia, a program of health, agriculture, and education is being carried on in about twenty-five communities.

At the time of this writing, we are working on plans for similar projects in Pakistan.

The concept of one world, while it has been vividly portrayed in oratory and on the printed page, comes into reality when men work and study and live together. Some people think that the most critical shortage in the world is a shortage of technicians, but the technique of living together creatively is the ingredient of which we stand in deepest need.

I know there is fear on the part of some of the peoples of "underdeveloped countries" that we of the United States will swamp them with our materialistic contribution, infecting them with the germ of gadget fever. Having seen the ruthlessly exploited labor of people in various parts of the world, I do not believe that the great danger at this moment is that of removing too much of the physical burden from their backs. Rather, I hope that we, who perhaps are overmechanized, by the very act of sharing our advantages with those who need to have their burdens eased, shall find ourselves less dependent upon the externals of life, in closer kinship with those who have kept alive qualities of spirit which our civilization all too often crushes.

In these areas of interchange lies the new call to missionary effort. It is not we going to those who are benighted, but we and they working together for common improvement in the enriched life that we both so deeply need.

8. Palestine

On Thursday, October 28, 1948, about 11 o'clock in the morning, Andrew Cordier, administrative assistant to the Secretary General of the United Nations, called me from Paris to say that the staff members of UN who were working on a one-year emergency relief program for Arab refugees in the Middle East wanted to know whether the American Friends Service Committee would undertake special responsibility for part of those in Palestine. Elmore Jackson of our Committee was arriving in London on other business that day, and I asked Andrew Cordier to call Elmore and request him to come to Paris for an interview on this important matter.

Our Committee's attitude toward the United Nations has from the beginning been one of most cordial co-operation in all efforts looking toward peaceful settlement of disputes. On principle, therefore, we were favorably disposed toward this invitation. However, we knew how bitter was the struggle between Jews and Arabs, and we were conscious of the fact that no quick and easy solution was likely to be found. We could not undertake a police operation, and we had had enough experience to know that in large-scale displacement of populations the sheer problem of order has to be considered. Then there is the perennial problem of suitable personnel.

Also we were anxious about the implications of such a service. We understood all that lay behind the setting up of the Jewish state, the long period of suffering and persecution in Europe, the high hopes and idealism connected with the return to the homeland. On the other side was the deep-seated bitterness not only of the Arab refugees but of all the Arab states surrounding the newly established state of Israel. It took little imagination to realize that this situation would test to the utmost both our administrative skill and our spiritual resources.

There was some history of Quaker participation in life in that part of the world. Just after the Civil War in the United States, Eli and Sybil Jones, American Friends of great capacity, had visited the Middle East and had succeeded in interesting the Society of Friends in establishing a boys' and a girls' school at Ramallah, a few miles north of Jerusalem. Somewhat later, Daniel Oliver, a Scottish Quaker, and his wife Emily, had developed a school for Arab orphan boys at Ras-el-Metn, then in Syria. In addition to supporting this effort, British Quakers had maintained a school at Brummana, and a very modern institution for the mentally ill (until recently the only one in the Middle East) not far from Beirut in Lebanon.

Our Committee's particular interests in Palestine during 1948 had naturally revolved around the emergence of the state of Israel, with its attendant conflicts and need for relief and reconciliation. In response to an appeal from Willard Jones of the Friends School in Ramallah we had made a small donation for medical aid for Arab refugees. More recently, having received assurances from Tel Aviv that such an emissary would be welcomed there, the AFSC had sent Moses Bailey to discuss with Israeli authorities the possibility of a small Quaker team's entering Israel to help in the resettlement of refugees. Moses's qualifications for this mission were particularly helpful. A Friend and a professor at Hartford Theological Seminary, he had the kind of personality that immediately establishes confidence, he had lived in Palestine, and had knowledge of both Hebrew and Arabic. The eventual result of his mission was initiation of Quaker work at Acre, north of Haifa, in Israel, where Arabs in the old walled city needed both physical relief and the reassurance which perhaps only "neutrals" could have given them at that time.

Also throughout most of 1948 we had been involved in Palestine on the level of negotiation. Back in February, a proposal had come to us from concerned persons: could any slight step, even, be taken toward stopping the cruel, destructive war that was raging in Palestine? Since Jerusalem was historically a great religious center for both Jews and Moslems, as well as for Christians, it was suggested that an appeal from religious leaders for at least a "Peace of God" in Jerusalem might be effective. Would Quakers assume leadership in such an effort?

Rufus Jones and I invited a few people to come to Quaker House in New York to discuss this possibility. While we were not so optimistic as to believe we could bring about an over-all peace in this way, we did feel that an effort aimed at a truce in Jerusalem might be successful, and that such success might in turn have some bearing on the wider reconciliation which must be achieved in time.

As a result of this meeting, and in consultation with those who had agreed to join him in signing the appeal, Rufus Jones drafted the following message:

> Those of us whose names are listed below, representing some of the most important Christian groups over the world, have a profound love for the land of Palestine and for the Holy City of Jerusalem. We devoutly wish that we could make peace and concord prevail over the entire land, but we are representatives of Religion, not of Politics or of Government Policies, and we can use only persuasion, in no sense the exhibition of force.
>
> In the spirit of Religion and in a united love for the City which is the mother of our religious faith and of the other religious faiths of the Western World, we are united in asking you to establish a "Truce of God," which means a holy area of peace and freedom from violence, in the City of Jerusalem, until once more this whole land which we love and cherish with devotion shall be blessed with peace.

On March 12, this appeal was dispatched to Rabbi Isaac Hertzog, chief rabbi of Palestine, Jerusalem, and to Amin Bey Abdulhabi, head of the Supreme Moslem Council, Jerusalem. Cosigners with Rufus Jones were the Most Reverend Geoffrey Francis Fisher, Archbishop of Canterbury; Bishop Eivind Bergraav, primate of the Church of Norway; the Right Reverend Henry Knox Sherrill, Presiding Bishop of the Protestant Episcopal Church of America; Archbishop Athenagoras of the Greek Orthodox Church, representing the Eastern Orthodox Church; Dr. John R. Mott, leader of the International YMCA; and Dr. Harry Emerson Fosdick, pastor emeritus of Riverside Church in New York. Unfortunately, it had not been possible to procure the signature of anyone representing the Roman Catholic Church.

James G. Vail was in Africa at this time. Although we felt that the united appeal to Jews and Arabs was appropriate, we also felt it was not likely to receive serious consideration unless it could be backed up by personal interviews. We therefore communicated with James Vail, who agreed to proceed to Cairo and Palestine on behalf of the Committee (1) to inquire into the possibilities of organizing some practical service which would involve an increasing element of reconciliation between Arabs and Jews, and (2) to inquire into the feasibility and means of securing a truce in the limited but clearly defined area of the Old City of Jerusalem and the immediately adjacent area of the Mount of Olives. English Friends co-operated by appointing Edgar B. Castle, a distinguished English educator, to join James Vail in this mission.

Meanwhile, as of Easter Sunday, March 28, the story of the united appeal was released to the press. Thus far no reply had reached us. But the next day we received the following cable from Rabbi Hertzog: "HEARTILY ENDORSE PROPOSED TRUCE OF GOD FOR CITY OF JERUSALEM. MY HEARTFELT BLESSINGS FOR SUCCESS YOUR EFFORTS."

The approach of May 15, the terminating date of the British mandate in Palestine, made this an acutely critical period in the life of that country. A cable received from James Vail and Edgar Castle after their visit to Jerusalem in April read in part as follows:

SAW JERUSALEM DISINTEGRATING BEFORE OUR EYES INTO PHYSICAL AND MORAL CHAOS. SITUATION CLOSE TO ANARCHY. DESTRUCTIVE HOUSE TO HOUSE CONFLICT DEMOLISHING HOMES AND CIVIC BUILDINGS. MURDER TO SECURE WEAPONS COMMONPLACE. FEAR AND SUSPICION DISRUPTING CIVIC LIFE ALREADY APPROACHING STANDSTILL. UNLESS FIGHTING CEASES BEFORE FIFTEENTH MAY JERUSALEM FACES DESTRUCTION. CUTTING OF WATER FUEL ELECTRICITY IMMINENT. DISEASE WILL SPREAD AND MULTI-PLY PRESENT SUFFERING. SERIOUS REFUGEE PROBLEM INEVITABLE. IMME-DIATE APPOINTMENT SUCCESSOR CIVIL AUTHORITY JERUSALEM VITAL. URGENT NEED FOR INITIAL SIGNIFICANT AND IMMEDIATE ACTION TO RELIEVE TENSION AND INTRODUCE ELEMENT OF STABILITY. URGE APPROACH AT HIGHEST LEVELS IMMEDIATE IMPLEMENTATION INTERNATIONAL AREA AROUND JERUSALEM UNDER GOVERNOR AND DISCIPLINED NEUTRAL POLICE.

Later cables recommended that our Committee co-operate with the YMCA and the Red Cross in refugee services in Jerusalem under the general sponsorship of the International Red Cross. We were also advised that truce possibilities for the Old City of Jeru-salem were being extensively explored.

Then on April 28 we received the very welcome information that the Secretary of the Arab League had informed James Vail and Edgar Castle that the League was announcing its sponsorship of a truce for the Old City of Jerusalem and the Mount of Olives.

Thus when a cease-fire order for Jerusalem became effective under the British High Commissioner early in May, with both Jews and Arabs co-operating, we had the satisfaction of knowing that, among others working for a truce, our delegates had played some part in the successful negotiations.

With this much accomplished, the next problem that emerged was the need for funds to support the use of the beautiful YMCA building in Jerusalem for refugee services. The YMCA was heart-ily behind this project, but could not assume total financial respon-sibility. We therefore undertook to raise extra funds. The Service Committee itself contributed $7500. I obtained a gift of $23,000, the

YMCA put in $10,000, and the Church of the Brethren $5000, making a total of $45,500. Part of this money was sent immediately, but rapid changes in the situation in Jerusalem soon made the project untenable. It was, however, resumed at a later date.

Meanwhile, on May 7 a new development had taken place. Andrew Cordier called me to say that the United Nations wished to set up a UN administration of Jerusalem on a temporary basis, and that Jews and Arabs had united in naming myself as one acceptable to both groups as municipal commissioner. From his description of the office, I understood that it would not be primarily administrative, as in the case of a mayor, but rather that the commissioner would stand between the two groups, Jews and Arabs, and try to see that the joint administration of the whole of Jerusalem was made to work.

While I was deeply moved by this request, I felt that probably I would be of greater use in the scene if I stayed by my present work. We were then asked to suggest another Friend, and succeeded in getting Harold Evans to accept the appointment. We also prevailed upon James Vail, who had just arrived in Philadelphia, to return to Palestine with Harold Evans on this uncertain but important mission.

One of my treasured memories of the period of preparation for their departure is an interview the three of us had with Rabbi Judah Magnes, who for twenty years had been chancellor of the Hebrew University in Jerusalem. He was one of the world's saints and prophets. The strain of the war period and the closing of his university proved too much for him, and it was not long after this interview that he was stricken, and died.

By the time Harold Evans and James Vail left the United States the latter part of May, the situation in Palestine had altered drastically. The British mandate had ended, the new state of Israel had been proclaimed and recognized by the United States among others, and there was war throughout Palestine, including Jerusalem. Count Folke Bernadotte had been appointed UN Mediator. Obviously, for the time being the office of municipal commissioner for Jerusalem could not be developed as planned, but it was thought that, because Harold Evans's appointment had been approved by both the Jewish Agency and the Arab Higher Committee, he and James Vail might be helpful in the work of mediation.

They were warmly welcomed by Count Bernadotte and his party, whom they met in Cairo, and with whom they proceeded to Jerusalem where they participated in a number of conferences aimed at a truce in the over-all conflict in Palestine.

This effort on the part of our Committee was one of those ventures that has to be undertaken in an emergency, and even though the particular object of the mission was not accomplished, it did probably help in the important work of negotiation.

The assassination of Count Bernadotte in September was a double blow to those of us in the Service Committee who had known him personally.

That the leadership passed into the hands of Dr. Ralph Bunche was one of those blessings all too rare in political history. When at a later date in Geneva I was talking with Elsa Cedergren, Count Bernadotte's sister, of her brother's death, she spoke in this same vein of warmest appreciation for Dr. Bunche.

I have thus sketched some of the earlier events of 1948, to show that, although our Committee had had small experience in that part of the world when the United Nations asked us to undertake a program of relief among Arab refugees in Palestine, the request did not arrive in a vacuum.

Emergency appeals during the past six months had served to focus the world's attention on the dire condition of what ultimately totaled nearly a million such refugees. As early as August, 1948, Count Bernadotte had made an urgent appeal to nations in the UN to divert supplies then on the high seas to the Middle East, to help avert colossal tragedy.

The UN plan now called for at least a nine months' emergency program, pending more permanent arrangements, at a cost of

$32,000,000. The International Committee of the Red Cross was asked to be the distributing agency in the main area of Palestine and in Israel, the League of Red Cross Societies in Arab states outside Palestine, and the American Friends Service Committee in that portion of southern Palestine which has come to be known as the Gaza strip. Supplies would be purchased and shipped by the UN agency, the distributing agencies assuming responsibility at Beirut and Port Said. (Later arrangements made with the Egyptian government resulted in that government's providing transportation for our supplies from Port Said to Gaza, as well as warehousing and exemption from customs duties.) Stanton Griffis, United States ambassador to Egypt, was appointed director of the over-all program, designated as United Nations Relief for Palestine Refugees.

After many conferences with Egyptian government officials and UN representatives both in this country and abroad, our Committee decided to undertake the assignment. The official invitation came to us from Secretary General Trygve Lie on December 7, 1948.

The next day I went to Washington, to the office of the Food and Agriculture Organization, to ask Norris Dodd, Director General, whether the FAO mission in Cairo might lend one or two men to help us get the southern Palestine program under way. He was most co-operative, and said he would ask the Egyptian head of mission there to comply with our request. Several other organizations came forward with offers of assistance. UNICEF (the United Nations International Children's Emergency Fund) called from Lake Success to say they had supplies of food at Port Said, which they would make available to us.

We had been working on the problem of personnel, and in this respect were greatly encouraged. Very excellent persons here and in England were volunteering to go if they could be of service.

Our first workers left for Palestine toward the end of December, after AFSC representatives had negotiated initial arrangements with the Egyptian government for entry of some fifty Quaker workers into the closed Gaza-strip area, and for other forms of co-operation and support which were vital to our effort. On their return, these representatives urged my going to Cairo to assist in cementing these agreements, since Quakers were barely known to the Egyptians, and the Gaza strip was an active war area occupied by the Egyptian army. They described a strip of land not more than twenty-two miles long and five miles wide, all of it sand, containing a local population of about 80,000, a superimposed refugee population of more than 200,000, and thousands of Egyptian troops.

The condition of the refugees, many with only the sky for shelter, was desperate. More than half of them were unskilled agricultural workers, 90 per cent were illiterate, more than half were women and children. The political-military climate was tense. Battle lines were not so far away but that the noise and illumination of exploding bombs and gunfire were a common experience. It was most important that the Egyptian government and army understand fully who we were, what we had undertaken to do, and why.

On January 7, 1949, Lilly Pickett and I were clipper-bound for Geneva, Cairo, and Palestine.

In Geneva I had an interview with Dr. Brock Chisholm, director of the World Health Organization, who was lending Dr. Jerome Peterson for our work in southern Palestine, plus another doctor to be co-ordinator of all medical services for the UN project.

Here it should be noted that Dr. Peterson, a Negro physician from New York, proved to be not only extremely competent, but highly valuable by very reason of his race. There was widespread distrust of America and Americans throughout the Arab population, and his presence did a great deal to inspire confidence in our mission. I am quite sure, also, that a majority of the refugees had better medical service during the period of his supervision than they had ever before enjoyed.

A few excerpts from the journal I kept in the Middle East might be helpful in giving a kind of everyday picture of what went on in connection with this program early in 1949. Perhaps the personal nature of these quotations should be modified for the purposes of a book, but on the other hand I think this very aspect of the entries demonstrates, far better than any explanation I could make, how the Service Committee functions through the individuals on its staff *as individuals*. The larger the operation, the more we feel the necessity to give personal content to the work, not only within the staff but as far as possible in relation to the persons with whom opportunities are being shared. Since my own contacts were pretty well confined to staff and public officials, the picture I give is one-sided, only scantily suggesting the arduous labors of the AFSC unit and the colorful personal contacts they had with the refugees themselves. Also I find that my journal entries give an exaggerated sense of my own importance in the early stages of the operation in Gaza. Delbert Replogle, who had taken a leave of absence from his business in New Jersey to work in the Acre mission, had now come south to help initiate the Gaza project. Emmett Gulley, who was to be head of mission in Gaza for six or eight months, had soon joined him. Nine or ten Quaker workers were starting relief distributions in and near Gaza by mid-January. I found in dealing with officials in Cairo that our representatives had done a remarkable job of establishing relations of mutual confidence and cordiality. What I did, therefore, was supplementary to their pioneering efforts.

(The first part of this journal has been written while we were in Egypt. As I go over it I realize how much color is lacking. For nearly two weeks when we first arrived, no one could see any government officials here because of fear of bombs. Heavy cordons of soldiers guarded every office. Then gradually that relaxed, and since then we have had plenty of opportunity. The press is so strictly censored that one knows very little of what is happening. In private conversations a great deal has been said to us which is of political nature and which I have not felt free to put in this journal. If the record is monotonous the events have not been. Here is an ancient civilization struggling to be reborn, and the birth pangs are painful. Egypt needs understanding and patience.

While in general America is mistrusted politically, we as individuals have everywhere been cordially received.)

January 16. Athens is the most colorful city we have seen from the air at night. It was a veritable blaze of lights even though we arrived at 2 A.M. We waited there about one and a half hours because military regulations forbid landing in Egypt before sunrise. We saw the delta of the Nile from about 4,000 feet — a patchwork of beautiful green ending sharply where water gives out. Elmon Benton and Avery Demond of the Quaker team and Mr. Ballou from the American Embassy met us at the Farouk Airport near Cairo.

January 17. Had a good talk with Abdel Halim Mahfooz Bey, M.D., of the Egyptian Red Crescent.

Had a brief visit with Stanton Griffis, Ambassador and UN Director of Palestine relief. He spoke with warm appreciation of the unit at Gaza. Invited Lilly and me to go with him to Gaza tomorrow since he has use of a UN plane.

In the evening at six had tea with the family of Dr. Mahfooz in their very charming home. His daughter came to get us in a car with a liveried chauffeur. She has been much in America, and speaks English well. After tea they drove us to the Pyramids — only five miles from their home. It was dark, but bright starlight, and very impressive.

January 18. Up early today. We went to the airport to fly to Gaza. The Ambassador had arranged to fly us up and back the same day. The round trip between Cairo and Beirut is made daily by UN planes — small military aircraft painted white. They are the only Cairo-Beirut planes allowed to land in Israel. Theodora Hodgkin, Elmon Benton, Lilly, and myself went for AFSC; and the Ambassador, his assistant, James Keen,* and Mr. Ballou went from the Ambassador's staff. It was interesting though dreary to fly for one and a half hours and see no vegetation — only sand — except along the Suez Canal. Emmett Gulley met us in the pasture at Gaza which serves as an airfield. He certainly looked prosperous in the new maroon Ford with *Quakers* written on it in Arabic and Eng-

* Whose co-operation we were to find most helpful.

lish. The Ambassador thought the Arabic looked like the word for Coca Cola!

First we saw where the staff lives — in a nice, almost new, modern house, very satisfactory but very crowded. We authorized taking another house which is available. We saw the warehousing facilities for food and blankets — total space for six or seven thousand tons, with about four thousand tons in stock now. Some of the warehouse space is donated by Iraq Petroleum Company.

Then we went to the camps — three of them. Here was the heart of our visit. These Arabs looked thin but mostly not diseased. The Egyptian Army has been helping them out more than I had realized, with both food and tents. But even so, they were a sorry lot. The Bedouin camp was separate — they hold themselves aloof from other Arabs. They have their own typical black tents; sheep, goats, donkeys, and people are all mixed up together. We saw three camps within four miles of Gaza. Blankets were being distributed today — 40,000 of them.

The civil affairs officer of the Egyptian Army gave us a huge lunch, and at three o'clock we were off back to Cairo. We encountered a sandstorm which made landing difficult, but we had a fine pilot from Alabama who brought us down safely just five minutes before airport curfew. . . .

We got the impression that Stanton Griffis is a good man for this job. He certainly is in strong support of our Unit.

January 19. Had a talk with Dr. M. S. Rafey, who was ten years in the United States, graduated at California Agricultural College — *re* diets. Have arranged for him to go to Gaza next week to help the staff in working out simple but important problems of diet to save money and give maximum nourishment. Present diet has too much oils.

January 20. Had fine visit with the Anglican Bishop here, Geoffrey Allen, who has collected money and clothing for us to use. He was formerly in China and knew the Friends Ambulance Unit there. Al Holtz and Kelly Peckham arrived today en route to Gaza. Bernie Klausener, a Swiss of 26 years, who is in charge of receiving our supplies at Port Said, came in for a good visit. He has been with AFSC in Italy and Germany, and is evidently on top of this job at Port Said.

January 22. Got Lilly's first inoculation for cholera at the Embassy. She didn't have time to get it in Philadelphia. Visited the Embassy Library. Got some reading material on Egypt. At ten, saw Mr. Griffis. He will go to Beirut tomorrow, so wanted to talk over Gaza operations. He urged prompt starting of feeding both because of refugee need and also he feared newspaper attack if operation was delayed. Wanted me to hurry up further personnel. I consulted Elmon Benton, who is just back from Gaza, and found feeding is already under way. Flour has begun to be distributed, also meat. Milk distribution will begin today. Attended press conference called by Stanton Griffis. About 50 persons present. UP, AP, *NY Times,* and *London Chronicle* present, as well as Egyptian press. He gave a factual statement about the three agencies, amount of money available — said there were about 650,000 refugees — probably a low estimate.

I sent telegram to Senator Paul Douglas and Congressman Herter, giving facts and urging their support of the bill now before Congress to appropriate $16,000,000. In afternoon, had talk with Azcarate, who is here en route to Jerusalem, where he will be Secretary of the UN Conciliation Commission.

January 23. Elmon Benton, Albert Chapel (just arrived from France), Avery Demond, and I held a Friends Meeting in the hotel parlor for about 40 minutes. Then I called on Hamed Bey Salim Soliman, Dean of the Faculty of Agriculture, Fuad I University. They have about 1400 students, most of whom go into government service, but some become farmers.

Delbert Replogle arrived today and we had a good talk. Also Dr. Peterson.

January 24. Long session this A.M. with Delbert Replogle. I talked out with him plans for final placement of authority. We plan to make Emmett Gully Chief of Unit, Elden Mills Chief of Khan Yunis Section, and Delbert Deputy Chief to consult with Government and to be liaison between Cairo and Gaza. Marshall Sutton and Ray Hartsough, a minister from Gilman, Iowa, arrived today.

Had fine group lunch with all Cairo staff and visitors. Cordelia Trimble is down to have a broken tooth fixed. There are no dentists in Gaza.

Had a good visit with Dr. Elder, head of the American

Mission. Found he came from Albia, Iowa, very near Oskaloosa, where Lilly and I went to college, and we have many
acquaintances in common.

January 25. Visited Ali Maher Pasha, President of the Egyptian Association of Social Studies, to ask him to let Abdul
Hamid Zaki, its Director, give half time to us at Gaza. He
warmly supported the proposed arrangement — would ask for
approval by mail, then let us know. The Pasha's son, who was
present in the interview, was just back from two years' study
at the University of Virginia. . . .

In the evening we had dinner with Ahmed Hussein Bey,
Under-Secretary of the Ministry of Social Welfare, who prom-
ises to help get an assistant for Abdul Hamid Zaki and let him
be with us full time. Also will find some educational materials.
He has a beautiful but simple home and a very beautiful wife.
Her sister is now a graduate student at Bryn Mawr College.

January 26. All-day trip to Gaza by train. It was green farms
almost to Ismailia, the Suez Canal. Irrigated from the Nile.
Very primitive — cows turning pumps to bring up the water
for irrigation. But more beautiful oranges, tangerines, cauli-
flower, cabbage, alfalfa, I've seldom seen. Camels, donkeys,
and water buffalo are the chief sources of power — but I did
see two tractors. The housing is indescribably bad.

With us on the trip were Dr. Rafey of the Egyptian Department of Agriculture, who is going to survey diets for us,
Bernie Klausener from Port Said, Richard Rhoads, who had
been dismantling an unused IRO camp at El Shatt, Delbert
Replogle, and Lawrence Skene just arriving from Newberg,
Oregon. The long train of about 15 cars was almost entirely
soldiers. It took from 11 A.M. to 9 P.M. to make the trip, and
across the desert it was very dusty. But we survived, and I
was warmly welcomed at the Church Missionary Society hospital where I was the guest of Dr. and Mrs. Alfred Hargreaves,
English missionaries. A good warm supper and a good warm
sleep. It has rained here today and is very chilly tonight. In a
recent bombing, 63 window panes were broken and no glass
is available, so the house does not lack for fresh air.

January 27. Went to Rafah and El Qantara Camps today.
Numbers go like this: 5 camps, about 15 miles south of Gaza,
have 70,000 people in them. Gaza has about 64,000. Camps

near Gaza, 75,000. It is appalling. The south camps are out on completely open desert. I saw a man buried, a baby born, hundreds of malnurtured children, a local farmer angry because the refugees are using his trees for firewood, which will leave the sands free to shift again. We saw the problem of the possible surrender of authority by the Army and our assuming it. This project is incredibly difficult. Tragically needed, and absorbingly interesting.

We had a good meeting of the whole Gaza unit in the evening. There are 23 foreign staff here now — 5 more to come, besides medical staff.

January 28. This morning after breakfast I went to prayers with the hospital staff. Before they were over, Delbert Replogle came to take me to the airport to meet Colonel Riley of UN truce-observer staff, who was flying in to head a convoy of food into Fālūja, the pocket of Palestine Arabs and Egyptian soldiers cut off from all communication with the outside world by Israeli forces. We sent 12 tons of food for the 3000 civilians, and the Egyptian Army sent food for the equal number of Egyptian soldiers. Emmett Gulley and Lee Dinsmore went on the convoy, representing AFSC. The whole convoy was arranged by UN truce observers.

They crossed the Egyptian-Israeli army lines not more than two miles east of Gaza. All mines had supposedly been cleared from a fully mined road, but one had been missed and exploded under Emmett's car, fortunately doing no damage. They received a great welcome from Fālūja, which had just reached the end of its supplies. The soldiers and Palestine Arabs caught in this little pocket are all in miserable condition. It is interesting that they had pooled what food they possessed, and had been rationing it strictly and equally. Arrangements are now made to deliver twelve tons weekly to Fālūja, and we hope next time we may be able to have someone from our staff participate in the distribution to civilians.

We called on the Gaza mayor today. He is a very able and well-to-do gentleman who has been Mayor of Gaza for more than thirty years — having served under the old Ottoman Empire. . . . He took us to a child-feeding milk station run by his wife. They are feeding about 600 children daily here, and this is one of four such stations in Gaza. But their supplies will be exhausted in three or four days and they hoped we could take over. We hope to be able to do this.

Spent most of the rest of the day talking with individual members of the staff. In the evening Emmett Gulley outlined the job assignments of all staff members — and did it well. I think all were pleased with the arrangements.

January 29. Up at 4.15. Breakfast at 5. Took the Diesel train at 6 o'clock for Cairo. An uneventful trip, arriving at 1.45. Lilly was much surprised to see me so early. She has been well, and has had some fine new Egyptian contacts since I left. With me came Delbert Replogle, Dick Rhoads, Bernie Klausener, and Dr. Rafey.

We found Dr. Peterson had just arrived from Beirut, and at once we began conferences *re* the medical program. Plans call for about 20 doctors and 30 or 40 nurses. Mostly refugee doctors will be used — some now in Gaza and some from North Palestine. I was asked to write a statement to be used in explaining to government officials "Who are the Quakers and what are they doing here." This I did in 100 words.

January 30. After a brief meeting for worship, met with Delbert Replogle and Cordelia Trimble to discuss the educational program. Continued the discussion at 5 with Dr. Zaki. He will direct the program which will hope to give some educational opportunity to the 65,000 children of school age in the camps. We will try to get teachers from among the refugees and will ask the Egyptian Ministry of Education to help us get blackboards, primers, slates, chalk, and pencils. That is about the only equipment we can expect to assemble.

In the afternoon, Abdul Ibrahim, who knew our daughter Rachel at Ohio State University, took us for a short visit to the Pyramids and the Sphinx. They are interesting, but for me chiefly as a monument to an immense program of slave labor.

January 31. Had conference with El Kibbani Bey, Under-Secretary of the Ministry of Education, and Abdul Hadi Bey, Director of Education in the Sudan, who made a study of education in Gaza before we were there. We asked if they could furnish primers, paper, pencils, slates, and blackboards. They have a big stock of second-hand Arabic primers which they will let us use. Must check to see about other items. El Kibbani Bey is a fan for progressive education and wanted us to try project method. He especially congratulated us on having no ministry of education or even school board to prevent free experimentation.

Called on the Foreign Minister, thanked him for co-operation. He spoke with deep feeling that we had come to help Palestine refugees, and assured us full help. Said he liked our call and hoped we would ask to see him whenever we needed his help. Had lunch with a group from the Egyptian Medical Association, about 10 doctors present, to discuss the medical problems of the refugees. All were interested, were sure we should use refugee doctors as far as we could, promised to help with getting a sanitary engineer. . . .

I have a feeling that these calls on government people may be of some value beyond their significance for Gaza. They are hungry for non-political contacts with people from the West.

February 1. This morning we called on the Under-Secretary of the Ministry of Health. He is also at present Chairman of the Board of the World Health Organization, A. T. Shusha Pasha. Dr. Peterson cleared with him certain financial matters *re* funds for the Gaza health program — he discussed the danger to health as it will come when warm weather arrives. Said malaria, dysentery, and even pneumonia will be much harder to combat due largely to flies. He is a very well-informed man, and will be a help in accepting the principle of using Palestinian doctors, not Egyptian.

Then Dr. Zaki and Mr. Sadhi, of Chase National Bank, joined me in a two-hour session with Abdul Rahman Azzam Pasha, Secretary of the Arab League. This League was organized in an attempt to get joint action by all of the Arab States. Trans-Jordan has now withdrawn from it, and Azzam evidently deeply resents this action. He feels that repatriation of at least 500,000 refugees is basic to any peace settlement. I asked whether he would advise Arab refugees to go back even though they would be a minority group. His answer was a clear *Yes.*

February 2. Had a long talk with the Minister of Education, Sanhouri Pasha. He is a lawyer of distinction, has revised the basic code of Egypt and of Iraq, but is really more interested in education. After we talked a while *re* schools at Gaza, he asked about Quakers. I described their origin, how the term

Quaker originated, the rise of AFSC, the non-priestly character of our ministry, and the voluntary character of our relief workers. He and Abdul Hadi Bey, who was with me, seemed genuinely interested and hoped we could talk further. He especially welcomed a chance to talk about matters of human welfare and not war and politics.

Lilly and I took a little time after lunch to see the old Citadel of Cairo, and especially the Mosque. It is a great work of art, quite as beautiful as any church we have ever seen. Very large, no seats, no pulpit — only a desk from which a scholar reads the Koran. The Moslem faith has no priesthood.

Home at 5 to meet Monsignor McMahon, whom I have known in New York as the director of activities of the Catholic Church in the Middle East, attached to the staff of Cardinal Spellman. He has been in the Middle East many times, and is just now completing a three-months visit. I am much impressed to find the Catholics giving considerable quantities of relief to Moslems, and willing to let the deed be the only means of spiritual message.

February 3. Lilly and I had lunch with Mr. and Mrs. Jefferson Patterson. (He is Chargé d'Affaires of the American Embassy.) They had several people — the Swedish Minister, Egyptian Minister of Health, the dean of the foreign correspondents, and several members of the Embassy staff. The Minister of Health, who sat by me, was especially concerned to discuss repatriation of refugees. He opposed it. Felt an Arab minority in Israel would be unwelcome and unhappy. But he proposed no alternative.

February 4. Mrs. Hussein came to drive us to a new agricultural development where Afifi Pasha, a distinguished Egyptian who was a doctor, then a diplomat, and now President of the Egyptian National Bank, has reclaimed pure desert land — 200 acres now and starting on a second 200. In eight years he has brought this pure sand to produce all kinds of vegetables in abundance, plus grapes, pineapples, oranges, and dates. He has model housing for workers, and a very charming though simple house for his family. He spends the week in Cairo, and Friday evening, Saturday, and Sunday on the farm. He employs 100 workers the year round — says that though hand-labor is low-paid it is expensive, and he looks toward gradual mechanization. He believes Arab refugees themselves and not Arab politicians should decide whether they should go back into Jewish-controlled territory. Also believes they need to learn that they will have to stand up for their rights and not be as dependent as they were. He does not share the usual fears of Jewish persecution. . . .

. . . . Met Norris Dodd, Director General of FAO, and Hefnawy Pasha, Chief of the FAO Mission in the Middle East, to talk over possible FAO help for the Gaza Mission.

February 5. Had a conference with Ambassador Griffis, who has just returned from the north and stopped at Gaza. He was impressed by the efficiency of the unit at Gaza. Wants us to get another house for workers to live in, so they can spread out. Wants to know how he can help Cairo service them better — ordered a car and driver to drive up one day, return next, and keep that up regularly to see they have all needs met.

Had a nice visit with Corrinne Hardesty, who came in from Gaza. She reports things going very well, high morale. They got possession of the third house today. Yesterday she went with the convoy from Gaza to Fālūja, where they made their second delivery of food — this time 14 tons. She reports people there listless and almost starving. Levinus Painter and Charles Freeman from the unit at Acre (in Israel) came down to meet them. It is the first time the two units have met. They brought Delbert Replogle some clothes from Acre where his wife, Ruth Replogle, is located.

Had dinner with Mr. Coates, local UNICEF (Children's Fund) representative, and Dr. Descoeudres, the Middle-East representative. We are to be the distributing agent for all UNICEF supplies in Gaza.

February 6. We had a meeting for worship this morning, then Delbert Replogle and I had a talk with the Prime Minister. We were quietly but very cordially received. We told him of some of the difficulties we were having with minor officials, and that specific cases had been presented to the Finance Minister, who would probably bring them up to the Cabinet. He assured us that he would ask his colleagues in the various Ministries to look into bottlenecks, such as delay in shipping gasoline to Gaza. He said the way was always open for us to come to him. He spoke of the great satisfaction it was to have a chance to aid a truly humanitarian effort, as contrasted with the usual political appeals. He said he envied us. We were quite moved by his evident sincerity and understanding of the religious motivation which he felt prompted us.

Ballou, of Mr. Griffis' staff, is taking 12 newspaper men to Gaza next Friday. Beds and sleeping items will not be easy, but Corrinne will look after that.

We made our farewells. . . . Just as we left, Cassius Fenton arrived fresh from Philadelphia. To the airfield, and a two-hour flight to Beirut. It was a slightly bumpy trip and cloudy, so we didn't see much. We flew, not over the land, but just offshore over the Mediterranean Sea. Beirut is certainly clean and quiet as compared with Cairo. We are housed in the Normandy Hotel on the shore — a clean, modern hotel and very reasonable rates. It is infinitely quiet as compared with Cairo, and thus far, no beggars!

February 7. Contacted UN representative and found that a plane leaves for Tel Aviv and Jerusalem tomorrow, and then no plane until Friday, so we decided to proceed to Tel Aviv tomorrow. We got our exit and re-entry permits from the Lebanese Government this morning. It has rained two thirds of the time today — quite a contrast to Egypt, where it almost never rains.

February 8. We had a pleasant flight, first to Haifa (30 minutes) then Tel Aviv (another 35 minutes). We were impressed with the density of population of Israel Palestine. Large and relatively modern villages are all along the coast — in the inland valleys. There are literally thousands of little new houses. They look very much like some of the Farm Security settlements which we know at home. I called James G. McDonald, our Ambassador here, as soon as we got in to the Kaete Dan Hotel where we are staying. He invited us to tea at 4.30. . . . UN truce observers are thick around the hotel, and, as we have found elsewhere, are a fine lot.

We had a good visit with McDonald and his wife. He showed me several documents from Washington which indicate their interest in resettlement of refugees. This was cheering. He agreed to ask President Weizmann and Foreign Secretary Shertok to see me. They are very busy this week, since next Monday they hold their first Constituent Assembly in 3500 years.

This has been the most unpleasant, stormy day here in 15 years. It has rained and been very cold and windy. Our hotel is crowded, cold, and drafty. We are told that it snowed in Jerusalem today — a very exceptional occurrence. . . .

Dr. Mohn, a Swedish acquaintance of ours, is here as personal representative of the Mediator, Ralph Bunche. The prevalence of soldiers and the constant drilling of boys and girls in the streets make us know we are in a country which is on a war footing.

February 9. Dr. Mohn loaned us his car and driver, who brought us 60 miles to Jerusalem this evening. It rained almost all of the way, and half of the distance is over a new road which has been built since the war because part of the regular highway is controlled by Abdullah's Arab Legion. It was full of holes and slow, but we made it safely. Within 15 miles of Jerusalem we found snow. It is a steep climb up the mountain to Jerusalem, and when we got here we found six or eight inches of snow and slush. Along the way we passed 15 or 20 former Arab villages completely demolished and deserted. A good deal of the land lies unused, though most of the orange groves are full of fruit. Olive trees, which seem to flourish on very stony and unpromising soil, looked fine. But the last 25 miles looked to us like desolate piles of rock with little promise of ever being productive.

February 10. In Jerusalem, we have stopped at the YMCA, the most beautiful Y building in the world, so they claim. James Sutton, a Friend, is in charge. The Y is used entirely by UN truce observers and soldiers from U.S., France, and Belgium, who do guard duty on neutral buildings, such as the Government House, the Y, the King David Hotel, and Consular offices.

We had a long talk with Mark Ethridge, American member of the United Nations Palestine Conciliation Commission. He is very much under the weight of our Arab refugee problems — believes some repatriation is possible and necessary — and also believes U.S. should finance some immigration projects, etc., in Syria, Jordan, and Iraq, as a long-time development. But the Commission has reached no conclusions yet. . . . I was favorably impressed with his grasp of the problem, and with two young aides whom he has with him.

Dr. Ollendorff, who heads a group of people, mostly Jews, concerned with reconciliation, came in for a talk. He can get Catholics, Protestants, and Jews together, but now no Arabs. Just now his group is buying mules for a few Arabs who are still in Israel but lost their livestock in the fighting. Most of the money he raises locally. He is a radiant and unconquerable spirit and I feel sure we should help him out.

Norman Bentwich of London came in and we talked about a small Service Committee of Jews he is getting started. He wants them to work with us at Acre. I hope to see two of their young people who are at Acre when we get there tomorrow.

This afternoon, Dr. Martin Buber, one of the greatest living Jewish religious scholars, formerly of Frankfurt, Germany, and now of Jerusalem, Dr. Ollendorff, and Norman Bentwich came to the King David Hotel, and we had a priceless talk.

Martin Buber is a man of deep discernment, an elderly seer, a prophet in the tradition of Isaiah, Jeremiah, Amos, and Hosea. I shall always remember him sitting in the rather solitary grandeur of the King David Hotel lobby, looking forward to the day when hopefully the political struggles will sufficiently subside so that he may again be permitted to teach oncoming generations in the Hebrew University from whose buildings he is now excluded because it is located in the Arab part of Jerusalem. Though he feels keenly that Israel for the moment is too preoccupied with physical rebuilding to turn toward the spiritual realities which alone can make the enterprise significant, he declared, with the confidence of a true prophet, "The time will come, and I must keep my faith in the persistent work of God. . . ."

Beirut, February 11. . . . This morning in Haifa we got our passage cleared on the UN plane for twelve o'clock, then got a taxi and drove to Acre. Got a permit from the military government to go into the walled city, where we found Levinus Painter, Charles Freeman, and Don Peretz. Ruth Replogle was in Haifa for a brief rest.

We went to the clothing room, then to the simple quarters where the staff live. They are clean and overlook the Mediterranean, but are certainly not luxurious. No food is yet there from the International Red Cross, and I will try to work that out with Dr. Escher of IRC. Some UNICEF milk is coming. But the population is pretty badly starved. It is touching to see how welcome our staff people are. They badly need supplies of food to distribute. But they do gradually get permission for people to go out to cultivate their gardens, tend their orchards, and do other work.

The three men drove us back to Haifa, fifteen miles, in their jeep. We located Ruth Replogle, and all then got in the truck and rode out with us to the UN plane. Thirty minutes later we were in Beirut.

February 14. Daniel Oliver (who with his wife has spent almost 50 years operating a school and orphanage for Arab children at Ras-el-Metn) showed up today — came down by bus. He had received none of my messages. He urged me to go with him to King Abdullah, but I couldn't. And, in fact, I don't feel such an interview is necessary. Much is being done by the Conciliation Commission that Daniel didn't know about. He agreed to go to see Weizmann and Shertok in Israel and, since he knows both of them well, this seems to me important. Daniel still has great vitality. At 79 he has never spent one day in bed with illness.

Delbert Replogle came in today and we had much reporting *re* Gaza, Fālūja, and personnel. On the whole the relief job is going well, and Delbert now is concerning himself with what next for the refugees. Also, he is very concerned to get food to Acre. In the evening we had dinner with the League of Red Cross people at St. George's Hotel. We agreed that basically what we are seeing here is the arrival of the industrial revolution to a people wholly or largely unprepared for it. They (especially the simple Arab farmers) are totally bewildered, but will never be able to return to their former isolated and primitive life. The question is, how can they be helped to adapt to this change with the least suffering and loss. And we all agreed that basically the spirit of religion is central in this adjustment.

This latter point, of the need for a fundamentally religious viewpoint if this part of the world's terrifically complex problems are to be worked through, I found shared by persons of many faiths — Jewish, Catholic, Protestant, Quaker, Moslem. On the level of politics, history, psychology (all of them important) the problem still seemed flatly insoluble unless there was brought to bear that deep communion in which all of us are one family. As I went about, talking with persons of the different faiths, it began to seem to me not impossible that the words of the great prophets would even yet prove to be the note which alone could bring peace within this great family of kindred peoples: the call of Allah in the Koran, "But I invite you to the Mighty, the Forgiving"; and of Micah in the Old Testament, "And what doth the Lord require of thee, but to do justly, and to love mercy, and to walk humbly with thy God?"; and of Jesus in the New Testament, "Love your enemies . . . do good to them that hate you, and pray for them which despitefully use you."

One of the most resourceful developments in our Unit's work in the Gaza strip was the school put together out of almost nothing. A few of the refugees, especially from Jaffa, had been engaged in business in a large, comfortable way. Others were professional men. The children of these families had had their education abruptly cut off. Add to these the majority of the 65,000 refugee children who had had little or no educational opportunity, and the need for schools was seen to be second only to the basic needs for food, blankets, and medicine.

Dr. Zaki worked with the director of our Unit in securing the co-operation of Gaza officials and teachers, and of refugee teachers. Approximately four hundred men from among the refugees volunteered their services as teachers. Of course most of these had only the most elementary type of schooling themselves. Special funds came from the Anglican Cathedral in Cairo, from Church World Service, and from UNESCO. Equipment arrived from the Egyptian Ministry of Education, and from other interested groups in Egypt, England, and Norway. In tents, with only straw mats or sand for seats, teachers went forward with the three R's in Arabic, in large part minus textbooks, blackboards, or slates. For most of the population it was an astonishing experience to have free education, and

for girls as well as boys, without economic, religious, or other discrimination, and — as nearly as we could make it so — without
political propaganda. The venture was highly popular. About 18,000
were enrolled in classes, with a daily average attendance of 16,000.

Weaving, sewing, embroidery, and carpentry were added to the
academic curriculum. More than 1000 metres of cloth were woven
in school-classes for relief distribution. In community weaving enterprises established by this program, about 450,000 metres were
woven.

A public laundry and bathing center constructed near one of
the distribution centers was a major morale-builder.

When the Unit's services were at their peak, more than a hundred doctors, nurses, and nurses' aides were conducting crowded
clinics (average monthly attendance, 200,000), running hospitals,
spraying persons and tents with DDT, giving inoculations and
vaccinations. During the entire UNRPR operation, no disease ac-
quired epidemic proportions — a high tribute to the thoroughness
of the medical teams and the co-operation of refugees.

Some five hundred Palestinians were employed to aid in distributions of food and blankets. (Shelter meant only tents and
blankets; hence the importance of blanket distributions.) Food
rations of 1500 to 1800 calories per day per person for more than
200,000 refugees included, principally, flour, beans, dried peas, rice,
sugar, meat, cooking oil or margarine, onions, dates, and salt. In
addition, on behalf of UNICEF, we administered a program involving more than 100,000 individual distributions of milk per day
for many months.

The AFSC worked in this program for sixteen months, from
January, 1949, through April, 1950. At least twenty-five agencies,
exclusive of UN member governments, assisted in one way or
another, some of them with great imaginativeness and vigor.

Such are the major over-all statistics. It was one of the most
difficult jobs our Committee ever undertook. Facilities which our
workers usually take for granted in setting up relief projects were

almost totally lacking: practically no tools or materials available in the desert locale, even wood being virtually nonexistent; with the exception of a few abandoned mosques, no public buildings available as distribution centers; no public-welfare or social-service organizations to build on; no local government outside the town of Gaza; communications possible only through UN truce observers' radio; no telephones; no regular mail delivery.

It is greatly to the credit of our staff of about fifty volunteers from nine countries that the program was actually carried out in a relatively effective and orderly manner. It is also a tribute to Egyptian government personnel and army officers, to the citizens of Gaza, and to the Arab refugees themselves, who co-operated with a remarkable degree of dignity, stability, and responsiveness. This does not mean there were not problems with government, or near-riots among refugees, nor does it mean there were not many complaints. But any relief agency going into a situation so fraught with tensions and insecurity must expect difficulties of this sort.

One thing which troubled our Unit during the entire operation was that it received such a consistently bad press in Egypt — a country in which the press was government-controlled. This is not the usual experience of Quaker overseas workers. Thirty-five years of service in some twenty-five countries have accustomed us to a considerable amount of co-operation from the press, which made this Egyptian experience stand out the more vividly. However, I am sure it was to be interpreted as part of the general feeling against the West, and not as directed against our Unit personally.

Back in the United States after our trip, I had conversations with a number of the American Jewish community and with certain Arab leaders, concerning what we had seen in Palestine. I tried to tell the same story to both groups.

The willingness to make concessions — Jews to allow Arabs to return, Arabs to be willing to believe in the integrity of Jews — was perhaps too much to expect so soon after the war. The establishment of the modern state of Israel was to loyal Zionists cause for rejoicing comparable only to the re-establishment of the little kingdom in Biblical times. Also, they saw it as fulfillment of their calling to bring the benefits of modern civilization to the Middle East. Their kinsmen, the Arabs, however, looked on the event as sheer aggression, a threat to the sovereignty of their state and their way of life, if not to life itself.

It seems clear that until settlement is made for properties taken by Jews from Arabs in Palestine, and until the refugees cease to be considered political pawns and are allowed to resettle with a chance at a reasonable standard of living, there is not likely to be stability and security in the Middle East. Israel must develop industries and the Arab states are her natural market; but trade cannot flourish between enemies.

There was a clear feeling among Arabs that the United States had taken the side of Israel in the conflict; therefore the long-standing good will between our country and the Arab states in the Middle East had greatly diminished. Whether or not it was just, our government would for a long time to come suffer a handicap because of this judgment against it. It seemed to us, therefore, the more important that private groups with no desire but to serve, and with an attitude of good will toward both Israel and the Arab states, should find concrete ways to help in the process of resettlement.

Early in 1950, before our Committee's service in southern Palestine was terminated, we were asked by the State Department to submit a program of social and economic projects for Arab refugees in the Gaza strip, which could be financed from UN funds. This was clear admission of the fact that the refugees' basic problem would remain unsolved for a long time to come. And it has proved to be so.

We responded to this request to the best of our ability before turning the work over to UN. After several postponements, the transfer finally occurred as of the end of April, 1950, and the new

UN organization — United Nations Relief and Works Agency — assumed complete responsibility for the Arab refugees, including the problem of their resettlement.

Meanwhile our Committee's continuing interest in the Middle East is at present expressed through two programs in the state of Israel, both of them designed to increase the mutual knowledge and understanding between Jews and Arabs. A neighborhood center in Acre has grown directly out of the early relief efforts. In its baby clinic, language classes, young people's groups, discussion and music groups, this center brings together many elements of the community of Old Acre. Then in a small experimental farming project in Tu'ran, a village in eastern Galilee, Quaker agriculturists help Arab farmers learn more advanced farming methods and thus move forward with their Jewish neighbors. Both of these activities have the complete co-operation of the government of Israel.

For a number of months British and American Friends have been exploring possibilities for a Friends' resettlement project among Arab refugees in West Jordan. At the time of this writing, plans are still in the formative stage.

III
From the Nameless
to the Nameless

It is the silent help from the nameless to the nameless which is their contribution to the promotion
of brotherhood among nations.

> — GUNNAR JAHN, Chairman of the Nobel
> Committee, in presenting the Nobel Peace
> Prize for 1947 to Friends Service Council
> and the American Friends Service Com-
> mittee

W HAT is this American Friends Service Committee, whose
work forms so large a part of the subject matter of this book?
   In considering how to describe it, I am reminded of the blind
men's attempt to describe the elephant. He who throws his arms
around the elephant's leg says he is like a telephone pole. He who
feels of his ears says he is like a fan. He who rubs the end of his
trunk says he is like a rope.
   To some people the Committee is about 250 persons nominated
by various groups of Friends in this country and Canada to serve
as Committee members. These members meet once a year to
transact Corporation business, and at least two other times to hear
reports of what has been accomplished, to pool their own ideas of
what might be done, and to discuss major matters of policy.
   Others think of the Service Committee as primarily the Executive
Board, which consists of fifty persons drawn from members of the
Corporation, including one representative from each of the thirteen
regional offices. This Board meets monthly to consider questions of
policy, and to make decisions in regard to new projects and issues.
   Still others, when AFSC is mentioned, see the multiplicity of
committees and subcommittees that discuss work camps, race re-
lations, school affiliation, seminars, rehabilitation enterprises, and a
score of other activities.
   To many people the American Friends Service Committee is one
of the thirteen regional offices in the United States, located in
Austin, Texas; Cambridge, Massachusetts; Chicago; Columbus,
Ohio; Des Moines; Greensboro, North Carolina; Pasadena; Phila-

delphia; Portland, Oregon; Richmond, Indiana; San Francisco; Seattle; Wichita, Kansas.

To hundreds of people, AFSC is the staff at 20 South Twelfth Street, Philadelphia, the Committee's home office since it came into being in 1917. At present about two hundred persons carry on the business of this central office, and all of them, from clerical beginners to the executive secretary, feel themselves, I hope, integral parts of the American Friends Service Committee.

Most of these Philadelphia staff members are paid workers, many with a certain amount of professional training. Salaries are not high, but neither, I believe, could they be said to be unduly low. We aim to make it possible for persons who share AFSC goals to work with us and at the same time have an adequately comfortable personal and family life. That an AFSC worker has to earn his living does not in itself mean less dedication, and sometimes I think that in stressing the amount of volunteer service in our program — particularly in the foreign field — we neglect to pay due tribute to the magnificent contributions made by hundreds of our paid staff over the years.

The ideal of AFSC, in line with Quaker practice, is that decisions on matters small and great should be made on the basis of unanimity within the group responsible for the decision. A full discussion of the issues involved is encouraged, and it is our conviction that if even one concerned member of the group feels a deep sense of doubt this should not be overridden but should be given further consideration. Usually if a group will go deep enough it can find ground acceptable to all, and one member's lack of convincement may be exactly the signal we need to go deeper. In this, as in all else, we do not attain to perfection, but in all the twenty-two years in which I have served with the Committee I have never known a deep and continuing dissension. Many times wide differences of opinion have existed, but in the end usually something better than anyone had at first conceived becomes the basis of action.

Of all the new steps taken by the Committee during the years of

my service as executive secretary, I think none was more difficult
than the decision to develop regional offices. There were those who
felt sure that the consequent added complications in raising funds
and in determining and controlling policy would threaten the very
life and integrity of the Committee. But all the time the urge for
this kind of expansion was growing stronger. It sprang from the
desire of local groups of Friends in different parts of the country
not only to make contributions and hear reports but to share in the
on-going life and activities of the Committee itself. Finally it
seemed quite clear that the home office and those who had participated in the founding and development of AFSC had no right to
stand in the way of other groups wishing to be part of it, and I can
now say that over the years nothing has added more to the strength,
expansion, and fellowship of the Committee than this step. The
vigor with which programs have been initiated and carried out by
regional offices — often leading the home office in certain directions
rather than following — would in itself make an exciting story. It
has never been our Committee's practice to aim for expansion, but
this kind of enlargement has been a matter of recognizing growth
and development in local groups and co-operating with it — a
process which adds to the cumulative strength of the Committee as
a whole rather than dissipating it. To learn how to accept growth
has been one of the continuous efforts of those of us who have
worked in this great adventure.

But there are other groups also who are the Service Committee.
There are the women who collect, clean, repair, make, and pack
clothing for use in other parts of the world. Today there are several
thousand women in a multitude of groups across the country who
with tender care and spiritual devotion continue this service, which
in its spirit comes as close to the heart of our intent as anything we
do.

For more than twenty years Eleanor Stabler Clarke, volunteering her services in the home office, has developed this work to
where it now uses four baling and shipping centers and a dozen or

so other large collection centers. More than once the year's intake has been valued at over a million dollars, the actual value being many times that figure. In recent years between one and two million pounds annually have been handled — clothing, bedding, shoes, textiles, leather, and soap. Shipments have been made to the Middle East, Africa, Asia, Europe, South America; to Jamaica and Puerto Rico; and, within the United States, to American Indians, Japanese relocation centers, coal regions, and groups of refugees and displaced persons. In scope, it is definitely "big business." But it is carried on almost entirely by volunteers, the greater part of them women.

Eleanor Clarke has an endless stock of stories as to ways in which dedicated persons have managed to give abundantly. A woman in New Jersey whose husband died a number of years ago, and whose children are married, last summer completed her one-thousandth little girl's dress for AFSC. She makes the dresses for overseas distribution with the same fine taste and loving care which she would bestow on her own children's clothing. She is not a Quaker. Both she and we know that, in the fellowship of suffering and sharing, labels are not important.

A woman in Iowa specializes in darning stockings. She has darned more than five hundred pairs for overseas shipment. A retired farmer in Iowa pieces quilts! A woman in Philadelphia focuses her efforts on beautiful layettes. Another woman gathers her neighbors' waste fats and makes soap; she has contributed more than three thousand cakes. A Quaker professor's wife has knit about one hundred children's sweaters.

Even where the gifts to this program are large quantities of fabrics from textile firms, the personal aspect is by no means lost. For these goods must be made up into garments. Sewing groups in Europe and Asia come together to provide gay new attire for children and other persons in need and not able to help themselves. The sense of common enterprise, the security of fellowship developed in these overseas sewing groups, has been an immeasurable blessing in countries devastated by war and permeated with bitter mistrust between neighbor and neighbor.

There are other things that happen in the handling of clothing gifts — sometimes amusing, unusual incidents. There are stories of fearsome and wonderful articles donated, though by and large the donated clothing is sturdy and practical, some of it new. There are out-of-the-ordinary projects, such as the time AFSC outfitted the Budapest Symphony Orchestra with dress suits donated in clothing drives. Then there is the story of how Henry J. Cadbury, chairman of the Committee, made personal use of the Philadelphia warehouse. It was when the 1947 Nobel Peace Prize was awarded jointly to Friends Service Council and the American Friends Service Committee, and the Committee decided that Henry Cadbury should be the one to go to Oslo, Norway, to receive its half of the prize. The presentation of this award is always a very formal affair, and Henry Cadbury was told it would be necessary for him to have a dress suit with tails. But he had no such suit, and he was not disposed to buy one. Then he had an inspiration. He wrote to the used-clothing warehouse, and was sent exactly the kind of suit he needed. What was more, it turned out to be a perfect fit. So that was what he wore to receive the Nobel Prize. Afterward it joined the other suits that were baled and shipped to Budapest.

But I am getting off my subject of what the Service Committee actually is. On the other hand, I am closer to its essence in relating small personal incidents than I would be if I tried to give a clear logical outline. The Committee has not grown according to a pre-established and therefore logically organized plan. Its work has sprung from the deep, personal concerns of innumerable individuals, and in terms of these concerns the organization is workable. But from the outside it must often appear to be a sprawling mass of the most heterogeneous activity.

For the Service Committee is also our foreign service workers who go on a maintenance basis to the far corners of the earth, and who ever afterward feel — and rightly so — that they are part of the Committee. Sometimes they even pay a part or all of their expenses. And there are the hundreds of volunteers in work projects in Mexico and the United States, among whom contributions toward their own expenses are common and even usual. I have often been interested to hear groups of this sort discussing Committee policy as though they were the sole determining policy makers. Sometimes I have had to remind myself that many of these matters are in the final analysis decided by an Executive Board. Surely it is a testimony to the inclusiveness which is represented by the AFSC family to find so many groups feeling that they are the Committee itself. I hope we shall never lose that sense of participation and integration.

I have had many discussions with people interested in this kind of work, concerning our personnel policies. Are we not exploiting labor in our use of volunteers? Among the many applicants for work with us, do we not get the unemployed who cannot find jobs anywhere else? Are we not pestered with square pegs trying to fit into round holes? These are pertinent questions, and there are other dangers, as well, which do not so readily occur to the average person. More than once I have had to caution volunteer overseas workers about spending too long a time abroad, because they may find it very difficult to settle back into life at home. Or they have responsibilities to their families which protracted service with us would not equip them to fulfill. Sometimes the unusual and dramatic nature of work abroad tends to hold the volunteer, seeming to represent a more vital contribution than he could make elsewhere. The greater conception is that all of our living is to be thought of as a contribution to society, and not just emergency assignments.

While there is the difficulty of having "misfits" volunteer or apply for a paid job with us because they can't find other work, it is not hard to establish minimum standards which automatically disqualify a large proportion of the incompetent. It would not be fair to our contributors, to the work, or to the workers themselves, if we were to appoint persons who proved unable to shoulder the required load. Of course this does occur in a few isolated cases, but far less frequently than one might imagine.

A more common experience is that of finding people of great capacity who wish to invest at least part of their life in the kind of work we undertake. Some of these persons are able to volunteer their time. There are those who have made it a practice to pull away from their regular business every few years, to give anywhere from six to eighteen months to the Committee on a volunteer basis. I believe one can easily feel that the enrichment of life that has come to them in this way has been well worth the adjustments they had to make. James Vail, who recently died in the course of duty for the Committee in India, pursued this in-and-out policy for many years. Vice-president of the Philadelphia Quartz Company, he was a highly skilled chemist, greatly respected for his technical knowledge. He carried out many missions for our Committee, and was secretary of its Foreign Service Section during World War II. Because of his deep religious commitment and his wide experience in dealing with people in distress in various parts of the world, and because of his high standing in the chemical field, he became a magnificent interpreter of the life of the spirit to men of science.

Others come onto our paid staff from successful careers in other fields, sometimes at lower salaries than they have been making, almost always because of a deep inner commitment to the values which we strive to realize. Margaret Frawley, an able newspaper woman, came to us in this spirit, serving for a number of years on our public relations staff and in emergency situations overseas until she was taken from us by a deadly disease — but only after she had earned the deep and abiding confidence of our Committee and of the distressed people of France among whom she worked valiantly in the early days of the Second World War and also immediately after liberation.

These are only two among many highly qualified men and women who have contributed generously of their gifts of spirit and ability. Over the years, some four thousand persons — exclusive

of summer-project workers, whose number is even higher — have
served with the Committee at home or abroad. If I were to attempt
to pay tribute to all those whose contributions have been of an
especially high order, there would be no stopping place, and besides, it would be humanly impossible to avoid errors of omission.
Here and there I have mentioned a name or several names as they
happened to come up in special connections. But at the same time
perhaps scores of individuals equally or even more important in
those immediate situations are not mentioned. I see no way around
this dilemma in a running account of this kind. All of us together
make up the Service Committee. That is the way we think of ourselves, that is how it is, and if, as I hope, my occasional mention of
an individual gives a sense of the quality of our service and the
climate in which we operate, I can only ask the reader to remember
that there are innumerable others who might just as aptly be
singled out. For probably, above all other definitions, the Service
Committee might be described as a host of men and women all
striving to put themselves at the service of an ideal big enough to
take anything any of us can give, and to call for much more. Daily
consciousness of this situation keeps feelings of self-importance at
a minimum, I think, and when such feelings do arise within us —
for we are abundantly human — they are apt to be soon put to
flight by predicaments beyond our power to meet in any way commensurate with our ideal.

Then, also making up the Service Committee, there are the contributors of money and gifts in kind other than clothing. From
time to time, sizable gifts have come from foundations and corporations, and from groups and communities, but it is the thousands of individual contributions that give the Committee its broad
base and its continuing stability. More than 100,000 persons have
participated in AFSC work in this way.

It is never sound to allow persons to determine major policies by
giving money, but it is always a good thing to listen to the concerns
of a contributor, and to try to explain to him the reasons behind

present policies. In the whole time of my connection with the Committee, we have had little if any of the trouble that sometimes comes to a college, for example, when contributing alumni seek to determine policy. It is quite possible to designate gifts for specific undertakings of the Committee, even to help it launch a new enterprise by making a specially designated contribution; but to attempt to determine the Committee's central policy, to put pressure on us to deviate from the group principles on which we operate, would be futile. In fact, it is almost never tried. Most of our contributors are in close sympathy with the way we work, and there is an enthusiasm and sense of belonging on their part which is a tower of strength to the Committee, quite aside from the money involved. Fundamentally we have not tried to solicit funds so much as we have tried to interpret what we are doing. Then if people want to be part of the undertaking — which usually represents services they couldn't carry alone — we are happy to have their contributions. High-powered salesmanship, whatever its merits may be in other walks of life, has no place when one is promoting a spiritual enterprise. Giving of money ought always to be accompanied by a sense of the giving spirit. I suppose that doesn't always happen, but it is the goal toward which we aim. Many contributors must feel this, or they would not give, as so often happens, out of their own scarcity.

Back in the 1920's, after the First World War, the Committee received a letter from Germany which read something like this: "The enclosed money represents approximately the amount of help which was given to my son after the war. I have now been able to save it and would like to return it, so that it can be used for other people who may now be in need." That kind of giving has been repeated many times in our history.

Then there was the Nisei couple in New York after World War II who had no savings except a hard-earned $137 which they had managed to bank for their child's future education. They withdrew the entire amount to give to one of the Committee's representatives, not at his urging but because they felt they wanted to help others through an agency which had been helpful to their own group under pressure of the war. I remember, too, a Japanese living in Chicago who had been comfortably off before he was taken from his home during the relocation. Now he was reduced to poorly paid routine work, with long hours. He insisted on giving $25 of his very meager income.

For several years after the war, there were thousands of students who once a week, or more frequently, went without a meal in order to save money for the program we were carrying on for students abroad.

This kind of expression of fellowship with others in suffering is the texture out of which a life of inner security is built. It may well be that the greatest contribution our Committee has made lies in its having afforded opportunities for people to give of self and substance to meet others' needs.

Sometimes it happens that a contributor with a real flair touches the imagination of a whole community. I remember when in January, 1944, Perry Hayden, a Quaker flour miller from Tecumseh, Michigan, came to tell me about an experiment he was carrying on. Three years before, he had taken a cubic inch of wheat and planted it. Devoted as he was to the practice of tithing, he had given one tenth of the harvest and planted the other nine tenths the following year. His proposal was to carry this plan through for six years, to see what happened. His third crop, in the fall of 1943, had been fourteen acres, planted on land lent him by Henry Ford. At the end of the first year he had cut the crop with a sickle hook and flailed it out in Biblical fashion. The second year he had used a cradle. The third crop he had harvested with a cradle and an old-fashioned reaper. The threshing had been done with a horse-power threshing machine taken from Henry Ford's Greenfield Museum. Perry told me he wanted AFSC to handle the tenth of his big crop the sixth year, if possible.

In the sixth year, his experiment really triumphed. Beginning with the cubic inch, or about 360 kernels, giving one tenth to the

Lord and replanting nine tenths, in the sixth year he couldn't find enough land in any one place to carry out his project, so he signed up 256 farmers in the surrounding community, and as far away as Tennessee, to grow the crop.

On August 1, 1946, all were to bring their crops in to Adrian, Michigan, threshed and ready to ship. I was invited to be present, to receive the Service Committee's tenth.

When I arrived in Adrian on that morning of August 1, farmers were already driving in from far and near, their trucks loaded with bags of wheat which they had threshed from acreage assigned to the "Dynamic Kernels Program," as it was called. Some were giving the tenth agreed upon, but others were giving the entire crop. So great was the contagion of the idea that many other people brought wheat not grown under the Hayden plan.

The governor of the state of Michigan had declared this Dynamic Kernels Holiday. All Adrian shops closed at noon.

The first event was a parade, with Perry Hayden, Mrs. Emma Clement, the "Mother of the Year," and myself riding in the front car of the procession. The American Legion had two or three cars, then came someone carrying the sickle which had been used the first year, another carrying the cradle, a third driving the reaper, pulled by a pair of beautiful black horses; then came the machinery used in the later harvests: a tractor pulling a binder, a tractor pulling a combine, finally a self-propelled combine. After this came a whole string of cars, trucks, and all kinds of vehicles hauling wheat. We went the full length of the town and into the fair grounds, where part of the sacked wheat was deposited in great piles.

Boy and Girl Scouts of Adrian had planted about fifteen acres in the middle of the race track, and this was now harvested before the throng of spectators. With the use of the sickle first, then the cradle, then the reaper, the binder, the combines, all was cut in short order. Then an old-fashioned steam threshing machine steamed into the middle of this race-track wheat field, and while all the people looked on it was put in order and proceeded to thresh the wheat that had not been cut by the combines.

Immediately after this, about one hundred pounds of the wheat was milled on an old-fashioned mill set up in front of the grandstand. The mill was two huge stones, which hadn't been used for over fifty years.

At this point a helicopter landed on the ground, picked up the meal, flew it to a bakery in Toledo, thirty miles away, where a baking company baked it into wafers, which were flown back to be passed out to the crowd.

It was one of the finest shows I have ever seen. It took place in the presence of some ten or twelve thousand people, mostly farmers and their families or other rural inhabitants. William Danforth, chairman of the Ralston Purina Milling Company of St. Louis, was there and took charge of the entire donation of wheat for our Committee; his company had agreed to mill it free of charge into cereal appropriate for overseas relief. The American Broadcasting Company over a national hookup gave wide coverage to the dramatic event. A radio commentator who had just returned from Europe told of the suffering he had seen; I spoke briefly of some of the situations our Committee knew about firsthand; Mrs. Clement, the Mother of the Year, a Negro woman from Louisville, Kentucky, widow of a Methodist bishop, spoke of the experience which she and her family had had in tithing throughout their lives, and what it had meant to them in terms of their own spiritual growth. In fact, the whole day took one into the very heart of the rich quality of the spiritual life of the people of this country.

Whatever may be the programs for assistance in other parts of the world paid for out of our government's tax receipts, the outpouring of people's own generosity typified by this experience is invaluable as an American heritage.

Only part of those participating in Perry Hayden's experiment were Quakers. In the Committee's summer projects among young people, the percentage of Friends is by the nature of things very small. Even on our regular staff in the United States and overseas, usually Friends form only about one third of the total number. In fact, the Service Committee has, it seems to me, come to be a movement of people rather than chiefly the instrument of a sect. We do have a requirement that members of the Corporation and the Executive Board must be Friends. Without being deeply grounded in the basic convictions that represent the ideal of the Religious Society of Friends, the Committee would lose its character. But its strength is likewise in its fellowship with the larger family. There was a time when Jesus was rebuked because he seemed not to give primary allegiance to his blood mother and brothers. It is recorded that he answered, "Who is my mother? And who are my brothers?" And he stretched forth his hand toward his disciples and said, "Here are my mother and my brothers! for whoever does the will of my Father in heaven is my brother, and sister, and mother." That is the inner essence of a movement such as the American Friends Service Committee.

An allegiance of this sort never operates in a vacuum. The AFSC is only one of many agencies which are carrying on relief and interpreting life in the terms in which their constituencies see it. Virtually from the beginning of our Committee's work, we have found ourselves in close relationship with Mennonites and members of the Church of the Brethren, our three groups representing what are often called the "peace churches." The Mennonite Central Committee dates back to the First World War relief period. I think our agency was the first to be called a Service Committee, but now the Brethren Service Commission,* the Unitarian Service Committee, and the Congregational-Christian Service Committee have come into being, and there is the relief arm of the Protestant churches, called Church World Service, which was born during the closing days of World War II. It has been my privilege to co-operate to a small extent in the establishment of these newer agencies, because I have been convinced that the American people would respond

* Formerly the Brethren Service Committee.

through channels which they helped to create. It may be true that there is strength in union, but there is also strength in diversity. The points of co-operation between such agencies and our Committee have been more numerous than perhaps I have indicated, and exceedingly fruitful in terms of fellowship as well as accomplishment.

I have already mentioned in some detail our close working relations with various Jewish groups. We have also been greatly strengthened by co-operative relations with the National Catholic Welfare Conference, particularly the War Relief Services branch of that agency.

These are but a few of the many relationships which constantly enrich the life of the American Friends Service Committee, outside of Friends' groups, and which must be carefully attended to if the work is to move smoothly.

Within the Society of Friends, there are the Meetings, which are at the very core not only of the Society but of the Service Committee as well. If ever the meeting for worship ceased to be the heart of our undertakings, no matter how great the latter might be, at that time our course would begin to go downhill. The close relationship between AFSC and Friends Meetings and schools and colleges is a relationship which must grow stronger with every expansion of program, if our growth is not to run away with our roots and so defeat itself in the end. Likewise the close relation between our Committee and Friends Service Council, which represents British and Irish Friends, is right at the heart of our work. This holds also for Friends' organizations which sprang up in wartime England to meet specific needs, notably Friends Relief Service and Friends Ambulance Unit. The co-operation between AFSC and British Friends' service groups goes back to the First World War, and has been so continuous and invaluable that it enters naturally into all our thinking about overseas programs. The Canadian Friends Service Committee has been another highly valued partner in much of our work. And Friends on the continent of Europe, in

Asia, and in other parts of the world, are a source of great strength and inspiration to us.

To draw a chart of all these relationships would be practically impossible. It would always be running off the page. But to trace a golden thread of common impulse toward the good of humanity is quite possible, and after all that is the important thing. If our Committee is thought of, not as a neatly self-contained organization, but as interlocking, interacting relationships, forever in a state of change, hopefully of growth — then the focus is where it should be, on the living contacts rather than on organizational machinery.

But what of the morality — or immorality — of so-called relief work, which from the budgetary point of view has been the Committee's largest service? One is on dubious ground unless there is clear experiencing of the reciprocity which is always involved if one will open to it. People who have lost all the usual daily supports of life — steady jobs, home, family, even country — must, if they are to survive as individuals, find security in the deepest levels of the human spirit. What such persons can give to the rest of us is very humbling in the healthy sense. One test of an AFSC worker's success among those needing relief might, I should think, be the measure in which he has caught for himself the quality of honesty, serenity, courage, and real humility which one so often finds among those who have been reduced to great need, especially under the impact of war.

It was with mixed feelings that our Committee received notification on October 31, 1947, that the Nobel Peace Prize for that year was being awarded jointly to Friends Service Council of London and the American Friends Service Committee. If we had contributed to the healing of the world, we had also received abundantly, and in what seemed to us more significant ways.

I think there was a general feeling of unworthiness among all who had participated in the life of the Committee. Insofar as the prize was deserved, it belonged to the entire Society of Friends, to many other groups who had worked with us, and to innumerable individuals, Quaker and non-Quaker alike. We immediately sent a letter to the Clerk of every Monthly Meeting of Friends in the country, calling their attention to the award and indicating that in some respects they as Friends also shared in it and in the responsibilities which it involved. Similar messages were sent to regional offices, summer work campers, foreign service workers, and others who had participated in the life of the Committee. Our minds went out especially to the Church of the Brethren and the Mennonites with whom we had so often been closely associated in common efforts in interpreting our faith.

What, exactly, was the basis on which our two organizations had received this prize? As we asked ourselves this question in the days following the announcement of the award, it seemed to us that in an age when increasingly the state was held to be supreme and the individual only a tool, the prize had gone, in a basic sense, to that way of life which holds each individual to be a child of God and therefore of supreme value. If this interpretation was correct, it really meant that people all over the world and of various creeds, who were of this fundamental faith, had received a striking vote of confidence.

We were reassured by the speech of award given by Gunnar Jahn, chairman of the Nobel Committee, in Oslo, Norway, on December 10, 1947. To be sure, he spoke of the practical works of the two service agencies and of Quakers as a whole over the three hundred years since the beginning of the movement. But he did not overlook the soil which has nourished the spreading tree of this service. He said, in part:

> The fact that Quakers have refused to take part in war has led many people to believe that this is the essential part of their religion. But the matter is not quite so simple. It is true that the declaration of 1660 contains the following words: "We utterly deny all outward wars and strife and fighting with outward weapons to any end and under any pretense whatever. This is our testimony to the whole world." In this decla-

ration there is implied much more than a mere refusal to take part in war. It amounts to the following: It is better to suffer injustice than to exercise injustice. In the end victory must come from within the individual man or woman. . . .

It is the silent help from the nameless to the nameless which is their contribution to the promotion of brotherhood among nations. . . . This is the message of good deeds, the message that men can come into contact with one another in spite of war and in spite of difference of race. May we believe that here there is hope of laying a foundation for peace among nations, of building up peace in man himself, so that it becomes impossible to settle disputes by use of force?

While Gunnar Jahn's speech focused attention on Friends' international activities, it touched just as surely on our work at home. That human brotherhood finds its full vitality in spanning gulfs of race prejudice and economic exploitation, that the young man who bears conscientious testimony against war must be ready to pay a high price for his faith — such suggestions are clear indication that groups like AFSC and FSC face their acid tests at home. Overseas, removed from the social pressures of his own United States milieu, being moreover a temporary resident in the foreign scene, an AFSC worker may find it fairly simple to champion the cause of brotherhood. It is really at home that his choices reach into the jugular vein. For often his convictions point in an opposite direction to that being taken by his natural companions — his boyhood and college friends, his business associates. In this present day, as in times past, his chances for promotion, his job or career, the regard of his fellow citizens, may be at stake. For this reason, we are conscious of the fact that in the final analysis we must be judged primarily in terms of our actions in our own country.

In all honesty it must be said that while early Quakerism was revolutionary and a deeply disturbing challenge to human society, in this latter time we Quakers as a group are much more comfortable in the generally accepted mores of society, much less inclined to find that our religion demands any radical behavior on our part. This is not to say we have lost all vitality of protest, and indeed the spark is capable of surprising new births. Particularly among the young men and women, often one sees fresh, exhilarating expression of the revolutionary message that the vicious circle of evil can be broken with positive good.

I V
The Moral Equivalent

So long as anti-militarists propose no substitute for war's disciplinary function, no *moral equivalent* of war, analogous, as one might say, to the mechanical equivalent of heat, so long they fail to realize the full inwardness of the situation. And as a rule they do fail. The duties, penalties, and sanctions pictured in the utopias they paint are all too weak and tame to touch the military-minded. . . . Meanwhile men at large still live as they always have lived, under a pain-and-fear economy — for those of us who live in an ease-economy are but an island in the stormy ocean — and the whole atmosphere of present-day utopian literature tastes mawkish and dishwatery to people who still keep a sense for life's more bitter flavors. It suggests, in truth, ubiquitous inferiority.
— WILLIAM JAMES, *The Moral Equivalent of War*

1. *The Conscientious Objector*

In January, 1940, the war in Europe was awaiting the coming of spring to explode into its full violence. It seemed obvious that United States "neutrality" would soon become participation, if more positive directions were not vigorously chosen. President Roosevelt was calling for stronger armaments; and conscription loomed as a definite possibility. We of the Service Committee, along with other pacifists, both Quaker and non-Quaker, were increasingly concerned about the problems conscientious objectors might have to face.

As is always the case under such circumstances, we were in a dilemma. We were against conscription. We were also concerned that any conscription measure adopted by our country should evince as much progress as possible in the way it dealt with conscientious objectors.

On January 10, a delegation made up of representatives of the three "historic peace churches," the Church of the Brethren, the Mennonite Church, and the Society of Friends, paid a visit to President Roosevelt. I was not a member of the delegation, but at the suggestion of the President's secretary I went along to introduce the members to the President.

Although he was under terrific pressures, the President, as always, was most affable, and took time to tell a story or two. The delegation then presented him with a memorandum containing general suggestions as to what might be done concerning conscientious objectors under conscription. He expressed appreciation that we had given thought to this problem, which he recognized the government would face. He advised us to have a talk with the Attorney General, Frank Murphy.

That afternoon we talked with Attorney General Murphy, and all of us were impressed with the religious character of his consideration of the subject. A devout Roman Catholic, he was profoundly committed to the right of conscience. He suggested that the matter should be brought before the Cabinet, and asked that we discuss our memorandum with Robert Jackson, who would succeed him as Attorney General when he moved on to the Supreme Court within a few days.

Both Murphy and Jackson agreed to see that our proposals were laid before any committee or individual members of Congress concerned in formulating a conscription act, but both men expressed the fervent hope that there would never be another military draft in this country.

Two days later we addressed a second memorandum to the government, making more specific recommendations, among them the following:

1. That a civilian board be appointed by the President to serve under him or under a cabinet officer, to judge the sincerity and weigh the claims of conscientious objectors, to assign to them a definite status, and to consider and authorize non-military service projects to which they might be assigned.

2. That draft boards be directed to route conscientious objectors directly to this civilian board, leaving them at all times under civilian direction and control. This might be facilitated by the issuance of certificates by our church organizations regarding the status of members who might be drafted.

3. That appropriate organizations of the historic peace churches be permitted to set up and administer, through their own personnel, service projects to which conscientious objectors might be assigned. The following forms of service might be considered as representative of the sort of projects we might undertake:

‧ Relief of war sufferers
Relief of refugees or evacuated civilian populations

Reconstruction of war-stricken areas

Resettlement of refugees

Reclamation or forestry services in the United States or elsewhere

Relief and reconstruction work in local communities in the United States

Medical and health services in connection with any of these projects

Farm service

In submitting the above proposals we realize that our organizations would have to be prepared to undertake difficult tasks and assume heavy burdens, but the type of projects we are suggesting are closely related to tasks in which we have been long engaged in times of peace. We would be willing to undertake an extension of these tasks up to the limit of our abilities to carry out these proposals and to offer our co-operation in working out details with the proper government agencies if occasion should arise.

We should like to call attention, however, to the fact that the procedures we have outlined apply only to those whose convictions permit participation in some form of alternative service. There are some whose consciences are unable to conform to the demands of any type of military conscription, however modified. These we should like to commend to the consideration of the responsible government officials, trusting that the consciences of such persons may receive due recognition.

By early June, 1940, three of us from the three peace churches were told by Francis Biddle, Solicitor General of the Department of Justice, that he considered the passage of a draft bill imminent. He wanted us to furnish him with statistics on our groups, and a record of our experience in the First World War and of British experience with conscientious objectors in the present war. He hoped that whatever was done could be kept within the framework of government, but he made every effort to understand our position when we explained to him that there would be possible objection to the state's right to conscript for any purpose whatsoever.

In such conferences with government officials I could not, of course, speak for the Society of Friends; but the next month there was to be a special conference of Friends, at which time we would try to see what we could agree to.

It should be noted here, perhaps, that while these discussions were going on, our Committee's efforts to get food through the blockade and to render relief service to France and the Low Countries were in full swing. There was a strong feeling within AFSC that conscientious objectors who wished to serve in overseas relief and were qualified to do so should be used in this way.

Although the draft act was not yet passed, on June 8 we decided to establish a camp to begin training C.O.'s for overseas service. A site near Philadelphia had been offered for this purpose.

Pursuant to this decision, Orie O. Miller of the Mennonite Central Committee and I had a talk with Sidney Hillman, whom I had always considered one of labor's real statesmen, and who was now a member of the President's National Defense Advisory Commission. He was eager to keep the service program for conscientious objectors on a volunteer basis, with the greatest possible freedom and flexibility, but he confessed he observed a continuous tightening of the lines and doubted whether it would be a possibility. He urged us to keep in close touch with him, and hoped it would be possible to keep the lines of control from becoming too all-inclusive. I have always greatly regretted that Sidney Hillman's health did not outlast the war. He was a man of rare spirit and unusual gifts.

On July 2, in Richmond, Indiana, a group widely representative of the Society of Friends gave consideration to the problems confronting Friends in case of a draft. While it was too early to make any final decision, it was clearly the sense of this group that Friends should assume heavy responsibility for providing alternative service opportunities for conscientious objectors who wished such assignments — this, of course, subject to the government's approval.

The Selective Training and Service Act was passed on September 14, 1940. One of its provisions was that it should not be construed to require any person to be "subject to combatant training and service in the land or naval forces of the United States, who, by reason of religious training and belief, is conscientiously opposed to participation in war in any form." The Act provided for local boards to handle the actual drafting of young men, and as a part of their duty they were to pass upon claims for C. O. classification. If such claims were sustained, the boards were to place the individuals involved, according to their wishes, either in noncombatant army training and service, or in "work of national importance under civilian direction."

It must not be inferred that all young men of draft age within the Society of Friends were conscientious objectors. More than half of those drafted did not claim conscientious-objector status. Among those who were unwilling to participate actively in war, there were a number of different points at which their consciences stopped them. There were those who found it within the dictates of their conscience to accept classification 1–A–O, which meant they were willing to perform noncombatant service within the armed forces, such as medical or ambulance work. There were those who, strong in their belief that the state had no right to conscript the individual, refused to register. Their course was clear. This was violation of the draft law, and they would go to prison. In between these groups was the third category — designated as 4–E — the men who registered as C. O.'s, whose consciences did not allow them to enter the armed forces, even as noncombatants, but who felt right about doing "work of national importance under civilian direction."

I will begin with this third group, since it was the one with which AFSC was most involved organizationally — with such endless ramifications that they can only be suggested here.*

* For a thorough account of American conscientious objectors during World War II, see Mulford Q. Sibley and Philip E. Jacob, *Conscription of Conscience: The American State and the Conscientious Objector, 1940–1947* (Cornell University Press, Ithaca, 1952). I have drawn on this book for some of my statistics and over-all facts, but the day-to-day experience of working out the problems as they confronted us in AFSC

The questions in the beginning were: What form should this "work of national importance" take, and under whose auspices should it be carried out? The Selective Service Administration was definitely interested in the possibility of the peace churches themselves taking care of the men who chose alternative service.

This situation as our Committee faced it, in consultation with as wide a representation of the Society of Friends as possible, seemed to us to involve at least five fundamental problems. First and foremost, suppose the Service Committee should establish camps or other projects in which drafted C. O.'s could perform work of national importance: did this imply approval of conscription? Secondly, would accepting this responsibility so qualify our relation with government that we would find ourselves not in a position to oppose the principle of conscription? Thirdly, there were those who felt, and rightly so, that, although in theory we might be in control of the camps, the fact that Selective Service would be in a position to inspect the camps might well mean that control was not actually in our hands. Then there was the very important question concerning funds to maintain the men in such camps. And finally there was the question of whether, if our Committee did administer camps, they would be for Friends only or — as Selective Service hoped — for any conscientious objector who wished to come.

In regard to the first two questions, we were certainly on record as opposed to conscription, and there was no doubt that the government understood this. We made it completely clear that if we undertook this kind of service we would do it under continuing protest against conscription.

Meanwhile, the National Service Board for Religious Objectors was established to meet the requirement of Selective Service that it have one agency to deal with instead of many. On this Board were representatives of the Brethren Service Committee, the Mennonite Central Committee, the American Friends Service Commit-

is a vivid personal memory. I am sure none of us who were involved in it need any prompting to recall its difficulties and its rewards.

tee, the Fellowship of Reconciliation, the Methodist Commission on World Peace, and other organizations whose constituencies would be directly involved. Soon after the passage of the Selective Service Act, this Board submitted to Selective Service a detailed proposal, recommending that both governmental and private agencies should administer service opportunities for C. O.'s, the government agencies offering maintenance plus wages in their services. This would give C. O.'s a choice of volunteer service with a religious group or paid service with the government. Selective Service looked with considerable favor on this plan, as did a large portion of the C. O.'s with whom we were able to confer.

A dozen or so members of the AFSC Board of Directors had met with Dr. Clarence A. Dykstra, Director of Selective Service, and in consultation with him had envisaged a wide range of possibilities of service. We had all been deeply impressed with Dr. Dykstra's understanding of our concern and of the C. O.'s eagerness to perform service of genuine significance.

It was not long until Dr. Dykstra was succeeded by General Lewis B. Hershey, who, though a professional soldier, had a Mennonite background. He believed in the draft as a means of assembling an army, but he had considerable understanding of the point of view of the conscientious objector.

Continued consultations with Friends throughout the country revealed that in general Friends felt that since a vast majority of the people of the United States had approved Selective Service, and since Congress had made provision in the Act for conscientious objectors to be allowed to do civilian work, the AFSC should accept responsibility for administering alternative services, at the same time continuing to protest conscription. It was felt that our testimony against conscription might even be more effective if we were willing to carry heavy responsibility in taking care of those who were recognized as conscientious objectors.

As far as control within the work projects was concerned, no one at the time envisioned as much interference by Selective Service as actually took place once we had entered into our administrative responsibilities. In spite of a good deal of understanding of our position on the part of the Selective Service Administration, there was also the bureaucratic habit of mind in some of the executives, and this almost always leads to more control than is anticipated in the beginning.

At one time the question had been raised as to whether government funds would be forthcoming to finance service programs run by church agencies. But it had become clear that such funds would not be available. Selective Service money was appropriated to finance military conscription, and our work would be of a civilian nature. This presented a very sobering prospect. None of the agencies concerned had the necessary funds in hand.

We of the Service Committee recognized the fact that our part of such a financial responsibility would have to be borne largely by Friends themselves, and not by the wider contributing public which supports so many of our enterprises. This was likewise true of the Brethren and Mennonites. We would be the three groups chiefly responsible for nongovernmental projects.

A further problem was the government's request that we accept C. O.'s who were not members of our own religious groups. There was a strong feeling in the AFSC that men who took the conscientious objector's position but who did not have the support of their community or their family or their religious denomination were in many respects in greater need of our support than were our own boys, and that therefore we should accept such additional responsibility. We did not suspect what a diversity of backgrounds this decision would bring into our camps and other units before the program came to a close!

In October, 1940, came the Five Years Meeting in Richmond, Indiana. This is a gathering of Friends from all over the country for worship and discussion.

The group was very widely representative; and in the course of the meeting a clear and strong opinion crystallized, supporting

AFSC (1) in undertaking to administer alternative service opportunities, and (2) in accepting responsibility for men who wished to come to our camps but who were not members of the Society of Friends. Also, this Meeting felt it would be wiser not to accept government funds even if they were available, but to bear the cost ourselves.

During these days when plans were in the making, one kept hearing from young men who were earnestly questioning themselves as to the position they should take in regard to the draft. One day I received a letter from the mother of a student at Union Theological Seminary. She was anxious about her son, who was one of a group of about twenty students who had announced they would refuse to register under the Selective Service Act. Although all of these men were eligible for exemption as candidates for the ministry, they felt they must take a more clear-cut stand against the method of war and in opposition to the draft. It was reported that the Seminary had threatened to expel them if they failed to register. I promised this mother to talk with her son, though of course I would not attempt to make his decision for him. I wired him to meet me the next Sunday morning as I passed through New York on my way home from Boston.

When I got off the sleeper in Grand Central Station that morning, I was met by not only the one boy, but nine of his associates as well. We had a two-hour session in the waiting room of the station, and then they requested that I stay over and meet with the whole group of twenty in the evening. These boys felt deeply the importance of the decision they were about to make, and I arranged to stay over for the larger meeting.

In the evening, I noticed that those with whom I had talked in the morning had done a good deal of thinking in the meantime. I had warned them against taking a dramatic position for the sake of the glamour, and had pointed out that the course they took, whether dramatic or undramatic, must be grounded deeply in their own consciences. I told them it was my belief that any of them who wished to come would be welcomed in our camps, but that this should not prejudice them against any other position they might take. It was most heartening to see them wrestling to make their action a true expression of their conscience. While none of them were members of the Society of Friends or other "peace church," they were deeply under the weight of the claims of Christian pacifism. I felt that for the most part their own religious bodies were not much in sympathy with the questions they were raising about conscription. In that respect they were typical of a great many devout young Christians, and this applies to some younger members of the Society of Friends who belonged to Meetings in which the peace testimony was not strong.

Details of the Service Committee's relationship to the National Service Board for Religious Objectors and to Selective Service were being worked out when suddenly, on November 29, quite to our surprise, President Roosevelt expressed to Dr. Dykstra aggressive opposition to the plan under consideration. He evidently felt it would involve too much leniency and lack of discipline, and advocated putting all the men to work under army direction.

This led to a long series of negotiations. Dr. Dykstra believed that if the church agencies would take responsibility for *all* alternative-service projects the President might then be willing to turn the men over to these agencies, for no government appropriation would be called for. In any case, it seemed the President did not favor paying wages, even in government camps.

If there were no government camps, the church agencies would be supervising even those "Civilian Public Service" men who did not wish to come under a religious agency's direction. This was a questionable procedure. Yet to consign all the men to government camps would be to deny those who preferred it the opportunity of working with a pacifist agency. In that case, as General Hershey himself recognized, the churches would be able to offer little more than chaplaincy service.

Groups represented in the National Service Board for Religious

Objectors hurriedly conferred among themselves and with government people. On December 10, twenty-five of us met with Dr. Dykstra, General Hershey, and other government representatives, and it was in this conference that an agreement was reached, whereby the Brethren Service Committee, the Mennonite Central Committee, the American Friends Service Committee, and possibly other groups, would undertake the administration and financing of all Civilian Public Service camps for a trial period of six months, at the end of which time the arrangement would be reconsidered. Though the door was thus left open for change, and though subsequently we committed ourselves for no more than a year at a time, no major alterations were ever made in the plan.

As finally approved and put into effect on December 20, 1940, this plan provided that C. O.'s choosing alternative service would be assigned to camps for soil conservation, reforestation, and other public works. The government would provide technical supervision and equipment, and would make available the camps in various parts of the country that had been used by the CCC (Civilian Conservation Corps) during the depression, together with cots, bedding, and other essential camp equipment. Selective Service would pay the men's transportation, and it reserved the right of general policy supervision and inspection. In each case the director of the work project would be a government employee. The running expenses and daily administration of the camps would be entirely in the hands of the church agencies.

I had a keen realization of the heavy responsibility which this decision laid on the Service Committee, and I shall never forget the sense of relief that swept through me when a member of the Board, C. Reed Cary, came to offer at least three or four hours a day of his very valuable service.

Later he came with us full-time on the dollar-a-year basis, though this meant withdrawing as vice-president of a large and important business concern for the duration of the war. It was impressive to read his letter of resignation from this firm, in which he had worked for nearly thirty years. It was now accepting government orders for the manufacture of combat equipment — just at the time when his son was claiming exemption as a C. O. — and he felt he could not go on, but must take a clear pacifist stand alongside his son.

This was not an isolated instance. Leslie Heath, who held an important engineering position in the same company, resigned to join our program for refugees in Casablanca. President Thomas E. Jones of Fisk University arranged to take a leave of absence to become the first director of our Civilian Public Service camps. Paul J. Furnas, a Philadelphia businessman, who had been a conscientious objector in World War I, later accepted this responsibility. There was in fact a deep pervading sense, as we entered into services for conscientious objectors, that older Friends were with the young men in spirit and in sacrificial giving, that all together were entering into a period of difficult demands.

There were high hopes for what might be accomplished through Civilian Public Service. Here was a chance to carry on an educational program among our own and other religiously motivated conscientious objectors while they were doing work of national importance.

Actually, it was far from easy, for there was a tendency for the program of physical work to seem unimportant to the men, more or less as if it were "made work." This led to a kind of disillusionment and disappointment, which is not a good frame of mind in which to take advantage of educational opportunities. Frequently there was unimaginative project direction by officials whose experience had been within the totally different framework of CCC. A further trouble was that some of the men whose C. O. position was not closely linked with a particular religious affiliation felt they should not be required to work under church-agency direction. Until late in the program, their only alternative was prison. On the other hand, many young men whose religious affiliation was important to them felt frustrated when they wanted to protest against certain Selective Service policies and found themselves in the position of protesting against the church agency which was in charge of their camp. The church agencies were often in the dilemma of being or seeming to be instruments for carrying out Selective Service policies.

Directors of camps reported great trouble in securing medical discharge for men who were mentally or physically unfit for participation in camp life, and the camps did not have facilities or flexibility for taking care of such men.

Still another difficulty was that, while the Board of the Service Committee had felt quite clear that the way ought to be opened for non-Friends to enter our camps, we had not anticipated that altogether there would be something like two hundred religious sects and denominations involved. Some of these held points of view differing widely from our own.

Denominational affiliations of *all* CPS men have been summarized as follows: *

Mennonites	4665
Church of the Brethren	1353
Society of Friends	951
Methodist	673
Jehovah's Witnesses	409
Congregational Christian	209
Church of Christ	199
Presbyterian, U.S.A.	192
Northern Baptist	178
German Baptist Brethren	157
Roman Catholic	149
Christadelphians	127
Lutheran (nine synods)	108
Evangelical and Reformed	101
Episcopal	88

* *Directory of Civilian Public Service* (Washington, 1947), pp. xviii ff., as quoted by Sibley and Jacob, *op. cit.*

Disciples of Christ	78
Russian Molokan	76
Evangelical	50
Southern Baptist	45
Unitarians	44
Other churches and sects	1695
Unaffiliated	449

Orie O. Miller, speaking on behalf of the Mennonites, had said that they would gladly pay their share of the bill, that they would do it even though every Mennonite farmer had to mortgage his farm. They did carry through on their heavy responsibilities, much in the spirit in which Orie Miller had spoken.

It was a little more complicated for Friends to make and carry out this kind of commitment. We are not ecclesiastically organized in such a way that central action can be taken on behalf of Friends as a group; our membership was much more divided on the issue of the war than were Mennonites; and, proportionately, our camps received more men not of our own religious affiliation. Up to January 1, 1944, the three peace churches shared equally in the cost of assignees who were not members of any one of them. After that date, each agency was responsible for all men in its own camps and units.

A number of the other denominations represented in the camps reimbursed the peace churches in full or in part for the cost of their men. Besides appreciating this financial help, we were sure this procedure was much better for the relationship between the individual man and his own church than if we had been his ultimate financial sponsor.

Friends Meetings, the families of C. O.'s, and the C. O.'s themselves, were all important sources of the funds spent by our Committee on CPS.

Final costs of CPS to the main administrative agencies were as follows:

Mennonite Central Committee	$3,188,578
American Friends Service Committee	2,332,176
Brethren Service Committee	1,681,495

In time we were able to expand the program's service opportunities somewhat, securing permission for detached units of men to work outside the camps — for example, on farms and in mental hospitals.

In all, there were 67 camps and more than 130 detached service units, of which Friends administered twenty camps and more than thirty units. Some 3400 men participated in these Friends' projects.

Final statistics for all services show that 11,950 CPS men gave over eight million man-days of work to their country. It must be noted that *gave* is the correct word here, since none of the men were paid.

The largest numbers of men were used in the United States Forestry Service, Soil Conservation Service, and National Park Service. These assignments ranged from the ridiculous to the sublime, from the men's point of view. "Manicuring the trees" in National Parks and planting little saplings in tree nurseries were among the most frustrating assignments. Constructing roads and trails was better, especially where it was for the purpose of fire prevention. Then there was the hewing of timber and clearing of underbrush and debris, the repairing of telephone lines to ranger stations, and the more dramatic work of the parachute-borne fire fighters.

In the spring of 1942 I visited the Coshocton, Ohio, camp, where the men were at work on important research projects having to do with the effect of moisture on soil, and with interrelations between soil, drainage, and crops. The enterprise was under the technical direction of about twenty representatives of the Department of Agriculture. The CPS men here seemed to me an especially interesting group — of high intellectual attainments, good discipline, and serious purpose.

The total accomplishment of CPS men in soil conservation was impressive; it included, among other things, the construction of 49 large diversion dams, 164 reservoirs, and 200 permanent check dams; 2870 miles of contour furrows dug, 2670 water-control structures built for irrigation, millions of square yards of banks sloped and gullies sodded and seeded, a million trees planted. Most of this was far from dramatic work, but its significance for our country was considerable.

A number of the CPS men helped on farms, mostly dairy farms. On the whole, these men were satisfied with their long hours of productive labor, and the farmers reported them to be steady, good workers. The going wage for such labor was paid by the farmer, but turned over to the United States Treasury instead of to the men. There was a tentative understanding between the church agencies and the government that such wages paid into the Treasury would be kept "frozen" for the time being, with the possibility that they might be used in relief and welfare services. But we have never been able to secure the use of these funds for any purposes we proposed.

One of the most significant services rendered by conscientious objectors was in connection with this country's mental hospitals. Before the war, 800,000 patients in such institutions had inadequate facilities and care, in large part due to the difficulty of finding adequately concerned and trained persons who would work for the wages and under the general conditions that prevailed. This situation was greatly aggravated by the war, which created dazzling wage-earning opportunities for even unskilled workers. "We are 150 attendants short out of 256," wrote one superintendent.

In response to such desperate pleas, and after the government had agreed to the church agencies' request for this service, two thousand C. O.'s eventually worked in 41 mental hospitals and 17 training schools for mental deficients, a majority of them serving as ward attendants. The work was hard and long, rarely less than 72 hours per week, often running to as much as 100 hours a week. It was as severe a test of the physical and spiritual energies of the men as anything that was undertaken. I visited some of these institutions, and had tremendous admiration for the way in which the C. O.'s were maintaining their morale, often in the midst of depressing conditions, lack of appreciation, and even overt antagonism.

In Byberry Hospital, on the edge of Philadelphia, the superintendent was able and co-operative, but here was what he was up against. The plant was designed to accommodate 2500 patients, and 6100 were in residence. There was only one doctor and one nurse for every 300 patients, one attendant for every 100. In the worst wing, 350 incontinent patients were virtually without care, in terms of what was needed.

While the presence of CPS men, with their genuine concern and "nonviolent" handling of patients, was in itself an invaluable contribution, the larger significance lay in their work of awakening the public to the need for drastic reform. It was a striking demonstration of what can be accomplished by a few persons if they care enough.

Even one man might set in motion substantial changes. A CPS attendant in the Veterans' Hospital at Lyons, New Jersey, outraged by what he saw of the treatment of war-shocked patients, went to the administration but got no satisfactory response. He then told his story to reporters, and the resulting newspaper and magazine articles shocked the public out of its ignorance as to how mental casualties of the war were being treated. The Veterans Administration took steps to investigate and clean up abuses.

In Cleveland, as a result of CPS men's stirring the pot, a grand jury handed down a scorching indictment, not only of the Cleveland State Hospital, but, more to the point, of all of us citizens who permit such conditions to obtain. The verdict said, in part, "The Grand Jury condemns the whole socio-political system that today allows this unholy thing to exist in our state of Ohio. The responsibility is widespread and it must be met. Our governor, the state welfare director, the commissioner of mental diseases, the legislators, the hospital superintendent, the least attendant, and we the people — all must share in the guilt for this social crime against these innocent and helpless people."

The CPS men at work as attendants early formulated a Mental Hygiene Program, which aimed to utilize the firsthand experience of C. O.'s in promoting (1) better training for attendants, (2) legal reforms, and (3) popular understanding of the nature of mental illness. This program had the blessing of the National Committee for Mental Hygiene. A monthly periodical, called *The Attendant,* was widely circulated, reaching almost every public mental hospital in the country. It sought to elevate the whole concept of an attendant's duties and opportunities, and was an innovation in the field of public mental-health institutions.

An ambitious development of this program was the creation of the National Mental Health Foundation, an agency which survived the dissolution of CPS. Another development was a survey of all existing state and Federal laws having to do with mental health, a survey which provided the framework for recommendations by various professional groups for revisions in laws and practices. A Public Affairs Pamphlet, "Toward Mental Health," was written by a CPS man, and given wide distribution.

It seems fair to say that the intense concern of a few CPS men had a measurable, permanent influence on the care of our mentally ill.

Then there were the units of men who became "guinea pigs" in medical experiments. In the search for causes and cures of diseases, these men were inoculated with suspected blood plasma, swallowed nose and throat washings and body wastes of infected patients, drank contaminated water, were bitten by infected mosquitoes, and took new drugs on an experimental basis. They caught jaundice, atypical pneumonia, malaria, and other diseases. One man, in the course of his assignment in infantile paralysis, contracted that disease and died of it.

There were those who underwent semistarvation, in order to help discover the physical, mental, and spiritual effects of undernourishment and the most effective methods of rehabilitation after such an ordeal. It was interesting that recovery proved to be much more trying than was the period of hunger. During semistarvation, the men had been praised by the scientists making the tests, for their persistent good spirits and wholehearted co-operation, even while their physical condition was sinking to a low level. But with the end of this negative phase of the ordeal, and the beginning of better rations, their morale slumped, energy returned more slowly than had been anticipated, they grew irritable and full of doubt as to the value of the whole experiment. In the process they certainly helped make more vivid to the world in general and especially to those of us who deal with relief the tragic effects of long and serious undernourishment. And they materially aided in the search for effective ways to bring underfed persons back to health and strength.

About five hundred CPS men thus became "guinea pigs" in medical and scientific research during the war.

Thirty C. O.'s died in the course of their CPS work, though not in every case as a direct result of it. Physical disabilities developed, sometimes as a direct result of assignments; disabled men were discharged as they would have been from the army.

While some of these services I have mentioned were as vitally useful as any we could have hoped for, the number of such opportunities was far more limited than we had anticipated. A tuberculosis hospital in Rhode Island, a crippled children's hospital, a number of cancer hospitals, a juvenile delinquency program in Virginia — more than a hundred such enterprises would have welcomed C. O.'s into programs in which because of their training and experience they might have been especially useful. But Selective Service said No to these opportunities. We had to acknowledge that at least half of the men in our program had been assigned to work which did not affect the wartime social emergencies of the nation and which could, if necessary, have been largely suspended until the drastic need for manpower had slackened. In the story of China

I have already reported the Act of Congress which prevented the use of conscientious objectors in overseas relief.

Selective Service was timid in reporting to Congress about what was happening in regard to conscientious objectors. I suppose it was because they did not want to raise the issue and subject themselves to probable criticism for being too "lenient" and "easy." From time to time, however, Congressmen and Senators asked specific questions. They were more than once shocked to learn the limitations that were being placed upon the use of C. O.'s. Less than ten per cent of the men in AFSC camps were unskilled. Fifty-five per cent had some professional training or experience, thirty per cent were skilled workers, five per cent had done technical work. From the viewpoint of the national welfare, there was a tragic waste of gifts and training.

Also, Congressmen were now and again shocked that there was no financial provision for these men, that not even their maintenance was provided for, save as the church agencies took care of it, largely through donations from the men themselves, their families, and their religious groups. "You are treating these fellows worse than the Japs!" a Senator exclaimed when he learned these facts. Even more difficult was the lack of any regular provision for the men's dependents, or for compensation in case of injury sustained in the course of duty. The church agencies supplemented the men's own efforts to meet such contingencies as they arose, but often the strain on the men was severe.

Because of the widespread peace program of AFSC, we tended to draw into our camps those CPS men who were more aggressively concerned with social measures that might prevent war and make for creative living. When such men found themselves in a camp far removed from the mainstream of life, this social impulse often seemed completely thwarted. They had successfully protested against participating in war. Now their protest began to go further: against the system of conscription that forced them to curtail their most heartfelt concerns; or against wastes and injustices which they found within the camps themselves. Now and again, such men used the slow-down technique, staged fasts or walkouts from camp, thus employing the only measures of protest that seemed left to them.

At times this confronted Quaker administrators of a camp with a very difficult dilemma. Must they discipline men for taking conscientious action to express their disapproval of war and conscription? Selective Service looked on these actions as aberrations, mild crimes being committed by men who had claimed to be religious objectors! The dilemma tended to increase the longer the camps were in existence, for the men were continuously thinking through their position, finding their own inner convictions, and becoming less and less satisfied with the solution offered by the camps. I never felt resentful when men reacted in this way. It was at least in part a sign of growing concern and conviction, and that is always valuable.

Then there were the men who objected to being in our camps because they were run by a religious body. Meetings for worship were held regularly, and while these were not made mandatory the religious motivation did prevail in the administration and educational programs of the camps. Finally, in response to the church agencies' request, some government camps were established for men not electing to be under church supervision. I might add that the men in these government camps were on the same no-pay basis as those in the church-sponsored projects.

On March 2, 1946, six months after the conclusion of hostilities with Japan, the American Friends Service Committee terminated its administration of Civilian Public Service. We took this action chiefly because conducting camps for drafted men in peacetime seemed to us and to most of the men undesirable. The Brethren and Mennonites continued their camps until March 29, 1947, when Selective Service closed the program.

With the end of CPS, many services were needed if the C. O.'s were to find their way back into regular channels of civilian life.

A good deal of vocational counseling was called for. Some men who had gone to camp uninterested in further education now wanted to continue into higher education. Some scholarship funds were solicited, and Quaker institutions offered scholarships on a relatively wide scale. Special loans were made available to young men wishing to enter into modest business ventures. These were repayable under circumstances which would not have interested banks. Once men were mustered out of CPS they were eligible, if they so desired and if they were qualified, to go abroad on relief and rehabilitation missions. A number of them chose to do this, and performed extremely useful work with the Committee, still serving without financial compensation.

While there was continuing and intimate contact between established Friends' groups in this country and young Friends in Civilian Public Service, it was not possible to maintain anything like as close contact with those who chose noncombatant service in the army (1-A-O). I know that these young men often felt a yearning for more attention than they received from their religious home. Some of them felt they could give full expression to the peace testimony in 1-A-O assignments. Others chose this path because, though they were unwilling to kill, they did not feel sufficiently convinced of their religious pacifist position to justify their asking for full exemption from army service. In still other cases, the convincing argument was the need for regular allowance for dependents, which was provided by the army, and which these men realized might otherwise become a burden upon their families or their Meeting or the Service Committee.

While in the early part of the war these men might be given any kind of noncombatant service, after January 21, 1943, they were all assigned to service in the Medical Corps.

The third group of conscientious objectors — those who refrained from registering or in some other way expressed refusal to co-operate with the whole system of conscription — were perhaps the most difficult group for the general American public to understand. Had not the government made provision for them to be exempt from military service and to do alternative work?

It should be observed that the other two groups — CPS and 1-A-O — were operating within the conscription law. The men who chose prison were taking a stand against the very right of the state to conscript. Here is one statement of this position, as given by Arle Brooks, a minister of the Disciples of Christ, before the court in Philadelphia, on January 10, 1941:

Democracy does not mean a blind following of the will of the majority. In a democracy the minority has a right and a duty to follow its ideals. Sometimes the ideals of the minority have eventually been adopted by the majority. Gandhi said, "We are sunk so low that we fancy that it is our duty and our religion to do what the law lays down. If man will only realize that it is unmanly to obey an unjust law, no man's tyranny will enslave him. . . . It is a superstition and an ungodly thing to believe that an act of a majority binds a minority."

I believe in and have worked for the brotherhood of man which is the highest form of democracy. I have worked with children of the slums in Chicago. I have worked with transients, with relief people, and prisoners in the State of Texas, and with sharecroppers in Mississippi.

Conscription is a denial of the democracy for which I have worked. Under conscription the individual is required blindly to obey his superior officer, even though his superior officer is wrong. Hitler could not have waged his wars if the people of Germany had not granted him the power to enslave them. The United States is adopting a system of conscription which may produce tyranny instead of freedom.

I cannot agree with those who believe that registration is a mere census. Registration is the first and necessary step for conscription. My conscience will not permit me to take that first step.

As a minister I could have received complete exemption. I felt it my moral duty to do all within my power to protest against conscription which will eventually weaken and destroy democracy. I am not evading the draft. I am opposing it. I am defending democracy.

This perhaps expresses the reasoned case for the absolute conscientious objector as well as any testimony I have heard. While it may shock some people to see young Christians going to prison rather than register, this is partly because we have so long forgotten the price which our forebears paid for the liberties we now enjoy. Certainly Quakers have a long-standing tradition in regard to going to prison for their convictions. Persons who take this course do not object to being imprisoned, for they realize and acknowledge that they have broken the law. But they do propose, by their position and conduct, to make way for higher law, the law of conscience based on religious thought and life. Almost every religious denomination has something of this in its background.

All in all, nearly six thousand conscientious objectors served time in prison. Only about three hundred of these were nonregistrants. The rest had refused to accept their draft board's decision denying them ministerial or C. O. status, or had otherwise been "non-cooperative." About 75 per cent of the total were Jehovah's Witnesses, penalized for not accepting the decision denying them ministerial status. It should be pointed out that the only channels for appealing an unfavorable Selective Service decision were Selective Service channels.

It is practically impossible in a society as highly organized as ours entirely to escape from some form of participation in the war effort. Those of us who pay taxes certainly participate; the men who did alternative service often were taking the places of men who fought in the army; even work done in the prisons might be helping the war effort. Knowledge of this dilemma created restlessness among a large part of the conscientious objectors. Now and again there were requests for reclassification, in both directions. Approximately five per cent of all CPS men asked for and received reclassification into noncombatant service in the army, and about the same number went into combat. Others, feeling that even CPS was too much of a compromise, voluntarily transferred to prison.

In the beginning, C. O.'s entering prison were often met by hostility on the part of prison officials and other prisoners; but in time, as they proved themselves, the tendency was quite the reverse. Sometimes, in fact, men were accused of choosing prison because it was easier. I know of no case, however, where the choice was made for this reason.

If the individual who chose prison believed that such personal action could alter the basic social patterns against which he was protesting — well, even in this extravagant hope he had considerable ground to stand on. In seventeenth-century England, Friends bore the brunt of much of the persecution of nonconformists. For refusing to take oath, for meeting as usual after their meetings had been prohibited, for saying what was not supposed to be said, probably about fifteen thousand Friends in England and Wales were imprisoned or otherwise punished during the Restoration period. Samuel Pepys wrote of some of these victims in his diary: "I would to God they would either conform, or be more wise, and not be catched!"

But it was the firm stand taken by these early Quakers and other dissenters which broke the back of authoritarianism in worship. Certainly the more recent experience of the followers of Gandhi in India demonstrates clearly the profound effect in terms of political change that can be wrought by a relatively small number of persons who go to prison for conscience's sake. There is ample justification, therefore, for belief that going to prison is not necessarily a negative act, but may be genuinely positive.

Among all of us who support the peace testimony in one way or another, there has been the continuing concern for amnesty for conscientious objectors who went to prison, which means the restoration of their voting and other rights as citizens. In December, 1946, the President, after many requests for general amnesty, appointed a Board to review the cases of all Selective Service violators whose civil and political rights had not been restored. Of C. O.'s, this involved some three hundred men still in prison and more than five thousand who had been released. No general amnesty resulted.

The Board reviewed individual cases, and there was restoration of civil rights to a relatively small number of the C. O.'s who had served time in prison. There are many who still do not have the right to vote, to hold public office, to be admitted to the bar, or to carry out other functions of the ordinary citizen. Efforts are still being made on their behalf.

Tides of fear are by no means assuaged by a military victory and by conscription of our manpower. We have emerged from World War II more fearful, more anxious, more committed to the use of physical violence for protection, than we have ever been before. For the first time in our history we have peacetime conscription. True, we are the chief participants in the Korean War, but conscription antedated our entrance into this conflict.

I have watched the movement of events since the conclusion of World War II, and have been greatly cheered by the growing conviction on the part of many men who objected in one way or another to participation in the Second World War. Equally cheering is the number of men who participated as soldiers but who now wish to join the ranks of those who will not again fight with outward weapons, choosing rather to throw their energies into the battle of the spirit to overcome those insidious enemies which are within all of us, and the root of our world trouble.

True, those who look at life this way are still small in number, but the real victory does not necessarily go to the most numerous. The social and spiritual achievements of humanity have come about not because of war but in spite of it; and it is an immense satisfaction to see a younger generation taking up with greater vigor and clarity of mind the opposition to war in all its forms, and, what is more, the task of participating in the kind of society which does away with the occasion for war.

This is the motive and heart of the efforts of the American Friends Service Committee. It is this which has lured me on from one year to another. If one allowed himself, he could become discouraged because as a nation we seem further from a recognition of the importance of good will, negotiation, and spiritual values than we did in 1929, when I became secretary of the Committee. But the tides of new life and creative spirit have a way of emerging when least expected. Certainly our spirits, our minds, and our morale will fritter away and wither if we put our confidence in arms. Already the signs of such weakness are upon us. Never have we been so afraid as we are now.

But in the midst of this fear, brave voices speak of a higher way which individuals and nations can find and follow. The place to begin considering one's attitude toward conscription is with the larger question, How can we most effectively, with a faith in men and God, expand the freedom of the human spirit? Those of us who object to conscription will continue to differ in our answers. But it may be of some service, at least, to have the right questions, clearly framed.

2. *Service Opportunities for Youth*

WORK CAMPS

THRESHING time on the Kansas farm where I grew up was for me the most joyous time of the year. Last of a family of eight children, and nine years last, I was almost like an only child. In perspective I can see that I was lonesome, though I hardly realized it at the time. One of our neighbors, who owed my father some money and who owned an old-fashioned horse-power threshing machine, worked out his debt by threshing our wheat in the fall. "Feeding the machine" was done by hand. Bundles were pitched onto a platform, and on each side of the feeder was a boy cutting the bands of the sheaves, so the wheat would be ready for the feeder. Being elevated to the position of cutter was one of the most exhilarating experiences of my life.

Threshing was a community event. Five or six neighbors came in with their hayracks and teams of horses to haul the bundles from the field to the threshing machine. In time I was able to handle one of the teams; and sometimes I worked at that incredibly hard job of stacking straw at the tail end of the machine. A dustier job no one ever had. Then there was the great threshing-crew dinner. The women of the community competed to see who could provide the most and the best food. But for the growing boy, the greatest joy was the chance to work with other people. There was no time when the farm boy worked harder; the sun was hot and hours were long; but how I enjoyed it!

In our home, following breakfast my father always read a passage from the Scriptures, and then we all knelt down by our chairs and Father, at least, offered a prayer. Sometimes other members of the family joined in that form of vocal worship. I can remember Father's making a special request of our protecting Heavenly Father that nothing we should do or say during this hurried period of threshing should in any way mar the purity of our thought and hearts. I am sure he had in mind, to some extent at least, the contagious nature of some of the picturesque language now and again used by certain members of the threshing crew!

What relevance does this have to Service Committee operations? Well, back about 1933 Ray Newton of our staff began talking with me about the work camps which had been initiated by Pierre Ceresole in Europe after the First World War. Pierre Ceresole, Swiss scientist, pacifist, and man extraordinary, had been impressed by Friends' reconstruction services in France in the wake of the war. Having served prison sentences in Switzerland for his pacifist stand, Pierre's thoughts were reaching out toward some form of service which might be performed by pacifists as an alternative to military service. In 1920 he brought his thinking to the Congress of the International Fellowship of Reconciliation in Holland, and met with warm response. With backing from this Fellowship and from Friends and other pacifists, he proceeded to organize a group of young men drawn from both sides of the recent conflict, to help in rebuilding devastated areas of northern France. "For a long time," wrote one of the German volunteers, "I have hoped for a chance to go and repair in France a little of what my brother (killed at Verdun) and his comrades were forced under military orders to destroy."

Rapidly this *Service Civil International* spread throughout Europe. It gave the youth of Europe a constructive outlet for their energies, and the comradeship of working together, living together, playing together. In Germany especially the movement became popular on a national scale during the years of the German people's attempt to restore their country physically and spiritually. At one time in pre-Hitler Germany, close to 300,000 young men and women were reported to be enrolled in the voluntary camps. One of the largest jobs ever done by the international movement was the work of reconstruction performed by more than seven hundred volunteers from many countries after the floods in Liechtenstein in 1928.

Now, in 1933, when our United States economy was on the rocks and open to all sorts of experimentation, Ray Newton was arguing for the merit of introducing work camps for American youth. As we discussed the idea, my experience in the fellowship of the threshing crews came back to me. I realized afresh that there is an exhilaration, a companionship, in working together, which I had never found in any other way. Conferences, study groups, meetings, all had their functions. But nothing took the place of working together.

Suppose we could get twenty-five or thirty young people, men and women, who would give a summer to doing a job in some maladjusted social situation — a job which needed doing and might not otherwise get done; and suppose that accompanying this there could be some study of the cause and possible cures of the social malady which lay behind the need of what we were inclined to call the "underprivileged community." Suppose, lastly, that in addition we experimented in this group with the relevance of worship, meditation, and singing. Ought this not to be an instrument for cultivating the sense of social responsibility and religious dedication?

During the days of these deliberations within our Service Committee staff, I paid a visit to a very dear elderly friend of mine who had decided she had too much money. I told her of our dream of work camps to be composed largely of young people who had the summer relatively at their own command, mostly college students. Some would doubtless be able to pay the cost of their part in the summer's work, but others would not.

When I came away from that visit, it was with a $30,000 check in my pocket — a three-year subsidy of $10,000 per year for work camps. I saw that check in terms of the social and religious development of an on-going generation, and I was exhilarated at the prospect.

This was during the period when government homesteads were being built. To co-operate with government in keeping costs down, and after many consultations with key government people, we decided as a first project to build a reservoir and water main for the new community in Westmoreland County, Pennsylvania, now named Norvelt.

The following summer, 1934, fifty-five young people (forty-one men and fourteen women) contributed 10,000 man-hours in digging a ditch a mile and a half long, laying the water-pipe, and constructing a 260,000-gallon reservoir. Some of the women also worked with wives in household arts, canning, health, and playground projects. During the summer the men lived in a large barn, the girls in a deserted tenant house. Housekeeping duties were shared by all. The evenings were largely given over to study of economic and social causes of the collapse which made these homesteads necessary, and to an exploration of pacifists' possible contributions toward a solution.

I am sure someone will ask, Why shouldn't unemployed men in that region have been used in constructing the water system, instead of importing young labor, even though it was free? It is quite true that there was a great deal of unemployment within the general community, but all the unemployed were now being used on existing WPA projects. For this they received sufficient pay to keep their families alive. The small water system at Norvelt was not set up as a WPA enterprise, and probably never would have been. In big, sweeping government programs, a great many things that need very much to be done cannot be included.

But more important than anything else was the manifestation on the part of these young people of a self-giving spirit, which was badly needed even where WPA prevailed.

Some persons may feel that though the results were socially beneficial the enterprise was a technical anachronism. In a matter of
days, if not hours, a mechanical ditchdigger could have done much
of the job that took weeks of hand labor. This is quite true. And
our work-camp program takes into consideration effective use of
machines when they can be obtained. But this again would have
added a great deal of expense to the waterworks project. We were
trying to reduce the total cost of the homestead to the individual.

And it seems to me important to keep in mind that simple and pure
economics is not where people live. When society gets so tightly
organized that there is no place for even a slightly inefficient use of
labor in the process of achieving spiritual values, then the virtue and
fun of living are gone.

I had not needed to go to a work camp to get fellowship in
physical work. My work camp was the threshing crew. The fact
remains that now with our more highly organized society and
largely urbanized young people it often takes a special effort to
bring to the more privileged among them the opportunity of sharing hard physical labor on needed projects, alongside people who
have not had their opportunities. The work camp moves into that
unoccupied area.

In 1934, the twofold aim of the voluntary work camp was stated
as follows: to render tangible service to part of the "stranded population" which was trying to establish itself in a new way of life, and
to bring young people face to face with one specific knot of the
economic tangle, enabling them to seek answers under Christian-
pacifist leadership.

Among the group of fifty-five the experiment had very wide re-
percussions. The directors of the camp, Wilmer and Mildred Young,
were permanently uprooted from their quiet berth of teaching at
Westtown School by this experience. In a talk which Mildred
Young gave to a group of Friends shortly after the close of camp,
she said, in part:

The Friends Service Camp meant to us a tiny experiment in training ourselves for the nonviolent revolution, for this repentance with our whole lives. The rough life and labor were a small effort toward the discipline of the flesh which opens a little the way for growth in that sense of unity with those millions who are born to unremitting, enforced discipline of the flesh. . . . One said to us, "Yes, Friends as pacifists could help very much in this conflict, with all their influence and people's belief in their good will; but not as neutrals. Not as neutrals!" No, not as neutrals. Not as people having no stake in the struggle, but as people who are giving all that they have and are, to raise up the partial truth on each side unto one TRUTH. . . . Friends, we deceive ourselves if we think this could be less than a revolutionary Quakerism. We deceive ourselves if we think we could keep our wide properties and our prestige in high places. Our only weapon and our only defense would be that nonviolence which involves participation to the last ounce of energy and resource that is in us. . . . One wonders sometimes if, while in all our meetings for worship we are striving to reach and unite our minds with the mind of God, it may not be that the reason the effort often seems so vain and the result so sterile of life, is that none of us has been down with our flesh and our bone and those things which we call security and our influence — down to lay them where, as Tagore says, "God's feet rest among the poorest, and the lowliest, and the lost."

This was not mere oratory. Mildred and Wilmer Young were never again satisfied until they put everything they had and were into an experiment of identifying themselves with a group of share-croppers in South Carolina. Over the years they have led a local co-operative enterprise, through which people have been able gradually to gain possession of the lands they worked and to improve their operations, their homes and facilities, their whole tenor of life. This is what our first work camp did to two persons.

David Richie, who was one of the student campers, also was propelled by the experience into thoroughgoing dedication. It was he who later conceived the idea of adapting work camps to a week-end span, so that students might be able to participate throughout

the year. Both in the United States and in Europe, David has proved
to be a most inspiring work-camp leader. Thus one student at least
had his life pretty much shaped by that first experiment in Westmoreland County. And there were others.

The next year eighty-four young people participated in four
camps — two in mining communities, one in a textile workers'
community, and one in an interracial community center in Philadelphia. The program soared on the wings of youth, who had the
time of their lives even while they worked themselves to the point
of exhaustion, who made new friends in areas of life new to them,
who, partly because they were young, welcomed the vision of "the
new order, whose name is brotherhood." By the third year, 190
campers were at work. All told, since the opening of the movement
in the United States, something more than three thousand young
people have participated in AFSC camps alone, and the movement
has spread so that we are now only one of many organizations sponsoring such camps. During my entire life so far, as a minister, a
teacher, and an administrator, I have seen many devices used for
the purpose of deepening religious life and broadening social concern, but I think I have never found any form of service that
enjoys a higher rate of spiritual achievement than the work camp.

Our camps have been in coal-mining communities, in overcrowded and underprivileged industrial areas, in sharecropper regions of the South, on TVA and other progressive social and technical experiments, on American Indian reservations, in migrant
camps, in burned-over parts of New England after forest fires, in
the Ozarks and other Southern hill country, in areas of special
racial tension, especially among Japanese-Americans, Chinese,
Mexicans, and Negroes, and notably in spots where Negro-white
tensions are acute. From the very first summer, camper personnel
has been interracial, and since the war it has also been progressively
international. In 1952 twenty-two foreign students participated in
our camps in this country.

Water mains have been laid; swimming pools and playgrounds

built; homes, barns, mills, bridges, dams, community centers, and schools constructed or renovated; roads have been made; forests cleared; soil conservation programs initiated; gardening and farm work done, especially during the war. Recreational programs and nursery schools have been established. . . . But there is no call to make an exhaustive survey; a few glimpses of specific projects through the years will better serve to suggest the range of work, the response of campers, and the problems that are faced.

In 1937 I visited a work camp at Penn-Craft, and recorded in my journal:

In the afternoon I worked with the gang hauling stone from the Beehive Coke Ovens, chiefly for road-making on the new project. I worked with two or three of the boys, one of the homesteaders, and Carl Landis of the Mennonite group, who is living in the community. I wasn't much good as a worker, although I carried about as much of a load as the boys. Walker Lawson of the homesteaders was the great worker of the crowd. It was interesting to hear the campers ask Walker Lawson, who is a long-time coal miner, about the union and the whole problem of mining from the miner's point of view.

In 1940 a girl wrote to her family from a work camp among migrants in California:

This is not the kind of town most of you think of when you think of California. It is a hot, dusty town with few trees.... A railroad divides the town into two sections; we are living in a schoolhouse on the west side of the tracks, which is the poorer section. . . . The county migrant camp looks just like the ones pictured in "Grapes of Wrath." . . . We were guests at the regular Saturday night dance which is held at the Visalia Federal Migratory Labor Camp. The floor was packed with energetic dancers, swaying and dashing to the rhythm of a lively fiddle and three guitars and the piano. . . . A mural has been drawn depicting the story of the Migrant from the time he left his home back in the Middle West, through the present, and then the life in California is expressed. We all had a swell time.

These work campers were helping migrants construct an athletic field, and were taking the lead in a recreational program for all ages. But what they were getting for themselves was much more: never would they speak of migrants with a complete outsider's viewpoint.

In 1945 a work-camp unit helped out in the Emergency Refugee Shelter at Fort Ontario, Oswego, New York, where refugees straight out of grueling experiences in Europe were being given temporary shelter. In making plans for this camp a director wrote: "One of the greatest problems will be to get the members of this unit to have a sense of positive direction without the ordinary American adolescent buoyancy which seems to disturb these people who have been through so much. The unit probably should be put through several days of special training on such points." I am sure that the young people who were eventually chosen for this service left Oswego at the end of the summer greatly chastened in heart and spirit.

In the summer of 1947 a work camp was set up in a southern Missouri community where racial segregation was deeply ingrained in the social pattern. The job of the camp was to help build a community center in a new housing project for Negroes, and run a recreation program for the children. One of the campers was a Negro boy. The wider community was not ready to accept interracial fellowship. The young people found themselves face to face with the stern realities of prejudice and threat of violence.

At first the campers and directors thought they might convince the community by taking it in slow stages. One evening after much soul-searching, the group, including the Negro camper, decided that the white campers should accept an invitation to the home of a local white family, though the Negro boy had to be left behind; their hope was that, if the white boys and girls could establish confidence in themselves, they might then be able to break the local taboos against the Negro boy.

After this social evening, a Finnish girl who was a member of the camp wrote a long letter to her family in Finland:

They are all good fellows and I think that the group life is "all right," — but there is one great difficulty. J. is a Negro, and this group can't take him with them if they are going to the town — and only because he is a Negro! Thursday night we were all invited to Reverend M.'s home, where were some white people from Charleston. *J. was at home alone,* and only because his skin was darker than ours! I can't tell you my feelings this night. I was angry, unhappy, disappointed, sad. I told to one visitor that I am unhappy, because one of us is not with us. He was a little surprised, but he said only, "You are lucky, you have no Negroes in Finland." . . . One lady from Charleston played *Finlandia* and I sang the words, "We would be building," . . . When we came home J. was sitting and reading. He was sad and I knew how he felt. He said that maybe it is better he go home. But I and some of the others asked him to stay. Before he left to sleep he said, "I will pray that the Lord will give me strength enough to be here."

This procedure of leaving J. behind was not one the group could go on with. Most of them felt badly that they had even tried it. There was talk of giving up the camp. But it was felt that there was a good deal of interracial value in the presence of white campers working with the Negro population on their homes. It seemed this was acceptable to the community, but not the presence of the Negro boy in the camp. There was continued threat of violence on the part of the more lawless elements of the white population. In the end, rightly or wrongly, it was the decision of the entire group that for that summer J. would leave and the rest of them would continue to work with the Negro community. A letter from one of the directors reported this decision:

J. felt no fear for himself, nor did we for ourselves, and the Negro community was game to take what might come. . . . But we were persuaded the step was one too many. . . . J. is a fine person, an independent thinker and very warm of spirit. He wants to come back some time. This area is a place where progress can be made in the next few years. I hope we keep very clear our ultimate aims, and not let fears and doubts and negative attitudes stop us from progressing at a rather rapid rate, since time is relatively short and the distance to Christianity and democracy so great.

This whole episode was, in a sense, one of our "failures." Neither AFSC nor the camp directors nor the campers felt very good about it. It was obvious that we had tried to go faster than we could; other errors may have been made, perhaps the final crisis was not met in the best way possible. But it was met by the group as a whole, and the educational value of the experience was enormous. A group of boys and girls who had arrived singing of brotherhood, full of the confidence of youth, had learned something about the agony of segregation which they would never forget. We knew that the situation had placed an excessive demand on the one Negro camper, and it was extremely fortunate that he had been unusually mature for his age, able to view the problem with impressive objectivity. We were careful not to let this kind of thing happen again. For the most part, we now go into communities where we are assured we can be interracial. Once in a while we will undertake a project on a noninterracial basis if there is hope that by so doing we can work into an interracial project in the near future.

Another work camp, in Indiana, had excellent interracial experience throughout its life as a camp and on the work project, but when the campers went on a holiday to the nearby State Park they ran into trouble. One camper wrote: "Thursday morning we ran up against an unpleasant experience with the Park Superintendent which prevented our swimming again; by this experience we learned more about race relations in one day than we had all the six weeks before in our camp. The experience made us a much closer group. . . . Monday evening we had an interesting seminar on 'legal aspects of segregation and discrimination,' led by Mr. Richardson, a colored lawyer."

In speaking with groups of students, I often find myself talking about earning the right to be a propagandist, and I use our work camps and other youth activities to illustrate the ways in which we are trying to get young people to dig in and get close to the social issues about which they are concerned.

As I see the work-camp movement, it is a kind of evangelism which aims to make it possible for young people (1) to perform physical labor and give of themselves in a social situation that needs the gift of service and love, with no remuneration involved; (2) to get acquainted with some of the situations in this and other countries where our fellow human beings have to live the year around under circumstances that cramp and stultify life; (3) through association with people of the community and other campers in this fellowship of service, to find anew the meaning of the commitment that Jesus made. Work camps certainly contain the element of service to man, and offer the opportunity for individual and group fellowship with God. It seems to me that any healthy society here or elsewhere must be rooted in the kind of motives that prompt one to throw himself into this type of experience.

FRIENDS SERVICE UNITS IN MEXICO

It was our peace-education program which was responsible for taking the work-camp idea into Mexico under AFSC auspices. Participants in our "Institutes of International Relations" — especially in the Southwest part of the country — began to feel a particular responsibility to do something about United States relations with Mexico. Young people of the United States who associated with young Mexicans in these Institutes became conscious that Mexicans had learned to fear their neighbors to the north. Was not our attack on Vera Cruz pure aggression? Did not most Mexicans take a dim view of certain United States groups' exploitation of Mexico's oil resources?

Again it was the imaginative Ray Newton who, together with the picturesque "red-headed Aztec," Heberto Sein of Mexico City, decided that something must be done to give United States youth a chance to know Mexican youth in their homeland, amidst their own problems. Mexicans came to our country to study, but for the most part people who traveled southward across the border went only as tourists, or, what was worse, as exploiters.

Heberto Sein's mother was a Quaker missionary, sent down as a young woman from Iowa to Mexico. There she met and married a Mexican Protestant minister. Heberto Sein grew up in a home devoutly religious, bilingual, and ardently interested in education. At an early age he decided to fit himself to be a language teacher. He already knew Spanish and English from his home life, and now, when he was ready to do further study, his parents arranged for him to go to Paris to study French. They knew that AFSC had a Center in Paris, and Heberto was instructed to go directly to that Center when he arrived.

He describes himself as a gangling, red-headed, freckle-faced youth, fresh from a long bicycle ride from the coast to Paris, hot and tired, when he walked into the Paris Center. The first person he met was a charming young French girl, who on first sight caught his fancy. We shall have to forego the delicious temptation to tell in detail the story of their developing friendship and eventual marriage, their journey back to Mexico after three years' study in Paris, and then the shipwreck near the Azores, when Heberto swam to shore carrying his bride! There followed the establishment of a home in Mexico City and the birth of three fine children, Heberto meanwhile being employed as a teacher of English and French at two of the state colleges of Mexico.

Here indeed was ground prepared, ready for full co-operation when Ray Newton made his first trip to Mexico City to explore possibilities for developing international projects in Mexico. Our work camps in the United States had been under way for several years, and it seemed clear that similar projects in Mexico would serve a useful purpose, if they could be initiated in the right spirit. The international aspect of such an undertaking highlighted considerations which were not even part of the picture in the United States.

Before actual planning was begun, certain principles were laid down as being fundamental to the right development of the enterprise, and these principles have been pretty well adhered to ever since. They are:

(1) Services of the campers are offered to the Mexican people for jobs THEY want done, in the way THEY want them done.

(2) The work-campers receive no pay.

(3) Units are located and work undertaken only on invitation of the Mexican authorities responsible in the given areas. (Most AFSC services have come under the jurisdiction of the Mexican Departments of Public Health and Education.)

(4) The Mexican Departments should provide any engineering skill and equipment necessary to the projects.

(5) On each project there should be at least an equal number of Mexicans participating with campers from the United States.

Anyone sensitive to the violations of good relationship between our country and Mexico over the years will comprehend the significance of all these points. A good illustration of their practical application is the conference in 1940, of Dr. José Bustos, head of the Department of Health in the state of Vera Cruz, his technical staff, Dr. George Payne of the Rockefeller Foundation, and an AFSC staff member. At this conference, it was decided that the drainage of a forty-acre swamp near Tolome was a job which should be undertaken. Dr. Bustos remarked that if the AFSC could furnish twenty men, he was sure he could get twenty Mexicans to come out from the village to help them. The AFSC staff representative immediately pointed out that he very much hoped this would not be done, suggesting rather that Dr. Bustos go to the people in the village, talk to them about the swamp and malaria, and tell them that if they wanted to drain the swamp, he was sure he could get twenty American men to help them.

For various reasons, it was 1942 before the drainage of the swamp could be undertaken. By that time, everyone interested in this program was greatly under the weight of the war, and there was an added urgency among young pacifists to prove themselves in constructive work that taxed their resources to the uttermost. Draining the swamp left little to be desired in the way of difficult conditions. It meant standing knee-deep in mud in steaming summer weather, mosquitoes and threat of malaria to contend with, and dysentery — not to mention snakes, tarantulas, and scorpions.

Ninety per cent of the people of that region had malaria. Another fact that added to the project's significance was that it was in the state of Vera Cruz, where bitterness against Americans was very deep.

In the beginning there was bound to be mistrust, a searching for ulterior motives. What could be wrong with these young people? No North Americans ever acted like this. They must be digging for oil.

In addition to the regular practice of meditation and worship within the group itself, which is part of the pattern of all AFSC work camps at home or abroad, the campers here attended the local Catholic Church, sang in the choir, pumped the organ, lent their station wagon to the priest, and all the time were proving themselves to be good hard workers. It became evident that the long ditch was for drainage purposes only. It also became known that these young people were volunteers, giving their time and their energy, and that all of it was a testimony on behalf of creative solutions as opposed to war.

It was inevitable that friendships should be formed between the Mexicans and North Americans who worked together. But it went further than that. Gradually, the campers established a relationship of confidence and affection with the larger community. When this is compared with the gratuitous attack of our Navy on the city of Vera Cruz, one begins to feel there is real justification in considering efforts of this kind as the moral equivalent of war.

From 1939, when the first unit in Mexico was established, up to the present time, 1700 young people from the United States and other countries have gone to Mexico to co-operate with Mexican communities in a variety of services. In return, Mexican young people have come to the United States, to take part in reclamation projects here. Nothing about the program is tinged by that wilting sentiment of benevolent good works. For one thing, the campers are much too bent on enjoying themselves for that. Besides, it is not in the philosophy of the program. One of the important aspects of the work-camper's experience in Mexico is the study of Mexican history and culture that goes on throughout the period, culminating in a seminar in Mexico City each year in August.

During the summer of 1942 our entire family spent two months in Mexico on vacation. We were not really studying the projects of the Service Committee, but I took occasion to talk with some of the people in government and other leading positions in Mexican life, about these voluntary work projects. I was especially impressed on a visit to the president of the Bank of Mexico to find that he knew about the AFSC work camps, had been much interested in them, and emphasized the very great importance they had for his own people as an interpretation of the inner meaning of Christianity. He himself was a Catholic.

In 1947–1948 the Mexican Ministry of Education invited the American Friends Service Committee to send down some young people from this and other countries to co-operate in the Mexican government's development project in the Santiago River Valley in the state of Nayarit in western Mexico. This fertile coastal region, as marked out by the government for the experiment, includes the city of Santiago with its 8500 people, and twenty-five villages with about 1000 inhabitants each. The villages have up to this time been extremely primitive, with no sanitation facilities, no pure water, no services, no roads to speak of. Malaria and intestinal parasites have persistently sapped the energy of both children and adults. The few schools there were did not usually go beyond the fourth grade. Village life was dull, with practically no facilities for recreation. Alcoholism was a serious problem. The area was recognized from the beginning as having within the valley and its people the potential force to bring new life and purpose to the inhabitants. UNESCO's interest and co-operation had been obtained. Our Committee understood the value of such a "pilot project," and was happy to accept the Mexican government's invitation to co-operate.

A member of one of the first AFSC units to arrive in Nayarit has described the beginnings:

> The boys arrived to find themselves in a rather sorry plight. Their home-to-be had been a schoolhouse, whose roof leaked to the extent that it could scarcely be called a roof at all, and whose front lawn bore close resemblance to a swimming pool. The girls came to the village of Santiago where, save for a flea-ridden box-like theater, there was no means of entertainment except drinking, for any but the elite.
>
> Mario explained to the boys that the rebuilding of their home, the plans they have for making it attractive, and the genial attitude with which they work, are not precursors to the project, but an intrinsic part of it, and an example. The girls work with the schoolteachers in helping to care for the children. . . . And both groups together will work in the evening schools, not only as teachers but as students. Plans are afoot to give Aristophanes' *Peace* in one of the ejidos where those on one side of the road don't speak to those on the other side. Our job, as Mario put it, is to live well, not minimizing our differences but enjoying them; and the fruitfulness of the venture will not be for the Mexicans alone.

"Mario" was Mario Aguilera, the director and driving force of the project in its initial period. He had a paid staff of some thirty people, but the rest of the workers were volunteers. Co-operating with more than two hundred Mexican villagers who were also volunteering their time, AFSC units rapidly became integrated into the life of the region on a year-round basis.

While the undertaking as a whole has suffered a number of setbacks, due partly to internal political interference, our units have been able to move forward with their participation in a way that has been most gratifying.

The Mexican Department of Agriculture was interested in the development of better breeds of livestock, better quality of seeds, vaccination of pigs against cholera, ways to make additional farm lands available, and the wider cultivation of honey bees. In the public-health program, malaria control was a big item. In one case this has meant moving a whole town to a new, more sanitary location, building new homes, draining streets. Pools and swamps throughout the region have been sprayed with DDT.

In villages in which there had been no schools, schools have been started not only for the children but for adults as well. English classes have been popular, as well as instruction in gardening and arts and crafts. And the North American young people have learned Indian dances and the Spanish language.

While this experiment aims to relax the heavy physical burden that rests on the people of this region, especially the women, by making available a good water supply, health services, and instruction in improved methods of labor, fundamentally it is a cultural and spiritual adventure. It seeks not to bring something from the outside and impose it upon the Mexican, but to help him realize the values he feels — values which he has longed to understand and see, but which he has felt helpless to bring about without some assistance. The dream that lies within is gradually coming to be a reality.

One day a nurse from El Salvador came to the AFSC camp at the Nayarit project. She had been sent by Dr. Allwood, El Salvador's Director of Public Health, who had learned of our Committee's co-operation with the Mexican government. She lived and worked in our camp for several months, and upon her return to El Salvador told her story to Dr. Allwood.

The result was an invitation from the El Salvador government to AFSC to participate in the United Nations Rural Demonstration Project which was then being launched in that country. In this plan, four international agencies are participating — UNESCO, FAO, ILO, and WHO; and the United States Technical Cooperation Administration gives some assistance from time to time through the Institute of Inter-American Affairs. The Service Committee has found it quite natural to take this further step, from Mexico on into El Salvador.

It has not been an easy matter to bring all of these agencies into full co-operation in a single project. But now it is largely accomplished. Again, the contribution of the willing hand and the dedicated spirit of the young worker, under experienced leadership, has been of great significance. The social and technical agencies of the United Nations are in their rightful role in carrying responsibility for laying the larger plans. But the spirit, "Come on, boys, let's go!" can often be better furnished by youth, who are not inhibited by knowing the difficulties which are in the way.

QUAKER INTERNATIONAL VOLUNTARY SERVICE

I remember walking along the streets of New York one day in May, 1945, and suddenly hearing whistles begin to blow all over the city. There had been sufficient warning in the press so that I knew what this meant. The war in Europe was at an end.

I stopped a moment, meditating what was the next step. We knew there would be a heavy undertaking of relief. But how could one start on the delicate task of reknitting the social and spiritual fabric torn apart by bitterness and violence of war? My mind went back to the movement started by Pierre Ceresole after World War I.

Now our country had participated in almost unparalleled destruction in Europe and Asia. We at AFSC knew full well that there would be some young men who had been in the armed forces, and many who had not, who would want to put their all into the job of reconstruction in such a way that the ties of fellowship and understanding might be re-established. It was with these thoughts in mind that our Committee began considering the possibility of extending its work-camp program beyond our own shores, taking it back to Europe where it originated.

We were not under the illusion that we would be the only ones to think of this; happily, it has turned out that many groups in this country have taken an active part in work camps abroad. I could think of large numbers of Americans going, in the earlier stages taking their own food with them, and with the freshness of energy that was theirs, having been largely spared the sufferings of Europe, joining hands with Europeans in rebuilding some of the waste places; but most of all showing their desire to stand alongside their European neighbors in an effort to build a world of fellowship and understanding which moved beyond wars.

One could scarcely help seeing the potentialities of this kind of movement. If it could become a widespread crusade of reconstruction of body and mind and spirit, its influence would be illimitable.

Our Committee made some start in the summer of 1946, but it was in 1947 that the program really came into its own. That summer, forty-three young men and women went from the United States to camps reaching across Europe from northernmost Finnish Lapland to the valley of the Aventino in Italy, and eastward to Brixlegg in the Austrian Tyrol and the banks of the Vistula in Poland.

Most of them went to Quaker camps in Italy, Austria, Poland, and Finland, but a few were assigned to camps of the *Service Civil International* in Holland, Belgium, and France, and one worked in the British Friends Relief Service camp in Berlin.

In Italy, one of the most colorful projects was the construction of a cable car at Lettopalena, to replace a dynamited bridge. This cable car, about which local engineers were skeptical, was designed to transport building stone from the ruins of the old village of Lettopalena to the new site across the river. Its construction was an enormous success. When American campers left, the car was making seventy-seven trips per day across the river, hauling two hundred pounds of stone and brick each trip. Twenty Italian youth had joined forces with young men from the United States, Belgium, France, Sweden, and Switzerland on this job. It was interesting that many of the Italian fellows came from the more privileged student groups, and in this camp were for the first time brought into functional relationship with Italy's poverty and material need.

The most extensive program was carried out in Finland. About 140 young people participated in seven camps cosponsored by AFSC and a Finnish work-camp organization. In Finnish Lapland, they helped rebuild devastated towns, and in the southern part of the country they assisted evacuees from the East in constructing new homes. A Finnish Karelian evacuee declared his life made over by the experience: "To forget oneself, one's selfishness, to dedicate one's eagerness to the work and to one's neighbor will be my effort." Living on the rations on which Finnish people at that time were living was at first a great shock to well-fed Americans. One of our campers confessed: "Sometimes I am ashamed because I am so hungry. Sometimes I feel as if I would give my soul for a good piece of meat, or slice of pie, or just a piece of candy . . . . "

The camp at Lucimia, Poland, south of Warsaw on the banks of the Vistula River, was sponsored by the Anglo-American Quaker Mission and by UNESCO. The volunteers were American, English, Finnish, Danish, Swiss, and Polish. Those of Polish nationality were Communist, Socialist, and Catholic Rightist. Barracks were constructed to serve as a schoolhouse, the town having had none since the old building was destroyed during the war. Meanwhile classes were held on the banks of the river; a medical clinic was established; homes were rebuilt for widows and old people. The Polish Ministers of Reconstruction, Health, Education, and Foreign Affairs gave every co-operation, and the people of the village brought eggs, poultry, apples, whatever they could furnish. Sometimes political or national tensions waxed strong. The one Communist camper was never "convinced," nor did he convince. But he was happy in that camp, perhaps happier than he had ever been before in his life. At the beginning of the season, when the brotherhood of the

Germans was mentioned, Polish campers got up and stalked out. By the end of the summer, a German camper could probably have been invited to participate.

It might be well to point out that this growing acceptance of our common brotherhood was not achieved by intellectual arguments; nor was it sentimentally imposed on deeper feelings — a futile procedure. It was a transformation which gradually took place as these young people of different persuasions and experience united to rebuild what had been destroyed, and at the end of the day contemplated the meaning.

One of the campers, struggling with newly learned English, groped toward expression: "It seems to me," she said, "that problems of understanding each other grow less in working together on some problem other than understanding one another."

During the past six years, Quaker International Voluntary Service has sent about four hundred young people into work camps in Algeria, Austria, Belgium, Denmark, Finland, France, Germany, Great Britain, Greece, Haiti, Holland, India, Israel, Italy, Jamaica, Norway, Pakistan, Poland, The Saar, Sweden, Switzerland, and Yugoslavia. As political lines have tightened and the "iron curtain" has become more impenetrable, it has been impossible to continue camps in Poland. However, work camps in Berlin continue to bring together students from both East and West zones.

All of us interested in the work-camp movement realize that one of its most serious limitations is the fact that young people must have a certain amount of leisure time in order to participate. This excludes a great many young men and women who must work for a living and who are needed in such a movement if it is to be more than a "middle-class" expression. Some scholarships are available, but this is no over-all answer. The practice of letting campers come for short intervals, such as week-ends or brief vacation periods, though it helps, still does not satisfy the requirement of a large, dynamic movement of world youth in the name of fellowship. And one feels that the alternative is likely to be the use of such youth by governments whose purposes are other than that of world fellowship.

In 1951 a work-camper wrote from Berlin:

As we walked through East Berlin to the S-Bahn on the way to Meeting, Willi said, "Hark! It is the same voice — the same as Hitler's." I heard no one and said so. "But listen," said Willi. Then I heard the drums. Soon the drums were followed by a fanfare of trumpets. As we came close to the square we saw marchers — a small group of teen-agers, dressed in the blue shirts of the F.D.J.,* marching back and forth across the Potsdamer Platz. Even during Meeting we could hear the insistent beat of the drums and sporadic singing. On the way home I mentioned to a girl from Western Germany what Willi had said. She said, "No, I do not think it is the same voice." "Not even the voice of the drums?" I asked. "Oh, the drums, yes. But wherever there are large gatherings of youth in the world today, do you not hear these things? I think it is not so much the voice of Hitler, but the voice of Power. Is it not?"

There are in Germany today, and in other countries as well, great masses of youth detached from home ties, from jobs, and from religious and cultural affiliations. Our small experiments with work camps have given us a glimpse of what might be done if there were a real crusade of fellowship in suffering and work. I venture to predict that the diplomacy and the religion of this kind of effort would go far toward rebuilding the world's confidence and hope. We can still further lift our sights as to the possibilities of movements of this sort.

INTERNE PROGRAMS

I have pointed out that one shortcoming of our work with young people is that we reach chiefly those who have a reasonable degree

* Freie Deutsche Jugend.

of leisure. But there is more than one way of being underprivileged. Boys and girls who grow up without a chance to know what hard work under conditions of monotony means are in this respect underprivileged; they have an acute need to share through actual experience the problems, emotions, and activities of those "workers" who form the great bulk of the world's population. We have found many college students, particularly, who were conscious of this need, who wished to partake of life exactly where it was most necessitous and difficult, and who, in addition, wanted to give study and thought to the significance of such experiences.

In response to this need, the AFSC has established a program of internships in industry and agriculture. The young people who participate find their own jobs, and live on what they make, the conditions of their life differing in two respects from those of the other men and women with whom they work.

In the first place, these internes live in groups in some co-operative house or other place where they can easily get together for discussions and lectures. A leader is in residence with them. Evenings and week ends they bring to bear on their work experience the most searching questions and reactions they can muster. In addition, there is a schedule of talks by labor leaders, representatives of management, and social scientists. This is not just a work experience, which each young person might obtain individually, but a work-and-study experience — a far cry from academic consideration of "labor problems," as most of the internes can testify.

The other respect in which these young people differ from most of those with whom they work in factory or field is that they have easy access to emergence from this life of routine labor into positions of management or professional responsibility and privilege. Now and again one will remain as a worker in industry, but for the most part this is not the case. Therefore their identification with the "workingman" may be said to be somewhat artificial. Nevertheless, I have found that these young people tend to be deeply and permanently impressed by their experiences in looking for jobs, deciding as to union membership, failing or succeeding in assembly-line assignments, enduring the heat, noise, smells, discouragements of an industrial community, trying to make their pay cover emergency dental and medical needs. Like work-campers, they learn that where you stand makes considerable difference in the stand you take.

Over a period of three hundred years, what a great transformation has come about in the Society of Friends! When we came into being in the middle of the seventeenth century, most of our members were of humble origin, farmers or small craftsmen, and there was not a very high average of education. Yet the Meetings of that time were more often than not profoundly moving; lives were transformed. Robert Barclay was able to say, when he entered one of these Meetings, he the great scholar, that he found the evil weakening in him, and the good raised up. Now as a Society we have achieved more education, more ownership of property, more respect from the world. It is good when we find individuals, especially young people, rising among us to emphasize the need for a new sense of reality in life and worship. On the whole, this is the direction in which the young internes point us.

One interne-in-industry wrote:

My work was packing cookies from a "perpetual motion" conveyor belt at a rate I calculated to be fifteen cookies per second, eight hours a day, with two 20-minute reliefs and a 45-minute lunch. . . . At the end of my second week I was "given the air." Being laid off, fired without any reason that the personnel office or I could divine, was really a soul-shaking experience. I trust that through it I gained a measure of emotional equilibrium, for it certainly tested whatever I had had. Whatever the temporal effects, I am glad it happened, as it gave insight into another facet of industrial life, which is all too prevalent. As a woman with whom I worked put it, "Gosh, if only I could go home at night knowing that my family would be able to eat the next day!" Social conscience is a term I've had enough of. Living in the insecurity, poverty, fatigue, morally destructive atmosphere that so many spend a lifetime under, you lose any need for collegiate dallying with the pros and cons of a "social conscience." You know that this is wrong and inhuman, and that if justice is ever to prevail you must help its coming, for indifference is a form of obstruction.

Another wrote: "For a native of conservative Virginia to attempt an appraisal of such a program as this by comparing his present knowledge of human industrial relations with that prior to the summer is beyond what can be expected of him, for in doing so it becomes necessary for him to reveal former attitudes."

At the close of his interne experience in Chicago in the summer of 1952, one young man wrote, in a striking report:

College students, especially those of idealistic mind, are too apt to repeat liberal clichés rather than hammer out on the anvil of experience their own personal stand. . . . The longer a person remains in contact with the workers' world, the more impossible seem the ambiguities arising from the Industrial Revolution. It seems inevitable that men are destined to be less than God intended them, as long as they must perpetuate our existing industrial structure. We cannot relapse into a preindustrial state, and it does not seem likely that we will mechanize to the point where men need not be made into machines to keep the wheels turning. Where is the answer?

In 1952, 117 young people participated in the interne program. All were seeking reality in relation to the problem of mass production in our society. How could religion and social values survive and thrive under conditions most of the people must face? Many of the internes were surprised at the intelligence and responsibility they encountered in both labor and management, and were all the more impressed by the complexity of the problem.

My own feeling is that there is one step yet to take. I believe we shall see the time when industries are broken up into much smaller units, located where life can be lived in community, and where production is by no means impeded but perhaps increased by a closer and more intimate sense of participation by the workers in both production and community life. It may be that the introduction of modern machinery into some of the technical assistance programs in other parts of the world will be the means of bringing about this kind of development. The aggregation of enormous populations for the sake of mass production will, I believe, in the long run prove socially wasteful, and much more imaginative ways will be tried.

INSTITUTIONAL SERVICE UNITS

During the war, when conscientious objectors began working as attendants in mental hospitals, many young women who shared their pacifist convictions, especially wives of the CPS men, wished to contribute their services also. The understaffed, sorely tried mental hospitals were delighted to have them. Of course they were paid the going wage, but this was small in comparison with what most of them could have made in other pursuits. Their presence in the mental hospitals was definitely a testimony to the way of loving service as an alternative to war.

They found themselves in the midst of the United States' Number One health problem, often working under supervision which was custodial in attitude rather than curative.

No one who has worked as an attendant in any of these institutions can ever be quite unconcerned about the way they are operated. As a citizen he will at least be better informed, and he is quite likely to pass on his information and concern, thus setting in motion ever-widening circles of awareness.

The young women who went into this work through AFSC went in small groups under able leaders. Some of their free time was used in study and discussion of the problems they faced, with lectures by doctors, nurses, psychologists, sociologists, and hospital management. This type of opportunity proved to be so popular that, far from ending with the end of the war, the program has continued to expand in both scope and vitality. It accepts young men as well as young women, functions in reformatories, mental hospitals, and institutions for the mentally retarded, and has both summer and year-round projects. In the summer of 1952, 143 members were participating in twelve units.

One of the most interesting aspects of this service is the way in which it has given practical expression to the Committee's concern that "race relations" shall be, quite simply, human relations. From the beginning, those responsible for Institutional Service Units have held to the principle of interracial units, not only on the basis of Quaker faith, but also because sound mental health requires release from prejudices, and because as units go into public institutions which are supported by taxation they must claim the right of all races to work there, subject only to professional and personal qualifications.

It has been most gratifying to see public institutions accepting this principle, though sometimes it is necessary to overcome a certain amount of skepticism in the beginning. In fact, there is often considerable resistance to the whole idea of a group of college students stepping into the trying routine of attendants. Will they not soon walk out on the job? Will they not take a superior attitude toward the other attendants? Will they not think they know better than the hospital management? In certain cases where doubt as to the possibility of using an interracial unit is combined with mistrust of the student group as a whole, ISU has offered to move into an institution with an all-white unit on a temporary basis, but always with the understanding that, once the unit has established confidence in itself, the hospital will reconsider an interracial unit, and, if it does not see its way clear to accepting this development within a reasonable time, ISU will withdraw.

This kind of approach has appealed to most hospital officials as being eminently reasonable, and the results have been even better than we had dared anticipate. Several outstanding hospitals in Illinois, after one-year tests of ISU, received interracial units, and then began adding Negroes to their regular staffs — a not uncommon sequence. In Iowa, after a three-year test of ISU, the whole state policy was changed in regard to hiring Negroes for professional and semiprofessional work in state institutions.

But perhaps the most interesting example is what took place in Austin, Texas. There the particularly forward-looking administrator of Austin State Hospital was quite eager to have an ISU unit, but felt that because of regional prejudices he could not possibly take a unit which included Negroes. Our ISU administrator in Philadelphia conferred with our race-relations division, and also with our regional office in Austin, and out of these conferences made the following proposal to the superintendent. If no Negroes were included in the unit the first year, would the hospital accept two provisions: (1) that a representative committee of citizens of Austin, both white and colored, should work with the unit, coming in as visitors to assist in recreation and therapy, and to advise on difficult situations (there are both white and colored patients in the hospital, though they are segregated); (2) that the possibility of including Negroes in the unit should be given serious consideration the second year.

The superintendent readily agreed to these provisions and was most anxious to be co-operative. He suggested it might be helpful if several members of the unit were from Texas.

A unit of nine young men and women was assembled. Three of them were Texans, and the others were from California, Oklahoma, Indiana, Florida, and Pennsylvania. One was a Japanese-American.

The proposed citizens' committee was organized, including both Negro and white professional men and women. For both racial groups it was an exhilarating experience and opened a new era in the relation of the total community to the institution.

The superintendent of the hospital was troubled about the apparent necessity to use mechanical restraints on the more violent patients, but the regular attendants were reluctant to try handling these patients otherwise. Now he talked with members of our unit concerning their "nonviolent" approach to patients, and accepted their offer to try caring for a group of overactive patients with the mechanical restraints removed.

The change was made. A few days passed, and there was a noticeable calm on that ward. The entire hospital staff was interested, not to say elated. It had worked far better than anyone had expected. In fact, there was no trouble at all. By the time our unit left at the end of the summer, regular attendants were ready to take over on the new basis.

It is interesting to note that by the next summer (1952) the hospital had added two Negroes to its regular professional staff, and was ready to try a unit which included Negro members. Also, a doctor in this Austin hospital had been made superintendent of the State Hospital in San Antonio, and he too requested a unit, saying it could be fully interracial from the beginning. His confidence had been won the first summer by the way in which those nine young people had gone about their work.

Then came the great blow. The loyalty oath in Texas was to be firmly enforced. ISU members preparing to go to Texas faced a tragic conflict. On the one hand was their desire to serve patients in mental institutions, particularly in a situation in the South where they were being given almost unheard-of co-operation in breaking down barriers of race prejudice; on the other hand was their unwillingness to perjure their own spiritual freedom by taking an oath which they did not believe should be required.

The two superintendents understood how fundamental was the issue at stake. Unit members, both white and Negro, wrestled with the problem. So did the citizens' committee, and AFSC staff. In the end it became clear that the unit would have to be discontinued.

Here we see a program which was born of the effort to provide conscientious objectors with alternative service opportunities, which grew beyond that into a peacetime service to the mentally ill, became a vigorous, constructive force in the field of race relations, and then found itself up against the loyalty oath. Thus one sees the devastating effect of the decline of civil liberties on the free growth of social conscience.

The idea of ISU has spread rapidly. In 1952 sixteen agencies were sponsoring similiar units. Six programs were church-sponsored, four were sponsored by social service agencies, and six by colleges.

The eagerness with which young people have responded to this kind of opportunity demonstrates, I believe, a search on their part for ways in which a religious life may be interpreted in terms of today's social structure and problems. Most of these young folks will not enter professionally into these fields. But their own lives in many cases will be sensitized and changed, their religious life will be made more articulate, and as citizens they will be much more intelligent and concerned about the "sore spots" in our society. Not least, their services have now made a place for themselves as an important ingredient in the treatment of our mentally ill.

3. Race Relations

Two familiar names come to mind in connection with Friends' protest against human slavery before the Emancipation Proclamation. John Greenleaf Whittier, born in Massachusetts just after the turn of the nineteenth century, became one of the leaders of the Abolition movement. As an editor, first in New England, later in Philadelphia, and as a political leader in his home state and carrying influence with national political figures, he was one of a small group of prominent American citizens who through editorials, poetry, and public speeches, helped bring to a climax the opposition to slavery in the United States. As the impending war between the North and South approached, he knew tragic conflict within his own soul. He did not believe in the use of violence, yet he was dedicated to freedom for the slaves. The time came when it was obvious that war would break out. He could not encourage it, but his influence on the side of Abolition was felt widely, both within his own little religious group, the Society of Friends, and throughout the whole country.

John Woolman was the earlier influence that left an indelible mark on the entire Society of Friends. It is a well-known fact that chattel slavery had been practiced by a good many Friends not only in the South but in the North. The way in which the Society purged itself of this evil, largely under the leadership of John Woolman during the second half of the eighteenth century, is an illustration of the way in which radical change can be brought about without violence.

As early as 1688, Francis Daniel Pastorius, a citizen of Germantown, Pennsylvania, a Mennonite by ancestry but a member of the Society of Friends, had succeeded in getting his own local Meeting to adopt the following minute:

There is a liberty of conscience here which is right and reasonable, and there ought to be likewise liberty of the body, except for evil-doers, which is another case. But to bring men hither, or to rob and sell them against their will, we stand against.

The Yearly Meeting in Philadelphia deferred action on this minute, but the yeast was at work among Friends.

It remained for John Woolman to carry the effort forward to fulfillment. A citizen of Mt. Holly, New Jersey, and a tailor by trade, John Woolman journeyed from place to place for about thirty years under a deep concern for slaves and slaveholders. How could the Society of Friends continue to carry its message of free access to God for all, so long as human freedom was denied to men and women of color?

It was perhaps as much his method as his message that was effective. It was a deep, personal matter with him. Not with preaching but in penitence for his own part in the evil of the world would he approach the slaveholder, sitting in solemn conference, sometimes with halting speech, sometimes in silence, until often the Friend's conscience was so deeply disturbed that even at great financial loss to himself he freed his slaves.

John Woolman found it difficult to eat food in a home in which slaves did the work, and on occasions when he did partake of such food he made a practice of leaving remuneration for the slaves. In his journal he recorded that few if any of the slaveholders manifested resentment at this behavior. "The fear of the Lord so covered me at times that my way was made easier than I expected."

He deliberately reduced the volume of his business, that he might have more time to carry on his ministry among Friends. He was a rather timid man, as indicated by these words from his journal:

"The prospect of so weighty a work, and of being so distinguished from many whom I esteemed before myself, brought me very low."

But though he carried on this ministry in great travail, penitence, and tenderness, his presentation was never weak. He recorded his participation in Philadelphia Yearly Meeting in 1758, thus:

> And though none did openly justify the practice of slave-keeping in general, yet some appeared concerned lest the Meeting should go into such measures as might give uneasiness to many brethren, alleging that if Friends patiently continued under the exercise the Lord in his time might open a way for the deliverance of these people. Finding an engagement to speak, I said, " . . . . Many slaves on this continent are oppressed, and their cries have reached the ears of the Most High. Such are the purity and certainty of His judgments, that He cannot be partial in our favor. In infinite love and goodness He hath opened our understanding from one time to another concerning our duty towards this people, and it is not a time for delay. Should we now be sensible of what He requires of us, and through a respect to the private interest of some persons, or through a regard to some friendships which do not stand on an immutable foundation, neglect to do our duty in firmness and constancy, still waiting for some extraordinary means to bring about their deliverance, God may by terrible things in righteousness answer us in this matter."

To some, this kind of testimony in Meeting and quiet personal conference may seem a small way to go about ridding humanity of a major evil. Yet it was just this method which awakened in slave-holding Quakers a willingness to free their slaves, so that seventy-five years before the abolition of slavery in the United States all Friends in good standing had ceased to own slaves.

This conviction and achievement among Friends, the previous practice of many slaveowning Quakers and their slaves in attending Meeting together, and the intimate acceptance of slaves or paid Negro servants into a large number of Quaker families, resulted in a strong Quaker influence among Negroes before the Civil War.

Many who never became members of the Society of Friends still dressed in Quaker garb and used the Quaker language. We know that some Negro children attended Friends' schools in the pre-Civil War period; and in certain places in the North, Friends were active and effective in bringing about the admission of colored children to the public schools.

But the Society of Friends in the United States remained largely white in membership. Among several contributing reasons, we must not fail to admit that a number of Meetings were slow to receive colored persons who requested admission as members, even when those persons' religious convincement and dedication were unquestioned. There were instances of highly valued Negro members of various Meetings, but, on the whole, white Friends in this country had not escaped involvement in the general social pattern of prejudice.

Immediately after the Civil War, Friends were active in establishing schools for the "freedmen." Especially those who had worked in the cause of Abolition or helped in the Underground Railway, enabling slaves to escape from their masters, now turned their attention to this new task.

The pattern of segregation took deep hold, and, for the most part, intelligent, alert, and continuing concern that Negroes should be received into full citizenship in this country gradually faded out among members of the Society of Friends.

President Grant had asked Friends to take considerable responsibility for work among Indians during his Administration, but in only a few regions — notably Oklahoma and New York State — did this participation continue through the years to be a vital daily part of Friends' lives. Generally speaking, in time the close relation between Friends and Indians became restricted to a few people and a few institutions. Meanwhile, Mexican, Japanese, and Chinese minorities were finding their way into the United States. Wholesome relations among all racial groups was one of the prime needs of the age, yet by the early part of the twentieth century there were few evidences among American Friends of an active concern in race relations. In general, we were not awake to the acute significance of the racial segregation that had become part and parcel of life in the United States, including Quaker as well as non-Quaker communities and institutions.

One of the factors in Friends' awakening to this situation was the passage of the Japanese exclusion clause of the Immigration Act of 1924. By that time, the American Friends Service Committee had brought to a close most of its postwar relief services in Europe, and was turning its attention to needs in the United States. Pamphlets were issued by the Committee, setting forth Friends' opposition to the Oriental exclusion policy, and pointing out its dangers. Dr. Inazo Nitobe, of the League of Nations Secretariat, was quoted: "When I went back to Japan I found the older men almost heartbroken. I have been a Christian for fifty years and after preaching brotherhood for all these years, to have our whole nation branded as inferior! . . . The earthquake was terrible, but the spiritual devastation caused in Japan by the Immigration Act was far worse."

An AFSC "Interracial Section" was established in 1924–1925. Two Japanese students were sponsored for study in the United States, and a Japanese Friend, Yasushi Hasegawa, traveled extensively in this country to present the Japanese viewpoint to American Friends and other groups. Crystal Bird, an outstanding young Negro woman, became a member of the AFSC staff and spoke before public forums, college groups, high-school students, and church bodies, in an effort to inform white Americans as to what the issues actually were, and how colored people felt about them. It may seem an anachronism that this kind of education was necessary in the United States in the first quarter of the twentieth century. That it is still necessary — among Friends as well as others — is one of the major tragedies of our time.

Later, in the 1930's, under the leadership of the two Philadelphia Yearly Meetings of Friends, the AFSC helped sponsor summer Institutes of Race Relations at Swarthmore College, Pennsylvania.

These were a beginning, and had far-reaching results through certain individuals. But the Service Committee in its own program was making only indirect attacks against the generally accepted pattern of racial segregation in the United States.

Meanwhile, we were in the midst of a catastrophic national depression. It may be appropriate to point out that during the critical depression years of the '30s, when our Committee was finding no real way to take hold in the field of race relations, Communists saw the issue of segregation and second-class citizenship, and became the foremost champions of equality of opportunity for the races. This is not to say that Negroes accepted that association, or that they did not seek other allies; but for the time being religious groups had forfeited their leadership by going to sleep.

With the coming of the Second World War and its accompanying shortage of manpower, recognition of the rights of Negroes and other racial minorities gained perceptibly in this country. By executive order President Roosevelt set up the national Fair Employment Practices Committee, which established standards for nondiscriminatory employment. And in the armed forces, long agitation has finally resulted in considerable recognition of the principle of no segregation. Yet the fact remains that in our country today there is widespread, agonizing segregation and other discrimination in housing, public services, employment, education, and worship. I believe that not until citizens locally show vigorous concern and take action on a neighborhood and community level will we of the United States be able to completely rid ourselves of a practice which is damaging not only to minority groups but to the sensitive spirit of those who form the dominant group.

As I see it, law is needed as a support. But law in itself is by no means enough.

Meanwhile, I have found outlets for my personal concern both within the Service Committee's program and aside from it. During the war, representatives of the Field Foundation and the Julius Rosenwald Fund called a meeting in Chicago, of people particularly interested in race relations. I was one of the group. For a period of five years, the American Council on Race Relations, which grew out of that meeting, functioned as a fact-finding agency, and furnished information and suggestions to local groups and communities wishing to rid themselves of racial discrimination.

As in many other cities, Philadelphia's mayor appointed a city Committee on Race Relations during the war, and I was asked to serve as a member. While this committee never had very much venture, it did explore certain phases of the violation of rights of Negroes in our own Philadelphia community — the higher interest rates being charged Negroes, chronic discrimination in employment and housing, overcrowding of public schools.

But the really vital development in Philadelphia during the early part of the war was the Fellowship Commission. This is a grouping of nine city-wide agencies which are concerned with those minorities in our large metropolitan community who are often denied equal rights with the majority. The agencies are: American Civil Liberties Union of Greater Philadelphia, Council for Equal Job Opportunity, Fellowship House, International Institute of Philadelphia, Philadelphia Area Office of the National Conference of Christians and Jews, Philadelphia Branch of the National Association for the Advancement of Colored People, Philadelphia Council of Churches Race Relations Committee, Philadelphia Jewish Community Relations Council, Society of Friends Committee on Race Relations. Coming to this concern for equality in citizenship for a wide variety of reasons, the leaders of all these movements meet together once a month to look at needs in Philadelphia. At present, most of the agencies are housed in a common building. Discrimination in housing, public schools, professional schools, and hospitals, police brutality — these and other violations of basic civil rights come before this body regularly.

Started as the vision of Marjorie Penney and Maurice Fagan, the Fellowship Commission has now made a city-wide impression, being one of the major influences behind the establishment of a

Commission on Human Relations as an integral part of the Philadelphia city government. Most satisfactory of all, the Fellowship Commission has become a point where inner struggles and distress of spirit can be poured out in the confidence that compassion and intelligence will be pooled in looking for a way to recognize dignity and worth in all our citizenry. As its president for the past two years, I have often been educated as to what is happening to many persons whose troubles would never reach my AFSC office or our suburban home.

In 1944 the American Friends Service Committee inaugurated a special race-relations program. Since 1929 our Committee's contributions in this field had been largely by-products of other activities. For example, AFSC work camps and other youth projects had been interracial from the beginning. There is, I believe, considerable justification for this kind of oblique approach. It still seems to me that the best way to bridge gulfs of prejudice and fear is perhaps not so much to tackle them directly as to bring the various groups together in common work, recreation, and worship.

Nevertheless, along with the rest of the country we had become increasingly aware of the seriousness of the racial tensions in our midst. We had been vitally involved in the relocation of Japanese and Japanese-Americans after Pearl Harbor; through a summer work camp we had established a close and fruitful year-round working relationship with Flanner House, a community center in a Negro neighborhood in Indianapolis, and this experience was leading us into a growing interest in the problems of the whole area surrounding the settlement; the Detroit race riots had brought home to us in vivid fashion how acute and combustible were the racial fears and antagonisms which lay just under the surface of our country's daily life.

When we set up our special race relations committee in 1944, with Nellie Lee Bok as its chairman, we were aware of the urgency of the need for effective action. But also we knew of the many agencies already attempting to fill that need, and we aimed to find ways to supplement rather than duplicate their efforts.

Securing the leadership of G. James Fleming, formerly regional director of the President's Fair Employment Practices Committee for Pennsylvania, New Jersey, and Delaware, we undertook first to make our own staff and our various programs demonstrations of what the "race relations" effort was all about. We had long been interracial and intercultural, but now we re-examined and strengthened ourselves on this score.

One of the earliest specific projects initiated was the "Visiting Lectureship," through which the ablest Negro scholars and artists we could find were brought to Quaker schools and colleges, and to non-Quaker educational institutions as well, for periods of about a week — not as "pleaders for their people," but to lecture in their chosen field, be it literature, art, social science, or physical science. It was anticipated that during the week their participation in the life of the institution on a more informal level would also be fruitful.

Hopes for this program have been more than fulfilled, for the men and women chosen have been persons of exceptional gifts and achievements, and the response of youth has been immediate and enthusiastic. One difficulty the lecturers have had is in protecting themselves from an inordinate demand on their time and energies during their periods of campus residence. After the experience, some of them have been offered and have accepted positions on the faculties of the institutions visited. Thus the project has played a substantial part in the general movement to open the doors of hitherto all-white institutions to Negro students and Negro faculty members. At present, probably more than a hundred Negroes are serving on the faculties of such colleges, having been selected on the basis of their pre-eminent intellectual and human qualifications, and neither because of nor in spite of their race. This kind of thing seems so obvious that it is embarrassing to have to make a point of it.

Early in the development of our race-relations program, we found that Frank S. Loescher, who was then on the faculty of Fisk University, had been giving special thought to the employment problems of Negroes. Through his daily contacts with Negro college students and graduates, he had come to realize how hard it was for well-trained Negroes to find employment at the level of their ability and preparation. This fact had been impressed upon me personally a number of times — once, I remember, when I got into conversation with a Pullman porter who had a Ph.D. degree from Columbia University, a man better educated than I was, and he could find no job in which he could use his training. So he had resorted to the Pullman Company, where he could at least earn money to support his family.

Furthermore, Frank Loescher pointed out that one of the best ways to change prejudiced attitudes, especially among the more educated white people, was to give them the opportunity to work with and come to know Negroes of similar educational background and interests.

Here our Committee saw a facet of race relations on which it might well concentrate, and arrangements were made for Frank Loescher to work with us in seeking employment opportunities for qualified Negroes in fields not usually open to them.

This effort moved slowly at first, partly because, under the stimulus of war conditions, highly trained Negroes were now finding employment more commensurate with their abilities. However, we soon took note that the situation had not improved appreciably for the normally intelligent young Negro man or woman with average training — for instance, the high-school or business-school graduate who, if white, would be able to find a job as a department-store clerk or a secretary. All around us, in the cities where AFSC offices were located, were thousands of business offices and scores of department stores which employed Negroes only as janitors, loaders, or elevator operators, regardless of their abilities. What this added up to was that most Negro young people of average capacity and schooling were definitely up against a "job ceiling" that had no relation to what they could contribute.

Curtis and Nellie Bok, who had recently become members of the Society of Friends, took a vital interest in this situation. They offered to give a dinner for the leading executives of the main department stores of Philadelphia, at which time the experience in one or two other cities where businesses were hiring on the basis of merit alone could be laid before the Philadelphia merchants.

There was no pressure brought to bear on anyone. Elmo Roper had come over from New York to share his thinking and experience with us, which he did extremely well. Simply and informally he told of the way in which his concern for this problem had come about, and expressed his conviction that, unless we gave the opportunities of our civilization to all groups, we couldn't make much progress in having democracy in other parts of the world. A record of the experience of businesses that had successfully started hiring on the basis of merit was laid before the guests.

With this dinner as a starting point, our race-relations staff members began to sit in conference with business executives who were interested in bringing their employment practices more in line with democratic values. Two large Philadelphia stores on their own initiative led the way in opening up employment opportunities on the basis of merit.

From samplings of customer reaction which have been taken from time to time it seems clear — as one would naturally suppose — that what customers want is courteous, efficient service, and that on the whole they are equally happy with such service whatever the color of the salesperson.

By the same token, Thomas B. Harvey of the Harvey Leather Company of Philadelphia testified somewhat later in hearings for a Philadelphia Fair Employment Practices ordinance: "As an employer I am definitely in favor of a Fair Employment Practices ordinance in Philadelphia. Employers are interested only in an efficient worker and do not care what race, color, or creed he or she may be."

In the same hearings, Frank Loescher was able to testify: "I have personally talked to the presidents of five banks, the personnel executives of two insurance companies, the heads or managers of five Market Street department stores. . . . In those interviews I have encountered this kind of reaction from employers themselves. They have said to me: 'I would welcome a Fair Employment Practices Commission because then I would know they are all doing the same thing. Without such a law it is unfair to make me a guinea pig.'"

As a matter of fact, the coming of the city FEPC resulted in visible, relatively rapid extension of the practice of employment on merit, opening the doors of businesses on a scale which is testimony to the helpfulness of such an ordinance in this field. The genius of FEPC lies in its combining with law and sanctions a provision that the Commission shall receive and wherever possible adjust complaints through conference, conciliation, and persuasion; and that it shall carry on community-wide educational programs. Within a year of the passage of the ordinance, our race-relations division had the experience of being approached by employers who wished to shift to a nondiscriminatory basis and came to consult our staff as to the best way to go about it.

After our employment-opportunities program was in operation, a further need was uncovered. We were told by many executives that both colored and white young people were constantly applying for jobs as cashiers or clerks or secretaries, without any idea of what their own skills were or what the jobs would require.

Therefore, in consultation with various personnel offices, our Committee set up (on a small-scale, experimental basis) a training course which was used by applicants of various racial and cultural backgrounds. It included instruction in vocational possibilities, how to apply for a job, and how to perform the required duties once a job was obtained.

It did not take long to understand what an initial handicap is suffered by young people of certain minority groups, especially Negro, because of their unequal educational opportunities, their restricted housing facilities, and other environmental obstacles. In fact, segregated housing protruded itself as perhaps one of the more basic factors, for out of it proceed many of the other segregations — of school, church, and social life. Not only is enforced segregation in itself discrimination, but it inevitably results in further discrimination. In testifying personally in hearings connected with Philadelphia city housing projects, I have lent what weight I could to the abolition of this stifling pattern.

As the training course for applicants proceeded and some placements were made, our race-relations staff was also setting up conferences with leaders in industry, banking, insurance, and education. More recently, the fields of medicine and nursing have been included.

In the meantime, and with the long and vigorous help of a committee of seventy citizens, Philadelphia had drafted a new charter which was accepted by a vote of the citizenry. Already the Philadelphia Council had established the Fair Employment Practices Commission for the city of Philadelphia, and Frank Loescher had become its director. With the establishment of the new city charter, provision was made for a city Commission on Human Relations, and Frank was asked to be its director. Thus through his widening services our Committee's experience was shared with an ever-increasing number of individuals and organizations.

In the state of Pennsylvania an heroic effort was made to get the legislature to establish a Fair Employment Practices Commission. Two different years I acted as chairman of a state committee sponsoring this legislation, and supported various bills in hearings before the House and Senate of the Pennsylvania Legislature. But this effort was the victim of internal politics, and did not succeed. However, one hopes that the endeavor has had some educational effect on employers, and that in time this great commonwealth will see fit to put itself on record in this respect.

Stating the case in its most elementary terms, I believe that what all of us concerned in this field would ask is that the way be cleared for each individual to be taken as an individual. It seems to me so simple and obvious a requirement that often when I have been called upon to testify — for FEPC, for example — it has been difficult for me to understand or comprehend the strength of the opposition. It is on this simplest ground of the individual that I must always base whatever contribution I may make in the field. When people are dealt with in any other way, all that I hold most precious in our human and divine heritage is being violated.

It is interesting how even small steps in a given direction tend to associate one with all others working in the same field. I have found myself sitting in conference with labor leaders and national government officials on issues of FEPC, and testifying in Washington as well as in Pennsylvania. Shortly after the war I met with a group called together in Washington by the Julius Rosenwald Fund to consider setting up a study of segregation and other discrimination in the nation's capital. This was a very strong committee of public-spirited citizens headed by Donald R. Young, then director of the Social Science Research Council. It included Protestants, Jews, Catholics, Friends, and people outside religious groups. It was with a deep sense of humiliation that we faced the fact that in our nation's capital were some of the worst violations of human rights anywhere in the country: housing conditions that would be a blot on any nation, segregated schools, Negro schools being seriously inferior and tragically overcrowded, segregation in swimming pools and in recreation generally, segregation in public eating places.

A careful study was made and revealingly presented in a graphic handbook, and this, together with the hospitable attitude of some members of the Federal government, has helped bring about certain alleviations in the over-all situation. But the sensitive person must still hang his head in shame at the racial practices in this city.

Meanwhile, AFSC work camps in Washington have successfully supervised interracial use of a public swimming pool, as well as interracial day camps and playground programs. International Student House in Washington, operated by AFSC assisted by a local committee, provides a place where both racial and national "gulfs" are easily bridged in gatherings of young people; and Davis House, given to the Committee to provide hospitality for visitors from foreign lands, often finds itself keeping diplomats who cannot find suitable quarters because of their color.

The Committee now has an interracial team working in Washington in co-operation with other agencies and individuals, toward the goal of integration of all groups in public education and recreation. The religious basis of this team's work is faith in the potential for reconciliation which lies in those deepest levels of the human spirit, even when people differ violently on the surface. Frankness and respect for each individual are indispensable aspects of such an approach.

Social practices in Washington have a peculiar significance. In taking stock of ourselves as a nation it is well to realize that many foreign visitors who come to the United States predisposed toward our democracy suffer a severe jolt as they see what we practice in our capital.

At the present writing, the American Friends Service Committee's employment-on-merit or job-opportunities program, formerly centered in the Philadelphia area, has been propelled outward through the enthusiastic activity of AFSC regional offices and a capacity in the home-office staff to recognize and co-operate with such local interest. This expansion has behind it a philosophy and conviction transcending the championing of the rights of minority groups. Rather, we think of it as an effort to help the entire community realize its full human assets and wholeness.

In Chicago, Dallas, Kansas City, Indianapolis, Columbus, Ohio, and Greensboro, North Carolina, regional offices are sponsoring vigorous programs. The Philadelphia community-relations staff co-operates, especially by putting at the regional office's disposal its cumulative experience.

In many cities other agencies are working in this field, and it is important to work with them instead of in competition. Also the co-operation of a wide range of local citizens is solicited. Housewives, teachers, clergymen, management and labor, become part of the movement. The aim is to discover and co-operate with "grass-roots" concern and energy, of which there are large quantities throughout the United States. In some cities an applicant-training program has become an important part of the project. In one or two cities, housing opportunities are the focus of an additional effort.

In connection with all this expanding activity, AFSC regional offices have been able to give the home office invaluable guidance in setting up some of its other programs, such as work camps and Institutional Service Units. For with their knowledge of local tension spots they can often save us from making grave errors, and at the same time show us where creative possibilities are only awaiting some catalytic enterprise.

In recent years the AFSC has also been considerably revitalized in connection with the changing scene of American Indian life. The Federal government's policy holds out the ideal of integration with the white population, but that does not come quickly, and there are grave dangers along the way. In all too many cases the values of the old Indian civilization are lost, and the movement of young Indians from reservations into industrialized communities plays havoc with the very foundations of their spiritual life as well as with their physical well-being.

In Rapid City, South Dakota, the Committee is working with the mayor and city organizations on a program of integration of the Indian and white populations. It is a long, slow-moving kind of project, undramatic in its day-to-day tasks, but deeply rewarding in long-term values, an opportunity to help create a truly American community in this specific locale.

California Friends have long had a particular interest in Indians of the Southwest. In 1948 the general American public was made suddenly conscious of the acute plight of the Navahos in particular, who had been pushed onto less and less good land until their flocks had overgrazed the pasture land left to them, and critical problems of survival had to be faced. The Service Committee sent relief shipments, especially of clothing. Over and over, Congress has made appropriations for relief, but the long-time solution is yet to come.

Meanwhile, the younger generation of the Navaho, Papago, Hopi, and other Southwest tribes have continued to leave their reservations to seek a better life in Los Angeles, among other cities, and there they are confronted with mechanized, impersonal forces which are the antithesis of most of their tribal values. In the summer of 1948 our Committee united with the California Yearly Meeting of Friends in its Indian Center project in Los Angeles, the AFSC regional office in Pasadena shouldering most of the Committee's part of the responsibility. Here cultural and recreational activities bring Indian and white people together in a climate of friendliness; young Indians are aided in finding their way in the bewildering city; and white people suddenly find themselves enriched by contacts with ancient cultures. "My own reaction is one of wonder," wrote a white woman who had been hostess to two Indian children for a two-weeks holiday, "extreme wonder that so very close to us — merely a day's journey — live people with such a different background, such limited facilities, such quietness, and yet such sameness."

The Advisory Board of the Los Angeles Indian Center is largely Indian. It seems particularly important in working with the American Indian people, who have been pushed back and still further back for many generations, that we should refrain from being one more force pressing on them. Our policy is rather to be on hand — in South Dakota, Los Angeles, Flagstaff, or wherever they are stirring, migrating, and seeking — and to stand by to co-operate in the ways in which they want us to. The need is within them, and exactly what it is can be known only as we give it space and time and a climate of patience and friendliness in which to unfold. Any other kind of help would be presumptuous and almost certainly harmful.

Surely it is true that the best race relations are achieved when "race relations" have become, simply, community relations, or human relations. And I must come back to the fact that this is one of the goals of all of our programs. When people of various racial and cultural backgrounds live and work together on some task beyond their relation to each other, intergroup problems are absorbed in the larger common problems; this is the ideal toward which we aim. "I can hardly believe it is true," said a young German boy in an international work camp in Europe, "I can hardly believe that there is a common goal; but the summer has shown it to me."

That our youth projects at home and abroad are interracial and intercultural; that in our Philadelphia office Jews, Protestants, Roman Catholics, Buddhists, Friends, Unitarians — and Negroes, Japanese, Chinese, Caucasians — have worked side by side in pursuit of common goals: none of this is irrelevant.

I think of William Stuart Nelson, dean of the School of Religion at Howard University, who was chosen as head of the Friends Service Unit in India, where he was volunteering his sabbatical year in AFSC service. That he was colored had nothing to do, either way, with the Unit members' selecting him as their leader. There was stern work to do, and the man best fitted for the job was needed. He was that man. Others come to mind in connection with foreign service: Jean Fairfax, former dean of women at Tuskegee Institute, serving in Vienna where she was called by the Viennese young people their "brown angel of mercy" — or Jerome Peterson, M.D., of the World Health Organization, working with our unit in Gaza. These are living demonstrations of "race relations" transformed into human relations, permitting the full and proper use of each individual's endowment and commitment. This is the Family-of-God conception at work, and it has always seemed to me difficult for a person of religious dedication to see race relations in any other way.

Yet the church as a whole still remains one of the most generally segregated institutions in our national community. And Quakers must bear their share of responsibility for this lag in religious leadership.

One begins to see the shape of things to come in the international scene, as regards races and cultures. The great untapped natural resources of the world are where the awakening populations are — notably, Africa and Asia. As education and consciousness of strength grow among these two thirds of the world's peoples, we will move in one of two directions. Will it be a continuation of the battle for white supremacy and for white exploitation of the resources of these lands? That way lies disaster for all.

But another course is still open to us. As differences in race and culture cease to be dividing lines in human society, human life on the whole is immeasurably enriched. When groups approach each other in fear, the creative life in both suffers. Because so many terrible wrongs have been done, overlaying our essential brotherhood with cruelty and hate, the way into the creative relation is often intricate and delicate. But full brotherhood awaits us in the deepest levels of the human spirit, and the issue seems to me abundantly clear. It presents itself to us in this century in the unequivocal terms of the instruction in Deuteronomy: "See, I have set before thee this day life and good, and death and evil. . . ."

4. Education for Peace

THE two decades covered by this book, are characterized by recovery from World War I, gathering of the forces which resulted in World War II, the war itself, and again the beginnings of recovery. For members of the Society of Friends it has been a period of deep searching of heart. For three hundred years we have professed a way of life which does away with the occasion for war, and yet the thirty-five-year period since the founding of the American Friends Service Committee has seen two of the world's worst wars. It is fitting, therefore, that we should cast up accounts. Have we been mistaken in believing that a world without war is possible? Have we been inept and ineffective in our efforts to prevent war? Or are we so tiny in numbers and in influence that, even joined with the much larger groups who share the peace testimony with us, we find it impossible to outweigh the continuing unwillingness, especially of the Christian Church as a whole, to act on the thesis that war is sin? Is there an alternative to war? Is the way still long? Are the needful sacrifices far greater than we have yet undertaken?

While Friends have never based their belief in the possibility of peace and the wickedness of war on Scripture quotations as such, it has seemed to me clear in reading from Amos that he saw the roots of conflict deeply imbedded in an unjust economic system. Isaiah and Jeremiah found the source of conflict in political ambition and dependence upon treaties of mutual assistance entered into on both sides from ulterior motives, showing lack of confidence in spiritual forces. In that great little book of Hosea, we have the story of a man who so deeply loved his wife that although she became a prostitute he bought her from her white-slave owners and brought her home to himself. In this searching experience of an unconquerable love Hosea saw a symbol of the love of God which included all men, even the most degraded.

A belief in peace rooted in the experience of these great Hebrew prophets, with no slavish literal insistence on Biblical texts, places one in the great mystical stream of religious faith, with deep confidence in its power and persuasiveness.

In the short three years of the recorded teachings of Jesus, he based his life on the thesis that love is stronger than hate, and that evil can be overcome by good. The thoughtful reader of the Gospels is brought up short and made to question whether here is not something new and transforming when it is really applied to human society. Jesus died rather than surrender his faith, his point of view which he believed had its origin in the very heart of God and in the nature of the universe. He did not die in despair but in hope, for he believed that, if men persistently followed this way, redemption of society from its corruption, its unholy political ambition, and its easy recourse to external force, could be achieved.

Most Christians would agree that this is the great Christian ideal. But there are all too few who are willing to say, "Now is the time and I am the person to put this into effect without compromise." Perhaps this is the weakness and the hope of those of us who inherit the tradition of the Society of Friends, and who in this tumultuous period are called upon to vindicate it by our conduct.

It is with this kind of re-examination of our own intellectual and spiritual roots that the American Friends Service Committee feels an obligation to educate as wide a constituency as possible in an understanding of the forces at work for peace and for war, especially giving opportunity to the younger generation to develop an attitude of mind and heart which makes for peace.

When I came to the Committee in 1929, my colleague, Ray Newton, was already conducting what were known as "peace caravans." College students volunteered their summers to go from community to community discussing international affairs, pacifism, and United States foreign policy, before church groups, service clubs, and any kind of organization that would give them a hearing. They traveled in teams of two to four, in third- or fourth-hand automobiles, usually living as guests in the homes of interested friends. Sometimes they may have been trying to teach people better informed than they were, but on the whole they made a favorable impression. Probably, however, the most profound effect of their undertaking was on themselves. A good many men and women now in the midstream of life date their abiding interest in international affairs and peace from the time when they ventured forth with great confidence to speak on these important issues.

Ray Newton dreamed up another idea. He wanted to hold institutes of international relations, where especially ministers, teachers, and other community leaders could listen to and enter into discussion with national and international leaders. Like the caravans, this would be an effort to make peace education a grass-roots affair. It has never been our belief that peace can be superimposed from above. It must grow out of the hearts of the people.

These institutes, starting in the summer of 1930, have consistently multiplied since that time, and taken on diverse forms. There are still the summer institutes for adults, running about ten days, held now in all parts of the country. Week-end institutes throughout the year have been added. The leadership is usually of very high caliber, representing many points of view. Specifically, as freedom of thought and speech seem to be waning, these institutes sometimes furnish a platform for unpopular prophets, making possible the kind of open discussion in an atmosphere of good will which in times past was assumed to be one of the marks of our democracy, but which is less and less common in these latter days.

Other variations of the original institute idea are special institutes for the whole family, where parents bring their children, and activities are planned for all; and, for teen-agers, institutes, seminars, and "world-affairs camps." The idea has even spread to Mexico, where a peace institute is held each year around Christmas time.

For the most part, AFSC regional offices and local groups of citizens, both Quaker and non-Quaker, shoulder responsibility for the adult summer institutes. In the course of laying plans, one question comes up over and over. Shall the discussions be "practical" from the viewpoint of the average citizen, admitting the possibility of the need for physical force, or shall they place primary emphasis on the religious basis of peace as conceived by the Society of Friends? If the first course is followed, are we not merely competing with other organizations which discuss foreign relations against a background of belief in "positions of strength"? As actually carried out, the institutes stress the religious pacifist viewpoint but afford ample opportunity for the expression of many other approaches on the part of men and women dedicated to the cause of creative international relations.

Out of the many thousands of people reached by these efforts, how many are deeply affected? No one can tell. Personal testimonies come from many quarters. "The more I visit such gatherings," wrote a college professor in the spring of 1952, "and participate in the very intimate experience of sharing and discussion, the more I realize their meaningfulness in our crucial times. Frankly, we do not have such warm and constructive exchange in the normal activities of a university campus or at important official levels where the facilities and external resources are so much greater." A woman wrote, "I think I have found here in these quiet morning half-hours of worship, in these fellowship experiences, this intellectual stimulation and renewal, the strength and courage I need to carry through in my community during the coming months." And at the close of a world-affairs camp, a teen-ager volunteered: "The great educational value of these experiences for us of the schools is the opportunity to live, even for a little time, in a free society."

From my own experience with institutes for various age groups, I would say that among teen-agers there is more eagerness to know what is really the religious basis for peace than there is in the older groups. It may be that this will prove to be the most fruitful age level for such education.

In 1936 the Service Committee became a kind of sponsor for the "Emergency Peace Campaign." This was an effort to pull together in a united front as many as possible of the groups in this country who were committed to peace, and to promote a general nation-wide educational campaign. One of the main efforts was to get the co-operation of people whose names were drawing cards and who, at the same time, had the peace message to give.

Rear Admiral Richard E. Byrd had only recently returned from his second expedition to the South Pole, where he had kept a long vigil entirely alone. Out of this experience came his book called *Alone*. Though by no means a pacifist, he was strongly committed to the effort to preserve peace, and in the course of the campaign he spoke for us a number of times. As I became acquainted with him I was struck by the evident depth of his religious experience during his isolation in Little America. He said that down there, alone, he had come into a vivid sense of the unity of all life, and especially all human life, and that he wanted to do something to help make this unity a reality in present-day living. He was very simple in his statements about this experience, and at times it seemed to me we were almost identical in our understanding of the nature of God and of man and religion. But family tradition and military experience had a strong hold on Admiral Byrd, and he never quite came to the position of being willing to surrender the possibility of using violence to achieve desired ends.

In 1935, when our government had proposed to hold extensive naval maneuvers in an area including Midway Island and the Aleutians, it had seemed to many of us that this was a deliberate effort to flex our muscles where Japan could see us, to warn her of what she might expect if she did not respect our power. I had arranged with President Roosevelt for a small group of concerned persons, under the leadership of Harry Emerson Fosdick, to talk with him about the danger of such threatening tactics. We were invited to tea in the Oval Room, and, as sometimes happened, the President was in a very talkative mood. He had a good array of stories, and we began to wonder whether we would ever get our concern expressed. Harry Fosdick is not easy to suppress, and finally he burst forth with an impressive presentation of the dangers of our assuming the posture of a threat to other nations. The President told us of an experience with an aristocratic Japanese classmate of his at Harvard, who talked freely about the time when Japan would become a conquering nation. The President felt this was in the blood of the Japanese leaders, and that it was desirable for them to see that their neighbors were prepared to resist any aggression. At the time, most of us questioned whether the President's experience at Harvard was terribly relevant. In perspective, I think that perhaps he was right as regards the aims of those who were determining Japan's path. We did not succeed in persuading him to move the navy's playground, and the maneuvers went forward in the proposed location.

If they were designed to discourage Japan from ever attacking the United States, they were a failure. One wonders whether they may not have even aroused the Japanese to greater defensiveness and antagonism. Here, it seems to me, was the real fallacy in the President's argument.

By the middle of 1937 the Emergency Peace Campaign had sponsored meetings of larger or smaller size in several thousand communities. In addition, there had been innumerable broadcasts. The most notable of these was on April 6, 1937, when Harry Emerson Fosdick, Rear Admiral Byrd, and Mrs. Roosevelt spoke on the need for international action to prevent war. Mrs. Roosevelt's talk on that occasion seems in retrospect prophetic of her present-day commitment to the United Nations. She said, "We must find a way whereby the grievances of nations, their necessities, their desires, can be heard by other nations and passed upon without recourse to force. . . . Surely if the nations of the world really had the will, a basis could be found for making a beginning."

The press gave wide publicity to this Emergency Peace Campaign in 1936–1937, and many interviews were held with government officials and members of Congress.

How are the results to be evaluated? The movement drew to itself large numbers of people who instinctively were interested in international problems but had had little opportunity to broaden their information in that field. It started many on the active search for ways into peace. It deepened the commitment of others who were already engaged in this search.

It was in part through his participation in the Emergency Peace Campaign that Harold Chance came to feel the importance of carrying much further the work for peace, particularly among Friends, staying close to the religious root of Friends' peace testimony. Harold had been in the army in the First World War, although he was a member of the Society of Friends. He had come out of that experience a deeply committed pacifist.

Over the years he has traveled widely among Friends, with patience and intelligence helping to develop a fund of information and stronger religious conviction, both of which are essential if we are to be effective in the cause of peace.

The more abiding values of this kind of religiously motivated effort are recognized when we see the ineffectiveness of trying to adapt ourselves to watered-down programs. It may well be that there is greater power in personal attitudes, greater capacity in the committed individual to meet the most intransigent enemy with good will and understanding, than most of us anticipate. In our time, through Gandhi's life and work we have seen the power of a movement which touches and releases the spiritual capacities of men. I think in the long run we are likely to find more hope for our little group by committing ourselves to ever-deepening experiments with this truth than by participating in large peace movements on a shallower base. I am certain that only as we commit ourselves to revealing this way of life in our own conduct do we earn the right to speak of it with confidence to others.

However, in maintaining our primary confidence in small and more personalized efforts, we may well develop a false modesty. And I am convinced that it is of great importance for individual Friends to give outspoken voice to their mistrust of hate and violence and their confidence in meeting evil with practical expressions of good. Especially as these words are being written, one sees the haunting shadow of suspicion and fear being thrown around educators, public officials, and other leaders to such an extent that to cry out against injustice and wrong and take the consequences may often be the most creative thing we can do. Sometimes opportunities for this kind of action are offered through mass media operated by persons other than ourselves, who may have greater organizing ability than we. The voice of conscience, of conviction, and of stirring concern can be stilled in us only at the expense of our losing all significance.

A more recent effort to lay foundations of peace is the Committee's international seminar program. In summer seminars we gather students from a number of countries, including our own, to spend three to seven weeks in thoughtful study of the problems of international life and morals which are of common interest and which often escape students in their regular college study. Simple group living, with all sharing in the housekeeping duties, is in itself part of the value of these projects. While this is a common practice among American students, it is far from common in countries from which some of these young people come. Another value lies in the consistent effort to develop a capacity for meditation and worship in these groups representing various religious backgrounds. For those who are willing and able to enter into this experience, often there comes a fresh comprehension of the creative forces in life which, when released, reveal new possibilities for peaceful living. For peace is not merely saying No to war. It involves penitence for our own share in the ways of living that provoke war, and finding fellowship at a new and deeper level of life with those who would fight us.

After one of these seminars a participant from Eastern Europe wrote: "We were frank with one another, and because of that we were friends. The seminar proved to me that the future is stronger than the past. We were all concerned with a better, peaceful world. The future of our nations was what interested us. Our past divided us, but our future united us."

At the close of another seminar, a Dutch student said: "I wrote a letter to my family. . . . I told them that with all our differences here, there were two things we all had in common: a belief in God, and a sense of humor. I have learned that making friends is different from agreeing. For instance, X [a Vietnamese] and I see things very differently. . . . We disagree. . . . But I think of him as a friend, and can call on him at any time." And the Vietnamese student said, "I want to say that for what I have done here, *I* am responsible. Do not judge my family or my country by me. I am a rebel. I am not what my father expected me to be. . . . I want to thank the staff. I want to thank Y [the Dutch student] for the friendship he expressed towards me."

At first these seminars were held only in the United States, in locations scattered from New England to the Southwest. About thirty-five students and a faculty of five or six outstanding men and women made up each seminar. Usually not more than seven or eight of the students were Americans.

In 1948, the seminars were extended overseas. The Berlin "airlift seminar" was one of the most colorful. Faculty, students, and supplies were flown into the city. There both East and West Zone Germans (including former Nazis), an R.A.F. officer interned in Germany during the war, Jewish young people, Poles, Finns, and Americans met together. By the summer of 1951, the program had developed to the point of including five regularly scheduled seminars in Europe, two or three in India, and two in Japan. The

European seminars are the result of co-operation of Friends Service Council, Continental Friends, and AFSC. In India, FSC and AFSC are jointly responsible.

Another program being carried on through AFSC is an inter-national-relations informational service to organized labor, farm, and church groups. For example, working with a national Labor Advisory Committee (CIO and AFL), we provide materials and speakers for labor groups exploring ways into peace. Similar service is extended to farm and church agencies desiring it.

A flourishing project of educational materials for children is still another facet of our general educational effort.

There is a real sense in which everything the Service Committee does is work for peace. The healing of the wounds of war, the succor of the refugee, youth joining with other youth across racial and national lines in serving the common good, these and the whole gamut of ministry to bodies, minds, and spirits of men caught in the aftermath of violence and hate are the stuff out of which a family of mankind is created. Like "race relations," education for peace is not a pigeonholed activity of the AFSC; insofar as we fulfill our function, it permeates all our activities.

But perhaps most important of all efforts toward peace are the private conversations one has from time to time with many sorts of people who feel that there is something essentially misdirected and false about our wanting peace but preparing for war. Such persons are quite likely to barge into one's home or office on the busiest of days, eager to talk, thus representing a threat to the schedule that one has so carefully made for the day's activities. One day it is a young man who has been disillusioned in the army, and who has learned to read the New Testament with fresh eyes, feeling that Jesus really meant what he said about the Kingdom of Heaven's being among us. How can this young man get back into the labor movement from which he came in such a way as to live out the life he is now glimpsing for the first time? Another day it is a young woman who has lost her position in a public school because of her too keen interest in the problems of race relations in her community. She needs help in defending her rights, and also in her effort to endure hardship and mistreatment with an unconquerable spirit of good will. Or perhaps we are confronted with a distraught man who has been carrying responsibility in government office and who is trying to find a way in which he can express his religious faith through his public acts.

How easy it is for most of us to indulge ourselves in a life that gets itself worked out on an appointment-pad basis! Thus we can easily find justification for not taking time to talk with those who need counsel, encouragement, and support, and by whom we might ourselves be drawn into the currents of intellectual and spiritual turmoil if we stopped to listen.

Often when I get into this kind of quandary I remember the priest and the Levite who went by on the other side of the road when they came to the man who had fallen among thieves and was beaten up and robbed. It was the Good Samaritan, he who forgot his appointment pad and stopped to bind up the wounds and take care of the abused traveler, who has been immortalized in this story. Sometimes the decision is not an easy one to make, for our appointments also may be vitally important. But it is at this point of daily personal weighing of values and decisions that most of us make or fail to make our greatest contribution to the cause of peace.

V
Witness in High Places

Let all nations hear the sound by word or writing. Spare no place, spare no tongue nor pen, but be obedient to the Lord God; go through the work and be valiant for the truth upon earth; tread and trample all that is contrary under. . . . Be patterns, be examples in all countries, places, islands, nations, wherever you come, that your carriage and life may preach among all sorts of people, and to them; then you will come to walk cheerfully over the world, answering that of God in every one.

— GEORGE FOX, from Launceston Prison to Friends in the ministry, 1656

In March, 1950, I retired as executive secretary and became honorary secretary of the American Friends Service Committee.

This Committee is a *service* agency. Whatever impact it may have made on the religious and social life of its time has been due almost entirely to acts of healing quality rendered without expectation of return or commendation. The fact that this final chapter speaks of "witness in high places" should by no means be taken as an indication that service is no longer the heart and soul of the Committee's life. Indeed, the "highest" places in terms of abiding values will probably continue to be awarded to the simple and often undiscovered deeds of loving kindness and generosity offered by the nameless to the nameless.

Yet anyone who has been involved in the administration of services designed to heal the wounds of war and bridge man-made gulfs of economic exploitation and racial and national prejudices would, I think, feel that his religious testimony was carried out even more thoroughly if he were able to help prevent the violations of our common brotherhood which make these services necessary. Indeed, almost always this further goal is implicit, if not explicit, in AFSC programs.

During the thirty-five years of the life of the Committee we have had experience in more than twenty countries of the world. These experiences have brought us into touch with the lowliest and most humble citizens of these countries, and also often with people in positions of power and influence in the various governments. Our testimony to the value of the individual, the sacredness of life, our belief in the presence of the Divine Spirit even in the midst of the human, have sometimes been understood and have come as a ray of hope in a world that looks meaningless and cruel. It is not an overstatement of fact, therefore, to say that at times government officials have turned to us with the hope that some new way out of chaos into creative international living might be found.

I glimpsed this during the days of the League of Nations. Though the United States was not a participant in the League, American Friends co-operated with British Friends in Geneva in maintaining a living contact with a great many people from a variety of countries who were trying to make the League of Nations an organ of peace in the world. But the upsurge of nationalism, the resentment against poverty, the ambition of dictators, and the growth of militaristic states, overwhelmed the League. To some extent, this came about because the United States failed to participate.

During the two decades which this book covers, there has been in our own country a tremendous increase in the impact of government upon the daily life of the people. Likewise there has been a decidedly broadening sense of United States participation in world affairs. The rapid growth of our country's influence in the international scene has seemed to imply a responsibility on the part of a voluntary group like ours to use what knowledge and contacts we have in an effort to preserve peace and understanding.

It was with these thoughts in mind that the Service Committee asked me in 1950 to give some attention to the international aspects of our work, particularly as they related to governments and to the United Nations. Although I am no expert in international affairs, these past two decades have offered me some opportunity to observe how governments can promote or hinder peace. I have also had a good many contacts with people who are influential in their governments. The same is true of a number of my AFSC colleagues in the United States and elsewhere. It seemed appropriate, therefore, that there should be an increasing effort to use whatever influence we might have at this important and tense moment in history to encourage those who are in policy-making positions to seek not so much national advantage as broad world understanding. Even more, we would seek to nourish the deep and abiding roots of religious faith that are in most if not all people.

It is true that to many Americans there has come an exceptional sense of international responsibility because of our country's enormous growth in power since the close of the First World War. It is also true that there are impulses in our national life that impel us to give assistance to weaker peoples, even those who are our late enemies. This we have done in an almost unprecedented way. Yet the failure to achieve real peace has become increasingly manifest since World War II.

We, together with other nations, have joined in a great power struggle. On one hand is the USSR, binding her neighbors to her as allies in the struggle; on the other hand is the United States, leading the Western world in opposition to the great power of the East. As the conflict has deepened we as a nation have largely moved away from assistance to people on the basis of need and into a policy of "mutual security," which all too often means giving aid to those who will promise in return to be our allies. Our hope now is said to be in "positions of strength" or in "total diplomacy." "Positions of strength" means using our economic and military potential to further the American cause, the Western cause. "Total diplomacy" means drawing into the orbit of the state all cultural and even religious influences that will help strengthen the cause of the West.

In part, this development is due to Communist states' accusation that we Americans have used our cultural and religious missions for imperialistic purposes. For instance, today in China the Western missionary enterprises of the past hundred years are interpreted by Chinese not as efforts of persons imbued by the spirit of Christ to render unselfish service but as an imperialist plot on the part of Christian nations to dominate and control unsuspecting peoples.

The West resents this. It may well be that a careful examination of the way in which we Americans have conducted ourselves, even in our religiously motivated efforts, will show that we have been more influenced by the American pattern of life and less deeply committed to the revolutionary, outgiving spirit of our religious faith than we have realized. I am thinking, not of any deliberate deceit, but of the unconscious influence of established social patterns upon our conduct. Now we are called upon much more carefully to examine our own inner spirits as well as our external programs.

However, as one reviews the record of experience of our AFSC workers in China, Japan, Germany, and elsewhere, he is conscious that they have usually sought with true sensitiveness to identify themselves as fully as possible with those among whom they worked. And even though they have not escaped criticism, especially in China, as representatives of the "Imperialist West," they have, one hopes, left a testimony to a genuine concern on the basis of brotherhood. That the upsurge of nationalism intermingled with Communism at the moment engulfs their efforts is not to be taken as necessarily the final outcome.

In fact, it seems to me that throughout the American effort and American life there is a refreshing flow of service and learning dedicated to the public good, to act as a saving force in our on-going society. This is our true stability and security.

There can be little doubt that the United States has a responsibility to share her abundance. But sharing without becoming arrogant is hard. The giver may easily think of himself as superior. Even when we talk about exporting our "know-how," we may well imply superiority. We may easily assume we are better than other peoples because we have a higher proportion of bathtubs and automobiles. We often seem to other peoples to be a boastful lot.

Much of this may be unfair to us. But it is a fact that has to be reckoned with. And it is one of the reasons for the special value that private, voluntary groups can have in helping the United States discharge her share of responsibility to a world that yearns for health, literacy, food, and shelter. It is one of the reasons why the United States needs to learn far better how to use the facilities of the United Nations. For through both of these resources she can diminish the overwhelming sense of power which unilateral governmental efforts often represent to receiving countries.

It is with this wider sense of responsibility that we of AFSC must approach our tasks of the present period. I do not mean to imply that Friends alone have felt this impulse. It is perhaps felt more keenly and interpreted more intelligently by many other groups. But I believe it is fair to say that within the Society of Friends there is an increasing sense that whatever weight we have should be thrown in the balance with as much understanding and dedication as we can command.

Erupting with violence in 1914 and continuing now at an accelerated pace, a great social revolution is taking place in our world. In this period of rapid change we must find our way into patterns of life which are creative and rooted in a commitment to the preservation of spiritual values. Nothing less than this is the quest in which we are engaged.

As Friends we have felt that our first line of responsibility in the political field is to our own American political leaders. A technical obstacle in the way of AFSC's rendering effective service of this sort is the fact that agencies supported by tax-exempt funds are legally prohibited from using any considerable proportion of their revenue in attempting to influence legislation. Therefore in 1943 the Friends Committee on National Legislation was established in Washington. Under the vigorous leadership of E. Raymond Wilson, it has worked among Congressmen and Senators and with other groups, both governmental and private, on behalf of legislation consonant with our Christian faith.

With the establishment of the United Nations and the location of its headquarters in New York, there was a growing sense among us at AFSC that we should give some direct attention to its efforts and problems. While this concern was on our minds, a generous contributor to the Committee agreed to make available to us an apartment near the new UN site. Here a family might live and represent the Committee in its concern to cultivate every opportunity to further international understanding. This offer led to the establishment of Quaker House, where we have made a beginning in the process of getting acquainted with the various national delegations. Quaker House is also a center to which nonofficial groups of people, Friends and non-Friends, are invited from time to time to consider how those dedicated to maintaining the peace of the world might more effectively let their concerns be felt.

As early as 1948 it was obvious that the formation of two power blocs was well under way. It was also increasingly evident that the capacity to think objectively both about ourselves and about the USSR was becoming more and more rare. After calling together a small group of people concerned by this growing tension, the Service Committee decided to create out of this group a working party which would attempt to analyze and publicize our point of view concerning Soviet-American relations. Meetings were held at Quaker House in New York, and resulted in the publication of a small book, *The United States and the Soviet Union: Some Quaker Proposals for Peace*.* Although this report did not follow the popular line of our own government in depending upon a policy of "containment," it has enjoyed a relatively wide circulation not only in the United States but in many foreign countries. Copies have been requested by several governments east of Berlin.

Meanwhile, Elmore Jackson, formerly assistant executive secretary of the American Friends Service Committee, had moved with his wife and two children to Quaker House, under appointment as representative of the American Friends Service Committee at the United Nations.

In the spring of 1950 Elmore Jackson went to England to discuss

* Yale University Press, 1949.

the possibility of fuller co-operation with British Friends in an effort to make the maximum use of Friends' resources in the field of international relations. As an instrument for pursuing this particular concern, British Friends created what has come to be known as the East-West Relations Committee. In our own Service Committee there has developed the Consultative Committee on Foreign Affairs.

During the Fourth Assembly of the United Nations, in the fall of 1949, members of a number of official delegations had been invited to have dinner with groups of Friends at Quaker House, so that we might know more about the desires especially of some of the newer and weaker countries, to further the cause of peaceful coexistence. By the time of the Fifth Assembly it was decided there should be an international team of Friends serving as representatives to the UN Assembly. (The UN Charter contains provisions for nongovernmental agency representation to the Economic and Social Council, and these provisions have been so interpreted as to facilitate attendance by representatives of the same organizations at sessions of the General Assembly.) Accordingly, under the general sponsorship of the Friends World Committee for Consultation, a delegation of six Friends was asked to attend the meetings of the Assembly and its committees during the autumn and early winter of 1950. Gerald Bailey and Agatha Harrison came from England; Elsa Cedergren from Sweden; Heberto Sein from Mexico; and Elmore Jackson and myself from the United States.

Although we constantly saw the power struggle going on between East and West, we also saw the heroic efforts of many states to face issues on the basis of their merit rather than as pawns in the political struggle. And this effort to retain independence seemed to us a valuable contribution to international action. India, especially, took a strong lead in this effort to maintain independence from the "cold war." The Scandinavian and Latin American states, too, could be freer from the power struggle than the United States and Western Europe, or the USSR and Eastern Europe. It was a great advantage to our little group that it included representatives from Mexico and Scandinavia.

The Korean war had broken out in June, 1950. Now at Lake Success hard, pressing questions emerged as to whether General MacArthur and his armed forces should be permitted to go north of the 38th Parallel. A proposal to permit UN forces to continue their advance in the effort to unite Korea was presented by the Western powers; the USSR called for a halt at the 38th Parallel and the appointment of a body to attempt a settlement. Our Quaker delegation was much impressed by the plea of Sir Benegal Rau, representing India, that an attempt should be made to see what merit there might be in each of these proposals, and to take this occasion, if possible, to stop the tragic slaughter in Korea. The greatest threat of all was the imminent participation of China in the Korean war if it was decided to allow United Nations troops to go north of the 38th Parallel.

While India and others who pleaded for time and moderation were listened to with respect, the vote went against them. And UN troops were authorized to proceed as far north as was necessary to fulfill the original purposes of the act against aggression. Yet there had been an impressive demonstration of a third influence attempting to assert itself in between two power blocs. While the effort was not successful in terms of the immediate issue, our Quaker delegation saw a considerable moral victory in the fact that twenty-four states voted with India. This was heartening to those who were trying to view issues on their merit, and not in the climate of the power struggle.

If the caution to pause and consider had been heeded, might the Korean war have ended then? At any rate, the good custom of Friends to wait quietly for a few days and let thought catch up with passion was encouraged by our delegation in its talks with various national representatives.

In all our efforts, it has seemed important to us that we keep in touch with our own national delegations and let them know what we are doing. We may not agree with them on the course of action to be followed, but there should not be any sense of secrecy in our efforts. In order to nourish the climate of confidence, we have undertaken from time to time to talk over with officials of our respective governments the views of our international Quaker group concerning issues before the Assembly.

Not infrequently I have found our United States official representatives to the UN conscious that our government's insistence on physical strength to back up our cause is one of the very sources of other nations' fear and mistrust of us.

Can it be that there are two sets of spiritual laws in the universe — one set for states and one for individuals? To me it seems abundantly clear that there is one moral order and purpose. I have yet to see evidence to the contrary. In this faith Gandhi supplied a kind of leadership in our twentieth-century world, in the light of which our reliance on arms seems to me to show up for the false hope it is.

During the Fifth Assembly, probably the tensest moment was when the invited delegation from Communist China arrived to attend Security Council meetings on Formosa and Korea. While these Chinese emissaries were accorded nominal courtesies, there was marked aloofness from them because they represented a Communist state and one which was increasingly critical of the West.

At this time the Service Committee still had representatives in China trying to carry on mobile clinic work but finding it impossible to get permits to travel from village to village. In the delegates' lounge one day, I saw General Wu, leader of the delegation from the People's Republic of China, sitting quietly alone except for his interpreter, so I approached him, to discuss this matter. Hardly had we begun when we were surrounded by a bevy of newspaper reporters and cameramen who mercilessly plied us in an attempt to get material for publicity. As I tried to complete my talk with General Wu, I was approached with the comment, "I suppose you have made a peace proposal to General Wu." "Peace proposal!" I replied.

"Not at all. I have talked with the General about a very practical matter in regard to our medical work in China."

Later on, after great effort, some of us were able to have a more deliberate talk with members of the Communist China delegation at their headquarters in the Waldorf-Astoria Hotel in New York. But the climate of suspicion and fear pervaded the Assembly all during the discussion of the important issues at stake. Perhaps it may have been of some value to have our Quaker delegation show at least ordinary courtesy to these visitors, which it seemed very difficult for the political representatives of most states to show without their acts being misinterpreted.

During these Fifth Assembly sessions it came to a member of our Quaker delegation that there should be a room for prayer and meditation at UN. True, plans called for such a room in the new headquarters. But the time is always now. Did not present tensions call for a place where delegates might repair for spiritual refreshment and guidance? We knew that among the various delegations there were some persons for whom religion had deep personal meaning, and who were striving to bring their faith to bear on their actions in UN. A Moslem delegate had told us that he had to resort to using Telephone Booth No. 4 for his prayers during the day.

When we consulted the Secretary General's office, we found a sympathetic interest, even though space was at a premium. We were told, however, that it would be a great help if representatives of a number of delegations were consulted as to how they would feel about it. We talked with representatives of more than twenty delegations, and without exception there was warm approval. A room was established and was used with considerable appreciation by people representing many religious faiths as well as a wide variety of political affiliations.

More recently, we have had occasion to hear a delegate speak forcefully in the UN Assembly to the effect that the problems before UN are perhaps wholly insoluble unless and until there is willingness to accept the guidance of our deepest religious insights. This was no merely pious utterance. It was the considered judgment of a practical man concerned for a way out of the present impasse.

The development of the Korean war and of an unparalleled arms race as basic in American foreign policy caused our Committee again to enter the pamphleteering field in 1951. We looked with hope on the growing sense of public responsibility for aid to recovery through programs financed largely by our own government; also public funds were being used to finance the exchange of persons (such as students, engineers, public administrators) between countries, especially late enemy countries, and in many other ways to reknit the social fabric so badly torn apart by war. But at the same time we saw our country's increasing dependence on military strength and the growing tendency to use material aid as a bargaining point. These latter emphases we felt had in them the very seeds of war. Since we felt this way, we must say so.

We set up a study group, whose work resulted in a pamphlet, *Steps to Peace*. In this we called for renewed confidence in negotiation instead of increasing military threat, as a means of settling political problems. We felt we saw in ourselves as a nation less evidence of willingness to negotiate as our physical strength increased. In the second place, while the United States supported the United Nations, it was often accused of ignoring UN or of using it to serve its own national purposes. Our study group tried to determine how far these accusations were accurate and how our country could effectively strengthen UN. Third, we studied problems and possibilities of disarmament, including atomic weapons. Finally, we called for a broader, more inclusive development of projects of mutual aid in an effort to lift the standard of living throughout the world.

As these issues are outlined, they may seem to be solely economic and political in nature. But the argument is maintained that creative international developments can take place only through the birth of a new moral and spiritual sense of obligation.

Two points in this program seemed to many of us to need elaboration. International negotiation has not been developed into as much of an art as has labor negotiation. We felt that considerable profit might derive from a careful study of the similarities and differences between labor negotiations and international negotiations. A group representing some of the most successful experience in both of these fields was drawn together at Quaker House in New York. Over a considerable period of time they have produced a book under the editorship of Elmore Jackson, called *Meeting of Minds.** Also, a further group has produced a special study in pamphlet form under the title, *Toward Security through Disarmament.*

The international team which had represented the Friends World Committee for Consultation at the Fifth Assembly of UN attended sessions of the Sixth Assembly in Paris in the fall of 1951, augmented from time to time by other Friends from England and the Continent.

It was a great satisfaction to me that Lilly Pickett could accompany me on this trip. We spent ten days in England before the opening of the Assembly on November 6.

The East-West Relations Committee of London Yearly Meeting arranged a week end, with Elmore Jackson and myself as guests, especially to consider further steps which Friends might take in improving relations between the USSR and the West. Seven English Friends had recently returned from a visit to Moscow, Leningrad, Kiev, and surrounding communities in the USSR. They had had more opportunities for contact with a wide range of Russians than they had anticipated, and their experience gave vigorous backing to our sense of the urgent need to open up channels of communication between East and West.

During our conferences with the East-West Relations Committee, we had a most interesting conversation with Dr. Radhakrishnan,

* McGraw-Hill, New York, 1952.

then Indian ambassador to Moscow. He was an unusual ambassador. He spent five months of the year as a lecturer on Eastern religions at All Souls College at Oxford, about a month in his own country, and six months in Moscow. His frankness, good humor, and an intense desire to foster matters of common interest between his country and the USSR endeared him to the Russian people and gave him the confidence of Russian officials. Since that time, he has become Vice-president of India.

One of the major issues before the Sixth Assembly in Paris was the effort of the native tribes of South-West Africa to avoid being annexed to the Union of South Africa. This issue was carried over from the Fifth Assembly, and the UN Trusteeship Committee was working on it, but found South Africa completely unco-operative.

Finally, in the course of the Sixth Assembly the Trusteeship Committee proposed that the Hereros, a South-West African tribe who had petitioned the UN, should be invited to send their own spokesmen to UN to present their case. It had already been presented most effectively by Michael Scott, an Anglican missionary, but the Trusteeship Committee felt that the people should be given an opportunity to speak for themselves.

After a long debate in the Assembly, it was Cuba, a small and relatively unimportant country politically, which led the way, followed by several Arab and Latin American states, in voting to ask the Hereros to come to Paris to state their own case. It was with regret that we noted that our own country abstained from voting and that Great Britain voted against the visit of the Hereros.

Unhappily, the Hereros never arrived, because South Africa refused to give any kind of travel papers for them. Chief Hosea Kutako, eighty-four years old, and two of his associates traveled several hundred miles to Windhoek, their capital, and there waited for weeks for permissions that never came.

While we were often distressed by the positions taken by our national delegations, we realized they were acting under instructions, and that perhaps our major task was to do all we could at home to develop a greater concern for a different kind of action.

As the United States moved with its great power toward rearming the Western world and bidding high for allies wherever they could be found, we sensed perplexity in the minds of a good many official UN delegations, especially at two points. How could we of the United States fight a war to rid Germany of militarism, then so quickly turn about and use our large influence to encourage her to rearm? And how could we encourage Japan to renounce war in her new constitution, then almost immediately ask her to accept a military contract allowing American soldiers and military equipment to be maintained in Japan? How could we be urging Japan herself to return to an armed state?

The "reservoir of good will" toward the United States, talked about with such enthusiasm by Wendell Willkie in 1942–1943, seemed to us to be emptying out at an alarming rate.

At this Sixth Assembly our delegation found itself deeply disturbed by the general spirit prevailing in the discussions on the question of disarmament. Early in the sessions the atmosphere was so highly charged with recrimination that one almost despaired for the survival of the United Nations. But though one is conscious of the great threat of the forces of destruction, one need not have a completely lonely feeling that God has abandoned His world to evil. It is well to remember the famous conclusion of the Old Testament story of Deborah: "The stars in their courses fought against Sisera."

Although I could continue the list of discouraging items that stood out at the close of the Sixth Assembly when it adjourned at the end of January, 1952, that would not be a fair picture. These issues, instead of being pent-up bitterness in the minds and hearts of peoples, had been openly discussed. Contacts between delegations had been made. Hopes that had not been realized were, even so, not yet extinguished. The United Nations continued to be a political agency for preserving the peace. If as a collective-security agency, in the military sense, its achievements in Korea were disappointing, that in itself even more strongly emphasized the great importance of developing its negotiating, mediating, and reconciling function.

Usually, delegates of about thirty nongovernmental agencies attend sessions of the UN Assembly. These delegations represent an outpouring of hope that peace may become a practical political achievement, as well as a personal aspiration. The way may be long. But increasingly men recognize that war does not settle — rather, it unsettles — the problems of human society. Also there seems to me to be a growing consciousness that our human endeavors must finally find their sanction in faith in God and in men.

We have had representatives of perhaps as many as twenty of the national delegations at Quaker House in New York, and in our Paris headquarters during the Sixth Assembly. Often one is surprised to find how much search there is for a religious answer to the issues at stake. As I see it, one of the chief functions of delegations such as ours is to discover, encourage, and unite such seeking on the part of official delegates. They are experts in matters of which we may know little; we seek always to learn. And sometimes it turns out that our companionship in the spiritual search is something for which they, in turn, hunger deeply. One hopes that this kind of combined effort of official and nonofficial groups may in the long run bear fruit in terms of the preservation of moral and spiritual values, in a way that might not otherwise be possible.

There is also a more detailed kind of work which can be done in helping governments consider the human effects of their actions. An illustration is the negotiation which has gone on in connection with various groups of refugees in the world.

For example, in July, 1951, representatives of twenty-four nations meeting in Geneva drew up a Draft Convention Relating to the Status of Refugees. This was the culmination of a long effort on the part of UN to draft a "bill of rights" for refugees, who all too often have found themselves the responsibility of no one, and without the possibility of obtaining identification papers, passports, jobs, property, court hearings, or any of the privileges of citizens.

At this Geneva conference, Friends were unofficially represented by James Read, an American Friend who is UN Deputy High Commissioner for Refugees, and officially by Colin W. Bell, director of the Friends International Center in Geneva, who took part in the conference as representative of the Friends World Committee for Consultation.

Among the national delegates to the conference, the sense of national responsibility toward refugees varied greatly. European countries fear refugees because they walk across borders, young and old, rich and poor, sick and well, regardless of the desires of the country into which they come. It is easier for countries farther away to be more liberal about refugees' rights in certain respects, for these countries can be highly selective when it comes to actually admitting refugees.

Another difference was that some delegates wished to frame a convention for European refugees only, insisting that one convention could not possibly be made applicable to all refugees, while others asked, "What about Arab refugees? And those driven from their homes in Korea, Malaya, and Indo-China?"

How could the delegates assembled at Geneva draft a document which would satisfy states with such widely divergent problems and viewpoints?

It is important in such a situation to keep in mind that the most likely way to reach a goal is to aim not at the goal itself but at some more ambitious goal beyond it. In this instance, the higher goal was to remember that he whom we call a refugee is a child of God. And we may well realize that it is not through any virtue of our own that it is not we who are in this predicament.

Along with other nongovernmental organizations, the Friends World Committee for Consultation through Colin Bell sought consistently to liberalize and humanize the final document. An article on the right of religious freedom was written into the Convention partly, at least, as a result of statements submitted by FWCC and other nongovernmental groups.

In reporting the work of FWCC at this conference, Colin Bell wrote: "One thing is certain — that the attention given to what Quakers may say in 'high places' is a direct result of countless acts of service by Friends everywhere over the years. After one FWCC statement the Egyptian delegate paid tribute to the help given by Friends to the Palestine refugees, and asked the Conference to recognize that we spoke out of ground-root experience."

So long as our representations to those in authority stay consciously rooted in our service experience, "high places" and "low places" are terms without meaning in reality.

In the fall of 1952 on President Truman's invitation I undertook service on a special commission which he was setting up to study and make recommendations concerning a desirable immigration policy for the United States. Here again, one is conscious that such opportunities come not because of one's own achievements, but because there is wistful hope that the experience and profession of faith of Friends for three hundred years may prove relevant to the critical problems of our time.

Meanwhile, Elmore Jackson has been serving with Dr. Frank Graham in his efforts as United Nations mediator to negotiate a settlement of the conflict between India and Pakistan over Kashmir.

The Seventh Assembly, convening in New York in the fall of 1952, found our Quaker delegation working with an increased sense of the danger of stagnation in international affairs.

The growing yearning for recognition and equal treatment on the part of the darker races, together with the upsurge of nationalism, is evident at almost every session of the UN. These factors are not transient. They will not pass quickly or quietly. And one has the feeling that, as Whittier's antislavery efforts seemed to help precipitate war over slavery, so now Quakers' belief in the inherent worth of men in the sight of God, regardless of color, status, or creed, may seem to some to give support to disruptive forces. It is hard for the white peoples of the West to understand and help to realization the urge of millions of darker-skinned peoples, not only for a fair share of the world's goods, but for recognition on the basis of equality and dignity of all men under God. This is the central public issue of our time. And it is to discover ways to share without being compelled to, to recognize potential ability and help it develop, to become understanding agents of reconciliation, that we are called.

Christians often shy away from any connection between politics and religion because they have seen the church become the tool of the political state, or in some instances the state made a tool of the church. Neither of these alternatives can be our goal. None, however, can deny that there is a place for the life of the spirit in political calculations. It is because the two have been kept in unholy celibacy that politics becomes corrupt and religion shallow and sentimental. In all of the work of the American Friends Service Committee we try to bring religion and life into one common endeavor. Religion finds its fullest expression in daily life, and not alone in worship.

In the ebb and flow of a period of rapid change in the world, it is well to remember that there are all kinds of individuals and little groups of people who find security in abiding spiritual values, and with complete dedication seek to find ways of preserving them. During the invasion of southern Europe by "the barbarians," copies of the original text of the Scriptures were hidden in various places so that they might not be destroyed. People in secret caves, in forests, and wherever they could find hiding places, kept alive the spirit of devotion to the needs of suffering humanity.

In modern times many of our workers, especially in the devastated countries of Europe, have come across such groups, and we have felt it was appropriate that a special effort be made to encourage, as well as to understand, what was going on in the life and spirit of people who might be the true preservers of Christian values.

It was with this in mind that we arranged for Douglas V. Steere, professor of philosophy at Haverford College, to spend six months every other year in Europe, going about among Protestant ministers, Catholic brotherhoods, Quaker groups, locating individuals committed to this kind of life. All during the Hitler regime and the ravages of war, such persons — usually in small groups — have nourished the seeds of spiritual life, even though it was often done in the midst of danger and physical privation. Amiya Chakravarty of India, now living in the United States, expressed a concern to do similar service, particularly with the Catholic brotherhoods in Germany. Both of these emissaries have found a warm and deep sense of fellowship among people whose lives give evidence that nothing can kill the light of the spirit of the Divine in people who dedicate themselves to its nourishment and expression.

This may not be witness in high places. Yet it may be one of the most rewarding forms of service. May one not see here developing the kind of unconquerable spirit that can preserve the abiding values of a true European civilization? Few really trust to war to do more than leave the country more desolate than when war began. But these quiet creative forces may be the voice of the future.

Throughout three centuries, Friends have never been able to ignore government. Many times we have been unable to conform to government's demands and have had to disobey. Also, from time to time we have felt we must express our disapproval of acts of government which seemed to us bad public policy. But often there are creative forces at work in government in which we can participate. And here, I believe, we feel an increasing sense of responsibility at the present time.

But such a concern can be effective only insofar as men see in our daily individual and group life, in our homes and communities, the values which we profess in "high places."

To live in that state of tension which enables us to be at the same time critic and friend of government, to study its workings sufficiently to be able to help religious insight become political action, remains part of our duty and call. And withal and beyond all, to maintain an abiding faith in the power of good to overcome evil, to live in that way of loving service for which we all most deeply yearn: nothing less than this kind of energetic commitment of our whole lives can satisfy the inner sanctuary of the human spirit.

Index

432INDEX

State Department. *See* United States (Department of State)
Stearns, Alfred E., 205
Steere, Douglas V., 419
Stettinius, Edward, 65, 66
Stimson, Henry L., 218
Stuart, John Leighton, 224
Subsistence Homestead Act, 43
Subsistence homesteads: in Austria, 97–98; European, 93; in Germany, 71, 101–102; in United States, 38, 41–64, 71, 79, 93, 101, 341 (*see also* Penn-Craft); "Allotments Scheme" in Wales, 103
Suhrawardy, Husseyn Shaheed, 254–255
Sulzberger, Arthur, 176
Sun Yat-sen, Madame, 225
Sutton, James, 280
Sutton, Marshall, 272
Swarthmore College, Institutes of Race Relations, 373
Sweet, Lennig, 223
Swift, Ernest, 172

TACHE, BLANCHE CLOEREN, xi
Taft, Charles P., 248
Tagore, Rabindranath, 250, 343; before London Yearly Meeting of Friends, 91–92; visit to the United States, 92–93
Taylor, Howard and May, 245
Taylor, Myron C., 65, 66, 67
Technical assistance programs: UN and U.S. programs, 40, 364, 411; Friends in China, 228–229; Friends in India and Pakistan, 258, 259; Friends in UN project in El Salvador, 355–356
Tennessee Valley Authority, 204, 344
Thomas, Norman, 3–4
Thomas, Wilbur K., 21
Thomsen, Hans, 178
Timbres, Harry, 92
Toronto, Canada, ix
Toynbee, Arnold, 184
Trimble, Cordelia, 272, 275
Truman, Harry S., 335, 417
Tygart Valley Subsistence Homestead, 45

UNION OF SOVIET SOCIALIST REPUBLICS. *See* Soviet Union

Unitarian Service Committee, 142, 303
Unitarians, 324
United China Relief, 212–213, 223
United Mine Workers of America, 47, 62; Welfare and Retirement Fund, 38
United Nations, 40, 90, 162, 164, 197, 232, 260, 393, 402, 405–418. *See also* Food and Agriculture Organization, International Refugee Organization, World Health Organization, and UN agencies listed immediately following this item
UN Educational, Scientific, and Cultural Organization (UNESCO), 283, 354, 355, 358
UN International Children's Emergency Fund (UNICEF), 267, 278, 282, 284
UN Office of High Commissioner for Refugees, 162
UN Palestine Conciliation Commission, 280, 282
UN Relief and Rehabilitation Administration (UNRRA), 162, 189–192, 196, 203, 204, 225, 227, 228
UN Relief and Works Agency, 287
UN Relief for Palestine Refugees, 267 ff.
UN Rural Demonstration Project in El Salvador, 355
United States: Department of State, 134, 140–141, 167, 169, 177, 178, 180, 181, 190, 215–217, 235, 248, 258, 286; immigration and naturalization policies, 148–149, 151–152, 234–236, 373, 417; Immigration Act of 1924, 234, 235, 236, 373
United States Children's Bureau, 19, 26
United States Committee for the Care of European Children, 152–154
United States Maritime Commission, 110
United States Steel Corporation, 65
United States Technical Cooperation Administration, 355–356
United Textile Workers, 5
University of West Virginia, 26, 32, 54

VAIL, JAMES G., 172, 177, 178, 179, 250, 263, 264, 265, 266, 297
Van Dusen, Henry P., 176
Van Etten, Henry, 90, 187